Let's Celebrate Today

Let's Celebrate Today

Calendars, Events, and Holidays

Second Edition

Diana F. Marks

Illustrated by Donna L. Farrell

LIBRARIES

U N L I M I T E D

A Member of the Greenwood Publishing Group

Westport, Connecticut • London

British Library Cataloguing in Publication Data is available.

Copyright © 2003 by Diana F. Marks

All rights reserved. No portion of this book may
be reproduced, by any process or technique, without
the express written consent of the publisher.

ISBN: 1–59158–060–9

First published in 2003

Libraries Unlimited, 88 Post Road West, Westport, CT 06881
A Member of the Greenwood Publishing Group, Inc.
www.lu.com

Printed in the United States of America

The paper used in this book complies with the
Permanent Paper Standard issued by the National
Information Standards Organization (Z39.48–1984).

10 9 8 7 6 5 4 3 2 1

Contents

Acknowledgments vii
Introduction ix
Strategies for Using This Book xi
Information on Time and Calendars xiii

January 1
    Month-Long Activities 2
    Special Days 2

February 27
    Month-Long Activities 28
    Special Weeks 28
    Special Days 29

March 51
    Month-Long Activities 52
    Special Weeks 52

April 77
    Month-Long Activities 78
    Special Weeks 78
    Special Days 79

May 107
    Month-Long Activities 108
    Special Weeks 108
    Special Days 108

June 133
    Month-Long Activities 134
    Special Weeks 134
    Special Days 134

July 159
    Month-Long Activities 160

August 183
    Month-Long Activities 184
    Special Days 184

September 207
    Month-Long Activities 208
    Special Weeks 208
    Special Days 208

October 231
    Month-Long Activities 232
    Special Weeks 232
    Special Days 233

November 257
    Month-Long Activities 258
    Special Weeks 258
    Special Days 258

December 283
    Month-Long Activities 284

    Bibliography 309
    Index 311

Acknowledgments

I thank my mother, Shirley Heuchemer, for all her love. I thank my husband, Peter, and my sons, Kevin and Colin, for all their help and support.

I want to thank the students and staff of Wrightstown Elementary School. I appreciate all their advice and their positive comments.

Introduction

The first edition of *Let's Celebrate Today* was published in 1998. So much has happened since then. The Internet has changed the way we communicate, conduct research, and manage day-to-day activities. The use of cell phones has increased exponentially; just about every teenager can communicate with every other teenager at just about any time. We live in an era of instant information. Today's students sometimes know more about what is happening in the Middle East than what is happening in their neighborhoods. Finally, the events of September 11, 2001, changed our lives. We, including children, are not so trusting, not so naïve, and not so carefree.

Today's children have grown up with sophisticated calculators, computers, fax machines, Web sites, and e-mail. They have no idea what a slide rule is, let alone an abacus. They also have very confused ideas about time. They do not understand why knights in shining armor did not use guns. They wonder why George Washington never met Abraham Lincoln. They have no concept of living in a home without electricity, telephones, running water, and, worst of all, television.

This book is about time. It is about children. Finally, it is about making history interesting and meaningful for children. First, the book describes calendars and gives information about important days for most cultures. Then the book lists every day of the year. It gives important historical events, inventions, unusual happenings, birthdays of important people, and scientific data for each day of the year. This book is about making children more educated and more aware. Was Henry Tanner an artist or a musician? Who figured out that Neptune had to be there even if we could not see it? *Let's Celebrate Today* goes beyond just information and gives teachers, librarians, and parents at least three suggestions per day as to what to do with the information. All the ideas are aimed at either creative thinking skills or higher-level thinking skills. Web sites have been included as much as possible.

Let's Celebrate Today was fascinating to write. Sometimes there was a plethora of ideas for a particular day. Some days were just not very busy. I had to make choices. What should children know? Is there a difference between that and what they need to know? Is Adolph Hitler in or out? Should I include the fact that Thomas Jefferson owned slaves or leave that out? Some facts were just plain interesting. For example, I had no idea that the signers of the Declaration of Independence faced so much danger for simply putting their names on the document.

George Santayana stated, "Those who cannot remember the past are condemned to repeat it." Children should not just remember the past; they should comprehend it. They should understand what it would be like to walk in the shoes of Benjamin Franklin. They should see today's world, but they should also perceive the worlds of Magellan and Cousteau. Children should realize that the past is part of them. So is the present. We want them to see what their ancestors did and what worked and what did not. Therefore, as they stride toward the future, they have the skills of generations behind them. Hopefully *Let's Celebrate Today* will help them to be confident, capable, and productive citizens.

Strategies for Using This Book

I created *Let's Celebrate Today* to appeal to a wide range of people. I believe it can be used in a number of different ways.

First, the book could be a reference book. It could sit on a shelf until someone wants to know when Pennsylvania became a state or what famous people were born on a certain child's birthday. The book could let you know more about the Jewish calendar or when Johnny Appleseed Day is.

It could also be used on a daily basis. The entries could be read as part of the morning routine or as a break between activities. Events could be featured on a "Today in History" bulletin board.

Let's Celebrate Today could form a substantial portion of the day. I listed at least three varied and hopefully interesting ideas as to what to do with the entries each day. Educators could use the ideas I have provided as a good portion of the language arts program. I have included a wide range of authors and reading sources. To me, reading and writing are one and the same. Lots of researching and lots of writing could come from the ideas in my book. Consider displaying a large timeline. Students could see that quite a few years separated the Revolutionary War from the Civil War. They could really understand the fact that computers have only been around a short time. A map of the United States could be placed permanently on a bulletin board. Students could note when states were admitted to the Union or where Mesa Verde National Park is. A world map would be fantastic too. Then students could locate Djibouti, and they would know where Tbilisi is.

Finally, my book could provide the foundation for a class's entire instruction. Excluding math, everything else is here, from reading to health, from science to art. For those teachers who wish for a springboard, here it is. Gone would be the basals and the standard texts. In their places would be computers and references and student-generated work. This would not be an easy route, especially the first year. However, it would make learning real, relevant, and exciting.

Spontaneity and creativity are to be encouraged. Feel free to invent a new holiday or historical event should some day seem too slow. Here are some ideas.

- The first worm born in captivity . . .
- The first recorded account of a teacher tap dancing in class was . . .
- The first discussion of which came first, the chicken or the egg, happened on . . .
- National Organize Your Schoolwork Day is . . .
- Try a New Food Day is . . .
- Today is Adopt a New Name Day.
- Today is Wear Clothes from a Different Decade Day.
- The first indoor recess occurred on . . .
- The first kid who wore his/her sweatshirt inside out and backward was . . .
- National Read to Someone Else Day is . . .
- National Favorite Mollusk Day is . . .
- National Ask at Least Ten Questions Day is . . .
- National Garage Cleaning Day is . . .
- The first person to draw a picture was . . .

I hope all who open this book will find it useful. I wish you good luck and good times.

Information on Time and Calendars

Almost every ancient culture developed a calendar. Many calendars evolved because people depended on agriculture. The calendar was a way of knowing when to plant and when to harvest. Other calendars came about as a result of religious observances. The Mayan calendar, for instance, let the people know when the gods needed to be pleased. Individuals needed calendars as well to record birthdays, rites of passage, weddings, and deaths.

Many calendars were based on lunar cycles. The word "month" derives from the word "moon." However, a lunar calendar needs to be adjusted every so often, because no number of lunar cycles equals a solar year. The Gregorian calendar, used in many parts of the world, is based on the earth's rotation around the sun. However, many religious and cultural calendars still depend on the moon.

Christian Calendar

The Christian calendar is somewhat based on the Gregorian calendar. Christmas is always December 25. However, some of the other holidays are based on the lunar cycles. Easter, the most important day for Christians, is the first Sunday after the first full moon after the vernal equinox. Good Friday, the day Jesus was crucified, is the Friday preceding Easter. Lent, beginning on Ash Wednesday, signifies a forty-six-day period of fasting and giving up pleasures. Shrove Tuesday, the day before Ash Wednesday, is also called Mardi Gras or Fat Tuesday. People often feast on Shrove Tuesday. Pentecost occurs on the seventh Sunday after Easter. The Holy Spirit came down to the apostles on Pentecost. Trinity Sunday is the Sunday right after Pentecost. It reminds followers of the Trinity: the Father, Son, and Holy Ghost. Last, Advent starts on the Sunday closest to November 30 and continues until Christmas. The following table establishes important Christian holidays for a number of years.

Table 1. Dates of Major Christian Holidays, 2003–2012

Year	Ash Wednesday	Good Friday	Easter	Pentecost	Trinity Sunday	Advent
2003	3/5	4/18	4/20	6/8	6/15	11/30
2004	2/25	4/9	4/11	5/30	6/6	11/28
2005	2/9	3/25	3/27	5/15	5/22	11/27
2006	3/1	4/14	4/16	6/4	6/11	12/3
2007	2/21	4/6	4/8	5/27	6/3	12/2
2008	2/6	3/21	3/23	5/11	5/18	11/30
2009	2/25	4/10	4/12	5/31	6/7	11/29
2010	2/17	4/2	4/4	5/23	5/30	11/28
2011	3/9	4/22	4/24	6/12	6/19	11/27
2012	2/22	4/6	4/8	5/27	6/4	12/2

Jewish Calendar

The Jewish calendar combines elements of the lunar cycles and the solar calendar. The months of the calendar are Tishri, Heshvan, Kislev, Tebet, Shebat, Adar, Nisan, Iyar, Sivan, Tammuz, Ab, and Elul. An extra month, Adar Sheni, is intercalated to keep the lunar calendar correct with the sun. The calendar begins at the creation, *anno mundi*, which equals 3761 B.C.E. (before Common era).

The major Jewish holidays follow the lunar calendar. Rosh Hashanah, or New Year, is held on the first and second days of Tishri. It is also called the Day of Judgment and Remembrance. Yom Kippur ends the ten-day period of Rosh Hashanah. This Day of Atonement is observed by fasting and praying. Sukkoth is the harvest festival and marks the time the Jews traveled through the wilderness to Israel. Hanukkah, the festival of lights, lasts for eight days. It celebrates the triumph of the Maccabees over the Syrians. An oil lamp miraculously burned for eight days. Thus on each day of Hanukkah another candle is lit. Purim celebrates Queen Esther's victory over Haman, the evil minister to Esther's husband, King Ahasuerus. Pesach, or Passover, celebrates the Hebrews' exodus from Egypt. God passed over (spared) the Jewish first-born during plagues. During Passover no leavened bread can be eaten. Finally, Shavuoth marks the appearance of the Torah at Mt. Sinai.

The following chart indicates major Jewish holidays.

Table 2. Dates of Major Jewish Holidays, 5783–5772

Year	Rosh Hashanah	Yom Kippur	Sukkoth	Hanukkah	Purim	Pesach	Shavuoth
5763	9/7/2002	9/16/2002	9/21/2002	11/30/2002	3/18/2003	4/17/2003	6/6/2003
5764	9/27/2003	10/6/2003	10/11/2003	12/20/2003	3/7/2004	4/6/2004	5/26/2004
5765	9/16/2004	9/25/2004	9/30/2004	12/8/2004	3/25/2005	4/24/2005	6/13/2005
5766	10/4/2005	10/13/2005	10/18/2005	12/26/2005	3/14/2006	4/13/2006	6/2/2006
5767	9/23/2006	10/2/2006	10/7/2006	12/16/2006	3/4/2007	4/3/2007	5/23/2007
5768	9/13/2007	9/22/2007	9/27/2007	12/5/2007	3/27/2008	4/20/2008	6/9/2008
5769	9/30/2008	10/9/2008	10/14/2008	12/22/2008	3/10/2009	4/9/2009	5/29/2009
5770	9/19/2009	9/28/2009	10/3/2009	12/12/2009	2/28/2010	3/30/2010	5/19/2010
5771	9/9/2010	9/18/2010	9/23/2010	12/2/2010	3/20/2011	4/19/2011	6/8/2011
5772	9/29/2011	10/8/2011	10/13/2011	12/21/2011	3/8/2012	4/7/2012	5/27/2012

Islamic Calendar

The Islamic calendar is organized on a lunar year. Twelve months alternate between having twenty-nine and thirty days. Therefore, the Islamic year is 354 days. A cycle of thirty years occasionally has leap years, where a day is added to the leap year. The months are named Muharram, Safar, Rabi I, Rabi II, Jumada I, Jumada II, Rajab, Sha'ban, Ramadan, Shawwal, Dhu'l-Qa'dah, and Dhu'l-Hijja. The first year of Islam corresponds to C.E. 622 and is called 1 A.H., meaning *anno hegirae*.

Ramadan is the most important holy period for the Muslims. The Koran was revealed during this time, so all physically capable Muslims fast between sunrise and sunset for the entire month. Eidul Fitri marks the end of Ramadan. People offer alms at the mosque during the early morning service. Eidul Adha, the Feast of Sacrifice, signals the start of a pilgrimage. Those who do not go on a pilgrimage must slaughter a sheep and donate at least a third of the meat to charity.

The following chart shows major Muslim holy days. However, it may not be accurate. Not all Muslim countries follow the same calendar. Certain people, the *muezzin,* watch for the rising of the moon at the end of each month. If the moon is not seen, then a day is added to the month. Thus, several months in succession might have thirty days each. Also, since the *muezzin* reside in different countries and since the moon may not be visible to all *muezzin,* the calendars vary.

Table 3. Dates of Major Muslim Holy Days, A.H.1424–1433

Year A.H.	New Year's Day	1 Ramadan	Eid al Fitr	Eid al Adha
1424	3/4/2003	10/26/2003	11/25/2003	2/1/2004
1425	2/21/2004	10/15/2004	11/13/2004	1/20/2005
1426	2/10/2005	10/4/2005	11/3/2005	1/10/2006
1427	1/30/2006	9/23/2006	10/23/2006	12/30/2006
1428	1/27/2007	9/13/2007	10/13/2007	12/20/2007
1429	1/10/2008	9/12/2008	10/2/2008	12/9/2008
1430	12/29/2008	8/22/2009	9/21/2009	11/28/2009
1431	12/18/2009	8/11/2010	9/10/2010	11/17/2010
1432	12/18/2010	8/1/2011	8/11/2011	10/18/2011
1433	11/27/2011	7/20/2012	8/19/2012	10/26/2012

Hindu Calendar

The Hindu calendar combines lunar aspects and solar aspects. Twelve months vary in length from twenty-seven to thirty-one days. Extra days are tacked on every three years. The twelve months are Caitra, Vaisakha, Jyaistha, Asadha, Sravana, Bhadrapada, Asvina, Karttika, Margasivsa, Pansa, Magha, and Phalguna.

Several holidays are marked by the sun's movement. Mesasamkranti starts the astrological new year when the sun enters the constellation Aries. Makaraj-Samkrani, the winter solstice, begins when the sun enters the constellation Capricorn. Mahavisuva is New Years Eve. Other celebrations are marked by the lunar calendar. Ramanavami (Caitra 9) honors the birth of Rama. Rama is an incarnation of Vishnu. Rathayatra (Asadha 2) begins the pilgrimage of the chariot festival of Orissa. Janmastami (Sravana 8) celebrates the birth of Krishna, a hero and an incarnation of Vishnu. Dasahra (Asvina 7–10) remembers the victory of Rama over Ravana. Laksmipuja (Asvina 15) is a day to pay homage to Laksmi, the goddess of good fortune. Diwali (Karttika 15) is the festival of lights and the giving of presents. It occurs around October and November. Mahasivaratri (Magha 13) pays tribute to Shiva, one of the most important Hindu gods. Shiva stands for both reproduction and destruction.

Chinese Calendar

The Chinese calendar is probably at least 5,000 years old. It also is a lunar calendar of twelve months. A month starts with the new moon. Every few years an extra month is appended. The year begins around January or February with the first day of the Chinese month.

In China people all become one year older on New Year's Day; individual birthdays are not celebrated. Each year is represented by an animal in a cycle of twelve years. Below is a chart showing the Chinese New Years and the twelve-year animal cycle.

Table 4. Chinese New Years and Animal Cycles, 4701–4712

Year	Gregorian Calendar	Zodiac Animal	Other Years of the Zodiac Animal
4701	2/1/2003	Ram/Sheep	1979, 1991
4702	1/22/2004	Monkey	1980, 1992
4703	2/9/2005	Rooster	1981, 1993
4704	1/29/2006	Dog	1982, 1994
4705	2/18/2007	Pig	1983, 1995
4706	2/7/2008	Rat	1984, 1996
4707	1/26/2009	Ox	1985, 1997
4708	2/14/2010	Tiger	1986, 1998
4709	2/3/2011	Rabbit	1987, 1999
4710	1/23/2012	Dragon	1988, 2000
4711	2/10/2013	Snake	1989, 2001
4712	1/31/2014	Horse	1990, 2002

Conclusion

Because these holidays can vary from month to month, they are not included in any of the following chapters. You might want to note these events in pencil on the margins of the particular days.

These days carry great weight. Each culture, of course, values its own traditions. However, children expand their horizons when they learn about other groups. They grow up with less prejudice and with more compassion. A terrific way to learn about other cultures is to participate in their holidays.

January

January, the first month of the year, was named in honor of the Roman god, Janus. Janus was a god who had two faces. He could look both into the past and into the future. His name derives from the Latin word *janua,* or "gate." Romans prayed to him especially at times of war. Originally the months of January and February were added to the end of a ten-month year. In 46 B.C., Julius Caesar made January the first month of the year. The snowdrop is often associated with January because it blooms early. The carnation can be January's flower as well. The garnet is the gem for January.

Month-Long Activities

National Soup Month honors one of America's comfort foods. Contact: Public Affairs, Campbell Soup Company, Campbell Place, Camden, New Jersey 08103. Telephone: (800) 257-8443. Visit a Web site at: http://www.campbellsoups.com.

 The children could make some soup and share it at lunch.

Oatmeal Month honors the cereal that is both healthy and delicious. Contact: The Oat Expert, 225 W. Washington, Suite 1625, Chicago, Illinois 60606.

 The children could make and eat oatmeal cookies one cold day.

Special Days

Martin Luther King, Jr. Day has been observed on the third Monday in January since 1986.

National School Nurse Day is celebrated on the fourth Wednesday in January. Contact: National Association of School Nurses, Inc., PO Box 1300, Scarborough, Maine 04070-1300. Telephone: (207) 883-2117. Email: nasn@aol.com.

Plough Day is celebrated in England the first Monday after Twelfth Day. Farmers return to their fields after the Christmas holiday.

January

New Year's Day is celebrated around the world. People make New Year's resolutions.

Emancipation Proclamation was declared by Abraham Lincoln in 1863, ending slavery.

Ellis Island opened its doors in 1892. Over twenty million people entered the United States through Ellis Island. It closed in 1954, becoming a national park in 1956. The island opened again as a museum in 1990.

 Children could find out if any of their relatives had ever come through Ellis Island. They could record interesting stories. Students would enjoy reading *Letters from Rifka,* by Karen Hesse.

Third Millennium officially started on January 1, 2001.

Fire engine was used in America for the first time in 1853.

Czechoslovakia officially became two countries, the Czech Republic and the Slovak Republic, in 1992.

Cuba celebrates Liberation Day. On January 1, 1899, Spain lost control of Cuba. For a time it was under U.S. rule. It became a country with a republican government until Fidel Castro overthrew the rulers on January 1, 1959.

Haiti celebrates its Independence Day. It was a Spanish colony from 1492 until 1697. Then it became a French colony until 1804, when it gained its freedom.

 Haiti is part of an island. Children could locate Haiti on a map and research it and its neighbor, the Dominican Republic.

Sudan celebrates its Independence Day. It has been a free nation since 1956, when Egypt and the United Kingdom gave up control.

Florida Citrus Bowl football game matches a team from the Big Ten Conference and a team from the Southeastern Conference.

Cotton Bowl Classic football game has been held annually since 1937. Dallas, Texas, hosts the game.

Tournament of Roses Parade is held in Pasadena, California.

Rose Bowl is a football game with the winner of the Big Ten playing the winner of the Pacific-10. The game, held in Pasadena, California, follows the Tournament of Roses Parade.

Euro was introduced as the currency of many European nations in 1999. On January 1, 2002, the Euro became the official currency of these nations, and all national currencies were removed in February of 2002.

Birthdays

J. Edgar Hoover (born Washington, DC, 1895; died Washington, DC, May 2, 1972) was the director of the FBI from 1924 to 1972.

Paul Revere (born Boston, Massachusetts, 1735; died Boston, Massachusetts, May 10, 1818) became famous for warning the people of Lexington and Concord, Massachusetts, that the British were arriving for military purposes. In addition to being a patriot, Revere was a distinguished silversmith and metalworker. He also made fine tools, such as surgical instruments.

 Children could read Jean Fritz's *And Then What Happened, Paul Revere?*

Betsy Ross (born Philadelphia, Pennsylvania, 1752; died Philadelphia, Pennsylvania, January 30, 1836) may have made the first American flag. Her grandson, in 1870, first proposed that George Washington came to her with specifications for the flag. There is little evidence to show she did make the first flag, but no one has found facts that someone else sewed the first flag.

 Children could look at a copy of our first flag. They could research the significance of the red, white, and blue colors and the symbolism of the stars and stripes.

J. D. Salinger (born Jerome David Salinger in New York, New York, 1919) is an author. One of his most famous books is *Catcher in the Rye.*

"Mad" Anthony Wayne (born Waynesboro, Pennsylvania, 1745; died Fort Presque Isle, Pennsylvania, December 15, 1796) was a hero during the Revolutionary War and continued to serve in the army after the war.

January

2 **Georgia became the fourth state in the United States by ratifying the Constitution in 1788.** Although one of Georgia's nicknames is the Peach State, the crops of peanuts and tobacco each bring in more revenue than peaches. Cotton, which was a very important source of revenue 100 years ago, now generates a little more than one percent of the state's income. Contact: (800) VISIT-GA. Visit an Internet site at: http://www.50states.com/georgia.htm.

 The children could make and enjoy a simple peach cobbler.

Haiti remembers Ancestors Day.

Canada and the United States began a joint project in 1929 to protect Niagara Falls.

Speed limit of 55 miles per hour was imposed in 1974.

First successful heart transplant was completed in 1968.

Louis Daguerre in 1839 became the first person to photograph the moon.

Birthdays

Isaac Asimov (born Petrovichi, Russia, 1920; died New York, New York, April 6, 1992) wrote more than 400 books. He was best known for his science fiction, but he also wrote about history and the world in general. One of his most well-known books is *I, Robot*.

 Children could find out how science fiction differs from other types of fiction. Then they could read a portion of a work by Isaac Asimov.

Nathaniel Bacon (born Suffolk, England, 1647; died Virginia Colony, October 26, 1676) led Bacon's Rebellion. The Virginia colonists were angry with the governor, Sir William Berkeley. They felt he was not properly protecting them from Indians. Nathaniel Bacon organized a group of people, and they burned Jamestown in protest. Berkeley fled to a nearby ship. Bacon died unexpectedly of a fever, and the rebellion fell apart.

Helen Herron Taft (born Cincinnati, Ohio, 1861; died Washington, DC, May 22, 1943) was the wife of William Howard Taft, twenty-seventh president of the United States. Nicknamed "Nellie," she and her husband lived in the Philippines, Japan, Cuba, Panama, and Italy before he became president. Visit a Web site at: http://www.whitehouse.gov/history/firstladies/ht27.html.

 Students could trace her travels on a map.

January

3 **Drinking straw was patented by Marvin Stone in 1888 in Washington, DC.** He covered paper with paraffin to make it waterproof.

Martin Luther was excommunicated from the Catholic Church in 1521.

Congress convenes at noon, according to the Constitution and the Twentieth Amendment. New members are sworn in on this day as well.

 Students could locate the names of their current senators and representatives.

Alaska became the forty-ninth state of the United States in 1959. Alaska is by far the biggest state, but only two states have smaller populations. The state has experienced booms in furs, fishing, whaling, gold, and oil. Contact: (907) 465–2010. Visit an Internet site at: http://www.50states.com/alaska.htm.

 Children could research Alaska more and predict its next economic focus.

Birthdays

Alma Flor Ada (born Camaguey, Cuba, 1938) is a children's author. One of her books is *Three Golden Oranges.*

Cicero (born Rome, 106 B.C.; died Rome 43 B.C.) was a writer, politician, and philosopher.

Grace Anna Goodhue Coolidge (born Burlington, Vermont, 1879; died Northampton, Massachusetts, July 8, 1957) was the wife of Calvin Coolidge, thirtieth president of the United States. The outgoing Grace Goodhue taught at the Clarke School for the Deaf, located in Massachusetts, before she married the shy Coolidge. Visit a Web site at: http://www.whitehouse.gov/history/firstladies/gc30.html.

Mel Gibson (born New York, New York, 1956) is an actor.

Bobby Hull (born Point Anne, Ontario, Canada, 1939) is one of the highest scoring hockey players on record. He played from 1957 to 1981. For nine of those years he scored fifty or more points each season.

Lucretia (Coffin) Mott (born Nantucket, Massachusetts, 1793; died Philadelphia, Pennsylvania, November 11, 1880) was an abolitionist and leader of the women's rights movement.

John Ronald Reuel Tolkien (born Bloemfontein, South Africa, 1892; died Bournemouth, England, September 2, 1973) wrote *The Hobbit* and *The Lord of the Rings.*

 Read to the children a passage from one of Tolkien's books.

January

4

Utah became the forty-fifth state of the United States in 1896. The state capital is Salt Lake City, and its state nickname is the Beehive State. Its Great Salt Lake, located in the northern part of the state, is really the remnant of an inland sea. Because its waters do not drain into another body of water, the lake is becoming saltier and saltier. Contact: (801) 538-1030. Visit an Internet site at: http://www.50states.com/utah.htm.

 Items float with more ease in salt water than in fresh water. Fill one container with fresh water, and fill another container with salt water. Try floating various objects. Record the results.

First appendectomy was performed in 1885 in Davenport, Iowa. Dr. William West removed Mary Gartside's appendix; she lived for at least another thirty years.

Union of Myanmar celebrates its Independence Day. It became free from British rule in 1948. The country was formerly called Burma.

Birthdays

Louis Braille (born Coupvray, France, 1809; died March 28, 1852) invented a raised type of writing that can felt and read by the blind. He was accidentally blinded at age three. When he was ten, he attended the National Institute for the Blind in Paris. He became an accomplished musician and served as a church organist. He also became a teacher at the Institute. He modified a military code system to develop Braille.

 Locate some materials written in Braille. The local library may have some works. Let the children feel the Braille.

Jacob Grimm (born Hanau, Germany, 1785; died Berlin, Germany, September 20, 1863) wrote, with his brother, *Grimm's Fairy Tales.*

 Children could read and enjoy some of the fairy tales. They could write fractured fairy tales.

Phyllis Reynolds Naylor (born Anderson, Indiana, 1933) is a children's author. One of her most famous books is *Shiloh,* the 1991 Newbery Medal winner.

Tom Thumb (born Charles Sherwood Stratton in Bridgeport, Connecticut, 1838; died Middleborough, Massachusetts, July 15, 1883) grew to a height of forty inches. He weighed seventy pounds. P. T. Barnum hired him to be a part of his museum and circus.

January

Nellie Tayloe Ross became the first woman governor. She became Wyoming's top executive in 1925.

 Children could compute some statistics of today's percentages of men and women governors.

National Audubon Society incorporated in 1905. Visit a Web site at: http://www.audubon.org.

Construction on the Golden Gate Bridge began in 1933.

George Washington Carver Memorial Day remembers his death in 1943 in Tuskegee, Alabama. His exact birthday is unknown, but he was probably born in 1864.

Twelfth Night signals the end of traditional Christmas celebrations. It is also the evening before Epiphany.

"Bozo the Clown," a live television show, aired for the first time in 1959.

Birthdays

Alvin Ailey (born Rogers, Texas, 1931; died New York, New York, December 1, 1989) was a choreographer and dancer. He created the Alvin Ailey American Dance Theater, and he strove to increase the importance of African Americans in dance.

 Children could learn more about different types of dancing.

Stephen Decatur (born Sinepuxent, Maryland, 1779; died Bladenburg, Maryland, March 22, 1820) was a naval officer. He is famous for saying, "Our country! In her intercourse with foreign nations may she always be in the right; but our country, right or wrong." He was killed in a duel with Commodore James Barron.

Zebulon Pike (born Lamberton, New Jersey, 1779; died near Toronto, Canada, 1813) was an explorer. In 1805 he investigated the source of the Mississippi River. In 1806 he became intrigued with a large mountain in Colorado. Thinking the mountain was nearby, he and his party started walking toward it. They were fooled by the mountain's height and its true distance from them. That mountain was named Pike's Peak. Later he signed up to fight in the War of 1812. He was killed in battle.

 Pike's Peak hosts a very important road race every year. Create a "road race" of questions regarding mountains. Each time a student answers a question correctly, he/she speeds farther up the mountain.

January

 6

Christmas is celebrated by members of the Armenian Church.

Epiphany is celebrated by some Christians. The magi visited Jesus on this day. In some cultures gifts are exchanged, and special dinners take place.

La Befana occurs in Italy. The "Befana," or witch, enters homes the previous night through the chimney. She leaves good children nice toys in their stockings. Bad children find coal in their stockings. The day is celebrated with parades and feasts.

New Mexico became the forty-seventh state of the United States in 1912. Santa Fe is the capital. Although New Mexico is one of the youngest states, it boasts some of the oldest American structures. Spaniards traveled on El Camino Real (the Royal Highway) in 1581; and Santa Fe was built in 1609 or 1610. Contact: (800) 545–2040. Visit an Internet site at: http://www.50states.com/newmexic.htm.

 Children could create some math problems regarding how long ago New Mexico's treasures were created.

Birthdays

Joan of Arc (born Domremy, France, 1412; died Rouen, France, May 30, 1431) led French troops against the British. Declaring she had religious visions, she persuaded Charles VII to give her an army. She was successful for quite some time. She was captured by the British. She was tried for heresy and burned at the stake in 1431.

 Children could research her battles and plot them on a map.

Sherlock Holmes (born 1854) was a fictional detective created by Sir Arthur Conan Doyle.

Tom Mix (born Driftwood, Pennsylvania, 1880; died Florence, Arizona, October 12, 1940) was a film actor known for his westerns.

Carl Sandburg (born Galesburg, Illinois, 1878; died Flat Rock, North Carolina, July 22, 1967) was a poet, writer, and historian. His free verse poetry depends on strong imagery. One of his books of poetry is *Corn Huskers,* written in 1918. He won the Pulitzer Prize in 1940 for his biographies on Abraham Lincoln.

 Share some of his poetry.

Jedediah Strong Smith (born Jericho, New York, 1799; died on the Santa Fe Trail, Kansas, May 27, 1831) was an American explorer. He claimed to be the first American to arrive in California.

anuary

 7 **Russia celebrates Christmas.**

Japan celebrates Nanakusa. The festival began in the seventh century when seven medicinal plants were offered to the emperor.

Dr. John Jeffries and Jean-Pierre Blanchard made the first balloon flight across the English Channel in 1785.

First U.S. commercial bank, the Bank of North America, opened in Philadelphia in 1782.

 Children could create their own class bank. However, instead of money, they could deposit acts of kindness.

Presidential elections occurred in America for the first time in 1789.

 Children could find out if George Washington had any opponents.

Transatlantic telephone calls could be made for the first time in 1927 between London and New York. A three-minute call brought a charge of $75.

Fountain pen was patented by William B. Purvis in 1890.

Birthdays

Katie Couric (born Arlington, Virginia, 1957) is a news commentator.

Millard Fillmore (born Cayuga County, New York, 1800; died Buffalo, New York, March 8, 1874) was the thirteenth president (1850–1853) of the United States. He succeeded Zachary Taylor when the latter died. Prior to being president, he had been a congressman for four terms. His party did not nominate him for the 1852 presidential contest. He campaigned during the 1856 race for the "Know-Nothing Party," but he lost. Visit a Web site at: http://www.whitehouse.gov/history/presidents/mf13.html.

Jacques Etienne Montgolfier (born Vidalon-lez Annonay, Ardeche, France, 1745; died Serrieres, France, August 2, 1799) was an inventor and balloonist. He and his brother, Joseph Michael, experimented with fabric balloons and smoke. Eventually they conducted the first hot air balloon flight.

 Since January 7 remembers two ballooning events, the children could conduct experiments with balloons. Consider having balloon races.

 anuary

8 **George Washington gave the first State of the Union message in 1790.**

Amendment Eleven to the Constitution was adopted in 1798. States could not be sued by people from another state or by other countries.

Herman Hollerith patented his tabulating machine in 1889. This machine, instrumental in calculating census data, was a precursor to today's computers. He went on to found IBM.

Children could make a timeline of inventions important to the development of the computer.

Dow Jones Industrial Average surpassed 2,000 in 1987, closing at 2,000.25.

 Children could graph regular intervals of the Dow Jones Average. They could also predict benchmarks for the future.

Greece celebrates Women's Day. Women take the day off from cooking and cleaning. The men take up the chores for the day.

Battle of New Orleans took place in 1815. General Andrew Jackson's American troops crushed the British. However, both sides later found out that a peace treaty had been signed two weeks prior to the battle.

Birthdays

Stephen Hawking (born Oxford, England, 1942) is a physicist.

Elvis Presley (born Tupelo, Mississippi, 1935; died Memphis, Tennessee, August 16, 1977) was a rock and roll star.

 Have an Elvis impersonation event.

Elisabetta Sirani (born Bologna, Italy, 1638; died Bologna, Italy, August 28, 1665) was one of a handful of women painters of the time. She painted almost 200 works of art and established a painting school for women.

January

9

Jean Pierre Blanchard made the first balloon flight in the United States in 1793. President George Washington and other officials watched the forty-six minute flight, staged in Philadelphia, Pennsylvania.

Connecticut became the fifth state in the United States by ratifying the Constitution in 1788. The state's name means, "beside the long tidal river." Connecticut is forty-eighth in size. Hartford is the state capital. Contact: (800) CT-BOUND. Visit an Internet site at: http://www.50states.com/connecti.htm.

 The state's song is *Yankee Doodle*. The children could play the song on kazoos.

American Baseball League and National Baseball League settled their differences in 1903.

Panama remembers Martyrs' Day.

Wind Cave National Park was established in 1903. The park is located in South Dakota. Visit a Web site at: http://www.nps.gov/wica.

Surveyor 7 **made a soft landing on the surface of Mars in 1968.**

 Children now know there are no "little green men" on Mars. However, they could do some research and create a skit about a meeting between Martians and Earthlings.

Birthdays

Clyde Robert Bulla (born King City, Missouri, 1914) is a children's author. One of his books is *The Chalk Box Kid*. Visit a Web site at: http://mowrites4kids.drury.edu/authors/bulla.

Carrie Lane Chapman Catt (born Ripon, Wisconsin, 1859; died New Rochelle, New York, March 9, 1947) was a women's rights advocate. She established the National League of Women Voters.

Bob Denver (born New Rochelle, New York, 1935) is an actor. He is famous for playing Gilligan in "Gilligan's Island."

 Children could discuss the possibility of being shipwrecked. They could make a list of essential items (for example, cups) and what they could substitute on a deserted island.

Richard Milhous Nixon (born Yorba Linda, California, 1913; died New York, New York, August 22, 1994) was the thirty-seventh president (1969–1974) of the United States. During World War II, he served in noncombat duty. He was elected to Congress in 1946 and to the Senate in 1950. He was Eisenhower's vice president. During Nixon's presidency the first moon landing occurred. Also, he made an important visit to China. He served from January 20, 1969, to August 9, 1974, when he resigned. He was about to be impeached. Visit a Web site at: http://www.whitehouse.gov/history/presidents/rn37.html.

January

 Common Sense **was published by Thomas Paine in 1776.** Some experts believe this small pamphlet was one of the major influences on the Revolutionary War. At least one half million copies were sold.

 Paine's words are very stirring. Older children would enjoy reading and discussing some of the passages.

Underground railway opened in London, England, in 1863.

League of Nations was formed in 1920. Over fifty countries worked together to try to end war. The United States was not a member. Permanent nations included France, Italy, Japan, and Great Britain. Later Germany and the Union of Soviet Socialist Republics became permanent members. It ceased to exist in 1946, but it became the basis for the United Nations.

United Nations General Assembly held its first meeting in 1946 in London, England.

 Children could discover why the United States did not join the League of Nations and why the United States was so active in the formation of the United Nations.

Birthdays

Ethan Allen (born Litchfield, Connecticut, 1738; died Burlington, Vermont, February 12, 1789) was a hero of the American Revolution and the leader of the "Green Mountain Boys."

Ray Bolger (born Dorchester, Massachusetts, 1904; died Los Angeles, California, January 15, 1987) was an actor and dancer. He played the scarecrow in *The Wizard of Oz*.

Robinson Jeffers (born Pittsburgh, Pennsylvania, 1887; died Carmel, California, January 20, 1962) was a poet and a playwright.

Willie "Stretch" McCovey (born Mobile, Alabama, 1938) was a famous baseball player. He played for the San Francisco Giants.

Bill Toomey (born 1939) was a decathalon champion. He won the gold medal in the 1968 Olympics.

 Children could create their own class decathalon, possibly a combination of mental and athletic events.

anuary

11 **Mount Etna in Sicily erupted in 1693.**

 Children could make a mock volcano by surrounding a plastic cup with papier mache. They can make the volcano "erupt" by first placing some baking soda into the cup and then adding vinegar.

William Herschel discovered Titania and Oberon, two moons of Uranus, in 1787.

Milk was delivered in glass bottles for the first time in 1878.

Nepal celebrates National Unity Day. King Prithvinarayan Shan united all of Nepal and established a dynasty of rulers existing still.

 Mount Everest and other formidable mountains lie within the borders of Nepal. Mountaineering has increased the country's prosperity, but it has also created problems. Children could list the pros and cons of this kind of tourism.

U.S. Surgeon General Luther Terry issued the first report, published in 1964, that cigarettes and smoking were health hazards.

 Children could make antismoking posters and display their works around school.

Birthdays

Alexander Hamilton (born British West Indies, 1757; died Weehawken, New Jersey, July 12, 1804) was an early American leader. He rallied for the causes of the Revolutionary War and served for a while as George Washington's aide-de-camp. He was secretary of the treasury while Washington was president and helped the new country become financially sound. Hamilton believed in a strong central government, and he wrote a large portion of *The Federalist*. He was mortally wounded after a duel with Aaron Burr.

Robert C. O'Brien (born Robert Conly in Brooklyn, New York, 1918; died Washington, DC, March 3, 1973) was an editor for *National Geographic* and a children's author. He won the Newbery Medal for *Mrs. Frisby and the Rats of NIMH*. Visit a good Web site at: http://www.edupaperback.org/pastbios/Obrienr.html.

anuary

12 **Zanzibar remembers its revolution day of 1935. Zanzibar is now part of Tanzania.**

X-ray photograph was first created in 1896 by Henry Smith in Davidson, North Carolina.

Hattie Caraway became the first woman to be elected a U.S. senator in 1932. She represented the state of Arkansas.

 Students could calculate the number of men and women senators. They could find out if the number of women senators has risen in recent years.

President Bill Clinton in 1994 signed an agreement to disarm some of America's nuclear arsenal.

Birthdays

Joe Frazier (born Beaufort, South Carolina, 1944) is a former boxer.

John Hancock (born Braintree, Massachusetts, 1737; died Quincy, Massachusetts, October 8, 1793) was an American patriot. He deliberately made his signature on the Declaration of Independence very prominent. His political activities irritated the British, and they started the famous march to Concord. After the war, he served as governor of Massachusetts for a number of years. Visit a Web site at: http://www.ushistory.org/declaration/signers/hancock.htm.

 Show the students a copy of the Declaration of Independence and his famous signature. Have a signature writing event where they copy his style. Jean Fritz wrote *Will You Sign Here, John Hancock?* Students would enjoy reading the book.

Jack London (born San Francisco, California, 1876; died Santa Rosa, California, November 22, 1916) was an author. He wrote more than fifty books, and one of his most celebrated works is *Call of the Wild.*

 Consider reading a portion of the book.

Charles Perrault (born Paris, France, 1628; died Paris, France, May 16, 1703) wrote several tales, including *Cinderella, Sleeping Beauty,* and *Little Red Riding Hood.*

John Singer Sargent (born Florence, Italy, 1856; died London, England, 1925) was a painter.

 Sargent's portraits flatter the subject, but they also tell much about fashion and home decor. Visit a Web site at: http://www.jssgallery.org. Look at some of his works. What conclusions can the children derive?

John Winthrop (born Edwardston, England, 1588; died Boston, Massachusetts, March 26, 1649) was the leader of the Massachusetts Bay Colony.

Jacqueline Woodson (born Columbus, Ohio, 1964) is a children's author. One of her books is *Miracle's Boys.*

January

 Elizabeth I was crowned queen of England in 1559. The ceremony took place in Westminster Abbey.

 Children could make the family tree of Elizabeth I.

National Geographic Society was created in Washington, DC, in 1888. Visit a Web site at: http://www.nationalgeographic.com.

Stephen Foster Memorial Day was established by Presidential Proclamation in 1951. It notes Foster's death on January 13, 1864, in New York, New York.

Radio show was broadcast for the first time in 1910. Lee Deforest arranged for Enrico Caruso and other celebrities to perform in New York City. Only a few people owned the necessary equipment to receive the performance, but it did mark the beginning of radio communication.

Accordion was patented in 1854.

Robert C. Weaver became the first African American appointed to the presidential cabinet. Lyndon Baines Johnson made Weaver Secretary of Housing and Urban Development in 1966.

Children could investigate the presidential cabinet and find out the roles of each advisor.

Douglas Wilder was inaugurated governor of Virginia in 1990. He was the first elected African American governor.

Birthdays

Horatio Alger, Jr. (born Revere, Massachusetts, 1834; died Natick, Massachusetts, July 18, 1899) was an author. He wrote more than 100 books where the young male hero fought tough times to find fame and fortune. Two of his most famous works were *Ragged Dick,* published in 1867, and *From Canal Boy to President,* published in 1881. Visit a Web site at: http://www.biography.com.

 Read a portion of one of his books.

Michael Bond (born Newbury, Berkshire, England, 1926) is an author. He wrote *Paddington Bear.* Visit a Web site at: http://www.oup.co.uk/oxed/children/fiction/authors/bond.

Salmon Portland Chase (born Cornish, New Hampshire, 1808; died New York, New York, May 7, 1873) was a politician, senator, and chief justice for the Supreme Court. He would have liked to be president, but his antislavery views put off many voters.

January

 Clarinet was invented in Germany in 1690.

 The music teacher or a child studying the clarinet could show how the clarinet works. The children could look at other woodwind instruments.

Massachusetts held a day of fasting in 1699 to atone for punishing "witches."

Ratification Day marks the day in 1784 when the Continental Congress ratified the peace agreement with Britain. The United States officially became an independent country.

Bulgaria celebrates Vinegrower's Day. Grape vines are trimmed, and wine is sprinkled over the plants in hopes that the season will be a good one.

Henry Ford pushed the button to start the first assembly-line production in 1914.

 Ford's first assembly line made cars. However, children could form an assembly line to make ice cream sundaes.

Soyuz 4 **docked with** *Soyuz 5,* **both Soviet spacecraft, in 1969, marking the first time spacecraft joined in space.** Cosmonauts went from one vessel to the other.

Franklin Roosevelt in 1943 became the first president to fly in an airplane.

Birthdays

Benedict Arnold (born Norwich, Connecticut, 1741; died London, England, June 14, 1801) was an American officer who became a traitor during the Revolutionary War.

Hugh Lofting (born Maidenhead, England, 1886; died Santa Monica, California, September 26, 1947) was an author. He is famous for his ten Dr. Dolittle books. His *Voyages of Dr. Dolittle* won the 1923 Newbery Medal.

Albert Schweitzer (born Kayserberg, Upper Alsace, 1875; died Lamboren, Gabon, September 4, 1965) balanced his love of music, theology, and medicine. As a young adult, he was a very accomplished organist. He also wrote about music and composers. In 1913 he went to Gabon as a missionary and as a doctor. He practiced there on and off, continuing to write and play concerts whenever possible. He received the 1952 Nobel Peace Prize.

 The children could research his life and decide which of the three areas benefited most from his work.

William Whipple (born Kittery, Maine, 1730; died Portsmouth, New Hampshire, November 10, 1785) signed the Declaration of Independence. He represented New Hampshire.

January

 15

Henry VIII declared himself to be the leader of the Church of England in 1535.

Democratic Party used the donkey as its party emblem for the first time in 1870. *Harper's Weekly* printed an article which included Thomas Nast's caricature of a donkey.

Swan Lake, **Tchaikovsky's ballet, opened in Saint Petersburg, Russia, in 1895.**

 Children could listen to a portion of the music and perhaps transfer what they hear to art.

Super Bowl I was played in 1967. The Green Bay Packers defeated the Kansas City Chiefs.

 Sports fans could compile statistics on the various Super Bowl games. Which team holds the most championships? Which person played in the most games?

Birthdays

Martin Luther King, Jr. (born Atlanta, Georgia, 1929; assassinated Memphis, Tennessee, April 4, 1968) was a civil rights leader and a minister. He was an excellent student and skipped two years of high school. He entered Morehouse College at age fifteen. He graduated in 1948 and decided to become a minister. He obtained a divinity degree from Crozer Theological Seminary and a Ph.D. in theology from Boston University. In 1954 he became the pastor of a congregation in Montgomery, Alabama. He became active in civil rights in 1955. He urged people to use nonviolent methods to obtain their rights. He was arrested and jailed several times. King and other leaders organized a march to Washington, DC, in 1963. There he gave his famous *I Have a Dream* speech. He won the Nobel Peace Prize in 1964. While supporting a strike of garbagemen in Memphis Tennessee, he was killed by James Earl Ray.

 The children could read excerpts from the *I Have a Dream* speech and illustrate his words.

Philip Livingston (born Albany, New York, 1716; died York, Pennsylvania, June 12, 1778) signed the Declaration of Independence. He represented New York.

Edward Teller (born Budapest, Hungary, 1908) is a renowned physicist. He is known as the father of the hydrogen bomb.

January

 16 *Hello, Dolly!* premiered on Broadway with Carol Channing in 1964.

 Students could compare a musical to other types of theatrical productions.

Persian Gulf War began in 1991 when the Allied Forces attacked Iraq after it had invaded Kuwait.

Birthdays

Jay Hanna "Dizzy" Dean (born Lucas, Arkansas, 1911; died Reno, Nevada, July 17, 1974) was a baseball pitcher and a baseball game announcer.

 Sports announcing is difficult. Tape a baseball game. Replay it, but eliminate the sound. Have students be the commentators.

Martha Weston (born Asheville, North Carolina, 1947) is an illustrator and author. One of her books is *Tuck's Haunted House.*

 Students could find out the name of her favorite monkey.

January

 17 James Cook in 1773 became the first person to cross the Antarctic Circle.

James Madison Randolph was born in 1806 in the White House. He was the first child born in the White House and the grandson of Thomas Jefferson.

Cable car was patented by Andrew Hallidie in 1871.

 Children could find out how a cable car differs from a train or a bus.

Poland remembers Liberation Day when in 1945 the Russians defeated the Nazis in Warsaw.

Birthdays

Muhammad Ali (born Cassius Clay in Louisville, Kentucky, 1942) is a former heavyweight boxer. He carried the torch for part of the opening ceremonies for the 1995 Olympic Summer Games in Atlanta, Georgia.

John Bellairs (born Marshall, Michigan, 1938; died Haverhill, Massachusetts, March 8, 1991) was a children's author.

Jim Carrey (born Newmarket, Ontario, Canada, 1962) is an actor and a comedian.

Robert Cormier (born Leominster, Massachusetts, 1925; died Leominster, Massachusetts, November 2, 2000) was a children's author. One of his works is *The Chocolate War.* Visit a Web site at: http://www.randomhouse.com/teachers/authors/corm.html.

Benjamin Franklin (born Boston, Massachusetts, 1706; died Philadelphia, Pennsylvania, April 17, 1790) was a statesman, writer, printer, and much more. He signed both the Declaration of Independence and the Constitution. He published *Poor Richard's Almanack.* He invented many items, including bifocal glasses and the lightning rod. He created the first fire company and the first free library.

 Children could make a timeline of his life and then decide whether he made the most contributions to science or to the freedom of America. *Ben Franklin of Old Philadelphia,* by Margaret Cousins, is an excellent source of information.

Shari Lewis (born Shari Hurwitz in New York, New York, 1934; died Los Angeles, California, August 2, 1998) was a puppeteer and a leader in children's educational television.

 Bring in materials to make puppets of various kinds. Consider sock puppets, stick puppets, even finger puppets. Have the children produce a puppet show.

January

 Tunisia celebrates its Revolution Day.

Polar bear was put on display in a zoo in Boston, Massachusetts, in 1733.

 Students could discuss why this would be a very big event for that time period.

An airplane landed for the first time on a ship, the USS *Pennsylvania,* in 1911.

Gold reached $1,000 per ounce in 1980.

Birthdays

Danny Kaye (born David Daniel Kaminski in Brooklyn, New York, 1913; died Los Angeles, California, March 3, 1987) was a television and movie star. He was also a spokesperson for UNICEF.

Kevin Costner (born Compton, California, 1955) is an actor and director.

A(lan) A(lexander) Milne (born London, England, 1882; died Hartfield, England, January 31, 1956) was an author. He is best remembered for his Winnie the Pooh stories.

 Have a Winnie the Pooh day. Children could bring in their stuffed creatures, and they could share some of his writing.

Peter Roget (born London, England, 1779; died West Malvern, England, September 12, 1869) wrote *Roget's Thesaurus.*

 Children could learn how to use a thesaurus. Each could create a page of a thesaurus regarding a certain word. Consider using colors and action verbs.

Daniel Webster (born Salisbury, New Hampshire, 1782; died Marshfield, Massachusetts, October 24, 1852) was a politician and a speaker.

January

 Tin can processing of food was patented in 1825 by Ezra Daggett and Thomas Kensett.

 Research and draw the steps to tin can processing.

Singapore celebrates its kite festival. Singapore is a country of one large island and fifty smaller islands. Located at the southern tip of the Malay Peninsula, it sits between the Indian Ocean and the South China Sea. Colonized by the British, today it is independent and an important commerce and transportation center.

 Children could make and fly their own kites.

Birthdays

Paul Cézanne (born Aix-en-Provence, France, 1839; died Aix-en-Provence, France, October 22, 1906) has been declared the father of modern painting. He did not become famous until after his death. He tended to convey the emotion of the object painted rather than its physical appearance. Visit a Web site at: http://www.oir.ucf.edu/wm/paint/auth/cezanne.

Robert E. Lee (born Westmoreland County, Virginia, 1807; died Lexington, Virginia, October 12, 1870) was the leader of the Confederate Army during the Civil War.

Edgar Allan Poe (born Boston, Massachusetts, 1809; died Baltimore, Maryland, October 7, 1849) was a poet and a writer. His most famous works include the poem *The Raven* and the tale *The Gold Bug.*

 Older children enjoy a choral reading of *The Raven.*

James Watt (born Greenock, Scotland, 1736; died Heathfield, England, August 19, 1819) was an inventor and a civil engineer. Although he did not invent the steam engine, he did make it more practical. The electrical unit, the watt, is named in honor of him.

 Children could look at different types of light bulbs and find the wattage. They could then discover the relationship between wattage and brightness.

January

 Aquarius the Water Bearer is the astrological sign for January 20 through February 18.

American Revolution ended informally when British and American diplomats signed a "Cessation of Hostilities" in 1783. The official documents concluding the war were signed September 3, 1783.

 Children could imagine how happy both the soldiers and their families would feel on this day. They could each become a person of the times and write letters to their loved ones.

Presidential Inauguration Day occurs every four years. The newly elected president and vice president take the oath of office at noon.

 Children could hear or read the oaths of office. They could compose an oath citizens could take that day.

Brazil celebrates San Sebastian Day. Sebastian is the patron saint of Rio de Janeiro.

First basketball game was played in 1892. James Naismith was working at the School for Christian Workers, now Springfield College, in Springfield, Massachusetts. He was told to develop a new game to keep athletes fit in the winter months. Using a soccer ball and two peach bushel baskets, he created the game of basketball.

Children could organize a basketball mini-tournament.

Republic of Guinea-Bissau remembers National Heroes Day.

Birthdays

Edwin "Buzz" Aldrin (born Montclair, New Jersey, 1930) is one of the first men to walk on the moon.

George Burns (born New York, New York, 1896; died Los Angeles, California, March 9, 1996) was a comedian and an actor.

DeForest Kelley (born Atlanta, Georgia, 1920; died June 11, 1999) was an actor famous for his roles in *Star Trek* movies and television programs.

January

Pineapple was brought to Hawaii for cultivation in 1813.

 Children could prepare and eat fresh pineapple. They could also find out how pineapples are grown.

Carrie Nation visited and destroyed a Kansas City saloon in 1901.

Automobile driver's licenses became legal requirements in 1937.

 Children could interview a police officer to find out how a license is obtained and how and why it could be taken away.

President Truman's inaugural parade was televised in 1949.

Concorde flew for the first time in 1976.

Birthdays

John Fitch (born East Windsor, Connecticut, 1743; died Bardstown, Kentucky, July 2, 1798) was an inventor and clock maker. He invented the steamboat and obtained American and French patents for it in 1791. Although Robert Fulton is often credited with inventing the steamboat, he actually just made it more practical.

 Children could discover how steam propels a ship.

Thomas Jonathan "Stonewall" Jackson (born Clarksburg, Virginia (now West Virginia), 1824; died in battle near Chancellorsville, Virginia, May 10, 1863) was a famous Confederate general during the Civil War.

Hakeem Abdul Olajuwon (born Lagos, Nigeria, 1963) is a basketball player.

January

Postal service between Boston and New York was started in 1673.

Children could investigate how postal services have changed over the years.

World's biggest cheese was made in Wisconsin in 1964. It weighed 15,723 kilograms.

 Children could convert the weight of the cheese into pounds.

Birthdays

Andre Ampere (born Lyons, France, 1775; died Marseilles, France, June 10, 1836) was a physicist specializing in electricity. The ampere, a measure of electrical current, is named for him.

 Students could find out how electrical circuits work.

January

National Pie Day is celebrated through tastings and competitions. Contact: American Pie Council, 512 Concord Avenue, Boulder, Colorado 80304. Telephone: (303) 449-0165. Visit an Internet site at: http://piecouncil.org.

 Children could bring in various kinds of pies. Everyone could sample the different types.

Elizabeth Blackwell became the first woman to receive a medical doctor's degree in the United States in 1849.

 Children could interview a doctor to find out how a person becomes a doctor.

The Twenty-Fourth Amendment to the Constitution was adopted in 1964. It eliminated poll taxes and other taxes designed to prevent people from voting.

National Handwriting Day stresses the importance of legibility.

 Students could write, using their best penmanship, a thank you note to someone.

Birthdays

Joseph Hewes (born Kingston, New Jersey, 1730; died Philadelphia, Pennsylvania, November 10, 1779) signed the Declaration of Independence. He represented North Carolina.

Edouard Manet (born Paris, France, 1832; died Paris, France, April 30, 1883) was an impressionist painter. Visit a Web site at: http://www.oir.ucf.edu/wm/paint/auth/manet.

January

Gold was discovered in California in 1848 by John Sutter and John Marshall. They were building a sawmill when they noticed flakes of gold in the water. The Gold Rush began as people flocked to the western foothills of the Sierra Nevadas. Over 90,000 people had reached California by 1849, and the population topped 220,000 by 1852. The rush had declined by 1854, and most prospectors turned to other jobs.

Children could find out how mine claims are made legal and how assays prove metal content of ore. Children would really enjoy reading Sid Fleischman's *By the Great Horn Spoon!*

The Newcastle Badminton Club, the first such club, was established in England in 1900.

 Children could play badminton and compare it to tennis.

***Voyager 2* sailed past Uranus in 1986.** It discovered new moons.

 Children could find out how newly discovered objects in space are named.

Togo celebrates Economic Liberation Day.

Birthdays

Mary Lou Retton (born Fairmont, West Virginia, 1968) is an Olympic gold medal winner in gymnastics.

Maria Tallchief (born Betty Marie Tall Chief in Fairfax, Oklahoma, 1925) is a noted ballerina. A member of the Osage tribe, she originally studied to be a pianist. She established the Chicago City Ballet in 1979.

January

25 **Largest diamond, the Cullinan, ever found was discovered in South Africa in 1905.** The stone was 3,106 carats.

 Have children illustrate how diamonds are made and how they are cut.

Fluoridation process was added to drinking water in 1945 in Grand Rapids, Michigan.

 Children could find out how fluoride makes their teeth stronger.

"Guiding Light," a soap opera, was broadcast over radio for the first time in 1937.

Birthdays

Robert Boyle (born Lismore, Ireland, 1662; died London, England, December 30, 1691) was a scientist. He developed Boyle's Law: If a gas is maintained at a constant temperature, the volume of the gas is inversely proportional to the pressure.

 Children could inflate a balloon and put it in a refrigerator. They could record the results.

Robert Burns (born Ayrshire, Scotland, 1759; died Dumfries, Scotland, July 21, 1796) was a poet. One of his most famous works is *Auld Lang Syne.*

January

26 **Backwards Day** is celebrated.

 Children could wear shirts or hats backward today.

Dominican Republic celebrates the birthday of Juan Pablo Duarte, a founding father.

India celebrates Republic Day. It gained its freedom from Great Britain in 1950.

Australia was founded in 1788. It may be the smallest continent, but it is the sixth largest country. Aborigines settled in Australia at least 40,000 years ago. The Dutch were the first Europeans to explore the area, and they called the continent New Holland. However, Captain James Cook declared in 1770 that the land belonged to Great Britain. Australia became a penal colony when 700 prisoners were transported there in 1788. Gold was discovered in 1851. It became a commonwealth in 1901.

 Australia is home to many marsupials. Children could research some of these animals and then make a play in which Captain Cook explores Australia and finds these animals.

Michigan became the twenty-sixth state of the United States in 1837. The state borders four of the five Great Lakes. It has more coastline than any other state except Alaska. The state capital is Lansing, and its nicknames are the Wolverine State and the Lake State. It ranks twenty-third in area and eighth in population. Contact: (800) 543–2937. Visit an Internet site at: http://www.50states.com/michigan.htm.

 Children could make a map of Michigan and the Great Lakes it borders. They could write a letter to the governor to ask whether having two distinct portions to the state is a problem.

Electric dental drill was patented in 1875 by George Green from Kalamazoo, Michigan.

Rocky Mountain National Park was created in Colorado in 1915. Visitors have to get used to its high elevations (8,000 to 14,000 feet above sea level). Visit a Web site at: http://www.nps.gov/romo.

Birthdays

Bessie Coleman (born Atlanta, Georgia, 1893; died Jacksonville, Florida, April 30, 1926) was the first African American woman to earn an airplane pilot's license.

Mary Elizabeth Mapes Dodge (born New York, New York, 1831; died Onteora Park, New York, August 21, 1905) was an author and an editor. Her most famous work is *Hans Brinker; or The Silver Skates*. The 1865 novel has had more than 100 editions and has been translated into at least six other languages.

 Read to the children a passage of the book. Compare it to some recent novels.

Jules Feiffer (born New York, New York, 1929) is a cartoonist. He illustrated *The Phantom Tollbooth*.

Julia Dent Grant (born St. Louis, Missouri, 1826; died Washington, DC, December 14, 1902) was the wife of Ulysses Grant, the eighteenth president of the United States. Grant was an army officer, and much of their married life was spent on the frontier in the garrisons. Mrs. Grant enjoyed the comparatively easy life of the White House. Visit a Web site at: http://www.whitehouse.gov/history/firstladies/jg18.html.

Douglas MacArthur (born Little Rock, Arkansas, 1880; died Washington, DC, April 5, 1964) was a general who became famous for his leadership in the South Pacific during World War II. He uttered his famous line, "I will return," when the Japanese forced him to leave the Philippines. He did return.

January

27 **Astronauts Virgil Grissom, Edward White, and Roger Chaffee were killed in the** *Apollo I* **fire in 1967.** The three were in a training simulator when a spark set off a fire in an oxygen-rich capsule. The hatch could not be opened fast enough, and the three perished. NASA suspended missions for two years to improve the safety of the space program.

Incandescent light bulb was patented by Thomas Edison in 1880.

 In a drawing a light bulb above someone's head indicates the person has developed a new idea. Children could draw light bulbs. They could surround the light bulbs with ideas of their own for new inventions.

Magnetic tape recorder was invented in 1948.

Birthdays

Lewis Carroll (born Charles Lutwidge Dodgson in Cheshire, England, 1832; died Guildford, Surrey, England, January 14, 1898) was a writer and a mathematician. He is best known for his works, *Alice's Adventures in Wonderland* and *Through the Looking Glass.*

 Have a Mad Hatter's tea party.

Wolfgang Amadeus Mozart (born Salzburg, Austria, 1756; died Vienna, Austria, December 5, 1791) was a composer and a musician. He was playing before audiences by age three. He created his first composition at age five. He composed over 600 pieces of music. Two of his most famous works are *Marriage of Figaro* and *The Magic Flute.*

 Play some of his works. Children enjoy *The Magic Flute.*

January

28 **Galileo in 1613 may have seen Neptune, but he probably did not realize what it was.**

Challenger **Space Shuttle exploded in 1986.** Just seconds into its flight, the spacecraft blew up over the Atlantic Ocean. The accident temporarily stopped the American space program, and it revamped space travel safety requirements. Killed were Christa McAuliffe (the first teacher in space), Francis Scobee, Gregory Jarvis, Ronald McNair, Michael Smith, Judith Resnick, and Ellison Onizuka.

Coast Guard was created by Congress in 1915. It was derived from the Life Saving and Revenue Cutter Service.

 Children could find out just what the Coast Guard does.

Louis Brandeis became the first Jew to be appointed to the Supreme Court in 1916.

Vietnam War ended in 1973. The peace agreement, signed in Paris, France, ended the longest war in American history. More than 46,000 Americans died in Vietnam.

Birthdays

Jackson Pollock (born Cody, Wyoming, 1912; died East Hampton, New York, August 11, 1956) was an abstract expressionist painter. He developed a style where he dribbled paint and enamels over canvas to create delicate, lacy designs. While he was alive, he was famous but not wealthy. Only after he died did the price of his works soar. Visit a Web site at: http://www.oir.ucf.edu/wm/paint/auth/pollock.

 Examine some of his works and assign an art project to imitate his style.

Arthur Rubenstein (born Artur Rubenstein in Lodz, Poland, 1887; died 1982) was a concert pianist. He performed for the first time as a teenager in 1901. When World War II became imminent, he moved to the United States. He enjoyed touring and performing for radio, television, and movies.

Henry Morton Stanley (born Denbighshire, Wales, 1841; died London, England, May 10, 1904) was an explorer. He organized an expedition to find the missing missionary, David Livingstone. Stanley found Livingstone on November 10, 1871, and asked the famous question, "Dr. Livingstone, I presume?"

Vera B. Williams (born Hollywood, California, 1927) is a children's author and illustrator. She wrote, among other works, *More, More, More, Cried the Baby* (Caldecott Honor Book), published in 1990.

 Children could read some of her works.

January

Kansas became the thirty-fourth state of the United States in 1861. Kansas is known chiefly for its agricultural products, including wheat and cattle. The state capital is Topeka. The geographic center of the contiguous United States is located near Lebanon, Kansas. The state animal is the buffalo. Contact: (800) 2KANSAS. Visit an Internet site at: http://www.50states.com/kansas.htm.

 The sunflower is the state's official wildflower. Children could toast and eat sunflower seeds.

American League of Baseball was formed in 1900.

Amendment Eighteen to the Constitution was adopted in 1919. It brought on Prohibition.

Seeing Eye Guide Dog Organization was founded in 1929 by Dorothy Harrison Eustis of Morristown, New Jersey.

 Children could interview a seeing eye dog trainer.

National Baseball Hall of Fame elected its first baseball players in 1936. The people were Walter Johnson, Christy Mathewson, Ty Cobb, Babe Ruth, and Honus Wagner.

 Study the biographies of these men. What accomplishments brought them to the Hall of Fame?

Walt Disney's *Sleeping Beauty* was released in 1959.

Birthdays

Anton Pavlovich Chekhov (born Taganrog, Russia, 1860; died Badenweiler, Germany, July 15, 1904) was a playwright and short story writer. Two of his plays were *The Sea Gull* and *The Cherry Orchard.*

William McKinley (born Niles, Ohio, 1843; died Buffalo, New York, September 14, 1901) was the twenty-fifth president (1897–1901) of the United States. He enlisted as a private in the Civil War. When the war ended, he was twenty-two years old and a major. One of the planks of his presidential platform was that every person should have a "full dinner pail." He was shot by anarchist Leon Czolgosz; McKinley died two weeks later. Visit a Web site at: http://www.whitehouse.gov/history/presidents/wm25.html.

Thomas Paine (born Thetford, England, 1737; died New York, New York, June 8, 1809) was a patriot and an author. His *Common Sense* influenced people's opinions regarding their right to freedom. Many experts believe it was a major catalyst for the American Revolution.

Bill Peet (born Grandview, Indiana, 1915; died Studio City, California, May 11, 2002) was an author and illustrator for Disney Studios. He was also the author of several children's books, including *Farewell to Shady Glen.*

Tom Selleck (born Detroit, Michigan, 1945) is an actor.

Rosemary Wells (born New York, New York, 1943) is a children's author. One of her books is *Noisy Nora.*

Oprah Winfrey (born Kosciusko, Mississippi, 1954) is a talk show host and actress.

January

Library of Congress was burned in 1815. Thomas Jefferson helped reorganize it with a contribution of 6,500 books.

 Students could investigate the size of today's Library of Congress. Visit a Web site at: http:www.loc.gov. How does a book get there? How can citizens use the facilities?

"Lone Ranger" was broadcast over radio for the first time in 1933.

 The theme music for the "Lone Ranger" is a famous classical piece. Children could listen to the music and find out more about its composer.

Birthdays

Lloyd Alexander (born Philadelphia, Pennsylvania, 1924) is a children's author. He wrote, among other works, *The High King* (Newbery Medal), published in 1968.

Richard Cheney (born Lincoln, Nebraska, 1941) is the forty-sixth vice president of the United States. He has served in various political capacities, including being Wyoming's congressman for five terms. Visit a Web site at: http://www.whitehouse.gov/vicepresident/vpbio.html.

Tony Johnston (born Los Angeles, California, 1942) is a children's author. One of her books is *The Cowboy and the Blackeyed Pea,* published in 1992.

Franklin Delano Roosevelt (born Hyde Park, New York, 1882; died Warm Springs, Georgia, April 12, 1945) was the thirty-second president (1933–1945) of the United States. Before he was president, he had been a state senator for New York. He was assistant secretary of the navy, and he was governor of New York. He took over the presidency during the Great Depression. He was the only president to serve more than two terms. He died in office during his fourth term. An amendment to the Constitution limited the number of terms. Visit a Web site at: http://www.whitehouse.gov/history/presidents/fr32.html.

 Discuss whether the president's number of terms should be limited when the senators' and representatives' numbers of terms are not limited.

January

 Nauru celebrates a national holiday. It gained its independence from Australia in 1968. Nauru is a small island, only 8.1 square miles. It has less than 1,000 inhabitants. People live along the shore of the country, and the interior holds reserves of phosphates. Phosphates are components of fertilizer. However, in a few years the phosphates will be exhausted.

First U.S. satellite *Explorer I* was launched in 1958, four months after *Sputnik* was sent into space.

A. G. MacDonald in 1905 drove an automobile for the first time faster than 100 miles per hour. Daytona Beach, Florida, was the location of the speed trial.

 Children could locate current speed records for various kinds of vehicles.

James Van Allen discovered the radiation belt in 1958.

McDonald's opened a franchise in Moscow, Russia, in 1990.

Birthdays

Zane Grey (born Zanesville, Ohio, 1872; died Altadena, California, October 23, 1939) was a novelist best known for his westerns. Two of his most famous works were *Riders of the Purple Sage* and *The Last of the Plainsmen.* He wrote more than fifty books.

Richard Henry Lee (born Westmoreland County, Virginia; died Chantilly, Virginia, June 19, 1794) signed the Declaration of Independence.

Gerald McDermott (born Detroit, Michigan, 1941) is a children's book author and illustrator. Visit a Web site at: http://www.geraldmcdermott.com.

Gouverneur Morris (born Morrisania, New York, 1752; died Morrisania, New York, November 6, 1816) was an American patriot. He attended the Continental Congress and after the war helped Robert Morris settle the United States financially. He was minister to England and France and was a senator from New York.

Robert Morris (born Liverpool, England, 1734; died Philadelphia, Pennsylvania, May 9, 1806) was an American patriot and a merchant. He was one of only two men who signed all three important papers, the Declaration of Independence, the Articles of Confederation, and the Constitution. After the Revolutionary War, he helped the new country get on its feet financially. He was also a senator from the state of Pennsylvania. Later he was forced into bankruptcy and had to go to debtor's prison. Visit a Web site at: http://www.ushistory.org/declaration/signers/morris_r.htm.

 Three famous patriots were born today (Richard Henry Lee, Gouverneur Morris, and Robert Morris). Using a Venn diagram, compare and contrast the three.

Jackie Robinson (born Cairo, Georgia, 1919; died Stamford, Connecticut, October 24, 1972) was a baseball player. He left the army in 1945 as a first lieutenant and played baseball for the

Monarchs, a team in the Negro American League. He was then signed to the Royals, a minor league team. After one season, he moved to the Brooklyn Dodgers and became the first African American to play for the major leagues. He played second base from 1947 to 1956. He was also the first African American to be elected to the Baseball Hall of Fame.

 Children could read a biography of Jackie Robinson and find out what obstacles he faced in his lifetime.

Nolan Ryan (born Refugio, Texas, 1947) is a former baseball pitcher. He struck out 5,714 players. He holds the career record of the most no-hitters (seven). He retired after the 1993 season.

Franz Schubert (born Vienna, Austria, 1797; died Vienna, Austria, November 19, 1828) was a composer. His music combined classicism and romanticism. He created over 600 pieces of music, but he was not popular during his own lifetime. His works include *Unfinished Symphony* and *Die Zauberharfe* (The Magic Harp).

February

February is the second month and the shortest month. Around 700 B.C., it was the last month of the year and it had thirty days. It derives its name from the Latin word *februare,* or "purifying." The people at that time purified themselves to be ready for the new year. Julius Caesar, around 46 B.C., decided the year should begin with January. This decision made February the second month. He also took one day away from February and gave it to July, the month honoring him. Later Augustus Caesar took another day from February and added it to the month celebrating him, August. The amethyst is February's birthstone. Primroses and violets are February's flowers.

Month-Long Activities

American Heart Month is celebrated through a Presidential Proclamation and by the American Heart Association. Contact: American Heart Association, 7272 Greenville Avenue, Dallas, Texas 75231. Telephone: (800) AHA-USA1. Visit a Web site at: http://www.americanheart. org.

Black History Month began in 1926 when Dr. Carter G. Woodson saw a need to remember and honor African Americans.

National Cherry Month emphasizes the sweet fruit. Contact: Cherry Marketing Institute, PO Box 30285, Lansing, Michigan 48909. Visit a Web site at: http://www.cherrymkt.org.

National Children's Dental Health Month emphasizes the importance of dental care. Contact: American Dental Association, 211 E. Chicago Avenue, Chicago, Illinois 60611. Telephone: (800) 621-8099. Visit a Web site at: http://www.ada.org.

National Wild Bird Feeding Month reminds us that February, close to the end of winter, provides little food for wild birds. Children are encouraged to put out food and water for the birds. Contact: National Bird-Feeding Society, 507 Broad Street, Lake Geneva, Wisconsin 53147. Visit a Web site at: http://www.birdfeeding.org.

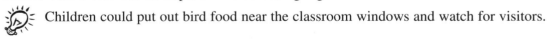 Children could put out bird food near the classroom windows and watch for visitors.

Responsible Pet Owners Month pinpoints issues of raising good pets, including nutrition and veterinary care. Contact: American Society for the Prevention of Cruelty to Animals, 424 E. 92nd Street, New York, New York, 10128.

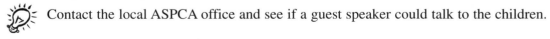 Contact the local ASPCA office and see if a guest speaker could talk to the children.

Special Weeks

Random Acts of Kindness Week counteracts violence in today's society. It stresses simple, unplanned acts of compassion. The week is held annually from Monday to Sunday of the week containing Valentine's Day. Contact: Random Acts of Kindness Foundation, 411 Scenic Road, Fairfax, California 94930. Telephone: (415) 456-0480. Visit a Web site at: http://www.readersndex.com.randomacts.

Special Days

Presidents' Day is celebrated on the third Monday in February. It was created to honor George Washington and Abraham Lincoln.

February

National Freedom Day marks the day in 1865 when President Abraham Lincoln approved the Thirteenth Amendment to the Constitution, abolishing slavery. The amendment was not ratified until close to the end of 1865.

Robinson Crusoe Day is the anniversary of Alexander Selkirk's rescue from the island Juan Fernandez in 1709. He landed on the island in 1704 after disagreeing with his ship's captain. His exploits may have inspired Daniel Defoe's *Robinson Crusoe*.

 Children could read an excerpt from the book and perhaps make a diorama of the scene.

Supreme Court opened its first session in 1790.

 Children could research where the Supreme Court met before its current building was completed.

United States' first dental college opened its doors in 1840.

Julia Ward Howe published "Battle Hymn of the Republic" as a poem in *The Atlantic Monthly* **in 1862.** The poem was inspired by a visit she made to a Union army camp during the Civil War.

Hale Telescope on Mount Palomar began operations in 1949.

Columbia **space shuttle broke apart as it reentered the atmosphere in 2003.** Debris was scattered over parts of Texas and other states. Its mission began January 16, 2003. Killed were Michael P. Anderson, David M. Brown, Kalpana Chawla, Laurel Blair Salton Clark, Rick D. Husband, William C. McCool, and Ilan Ramon.

Birthdays

Michelle Akers (born Santa Clara, California, 1966) is a soccer player.

Hattie Wyatt Caraway (born Bakersville, Tennessee, 1878; died Falls Church, Virginia, December 21, 1950) finished her husband's term in the Senate when he died in 1931. She then ran for the office when that term expired. She became the first woman to be elected to the Senate, and she worked ceaselessly for women's rights and Prohibition.

Langston Hughes (born Joplin, Missouri, 1902; died New York, New York, May 22, 1967) was a writer. He is famous for his poetry, and he experimented with meter. He wrote or edited at least fifty books, and he also created dramas.

 Students would enjoy reading Floyd Cooper's *Coming Home: From the Life of Langston Hughes*.

Jerry Spinelli (born Norristown, Pennsylvania, 1941) writes for children. His *Maniac McGee* won the 1990 Newbery Medal. His *Wringer* was a 1998 Newbery Honor Book. Visit a Web site at: http://www.carr.lib.md.us/authco/spinelli-j.htm.

February

 2 **Groundhog Day** delights children. If a groundhog sees his shadow, then winter will last another six weeks.

 Gather statistics as to whether the event really predicts the arrival of spring.

New Amsterdam was incorporated in 1653.

George Walton died in Augusta, Georgia, on February 2, 1804. He was born near Farmville, Virginia, 1741, but his exact date of birth is unknown. He signed the Declaration of Independence, representing Georgia. He fought for his state militia during the Revolutionary War and was caught by the British in late 1778. He was imprisoned until September 1779, when he was exchanged for a British officer.

Treaty of Guadalupe Hidalgo was signed in 1848, ending the war between Mexico and the United States. In return for $15 million from the United States, Mexico gave up the land that became California, Nevada, Utah, and parts of Arizona, Wyoming, Colorado, and New Mexico. Texas also became part of the United States.

 Students could locate the territory affected by the treaty. They could calculate the amount of land involved and thus the dollars per square mile.

Crown bottle cap was patented in 1892.

Mexico celebrates Día de la Candelaria with parades and bullfights.

National League of Baseball was formed in 1876.

Lie detector was tested for the first time in 1935.

 Students could find out how a lie detector works.

Birthdays

Jascha Heifetz (born Vilna, Lithuania, 1901; died Los Angeles, California, December 10, 1987) was a violin virtuoso. He started to play at age three and was performing at age six. At age thirteen he played in Berlin and found international fame. During the Russian Revolution he escaped to the United States, where he became a citizen in 1925. He recorded many great pieces and arrangements. Because of his technical skills, he was often the first person to play new pieces by present-day composers.

James Joyce (born Dublin, Ireland, 1882; died Zurich, Switzerland, January 13, 1941) was a writer. One if his most famous works is *A Portrait of the Artist as a Young Man.*

Judith Viorst (born Newark, New Jersey, 1931) is a children's author. One of her books is *Alexander and the Terrible, Horrible, No Good, Very Bad Day.* Visit a Web site at: http://www.edupaperback.org/authorbios/Viorst_Judith.html.

February

 3 **Paper money was used for the first time in 1690 in the colony of Massachusetts.**

 Students could debate the pros and cons of using paper money as opposed to coins.

Challenger STS-10 **lifted off into space in 1984.** The crew included Robert Gibson, Vance Brand, Ronald McNair, Robert Stewart, and Bruce McCandless. Two of the five astronauts became the first people to move freely in space without tethers. They were able to move about by using backpack jets.

Endangered Species Act became a law when it was signed by President Richard Nixon in 1973.

Birthdays

Elizabeth Blackwell (born Bristol, England, 1821; died Hastings, England, May 31, 1910) was the first woman doctor. During the Civil War, she trained nurses.

Horace Greeley (born Amherst, New Hampshire, 1811; died New York, New York, November 29, 1872) was a journalist and an antislavery advocate prior to the Civil War. He started the *New York Herald,* and he encouraged settlement of the American West. He is known for his statement, "Go west, young man."

Felix Mendelssohn (born Hamburg, Germany, 1809; died Leipzig, Germany, November 4, 1847) was a pianist and a classical composer. He was playing in concerts by age nine and was performing his own compositions by age eleven. One of his most famous pieces of music is *Wedding March.*

 Play some of his music and compare him to other composers.

James Michener (born New York, New York, 1907, died Texas, October 16, 1997) was a novelist. His book of short stories, *Tales of the South Pacific,* published in 1947, was the basis for the musical, *South Pacific.* The book won the Pulitzer Prize for fiction in 1948. Other works are *Hawaii* and *Texas.* Visit a Web site at: http://www.geocities.com/Heartland/4547/michener.html.

Joan Lowery Nixon (born Los Angeles, California, 1927) writes for children. One of her most well-known works is the series *A Family Apart,* published in 1987. Visit a Web site at: http://teacher.scholastic.com/writewit/mystery.

Norman Rockwell (born New York, New York, 1894; died Stockbridge, Massachusetts, November 8, 1978) was an artist. He is probably most famous for his illustrations for covers of the *Saturday Evening Post.*

 Students could view some of his works. They could list the works' qualities that endeared him to so many people.

Gertrude Stein (born Allegheny, Pennsylvania, 1874; died Paris, France, July 29, 1946) was a writer and friend to many avant-garde artists. She is famous for her saying, "A rose is a rose is a rose."

 February

4 **Sri Lanka celebrates its Independence Day.** The United Kingdom relinquished control of the island in 1948. The country, located southeast of India, exports tea, coconuts, and rubber. Colombo is the capital.

 Students could open up coconuts and enjoy the milk. They could toast the coconut flesh and taste it.

George Washington was elected president by the electoral college in 1789.

Olympic Winter Games were held for the first time in 1932.

 Find a list of events for the first winter Olympics and compare the events to today's list.

Confederate States of America came into being in 1861.

Birthdays

Russell Hoban (born Lansdale, Pennsylvania, 1925) is an author and an artist. One of his books is *Bedtime for Frances.*

 Students could read and enjoy some of his works.

Charles A. Lindbergh (born Detroit, Michigan, 1902; died Kipahula, Maui, Hawaii, August 27, 1974) was the first person to fly solo across the Atlantic Ocean. He made the trip May 20–21, 1927.

Thaddeus Kosciuszko (born Lithuania, 1746; died Solothurn, Switzerland, October 15, 1817) is often called the "Hero of Two Wars" because he fought for freedom in both America and Poland. He came to America in 1776 and presented himself to the Continental Congress. He had excellent engineering skills and built fortifications near Saratoga, West Point, and other locations. After the war, he received the rank of brigadier general. In 1784 he returned to Poland and became embroiled in a fight for freedom there. Although his side won for a time, ultimately he was imprisoned. Visit a Web site at: http://www.kosciuszkofoundation.org/common/thad.shtml.

 Compare and contrast his activities in America with his duties in Poland.

Rosa Louise Parks (born Tuskegee, Alabama, 1913) is a civil rights leader. She refused to give up her bus seat and was arrested.

February

5

Mt. Vesuvius in Italy erupted in A.D. 62. Major buildings in Pompeii were destroyed. In A.D. 79 Mt. Vesuvius erupted again and buried Pompeii and Herculaneum.

 Students could find out how and why the volcano erupted.

Roger Williams landed in America in 1631. He came for religious freedom, but he found the Massachusetts colony restrictive. Banished by Massachusetts leaders, he founded the colony of Rhode Island and the city of Providence.

Weatherperson's Day honors the birth of John Jeffries, one of America's first meteorologists. He was born in 1744 and died on September 16, 1819. Visit a Web site at: http://www.weather.com.

Mexico celebrates its Constitution Day. The document became official in 1917.

National Wildlife Federation was established in 1936.

 Discuss the goals of the organization.

Birthdays

Henry Louis "Hank" Aaron (born Mobile, Alabama, 1932) is a baseball Hall of Famer. He broke Babe Ruth's home run record, hitting 755 home runs.

David Wiesner (born Bridgewater, New Jersey, 1957) is a children's book author and illustrator. *The Three Pigs* won the 2002 Caldecott Medal.

John Witherspoon (born near Edinburgh, Scotland, 1723; died Princeton, New Jersey, November 15, 1794) signed the Declaration of Independence. A clergyman, he was also president of the College of New Jersey. The school changed its name to Princeton University.

 Students could learn more about Witherspoon's many accomplishments.

February

 Massachusetts became the sixth state in the United States by ratifying the Constitution in 1788. The word Massachusetts means, "at or about the great hill." The state ranks forty-fifth in size and thirteenth in population. Its state beverage is cranberry juice. Contact: (617) 727-3201. Visit an Internet site at: http://www.50states.com/massachu.htm.

 Toast Massachusetts's birthday with cranberry juice.

France in 1778 became the first foreign power to recognize the United States as a new nation.

The Twentieth Amendment of the Constitution was adopted in 1933. It moved the inauguration day of the president to January 20 at noon. It also changed the first day of a congressional session to January 3.

New Zealand remembers Waitangi Day. In 1840 the Maori and the Europeans signed the Treaty of Waitangi, permitting Great Britain to develop New Zealand.

Spanish-American War ended in 1900.

Queen Elizabeth II became England's monarch when her father, King George VI, died in 1952.

Alan Shepard in 1971 became the first person to play golf on the moon. He took three golf balls on the *Apollo 14* flight. Visit a Web site at: http://www.pasturegolf.com/archive/shepard.htm.

Birthdays

Tom Brokaw (born Yankton, South Dakota, 1940) is a television reporter and anchorperson.

Aaron Burr (born Newark, New Jersey, 1756; died Staten Island, New York, September 14, 1836) was a senator and the third vice president of the United States. He ran against Thomas Jefferson for the presidency in 1800. Each received the same number of electoral votes. According to the Constitution, the House of Representatives decided who was to be president, and Jefferson won. He was not renominated in 1804, and he did not win the governorship of New York. Burr blamed Alexander Hamilton for these losses and challenged him to a duel. Burr killed Hamilton, but his career was ruined.

Ronald Reagan (born Tampico, Illinois, 1911) was the fortieth president (1981–1989) of the United States. One of his first jobs was radio sports announcer. He became an actor and appeared in over fifty movies. He was elected governor of California, although he had no political experience. He became president in 1980 and created the term "Reaganomics." Visit a Web site at: http://www.whitehouse.gov/history/presidents/rr40.html.

Ronald Reagan was the country's oldest president when he left office. Children could debate whether there should be an age limit to the office.

George Herman "Babe" Ruth (born Baltimore, Maryland, 1895; died New York, New York, August 16, 1948) was one of baseball's greatest players. Nicknamed the "Great Bambino," he was an outstanding pitcher with a record of 94 games won and 46 games lost. He was also a greater batter, hitting 714 home runs during his career. He also played in the outfield. He played for the Boston Red Sox, the New York Yankees, and the Boston Braves.

 Students could discuss whether Babe Ruth was the greatest baseball player of all time.

February

 Ballet was performed for the first time in America in 1827. The Bowery Theater in New York City hosted a performance of *The Deserter* by Madame Francisquy Hutin and her troupe.

 Invite a ballet student to visit the class and demonstrate some basic ballet moves.

Grenada celebrates its Independence Day. Although it became free of British rule in 1974, it still recognizes Queen Elizabeth II as its head of state. St. George's is the capital. Carib Indians inhabited the territory in the 1600s. Nutmeg and mace are leading exports.

 Students could learn how nutmeg and mace are produced. Are nutmeg and mace different?

Stardust **was launched by NASA in 1999.** It will travel three billion miles before returning to Earth January 2006, with samples it will take from comets.

Birthdays

Shonto Begay (born Kayenta, Arizona, 1954) is a children's author. He wrote *The Mud Pony,* published in 1988.

Eubie Blake (born Baltimore, Maryland, 1883; died Brooklyn, New York, February 12, 1983) was a pianist and composer. He wrote almost 1,000 songs, including *I'm Just Wild about Harry.*

Garth Brooks (born Tulsa, Oklahoma, 1962) is a singer.

Charles Dickens (born Portsmouth, England, 1812; died Gad's Hill, England, June 9, 1870) was an English novelist. His works include *A Christmas Carol* and *Oliver Twist.* He is buried at Westminster Abbey.

(Harry) Sinclair Lewis (born Sauk Center, Minnesota, 1885; died Rome, Italy, January 10, 1951) was a novelist. His works include *Main Street.* He won the Nobel Prize for literature in 1930.

Sir Thomas More (born London, England, 1478; beheaded London, England, July 6, 1535) was a scholar, author, and martyr. The play *Man for All Seasons* is based on his refusal to grant Henry VIII's divorce from Catherine. He was canonized in 1935.

Laura Ingalls Wilder (born Pepin, Wisconsin, 1867; died Mansfield, Missouri, February 10, 1957) was an author. She wrote nine novels called the "Little House" books. The works are somewhat based on actual events from her life and that of her husband, Almanzo Wilder. Works include *Little House in the Big Woods* and *Farmer Boy.*

 Students could read and dramatize portions of her books.

February

8 **Boy Scouts of America was started in 1910 by William Boyce in Washington, DC.** The foundation was the work of Sir Robert Baden-Powell and the British Boy Scouts.

Opera was first performed in America in 1735 in Charleston, South Carolina. Colley Cibber wrote the opera, *Flora; or the Hob in the Well.*

 Students could learn about the components of opera.

First radio in the White House was installed in 1922 during Warren Harding's administration.

Birthdays

William Tecumseh Sherman (born Lancaster, Ohio, 1820; died New York, New York, February 14, 1891) was a Civil War general best known for his march through Georgia.

Jules Verne (born Nantes, France, 1828; died Amiens, France, March 24, 1905) was a French novelist and the "father of science fiction." His works include *Around the World in Eighty Days* and *Twenty Thousand Leagues Under the Sea.*

 Students could read portions of his works. Which of his ideas have become real inventions?

John Williams (born New York, New York, 1932) is a composer, conductor, and pianist. His works include the scores for *Star Wars* and *Jurassic Park.*

 Show a clip from a movie that includes some of his music. How does his music contribute to the mood of the scene?

February

9 **Jefferson Davis and Alexander Stephens were elected president and vice president, respectively, of the Confederate States of America in 1861.**

United States Weather Service was created in 1870.

Volleyball was invented by W. G. Morgan of Massachusetts in 1895.

 Organize a game of volleyball.

The Beatles appeared for the first time on the *Ed Sullivan Show* in 1964. Over 73 million people watched the program.

 Have the class create acts for a variety show.

Halley's Comet was visible in 1986. It will return in 2061. Visit a Web site at: http://seds.lpl.arizona.edu/nineplanets/nineplanets/halley.html.

Shimon Peres and Yasser Arafat signed a peace accord in 1994 to reduce tensions in the Middle East.

Birthdays

Paul Laurence Dunbar (born Dayton, Ohio, 1872; died Dayton, Ohio, February 6, 1906) was the son of former slaves. He wrote novels, but he is best remembered for his poetry. He published twelve books.

William Henry Harrison (born Berkeley, Virginia, 1773; died Washington, DC, April 4, 1841) was the ninth president (1841) of the United States. After a successful military career, he served in the House of Representatives, the Senate, and as ambassador to Colombia. His presidential campaign slogan was "Tippecanoe and Tyler Too." His inaugural address was delivered in the cold and rain. He developed pneumonia and died a month later. Visit a Web site at: http://www.whitehouse.gov/history/presidents/wh9.html.

 Students could find out what happened at Tippecanoe.

Amy Lowell (born Brookline, Massachusetts, 1874; died Brookline, Massachusetts, May 12, 1925) was a poet.

Lydia Estes Pinkham (born Lynn, Massachusetts, 1819; died Lynn, Massachusetts, May 17, 1883) produced and sold Lydia Pinkham's Vegetable Compound. Containing about 18 percent alcohol, the medicine was supposed to be therapeutic. After her death, the business became quite sound financially.

Shakira (born Barranquilla, Colombia, 1977) is a singer.

Alice Walker (born Eatonton, Georgia, 1944) is an author. One of her books is *The Color Purple.*

February

 French and Indian War ended in 1763.

 Students often confuse the sides of the French and Indian War. Students could locate more facts about the war and its causes.

Fire extinguisher was patented in 1863.

 Students could illustrate the different types of fire extinguishers.

The Twenty-Fifth Amendment to the Constitution was adopted in 1967. It delineated presidential succession requirements.

Birthdays

Jimmy Durante (born New York, New York, 1893; died Santa Monica, California, January 29, 1980) was an actor and comedian.

Leonard Kyle "Lenny" Dykstra (born Santa Ana, California, 1963) is a former baseball player.

Elaine Lobl Konigsburg (born New York, New York, 1930) is a children's author. She wrote, among other works, *From the Mixed-Up Files of Mrs. Basil E. Frankweiler* (Newbery Medal), published in 1967.

 Students could read and enjoy her works.

Boris Leonidovich Pasternak (born Moscow, Russia, 1890; died Moscow, Russia, May 30, 1960) was an author. One of his most famous works is *Doctor Zhivago.*

Leontyne Price (born Laurel, Mississippi, 1927) is an opera singer.

Ira Remsen (born New York, New York, 1846; died March 4, 1927) discovered saccharine.

February

11 British Parliament met for the first time in 1254.

Philadelphia established the first hospital in the United States in 1751.

Vermont became, in 1777, the first state to abolish slavery.

Boston Bicycle Club became America's first bicycle club in 1878.

Weather reports were issued on a weekly basis for the first time in 1878.

Vatican achieved its independence from Italy in 1929. Visit a Web site at: http://www.cia.gov/cia/publications/factbook/geos/vt.html.

Archie **comic books premiered in 1942.**

 Bring in some of the comic books. How are some of the terms and names in the old comic books used today in reference to computers and the World Wide Web?

Nelson Mandela was freed from prison in South Africa in 1990. He had been in prison for 27 years.

Birthdays

Jennifer Aniston (born Sherman Oaks, California, 1969) is an actress.

Thomas Alva Edison (born Milan, Ohio, 1847; died Menlo Park, New Jersey, October 18, 1931) held more than 1,200 patents. He invented the incandescent light bulb, the phonograph, and part of the telephone transmitter.

 Students could list more of his inventions and rank some of them in importance.

Jane Yolen (born New York, New York, 1939) is a children's author. She wrote, among other works, *Owl Moon* (Caldecott Medal), published in 1987. Visit a Web site at: http://www.janeyolen.com.

 Students could read and enjoy some of her work.

February

12 **Luxembourg celebrates Bursonneg.** A huge bonfire is lit, signifying the importance of the sun and the end of winter.

Oglethorpe Day is celebrated in Georgia. General James Oglethorpe and 100 other men set foot on what became Georgia in 1733. The colony was named after King George II. Eventually Oglethorpe became governor of Georgia.

Baseball catcher's mask was patented in 1878 by F. W. Thayer.

 A baseball catcher could come in and demonstrate how different pieces of equipment protect him/her.

Bill Clinton was acquitted at his impeachment trial in 1999.

Birthdays

Louisa Catherine Johnson Adams (born London, England, 1775; died Washington, DC, May 14, 1852) was the wife of John Quincy Adams, sixth president of the United States. She was the only first lady not born in the United States. A few years after Adams's presidency, he was elected to the House of Representatives. They lived in Washington, DC for another seventeen years. Visit a Web site at: http://www.whitehouse.gov/history/firstladies/la6.html.

Judy Blume (born Elizabeth, New Jersey, 1938) is a children's author. She wrote, among other works, *Fudge-a-Mania,* published in 1990.

 Students could read and enjoy some of her works.

Charles Darwin (born Shrewsberry, England, 1809; died Down, Kent, England, April 19, 1882) was a writer and a naturalist. He proposed the theory of natural selection after visiting the Galapagos Islands. One of his most famous works is *The Origin of Species by Means of Natural Selection.*

John Llewellyn Lewis (born Lucas, Iowa, 1880; died Washington, DC, June 11, 1969) never finished the seventh grade because he had to work in the mines. He became the head of the United Mine Workers of America and fought for better and safer working conditions for miners.

Abraham Lincoln (born Hodgenville, Kentucky, 1809; died Washington, DC, April 15, 1865) was the sixteenth president (1861–1865) of the United States. He was born in a log cabin, and his formal schooling added up to one year. He taught himself law and fought in the Black Hawk War of 1832. He served in the state legislature and became a Congressman in 1846. His debates with Stephen A. Douglas made him a more well-known figure. The Civil War brought him terrible sorrows. He was shot five days after the end of the Civil War. Visit a Web site at: http://www.whitehouse.gov/WH/glimpse/presidents/html/al16.html.

 Assign students to read Russell Freedman's book, *Lincoln: A Photobiography.*

Anna Pavlova (born St. Petersburg, Russia, 1881; died The Hague, The Netherlands, January 23, 1931) was a ballerina. She toured worldwide and popularized ballet. She also studied dance of different countries. Even when she was famous, she practiced fifteen hours a day.

David Small (born Detroit, Michigan, 1945) is a writer and illustrator. His *So You Want to Be President?* won the 2001 Caldecott Medal. Visit a Web site at: http://www.nccil.org/exhibit/davidsmall.html.

February

 Boston Latin School opened its doors in 1635, making it the first public school to operate in the colonies.

American Magazine, the first magazine to print in the United States, was published for the first time in 1741 by Andrew Bradford.

First recorded birth of quintuplets occurred in 1875.

Moving picture projector was patented in 1895.

National Negro Baseball League was formed in 1920.

Barbie doll premiered in 1959.

Find out how many different types of Barbie have been produced. What are the values of some of the old Barbies?

Birthdays

Randy Moss (born Rand, West Virginia, 1977) is a football player.

Simms Taback (born New York, New York, 1932) is an author and illustrator. His book *Joseph Had a Little Coat* won the 2000 Caldecott Medal. Visit a Web site at: http://www.cbcbooks.org/html/simms_taback.html.

Elizabeth "Bess" Virginia Wallace Truman (born Independence, Missouri, 1885; died Independence, Missouri, October 18, 1982) was the wife of Harry S Truman, thirty-third president of the United States. She did not like being first lady because she found so little privacy. Also, many people compared her to Eleanor Roosevelt, the previous first lady. She lived the longest of all first ladies. Visit a Web site at: http://www.whitehouse.gov/history/firstladies/et33.html.

 Have students pretend she wrote a diary. They could write some of the diary entries for her.

Grant Wood (born near Anamosa, Iowa, 1892; died Iowa City, Iowa, February 12, 1942) was an artist and a teacher. One of his most well-known works is *American Gothic*.

 American Gothic is often parodied. Students could update *American Gothic*.

Charles "Chuck" Yeager (born Myra, West Virginia, 1923) is a former test pilot who broke the sound barrier in 1947.

February

14 **St. Valentine's Day** is celebrated in parts of the world. Three factors may contribute to the creation of Valentine's Day. It may have roots in an ancient Roman festival, Lupercalia. One saint named Valentine secretly married couples against a Roman emperor's wishes. Another saint named Valentine refused to worship Roman gods and was arrested. Children tossed him notes, and thus the idea of exchanging valentines began. Other people believe birds choose their mates on Valentine's Day.

 Instead of buying valentines, students could make them.

Apple parer was patented in 1803 by Moses Coats.

Oregon became the thirty-third state of the United States in 1859. Salem is the state capital, and the state's nickname is the Beaver State. It is the leading state in the production of Christmas trees. It is also one of the strongest states in regard to environmental protection. The square dance is the state's official dance. Contact: (800) 547-7842. Visit an Internet site at: http://www.50states.com/oregon.htm.

 Teach students to square dance.

Arizona became the forty-eighth state of the United States in 1912. The word Arizona derives from a Pima or Papago word meaning "place of small springs." It was relatively unpopulated until the widespread use of air conditioners. It still faces the problem of water scarcity. The bola tie is the state's official neckwear. Contact: (800) 842-8257. Visit an Internet site at: http://www.50states.com/arizona.htm.

 Students could make variations of bolas.

League of Women Voters was organized in 1920.

Porpoise was born in captivity for the first time in 1940.

Lawrencium, element 103, was produced for the first time in 1961.

Birthdays

Jack Benny (born Benny Kubelsky in Chicago, Illinois, 1894; died Beverly Hills, California, December 26, 1974) was a comedian. He created a radio show in 1932, and it ran for twenty years. He followed that with a hit television series.

Drew Bledsoe (born Ellensburg, Washington, 1972) is a football player.

George Washington Gale Ferris (born Galesburg, Illinois, 1859; died Pittsburgh, Pennsylvania, November 22, 1896) invented the Ferris wheel. He created the first Ferris wheel for the World's Columbian Exposition in Chicago in 1893. It was made to rival the Eiffel Tower.

Paul O. Zelinsky (born Evanston, Illinois, 1953) is a children's book author and illustrator. His *Rapunzel* won the 1998 Caldecott Medal. Visit a Web site at: http://www.cbcbooks.org/html/pozelinsky.html.

February

Remember the *Maine* Day dates back to 1898. The *Maine,* anchored in the harbor in Havana, Cuba, was blown up. Over 200 Americans died, and the United States felt Spain was responsible. The United States declared war against Spain on April 25, 1898.

Adhesive postage stamps were used for the first time in 1842.

 Discuss the importance of stamps and what they were like before 1842.

Birthdays

Susan Brownell Anthony (born Adams, Massachusetts, 1820; died Rochester, New York, March 13, 1906) fought for women's rights. She was arrested in 1872 for voting, which was illegal for women at that time. A dollar coin has her image imprinted on it.

 Students could make a timeline of her life.

Abraham Clark (born Roselle, New Jersey, 1726; died Rahway, New Jersey, September 15, 1794) signed the Declaration of Independence.

Galileo (Galilei) (born Pisa, Italy, 1564; died near Florence, Italy, January 8, 1642) was a scientist. Although he did not invent the refracting telescope, he was the first person to put it to good use. By using the telescope, he found that the moon is not smooth but covered with mountains and valleys. In 1610 he located four moons around Jupiter. He was accused of being a heretic by the Catholic Church in 1633 because he believed that the Earth revolved around the sun. He was placed under house arrest for the remainder of his life.

 Students could play with different kinds of lenses and find out how telescopes work.

Matt Groening (born Portland, Oregon, 1954) is a cartoonist. He created *The Simpsons.*

Cyrus H. McCormick (born Rockbridge County, Virginia, 1809; died Chicago, Illinois, May 13, 1884) invented the reaper.

John Augustus Sutter (born Kandern, Germany, 1803; died Washington, DC, June 18, 1880) owned the California land where gold was first discovered. He died bankrupt.

February

 16

Halley's Comet made its ninth recorded perihelion in 374.

First Chinese newspaper in America was printed in San Francisco in 1900.

Lithuania celebrates its Independence Day of 1918. It became free of Russian and German rule. People celebrate this day even though Lithuania was annexed into the Soviet Union in 1940. In 1991 Lithuania became the first nation to break away from the Soviet Union.

First fruit tree patent was granted in 1932 to James Markham. The patent concerned a peach tree.

 Have students find out how trees can be patented.

Nylon was patented in the United States in 1937.

 Students could research how nylon is made.

Birthdays

Robert Joseph Flaherty (born Iron Mountain, Michigan, 1884; died Dummerston, Vermont, July 23, 1951) is known as the father of documentary motion pictures. He started out making silent films, including the 1922 *Nanook of the North.* Later he made sound films. *The Land* demonstrated erosion effects.

 Students could plan and produce a short documentary.

February

 17

Sardines were first canned in 1876 in Eastport, Maine.

Baltimore, Maryland, in 1816, became the first city to have its streetlights lit by hydrogen gas.

National PTA Founder's Day honors the group's creation by Phoebe Hearst and Alice McLellan Birney in 1897. Contact: National PTA, 330 North Wabash, Suite 2100, Chicago, Illinois 60611. Telephone: (312) 670-6782. Visit a Web site at: http://www.pta.org.

Alice Roosevelt, daughter of Theodore Roosevelt, was married in the White House in 1906.

Vanguard 2 **was launched in 1959.** The 21.5-pound satellite became the first weather station in space.

Birthdays

Walter Lanier "Red" Barber (born Columbus, Mississippi, 1908; died Tallahassee, Florida, October 22, 1992) was one of the pioneer baseball broadcasters.

Students could speak about some of his career highlights.

Michael Jordan (born Brooklyn, New York, 1963) is a basketball player.

René Theophile Hyacinthe Laennec (born Quimper, France, 1781; died Quimper, France, August 13, 1826) was a doctor. He also invented the stethoscope.

 Students could make stethoscopes.

Raphael Peale (born Annapolis, Maryland, 1774; died March 4, 1825) was an artist and a member of the famous Peale family.

Robert Newton Peck (born Vermont, 1928) is a children's author. One of his books is *A Day No Pigs Would Die*. Visit a Web site at: http://my.athenet.net/~blahnik/mpeck.

 Students could read excerpts from his books.

Aaron Montgomery Ward (born Chatham, New Jersey, 1844; died Highland Park, Illinois, December 7, 1913) was one of the first people to sell via mail order. He started Montgomery Ward in 1872 with George R. Thorne. Their first business was located in the loft of a livery stable.

February

 18 *Pilgrim's Progress* **was published in 1678.**

Gambia celebrates its Independence Day. It gained its independence from Great Britain in 1965. Banjul is the capital of this small country, located on the northwestern coast of Africa.

Pluto was discovered in 1930 by Clyde W. Tombaugh. As far back as 1905, Percival Lowell felt that an unknown planet was influencing the orbits of Neptune and Uranus. However, he died without finding the planet. Tombaugh used Lowell's work to predict the location and was successful in 1930. Its day is about six Earth days, and its year is about 248 Earth years. The average temperature is about −342 degrees to −369 degrees Fahrenheit. Pluto is named after the ancient god of the underworld.

 Sometimes Pluto is closer to the sun than Neptune. Students could find the dates of these cycles.

Elm Farm Ollie in 1930 was the first cow to be milked while flying in an airplane. The milk was placed in a container, and the container was dropped by parachute over St. Louis, Missouri.

 Have students write a newspaper account of this story.

Birthdays

Count Alessandro Giuseppe Antonio Anastasio Volta (born Como, Italy, 1745; died Como, Italy, March 5, 1827) developed the voltaic pile, an early battery. The unit of electrical measurement, the volt, is named after him.

 Students could find out more about volts and electrical current.

Toni Morrison (born Lorain, Ohio, 1931) is an author. She won the 1998 Pulitzer Prize and the 1993 Nobel Prize in literature.

John Travolta (born Englewood, New Jersey, 1955) is an actor.

February

Pisces the Fish is the astrological sign for February 19 through March 20.

Tin-type camera was patented by Hamilton Smith of Gambier, Ohio, in 1856.

 Learn how the tin-type was different from other kinds of cameras.

Gramophone, later called the phonograph, was patented by Thomas Edison in 1878.

President Franklin Roosevelt ordered the internment of about 110,000 Japanese Americans in 1942. They were sent to concentration camps in western states. They lost their property, valued at about $400 million.

 Students could find out more about the reasons behind Roosevelt's decision. What was life like in the concentration camps? Students might also read *Farewell to Manzanar* by Jeane W. Houston and James D. Houston.

Birthdays

Nicolaus Copernicus (born Torun, Poland, 1473; died Fromborck, Poland, May 24, 1543) was an astronomer and priest. He caused great upheaval among authorities when he proposed that the sun and not the Earth was the center of the planetary arrangement.

 Students could read more about his theories. Were all his ideas right?

February

U.S. Post Office was created in 1792.

First American cantilever bridge was finished in Harrodsburg, Kentucky, in 1877.

 Students could create cantilevers. They could find out how cantilevers work.

Frederick Douglass died in Anacostia Heights, DC, in 1895. He was born in Tuckahoe, Maryland, probably in February 1817. He escaped from slavery and became a popular abolitionist and speaker.

 Students could find out how he escaped from slavery.

Paracutín in 1943 became an active volcano in Mexico.

 Find out if Paracutín gave any warning signs.

***Batman and Robin* appeared in newspaper comics in 1944.**

John Glenn in 1962 was the first American and the third person to orbit the Earth. He circled the Earth in *Friendship 7* three times. In 1998 he returned to space on the space shuttle *Discovery.*

***Mir* space station was launched by the Soviet Union in 1986.** It was home to both Russian and American scientists until March 2001.

Birthdays

Ansel Adams (born San Francisco, California, 1902; died Monterey, California, April 22, 1984) was a photographer. Visit a Web site at: http://www.zpub.com/sf/history/adams.html.

Charles Barkley (born Leeds, Alabama, 1963) is a former basketball player.

William Prescott (born Groton, Massachusetts, 1726; died Pepperell, Massachusetts, October 13, 1795) was a Revolutionary War hero. He has received credit for the statement, "Don't fire until you see the whites of their eyes." He fought at the Battle of Bunker Hill on June 17, 1775.

February

21

The *Cherokee Phoenix,* published on a weekly basis in Georgia, became in 1828 the first Indian newspaper.

Lucy B. Hobbs became the first woman dentist when she graduated from an institute in Cincinnati, Ohio, in 1866.

Washington Monument was dedicated in 1885.

 Students could learn more about the history of the Washington Monument.

First telephone directory was published in 1878 in New Haven, Connecticut. It contained fifty names.

Last green and yellow Carolina parakeet died in 1918.

 Find out why the species became extinct.

Sarah G. Bagley became the first woman telegraph operator in 1946.

Polaroid camera was patented in 1947 in New York, New York.

 Take pictures with a Polaroid.

Richard Nixon in 1972 became the first U.S. president to travel to China.

Birthdays

Kelsey Grammer (born Saint Thomas, U.S. Virgin Islands, 1955) is an actor.

February

22

Saint Lucia celebrates its Independence Day. Although it became an independent country in 1979, it is still part of the British Commonwealth. The island, located in the Caribbean Sea, exports bananas and cocoa. Its area is 239 square miles. Castries is the capital.

Florida became a part of the United States in 1819. Spain gave the land to the United States under the condition that the United States would assume $5 million of claims of U.S. citizens against Spain.

Birthdays

Robert Baden-Powell (born London, England, 1857; died Nyeri, Kenya, January 8, 1941) established the Boy Scouts and Girl Guides.

Frederick Chopin (born Zelazowa-Wola, Poland, 1810; died Paris, France, October 17, 1849) was a classical pianist and composer. He created more than 200 pieces for the piano as well as chamber music and orchestral arrangements. He played his first concert at age eight and began composing after that. He spent most of his adult life in Paris. He died of tuberculosis. His works, influenced by his Slavic background, are full of melody and rhythm.

 Play some recordings of his music.

Julius Winfield "Dr. J" Erving (born Roosevelt, New York, 1950) is a former basketball player.

Rembrandt Peale (born Bucks County, Pennsylvania, 1778; died Philadelphia, Pennsylvania, October 3, 1860) was a painter, mostly of portraits. He was a member of the artistic and famous Peale family.

Horace Pippin (born West Chester, Pennsylvania, 1888; died West Chester, Pennsylvania, July 6, 1946) was a painter.

 Compare the works of Peale and Pippin.

George Washington (born Westmoreland County, Virginia, 1732; died Mt. Vernon, Virginia, December 14, 1799) was the first president (1789–1797) of the United States. He fought in the French and Indian War as an officer of the Virginia militia. He led the Continental Army to victory during the American Revolution. He helped organize the new country by presiding over the Constitutional Convention. He was elected president unanimously by the electoral college twice. He refused to run for a third term. He has been called the father of our country. Visit a Web site at: http://www.whitehouse.gov/history/presidents/gw1.html.

 Read about the portion of his life when he was a British officer.

February

Brunei Darussalam celebrates a national holiday. This small country is governed by a sultan. Extremely rich deposits of oil have made Brunei a wealthy country. The capital is Bandar Seri Begawan. Located on the island of Borneo, it became free of British rule in 1984.

 Students could find out more about the government of Brunei.

Guyana celebrates Republic Day. Various European countries laid claim to the country, located on the northeastern coast of South America. Georgetown is the capital.

Mt. Kilauea in Hawaii erupted in 1985.

Battle of the Alamo started in 1836.

 Children could learn more about the battle. Did any Texans survive?

First mass inoculations of Salk antipolio vaccine took place in 1954.

George Taylor, a signer of the Declaration of Independence, died in Easton, Pennsylvania, in 1781. He was born in Ireland, probably in 1716. He also helped the cause of the Revolutionary War because his forge produced grapeshot, cannonballs, and cannon.

 Students could find out how grapeshot and cannonballs were made.

Dolly, a lamb, was cloned in Scotland in 1997. Her creation led to many discussions regarding human cloning. She was put to sleep February 14, 2003, because she was suffering from a progressive lung disease.

Birthdays

W.E.B. DuBois (born Great Barrington, Massachusetts, 1868; died Accra, Ghana, August 27, 1963) was a famous African American leader striving for equality.

George Frederick Handel (born Halle, Saxony, Germany, 1685; died London, England, April 14, 1759) was a composer of Baroque music. One of his best-known works is *Messiah,* first performed in 1742.

 Students could enjoy some of his music.

February

 Pope Gregory XIII in 1582 issued a ruling stating the Julian calendar would be corrected in October 4 of the same year. The Julian calendar was erring by ten days. The new Gregorian calendar was named after Gregory.

Estonia celebrates its Independence Day. Located along the Gulf of Finland, Estonia has had a complicated history. Tallinn is the capital. In 1918 it became free of Soviet rule, but then it was conquered again. It became free of Soviet rule for the second time in 1991.

Birthdays

Wilhelm Karl Grimm (born Hanau, Germany, 1786; died Berlin, Germany, December 16, 1859) and his brother, Jacob, wrote *Grimm's Fairy Tales.*

 Students could read portions of *Grimm's Fairy Tales.* They could dramatize some of the stories.

Winslow Homer (born Boston, Massachusetts, 1836; died Prout's Neck, Maine, September 29, 1910) was an artist known for his outdoor scenes.

 Students could look at some prints of his work. They could paint an outdoor scene.

Steven Jobs (Born Los Altos, California, 1955) created the Apple computer.

John Peter "Honus" Wagner (born Carnegie, Pennsylvania, 1874; died Carnegie, Pennsylvania, December 6, 1955) was a famous baseball player. He was nicknamed the "Flying Dutchman."

 Have students find out why Honus Wagner was so famous.

February

 Kuwait observes a national holiday. This small country is located on the northeastern Arabian Peninsula. Kuwait City is the capital, and petroleum products compose the largest industries.

 Students could find out about Kuwait's role in Operation Desert Storm and Operation Desert Shield.

Suriname celebrates its Revolution Day.

Hiram R. Revels in 1870 became the first African American to be elected to the Senate.

The Sixteenth Amendment to the Constitution was adopted in 1913. Congress could implement an income tax.

Birthdays

Jim Backus (born Cleveland, Ohio, 1913; died Santa Monica, California, July 3, 1989) was an actor. He was the voice of Mr. Magoo. He was also Thurston Howell III on *Gilligan's Island.*

 Study how cartoon voices are recorded and combined with the animations.

Enrico Caruso (born Naples, Italy, 1873; died Naples, Italy, August 2, 1921) was a famous operatic tenor.

George Harrison (born Liverpool, England, 1943; died Los Angeles, California, November 29, 2001) was a musician. He was one of The Beatles.

Pierre Auguste Renoir (born Limoges, France, 1841; died Cagnes-sur-Mer, Provence, France, December 17, 1919) was an impressionist painter. One of his most famous works is *The Luncheon of the Boating Party.* Later in his life, arthritis crippled his hands. He had paintbrushes tied to his hands and learned to paint in broader strokes. Visit a Web site at: http://www.oir.ucf.edu/wm/paint/auth/renoir.

 Examine prints of his works and compare and contrast earlier and later paintings.

Cynthia Voigt (born Boston, Massachusetts, 1942) is an author who writes for children and young adults. She wrote *Dicey's Song,* the Newbery Medal winner for 1982.

February

 Grand Canyon National Park was created in 1919. Over millions of years the Colorado River has cut a deep gorge through Arizona. The park occupies over one million acres of land. Visit a Web site at: http://www.nps.gov/grca.

 Have students research exactly how the Grand Canyon was formed. Will it become even deeper and wider?

The Twenty-Second Amendment to the Constitution was adopted in 1951. It limited the number of terms a president could serve to two.

 Have the students debate term limitations, especially since senators and congresspeople do not have term limits.

First U.S. subway began operating in New York in 1870.

Birthdays

William Frederic "Buffalo Bill" Cody (born Scott County, Iowa, 1846; died Denver, Colorado, January 10, 1917) was a frontiersman and showman.

Johnny Cash (born Kingsland, Arkansas, 1932) is a singer.

Victor Hugo (born Besançon, France, 1802; died Paris, France, May 22, 1885) was an author. One of his best-known works is *Les Miserables.*

Levi Strauss (born Buttenheim, Bavaria, Germany, 1829; died San Francisco, California, September 26, 1902) invented tough, durable pants for California gold miners. These pants are now known as jeans.

 Compare and contrast denim with other fabrics.

February

 Dominican Republic celebrates its Independence Day. In 1844 the Haitians gave up control after dominating the country for 22 years.

 Students could draw and label the island that the Dominican Republic and Haiti occupy.

Gulf War ended in 1991 when the Allies liberated Kuwait.

Birthdays

Marian Anderson (born Philadelphia, Pennsylvania, 1897; died Portland, Oregon, April 8, 1993) was a singer and a diplomat. She was the first African American soloist at the Metropolitan Opera. In 1939 the Daughters of the American Revolution would not allow her to perform in Constitution Hall in Washington, DC. She sang before 75,000 people in front of the Lincoln Memorial. Her courage and talent brought her great fame. She was a U.S. delegate to the United Nations in 1958. She received the United Nations Peace Prize in 1977.

 Students could listen to recordings of her voice.

Ralph Nader (born Winstead, Connecticut, 1934) is an advocate on safety and consumer issues. He is famous for his studies in automobile safety.

 Students could research how cars have become safer in recent years.

Henry Wadsworth Longfellow (born Portland, Maine, 1807; died Cambridge, Massachusetts, March 24, 1882) was a poet and writer. His works include *The Song of Hiawatha* and *The Wreck of the Hesperus.*

 Students could read and recite some of his poetry.

John Steinbeck (born Salina, California, 1902; died New York, New York, December 20, 1968) was an author. His works include *Of Mice and Men* and *The Grapes of Wrath.* He was the Nobel Prize winner in literature in 1962.

James Ager Worthy (born Gastonia, North Carolina, 1961) is a former basketball player.

February

 Westminster Abbey opened in 1066.

 Find out the names of some of the people who are honored in Westminster Abbey. Visit a Web site at: http://www.westminster-abbey.org.

Republican Party was created in 1854 as an antislavery response to the Kansas-Nebraska Bill of 1854. Congress had voted to let the citizens of Nebraska and Kansas vote on the issue of slavery for their own areas. Alvan E. Bovay, a Whig, and others felt the only way to make a change was to create a new political party.

Territory of Colorado was created in 1861.

First televised basketball game occurred in 1940. The game took place in Madison Square Garden and showcased two college teams.

First killer whale was born in captivity in 1977.

 Students could learn whether killer whales are really killers.

Birthdays

Mario Andretti (born Montona, Trieste, Italy, 1940) is a race car driver.

Eric Lindros (born London, Ontario, Canada, 1973) is a hockey player.

Linus Pauling (born Portland, Oregon, 1901) is a scientist. He received a Nobel Prize for chemistry in 1954 for research in molecular structure. He won the Nobel Peace Prize in 1962 for his work in trying to stop nuclear testing. He is also famous for his claims that large amounts of vitamin C reduce the effects of colds and other diseases.

 Children could find out more about vitamin C.

February

 Leap Day is added to the year every four years.

 Students could figure out a way to know whether any given year contains a leap day.

Columbus used his knowledge of lunar eclipses to scare Jamaican natives in 1504.

 Do tables exist to predict lunar and solar eclipses?

Great Britain and the United States signed a pact regarding seal hunting in the Bering Sea in 1812.

Dick Button won his fifth consecutive world title in figure skating in 1952.

Jocelyn Burnell discovered the first pulsar in 1968.

Birthdays

John Phillip Holland (born County Clare, Ireland, 1844; died Newark, New Jersey, August 12, 1914) invented the submarine.

 Explain to the class how a submarine works.

March originally was the first month of the year, and it was named *Martius*. The name honors the Roman god of war, Mars. Julius Caesar modified the calendar and made January the first month of the year. Therefore, March moved to the third month. The violet is the flower for March. Birthstones for the month are bloodstone and aquamarine.

Month-Long Activities

American Red Cross Month recognizes the importance of the 1,600 local Red Cross chapters. Contact: Red Cross National Headquarters, Public Inquiry Center, 431 18th Street NW, Washington, DC 20006. Visit a Web site at: http://www.redcross.org.

Music in Our Schools Month celebrates the role of music education. Over eight million students benefit from the programs. Contact: Music Educators National Conference, 1806 Robert Fulton Drive, Reston, Virginia 20191. Telephone: (800) 336-3768. Visit a Web site at: http://www.menc.org.

National Peanut Month lauds the peanut, a favorite of children. Contact: National Peanut Council, Inc., 1500 King Street, Suite 301, Alexandria, Virginia 22314. Telephone: (703) 838-9500.

National Nutrition Month reminds children to eat right. Contact: The American Dietetic Association, National Center for Nutrition and Dietetics, 216 W. Jackson Boulevard, Chicago, Illinois 60606-6995. Telephone: (312) 899-0040. Visit a Web site at: http://www.eatright.org.

National Noodle Month celebrates pasta. Contact: National Pasta Association, Fleishman-Hillard, 1330 Avenue of the Americas, New York, New York 10019.

National Women's History Month reminds us of the roles American women have played in our history. Contact: National Women's History Project, 7738 Bell Road, Department P, Windsor, California 95492. Telephone: (707) 838-6000. Visit a Web site at: http://www.nwhp.org.

Youth Art Month stresses the importance of art in the development of children. Contact: Council for Art Education, Inc., 128 Main Street, Hanson, Massachusetts 02341. Telephone: (781) 293-4100.

Special Weeks

Newspaper in Education Week is the first full week in March. Contact: Manager of Education Programs, Newspaper Association of America Foundation, 1921 Gallows Road, Suite 600, Vienna, Virginia 22182. Visit a Web site at: http://www.naa.org.

March

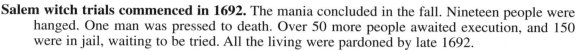

1

Salem witch trials commenced in 1692. The mania concluded in the fall. Nineteen people were hanged. One man was pressed to death. Over 50 more people awaited execution, and 150 were in jail, waiting to be tried. All the living were pardoned by late 1692.

Articles of Confederation were ratified in 1781. This document consolidated the thirteen colonies into one country and was the early nation's governing document until the Constitution was written in 1789.

Iditarod sled dog race begins. The sixteen-dog teams race from Anchorage to Nome, Alaska, a distance of 1,049 miles. Contact: Iditarod Trail Committee, Mile 2.2—Knik Road, PO Box 870800, Wasilla, Alaska 99687.

 Locate a map of the course and follow each day's news.

Korea celebrates Samiljol, Independence Day. In 1919 the country became free from the rule of Japan.

Wales celebrates St. David's Day. St. David is Wales's patron saint, and everyone wears a leek.

National Pig Day celebrates an animal many people claim is intelligent and beneficial to people.

Ohio became the seventeenth state of the United States in 1803. The state's nickname is the Buckeye State, and the state tree is the buckeye. The official state beverage is tomato juice. Contact: (800) BUCKEYE. Visit an Internet site at: http://www.50states.com/ohio.htm.

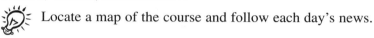 Children could make and drink some tomato juice.

Nebraska became the thirty-seventh state of the United States in 1867. The word Nebraska means "flat water." Its nickname is the Cornhusker State, and it is a leading producer of corn and cattle. Lincoln is the state capital. Nebraska ranks fifteenth in area and thirty-seventh in population. Contact: (800) 228-4307. Visit an Internet site at: http://www.50states.com/nebraska.htm.

 As a class, brainstorm a list of what to do with all those cornhusks.

Yellowstone National Park was established in 1872. Visit an Internet site at: http://www.nps.gov/yell.

Peace Corps was created in 1961 by President John Kennedy. The Peace Corps has sent over 140,000 people to over 130 third world countries. These volunteers work on projects ranging from nutrition to forestry. Contact: Office of Publications and Public Affairs, Peace Corps, 1990 K Street, Washington, DC 20526. Telephone: (800) 424-8580. Visit a Web site at: http://www.peacecorps.gov.

Switzerland celebrates Chalandra Marz. People in traditional costumes try to drive away winter by ringing bells and cracking whips.

Rebecca Lee became the first African American woman to get a medical degree in 1864.

Birthdays

Ron Howard (born Duncan, Oklahoma, 1954) is an actor and a director.

Glenn Miller (born Clarinda, Iowa, 1904; disappeared over the English Channel, December 15, 1944) was a bandleader and a composer. His big band sound was especially popular before and during World War II. On a flight to Paris to perform for troops, his plane vanished.

Donald "Deke" Slayton (born Sparta, Wisconsin, 1924; died League City, Texas, June 13, 1993) was one of the original seven astronauts. A heart condition kept him from traveling in space for some time, and he became chief of flight operations. In 1971 the heart condition disappeared, and he flew on the last *Apollo* mission. His crew docked for the first time with a Soviet *Soyuz* vessel.

 March

 2

Texas declared its independence from Mexico in 1836.

"Horseless carriage" was driven for the first time in Detroit in 1896.

 Students could find out what this "horseless carriage" looked like.

Mount Rainer became a national park in 1899. It is located in the state of Washington. Visit a Web site at: http://www.nps.gov/mora.

Puerto Rico became a U.S. territory in 1917.

Time **magazine published its first issue in 1923.**

 Visit a Web site at: http://www.pathfinder.com/time.

Birthdays

Dr. Seuss (born Theodor Seuss Geisel in Springfield, Massachusetts, 1902; died La Jolla, California, September 24, 1991) was an author and an illustrator. He wrote, among other works, *Green Eggs and Ham,* 1960. His birthday is celebrated by the Read Across America program. Visit a Web site at: http://www.nea.org/readacross.

 Make and eat green eggs by adding a few drops of green food coloring to the scrambled eggs before cooking.

Leo Dillon (born Brooklyn, New York, 1933) is a picture book illustrator with wife Diane Dillon. He illustrated, among other works, *Why Mosquitoes Buzz in People's Ears: A West African Tale* (Caldecott Medal), published in 1975.

 Students could look at some of his work.

Sam Houston (born Rockbridge County, Virginia, 1793; died Huntsville, Texas, July 26, 1863) is one of Texas's greatest heroes. He defeated General Santa Anna at the Battle of San Jacinto in 1836. He was elected to the U.S. Senate and served as governor of Texas until 1861, when he declined to swear allegiance to the Confederacy.

March

3

Hinamatsuri is celebrated in Japan. A special festival is held for girls and dolls.

United States declared war on Algiers in 1815.

 Encourage students to learn more about this little-known altercation.

National Academy of Sciences was created by Congress in 1863.

Belva Ann Lockwood became the first woman to argue before the Supreme Court in 1879.

Florida became the twenty-seventh state of the United States in 1845. Juan Ponce de Leon named the state *Pasqua Florida,* "Easter festival of the flowers." The state capital is Tallahassee, and the state's nickname is the Sunshine State. Most of the state is just above sea level. It is home to the Kennedy Space Center and Lake Okeechobee. Contact: (904) 487-1462. Visit an Internet site at: http://www.50states.com/florida.htm.

 Design a brochure regarding tourism in the state.

Malawi remembers Martyr's Day.

"The Star-Spangled Banner" became the national anthem in 1931.

"Mr. Wizard" premiered on television in 1951. The science show lasted fourteen years.

Birthdays

Alexander Graham Bell (born Edinburgh, Scotland, 1847; died Baddeck, Nova Scotia, Scotland, August 2, 1922) invented the telephone. He also investigated causes of deafness.

Jacqueline Joyner-Kersee (born East St. Louis, Missouri, 1962) is an Olympic gold medalist in the heptathalon.

Patricia MacLachlan (born Cheyenne, Wyoming, 1938) is a children's author. She wrote, among other works, *Sarah, Plain and Tall* (Newbery Medal), published in 1985.

 Students could read and enjoy some of her works.

George Pullman (born Brocton, New York, 1831; died Chicago, Illinois, October 19, 1897) invented the Pullman sleeping car for the railroad.

March

4

William Penn received the deed to Pennsylvania from King Charles II in 1681. The deed was in lieu of paying a debt of £16,000.

Vermont became the fourteenth state of the United States in 1791. A translation of the state's name leads to its nickname, the Green Mountain State. Montpelier is the state capital. Two of its products are maple syrup and maple candy. Contact: (800) VERMONT. Visit an Internet site at: http://www.50states.com/vermont.htm.

 Students could enjoy pancakes and real maple syrup.

Serfdom was prohibited in Russia in 1861.

 Compare and contrast serfdom and slavery.

Presidential inaugurations were held on this day until 1933, when the Twentieth Amendment to the Constitution changed the date to January 20.

Slinky was patented by Richard and Betty James in 1947.

***Ogo 5* was launched in 1968.** The orbiting geophysical spacecraft collected information on the relationship between the Earth and the sun.

Leaded gas was banned by the Environmental Protection Agency in 1985.

Birthdays

Prince Henry the Navigator (born Portugal, 1394; died November 13, 1460) encouraged and expanded exploration of Africa and other lands. He planned more than fifty expeditions, but he never went on any of these trips himself. He brought in experts in cartography, astronomy, and mathematics. Through his work, Portugal became a leading force in exploration.

Dav Pilkey (born Cleveland, Ohio, 1966) is an author. He wrote the Captain Underpants series.

Casimir Pulaski (born Winiary, Mazovia, Poland, 1747; died on the warship *Wasp,* October 11, 1779) was a military leader in his native Poland. He came to America after Poland was partitioned. He became a hero during the Revolutionary War. Pulaski was mortally wounded during the siege of Savannah.

Peggy Rathmann (born St. Paul, Minnesota, 1953) is a children's book author and illustrator. Her *Officer Buckle and Gloria* received the Caldecott Medal in 1996. Visit a Web site at: http://www.peggyrathmann.com/index.html.

 Students, like Officer Buckle, could make a list of safety tips.

 March

5 **Crispus Attucks Day** may have been one of the contributing factors to the Revolutionary War. The Boston Massacre occurred in 1770 between colonists and British soldiers. Crispus Attucks, possibly a fugitive slave, was the first person killed in the fight. Several other men died, and others were wounded.

 Read accounts of the event. Each side claimed the other side started it. Students could sift through the information.

Andrew Johnson's impeachment proceedings started in 1868. Supreme Court Chief Justice Salmon Chase presided over the sessions.

President Franklin Roosevelt made his famous statement, "The only thing we have to fear is fear itself." This sentence was part of his first inaugural address in 1933. In the same speech, he declared a "bank holiday" of ten days to try to save the slipping banking system.

 Students could reflect in writing about his statement.

Stapler was patented by C. H. Gould in England in 1868.

Birthdays

Mem Fox (born Melbourne, Australia, 1946) is an author. Visit a Web site at: http://www.memfox.net/intro.html.

James Merritt Ives (born New York, New York, 1824; died 1895) was part of the lithographic team of Currier and Ives. They published more than 4,000 scenes ranging from the commonplace to the historic. At the time, the prints were used for decoration or book illustration. Now originals are rare and expensive.

Gerhardus Mercator (born Rupelmonde, Flanders, 1512; died Duisburg, Germany, December 2, 1594) invented the Mercator projection for maps. He was able to portray more accurately the Earth on a flat piece of paper. He also used the term "atlas" for the first time to refer to a compilation of maps.

 Compare and contrast Mercator projections with other types of maps.

William Oughtred (born Eton, Buckingham, England, 1575; died near Guildford, Surrey, England, June 30, 1660) invented the slide rule.

Howard Pyle (born Wilmington, Delaware, 1853; died Florence, Italy, November 9, 1911) was an illustrator.

Marcharch

 6

Magellan discovered Guam in 1521.

Dred Scott **case decision was delivered by the Supreme Court in 1857.**

 Conduct research on the decision and the impact it had on slavery.

Alamo fell to Mexico in 1836. The Texas fort had been under siege since February 23, 1836. The last of the soldiers died, and General Santa Anna was victorious for a short time.

 Children might want to read Sherry Garland's *A Line in the Sand: The Alamo Diary of Lucinda Lawrence.*

Oreo went on sale in 1912. Today 2,000 Oreos are produced a minute.

Ghana celebrates its Independence Day. It became free from the rule of Great Britain in 1957. Accra is the capital, and it is located on the southern coast of West Africa. Farmers there grow cocoa, rice, and coffee.

Birthdays

Elizabeth Barrett Browning (born near Durham, England, 1806; died Florence, Italy, June 29, 1861) was a poet. One of her most famous works is *Sonnets from the Portuguese.* She was married to Robert Browning, also a famous poet. One of her most famous lines is "How do I love thee? Let me count the ways."

 Students could read and discuss some of her poetry.

L. Gordon Cooper (born Shawnee, Oklahoma, 1927) is a former astronaut.

Alan Greenspan (born New York, New York, 1926) is an economist.

Shaquille O'Neal (born Newark, New Jersey, 1972) is a basketball player.

Anna Claypoole Peale (born Philadelphia, Pennsylvania, 1791; died Philadelphia, Pennsylvania, December 25, 1878) was an artist. She was a part of the famous Peale family of artists.

Michelangelo (Buonarroti) (born Caprese, Italy, 1475; died Rome, Italy, February 18, 1564) was an artist, an architect, and a poet. Among his accomplishments are the painting of the Sistine Chapel and the sculpture *David.* Visit a Web site at: http://www.michelangelo.com/buonarroti.html.

 Students could learn about the rivalry between Michelangelo and Leonardo da Vinci.

March

7 **Suez Canal was opened in 1869.** It connects the Mediterranean Sea and the Red Sea.

Distinguished Service Medal was created under the authorization of Woodrow Wilson in 1918.

 Discuss what one did to receive the medal.

Transatlantic radio and telephone service between London and New York began 1926.

Birthdays

Luther Burbank (born Lancaster, Massachusetts, 1849; died Santa Rosa, California, April 11, 1926) developed new types of fruits, vegetables, and flowers.

 Study how new plant species are developed.

Michael Eisner (born Mount Kisco, New York, 1942) is a Disney executive.

Janet Guthrie (born Iowa City, Iowa, 1938) is a former race car driver.

Franco Harris (born Fort Dix, New Jersey, 1950) is a former football running back. He is a member of the Pro Football Hall of Fame.

Stephen Hopkins (born Providence, Rhode Island, 1707; died Providence, Rhode Island, July 13, 1785) was a governor of the colony of Rhode Island and a signer of the Declaration of Independence.

Piet Mondrian (born Amersfoort, the Netherlands, 1872; died New York, New York, February 1, 1944) was an artist. He is most known for his abstract studies of color.

Maurice Ravel (born Cibourne, France, 1875; died Paris, France, December 28, 1937) was a composer. One of his most famous works is *Bolero,* a ballet composed in 1928.

 Play some of his music to the class and tell students to listen for the Spanish influences or the jazz overtones.

March

8 **William Caxton published the first illustrated book in England in 1481.** The book, entitled *The Mirror of the World,* was about the sciences.

International Women's Day is celebrated by the United Nations. Contact: United Nations, Department of Public Relations, New York, New York 10017.

 Students could choose a woman, famous or not, and tell about her life.

Birthdays

Howard Hathaway Aiken (born Hoboken, New Jersey, 1900; died St. Louis, Missouri, March 14, 1973) invented the digital computer.

Hannah Hoes Van Buren (born Kinderhook, New York, 1783; died Albany, New York, February 5, 1819) was the first wife of Martin Van Buren, eighth president of the United States. She died from tuberculosis before he was elected to office. Visit a Web site at: http://www.white house.gov/history/firstladies/hvb8.html.

Kenneth Grahame (born Edinburgh, Scotland, 1859; died Pangbourne, Berkshire, England, July 6, 1932) was an author.

 Children might enjoy reading portions of his *Wind in the Willows.*

Oliver Wendell Holmes, Jr. (born Boston, Massachusetts, 1841; died Washington, DC, March 6, 1935) was one of the most important judges in American history. He was the son of Oliver Wendell Holmes, a distinguished writer. He fought in the Civil War and was wounded three times. He became a lawyer and was appointed to the Supreme Court in 1902 by President Theodore Roosevelt. He served on the Supreme Court for almost thirty years.

 Students could read more about his philosophy and his court decisions.

March

9

Belize remembers Baron Bliss Day. Sir Henry Edward Ernest Victor Bliss greatly helped the development of Belize.

False teeth were patented in 1822 by Charles Graham of New York, New York.

 Get the class to find out whether George Washington really did have false teeth.

Monitor **and** *Merrimac,* **two ironclad ships, battled in 1862.** The *Merrimac,* a Confederate vessel, and the *Monitor,* a Union ship, exchanged fire. Both pulled away after about two hours. Neither ship was severely damaged.

 Students could find out more about the ironclads and how they were built.

Sputnik 9, **a Soviet spacecraft, ventured into space in 1961.** Its voyager was a dog named Chernushka (Blackie).

Work on the Alaskan Oil Pipeline began in 1975.

Birthdays

Bobby Fischer (born Chicago, Illinois, 1943) is a world chess champion.

Yuri Alexseyevich Gagarin (born Gzhatsk, Russia, 1934; died in a plane crash near Moscow, Russia, March 27, 1968) was the first man to travel in space.

Benito Santiago (born Ponce, Puerto Rico, 1965) is a baseball player.

Amerigo Vespucci (born Florence, Italy, 1451; died Seville, Spain, February 22, 1512) was an Italian explorer. Even though Columbus reached the New World before Vespucci, the latter was the first to realize it was a new continent. Vespucci traveled at least twice to the New World around 1499 to 1502. Columbus continued to believe he had landed near India. Martin Waldseemuller, an early cartographer, named the new land America in honor of Amerigo Vespucci.

 Have the class brainstorm some other names Waldseemuller could have used.

March

10 Daniel Boone was hired in 1775 to cut the Wilderness Road.

 Trace on a map the Wilderness Road. Why was it created?

Rings around Uranus were discovered in 1977. Visit a Web site at: http://solarsystem. nasa.gov/features/planets/uranus/rings.html.

Thomas Jefferson became minister to France in 1785.

Salvation Army of the United States was created by Commissioner George Railton and seven other officers in 1880.

Telephone was invented by Alexander Graham Bell in 1876 in Cambridge, Massachusetts. His first message was "Mr. Watson, come here. I want you."

 Discuss how the telephone has changed over the years and have students predict its future appearance.

Harriet Tubman died in Auburn, New York, in 1913. Her exact date of birth is unknown. She was born around 1820 in Dorchester County, Maryland. A slave, she escaped to Philadelphia in 1849. She then became the most famous conductor for the Underground Railroad, probably saving about 900 people. During the Civil War, she was a spy and a scout. After the war, she cared for orphans and the aged.

 Create a play about this famous woman. Students may want to read Ann McGovern's *Wanted Dead or Alive: The Story of Harriet Tubman.*

Birthdays

Laurel Blair Salton Clark (born Ames, Iowa, 1961; died in *Columbia* disaster, February 1, 2003) was an astronaut.

Clare Booth Luce (born New York, New York, 1903; died Washington, DC, October 9, 1987) was a writer and politician. She edited two magazines and wrote a number of plays. She was elected to the House of Representatives and was the first woman ambassador to an important country.

Lillian D. Wald (born Cincinnati, Ohio, 1867; died Westport, Connecticut, September 1, 1940) was a nurse and social worker. She founded the Henry Street Settlement. It became an important public health nursing center. She campaigned actively to make Congress create the United States Children's Bureau.

March

11 Shakespeare believed this day in 1302 was Romeo and Juliet's wedding day.

 Students could learn more about the story of Romeo and Juliet.

London's first daily newspaper appeared in 1702.

Johnny Appleseed Day is celebrated. John Chapman, better known as Johnny Appleseed, died in Allen County, Indiana, in 1845. Stories say he helped plant fruit orchards all along the frontier. He was a friend to both the Indians and the settlers.

Have students plant some apple seeds in small containers. They could also dry apple rings.

Frankenstein **was published by Mary Shelley in 1818.**

Reginald Weir in 1948 became the first African American to play in the United States Tennis Open.

Birthdays

Ralph Abernathy (born Linden, Alabama, 1926) is a civil rights leader.

Ezra Jack Keats (born Brooklyn, New York, 1916; died New York, New York, May 6, 1983) was a children's author and illustrator. He wrote, among other works, *The Snowy Day* (Caldecott Medal), published in 1962.

 Students could read and enjoy some of his works.

Robert Treat Paine (born Boston, Massachusetts, 1731; died Boston, Massachusetts, May 11, 1814) signed the Declaration of Independence. He was also elected to the Constitutional Convention. He served on the Massachusetts State Supreme Court from 1790 to 1804.

Antonin Scalia (born Trenton, New Jersey, 1936) is an Associate Justice of the Supreme Court.

12 **Lesotho celebrates Moshoeshoe's Day.** Moshoeshoe I united the people of Basotho.

Mauritius celebrates Independence Day. It became a free nation in 1968, but it is still part of the British Commonwealth. This small country is located in the southwestern portion of the Indian Ocean. Port Louis is the capital.

 Locate Mauritius on a map and have students research major crops and sources of income.

Girl Scouts of the United States of America was established in 1912. A week of celebrations usually takes place around March 12. Visit a Web site at: http://www.girlscouts.org.

 Compare and contrast the Girl Scouts and the Boy Scouts.

"Fireside Chats" were held for the first time by Franklin Roosevelt in 1933. These radio broadcasts from the White House were his way of communicating his concerns and triumphs to America.

Steam engine was operated for the first time in 1755.

Birthdays

Charles Cunningham Boycott (born Norfolk, England, 1832; died Suffolk, England, June 19, 1897) is famous because his last name is so much a part of our language. He owned a number of properties. He charged high rents, and he evicted those who could not pay the money. The tenants refused to rent from him, and thus the word "boycott" came into being.

 Brainstorm as a class a list of words that have come from someone's name.

Virginia Hamilton (born Yellow Springs, Ohio, 1936; died Yellow Springs, Ohio, February 19, 2002) was a children's author. She wrote, among other works, *In the Beginning: Creation Stories from Around the World* (Newbery Honor Book), published in 1988. Visit a Web site at: http://www.virginiahamilton.com.

 Students could read and enjoy some of her works. They could consider reading *M. C. Higgins the Great,* Newbery Medal for 1975.

Jane Means Appleton Pierce (born Hampton, New Hampshire, 1806; died Andover, Massachusetts, December 2, 1863) was the wife of Franklin Pierce, fourteenth president of the United States. She did not want her husband to run for the office. Visit a Web site at: http://www.whitehouse.gov/wh/glimpse/firstladies/html/jp14.html.

Wally Schirra (born Hackensack, New Jersey, 1923) is a former astronaut. He was commander of *Apollo 7.*

Andrew Young (born New Orleans, Louisiana, 1932) is a civil rights leader.

arch

 Uranus was discovered by Sir William Herschel in 1781. The planet is actually a gas giant, composed of methane, helium, and hydrogen. Its temperature hovers around -355 degrees Fahrenheit. Some scientists believe that, despite the cold surface temperatures, a core about fifteen times the size of Earth has a temperature of approximately 12,000 degrees Fahrenheit. It possesses at least five moons and nine faint rings.

 Encourage students to develop some kind of craft that could land on the gas giant.

Earmuffs were patented by Chester Greenwood of Farmington, Maine, in 1877.

"Uncle Sam" cartoon was published for the first time in 1852.

World Standard Time was accomplished in 1884.

 Review the different time zones and construct word problems.

Birthdays

Diane Dillon (born Glendale, California, 1933) is a picture book illustrator with husband Leo Dillon. She wrote, among other works, *Why Mosquitoes Buzz in People's Ears: A West African Tale* (Caldecott Medal), published in 1975.

Percival Lowell (born Boston, Massachusetts, 1855; died Flagstaff, Arizona, November 12, 1916) was an astronomer. Lowell instigated the research that ultimately found Pluto. The planet was found fourteen years after he died. He created Lowell Observatory in Flagstaff, Arizona.

Abigail Powers Fillmore (born Stillwater, New York, 1798; died Washington, DC, March 30, 1853) was the first wife of Millard Fillmore, thirteenth president of the United States. She was the first first lady to work before and after she was married. She was a teacher. After they moved into the White House, she created its first library. She also had the first bathtub installed and the first kitchen stove added. Prior to that, cooking had been accomplished by using an open fireplace. Visit a Web site at: http://www.whitehouse.gov/history/firstladies/af13.html.

 Students could make "before" and "after" illustrations of the White House.

Joseph Priestley (born Fieldhead, England, 1733; died Northumberland, Pennsylvania, February 6, 1804) was a scientist and a cleric. He discovered oxygen.

Ellen Raskin (born Milwaukee, Wisconsin, 1928; died August 8, 1984) was a children's author. One of her most well-known books is *The Westing Game*. Visit a Web site at: http://soemadison.wisc.edu/ccbc/wisauth/raskin/main.html

March

14 **Cotton gin was patented by Eli Whitney in 1794.** It changed the way cotton was raised and processed in the southeastern United States. Visit a Web site at: http://inventors.about.com/library/inventors/blcotton_gin.htm.

United States war bonds were created by Congress in 1812.

 Have students research the purposes of war bonds.

Gold standard became the law in 1900.

Pi Day is celebrated because today is 3.14.

 Students could measure the circumference and diameter of various circular objects and then divide the circumference by the diameter. Do the results approach 3.14?

Birthdays

Frank Borman (born Gary, Indiana, 1928) is a former astronaut.

Albert Einstein (born Ulm, Germany, 1879; died Princeton, New Jersey, April 18, 1955) was a physicist who revolutionized theories about the universe.

 Students could learn more about his theories on relativity.

Marguerite de Angeli (born Lampeer, Michigan, 1889; died Detroit, Michigan, June 16, 1987) was a children's author. One of her books was *The Door in the Wall* (Newbery Medal, 1950). Visit a Web site at: http://www.deangeli.lapeer.org.

John Luther "Casey" Jones (born near Cayce, Kentucky, 1864; died in a train wreck near Vaughn, Mississippi, April 30, 1900) is the subject of the ballad.

 Have the students read and recite the ballad.

Hank Ketcham (born Seattle, Washington, 1920; died Pebble Beach, California, June 1, 2001) created *Dennis the Menace*. Dennis was created in the early 1950s. Ketcham retired in 1995, and other people draw Dennis today.

Kirby Puckett (born Chicago, Illinois, 1961) is a baseball player.

March

15 **Ides of March occurred when Julius Caesar was assassinated in 44 B.C.**

 Students could locate more facts about his death and discuss the saying "Beware the Ides of March."

Cincinnati Red Socks in 1869 became the first professional baseball team in the United States.

Escalator was patented in 1892 by Jesse Reno of New York City.

Maine became the twenty-third state of the United States in 1820. Vikings explored the area around A.D. 1000. Originally Maine was a part of the Massachusetts colony. Augusta is the state capital, and the state nickname is the Pinetree State. People who live in Maine are called Down-Easters. Today fishing, lumbering, and growing potatoes are strong sources of income. It is home to Acadia National Park. The moose is the state mammal. Contact: (207) 623-0363. Visit an Internet site at: http://www.50states.com/maine.htm.

 Students could find out when and why Maine separated from Massachusetts.

Blood bank was created in 1937.

Woodrow Wilson spoke before a formal presidential press conference in 1913. The press conference was the first of its kind.

Lymon Gilmore built the first commercial airfield in 1907.

Birthdays

Ruth Bader Ginsburg (born Brooklyn, New York, 1933) is an Associate Justice of the Supreme Court. She is the second woman to hold the office.

Andrew Jackson (born Waxhaw, South Carolina, 1767; died Nashville, Tennessee, June 8, 1845) was the seventh president (1829–1837) of the United States. He was nicknamed "Old Hickory" after his leadership in the War of 1812, especially in the Battle of New Orleans. He was the first president to be born in a log cabin, the first to travel by train, and the first to survive an assassination attempt. While he was not a polished man, he did care about the country's economy and was able to pay off the entire federal debt. Visit a Web site at: http://www.whitehouse.gov/history/presidents/aj7.html.

 Discuss how the federal government can go into debt and trends about government debt.

March

16

Robert Goddard fired the first liquid-fueled rocket in 1926 in Cambridge, Massachusetts.

Gemini 8 **was the first spacecraft to dock with another craft, the** *Agena,* **in 1966.**

Birthdays

George Clymer (born Philadelphia, Pennsylvania, 1739; died Philadelphia, Pennsylvania, January 24, 1813) was an American patriot. He was one of six men to sign both the Declaration of Independence and the Constitution. Later he served as a representative from Pennsylvania at the first House of Representatives.

Sid Fleischman (born Brooklyn, New York, 1920) is a children's author. He won the 1987 Newbery Medal for *The Whipping* Boy. His son is Paul Fleischman.

 Children could read and enjoy some of his works.

James Madison (born Port Conway, Virginia, 1751; died Montpelier, Virginia, June 28, 1836) was the fourth president (1809–1817) of the United States. He is known as the father of the Constitution because he continually pushed and pulled the delegates into meeting and resolving differences. He also wrote the first draft of the Bill of Rights. He was a Congressperson for four terms. While he was president, he had to contend with the War of 1812. Visit a Web site at: http://www.whitehouse.gov/history/presidents/jm4.html.

 Children could recite portions of Jean Fritz's *The Great Little Madison.*

Thelma Catherine Patricia Ryan Nixon (born Ely, Nevada, 1912; died Park Ridge, New Jersey, June 22, 1993) was the wife of Richard M. Nixon, thirty-seventh president of the United States. She met Nixon when she was teaching in Whittier, California. During World War II, she worked as a government economist. Visit a Web site at: http://www.whitehouse.gov/history/firstladies/pn37.html.

Georg Simon Ohm (born Erlangen, Germany, 1787; died Munich, Germany, July 6, 1854) was a physicist. He originated Ohm's Law. The ohm, a measure of electrical resistance, honors him.

 Find out more about Ohm's Law and electrical resistance.

March

17

St. Patrick's Day remembers the birth of Bishop Patrick, patron saint of Ireland. Bishop Patrick was born in 389 and died in 461. Born in England, he brought Christianity to Ireland.

 The class could make shamrocks and eat Irish potatoes.

First glider flight occurred in 1894.

Campfire Boys and Girls of America was created in 1910. Contact: Camp Fire Boys and Girls, 4601 Madison Avenue, Kansas City, Missouri 64112. Telephone: (816) 756-1950.

National Gallery of Art opened in 1941. It has a fine collection of artwork, ranging from the medieval period to the present. Visit an Internet site at: http://www.nga.gov.

 Students could pretend to be curators for the National Gallery of Art and decide which works of art to add to the collection.

First submarine was launched in 1898.

Birthdays

Jim Bridger (born Richmond, Virginia, 1804; died near Kansas City, Missouri, July 17, 1881) was a scout and pioneer. He built Fort Bridger in Wyoming as a fur trading post and rest station for settlers traveling on the Oregon Trail.

(Nathaniel Adams) Nat "King" Cole (born Montgomery, Alabama, 1919; died Santa Monica, California, February 25, 1965) was a singer. He was the first African American to host a television show. One of his most famous songs was *Unforgettable.*

Gottlieb Wilhelm Daimler (born Schorndorf, Wurttenberg, Germany, 1834; died Bad Cannstatt, 1900) is known as the father of the automobile. He invented the internal combustion engine.

 Help students discover how a car engine works.

Kate Greenaway (born London, England, 1846; died November 6, 1901) illustrated children's books. The Kate Greenaway Medal is given each year to the best-illustrated book published in the United Kingdom.

March

18 First railroad tunnel in the United States was completed in 1834.

Lord Stanley proposed the idea of a silver challenge cup for hockey. This cup became known as the Stanley Cup.

Pluto was discovered by Clyde Tombaugh in 1930.

 Have students find out much more about Pluto. How is it different from the other outer planets?

Schick patented the first electric razor in 1931.

Supreme Court in 1963 ruled on the *Miranda* case. They favored Miranda. Thus, defendants have the right to be represented by an attorney.

 Locate more information on *Miranda*. Does the class agree with the Supreme Court?

Aruba celebrates Flag Day.

Aleksei Leonov, a Soviet cosmonaut, became the first person to walk in space in 1965.

Birthdays

Bonnie Blair (born Cornwall, New York, 1964) is a speed skater. She won an Olympic gold medal.

John Caldwell Calhoun (born Abbeville District, South Carolina, 1782; died Washington, DC, March 31, 1850) was a politician. He was the first vice president to resign from the position.

 Students could find out why he resigned.

Grover Cleveland (born Caldwell, New Jersey, 1837; died Princeton, New Jersey, June 24, 1908) was the twenty-second and twenty-fourth president of the United States. He was president from 1885 to 1889 and from 1893 to 1897. A minister's son, he was mayor of Buffalo and governor of New York. He was not a very popular president. He applied his veto power over 300 times, more than double the total vetoes of all previous presidents. Visit a Web site at: http://www.whitehouse.gov/history/presidents/gc2224.html.

Rudolph Diesel (born Paris, France, 1858; died English Channel, September 29, 1913) invented the diesel internal combustion engine.

March

19 Ptolemy in A.D. 72 made the first recorded reference to a lunar eclipse.

Swallows return to San Juan Capistrano, California. They stay until October 23, when they fly to Goya, Argentina. Visit a Web site at: http://www.sanjuancapistrano.net/swallows.

Australia celebrates Canberra Day.

Students could locate information about Canberra.

Birthdays

William Bradford (born Yorkshire, England, 1589; died Plymouth, Massachusetts, May 9, 1657) was the second governor of Plymouth Colony, serving from 1621 to 1657. He organized the first Thanksgiving. Much of what we know of Pilgrim life comes from his book *Of Plimmoth Plantation.*

William Jennings Bryan (born Salem, Illinois, 1860; died Dayton, Tennessee, July 26, 1925) was a politician known as the "Silver-Tongued Orator."

Wyatt Earp (born Monmouth, Illinois, 1848; died Los Angeles, California, January 13, 1929) was a frontiersman and a deputy sheriff. At one time he was a buffalo hunter. He and his two brothers were responsible for the fight at the O.K. Corral in Tombstone, Arizona, in 1881.

 Students could find out exactly what happened at the O.K. Corral.

David Livingstone (born Blantyre, Scotland, 1813; died in Africa, May 1, 1873) was a physician, missionary, and the famous missing adventurer. A search party, headed by Henry Stanley, found him near Lake Tanganyika, Africa.

Thomas McKean (born New London, Pennsylvania, 1734; died Philadelphia, Pennsylvania, June 24, 1817) signed the Declaration of Independence. He represented Delaware. Visit a Web site at: http://www.ushistory.org/declaration/signers/mckean.htm.

Charles Russell (born St. Louis, Missouri, 1864; died Great Falls, Montana, October 26, 1926) was an artist. He was a cowboy before he began to paint. His art reflects his interest in the West.

 Compare and contrast his work to Frederic Remington's work.

Bruce Willis (born Penn's Grove, New Jersey, 1955) is an actor.

March

20 **First Day of Spring** occurs today or on March 21. It marks the vernal equinox in the Northern Hemisphere. The length of the day equals the length of the night.

Uncle Tom's Cabin, **written by Harriet Beecher Stowe, was published in 1852.**

 Students could read and dramatize passages from the book.

Tunisia celebrates its Independence Day. France gave up control of Tunisia in 1956. Slightly smaller than the state of Wisconsin, Tunisia is located on the northern coast of Africa. Tunis is the capital.

Birthdays

Mitsumasa Anno (born Tsuwano, Japan, 1926) is a picture book author and illustrator. He wrote, among other works, *Anno's Journey,* published in 1977.

 Students could read and enjoy some of his works.

Henrik Ibsen (born Skien, Norway, 1828; died Oslo, Norway, May 23, 1906) was a playwright. One of his most famous plays is *Peer Gynt.*

Lois Lowry (born Honolulu, Hawaii, 1937) is a children's author. She wrote, among other works, *Number the Stars* (Newbery Medal), published in 1990. Visit a Web site at: http://www.ipl.org/youth/askauthor/lowry/html.

Bill Martin, Jr. (born Hiawatha, Kansas, 1916) is a children's author. He wrote *Knots on a Counting Rope.*

Fred Rogers (born Latrobe, Pennsylvania, 1928; died Pittsburgh, Pennsylvania, February 27, 2003) was the producer and host of "Mr. Rogers' Neighborhood."

 Compile a list of reasons why this show was so successful.

Louis Sachar (born East Meadow, New York, 1954) is a children's author. His book *Holes* won the 1999 Newbery Medal. Visit a Web site at: http://www.cbcbooks.org/html/louissachar.html.

arch

 Pocahontas died in Gravesend, Kent, England, in 1617. She was probably born in 1595. She had accompanied her husband, John Rolfe, on a trip to England to meet his family and friends. Visit a Web site at: http://www.apva.org/history/pocahont.html.

Lesotho celebrates National Tree Planting Day.

Namibia celebrates its Independence Day. It declared itself free from South Africa in 1990. The Kalahari Desert is one of the geographic features of this fairly large country. Windhoek is the capital.

 Have students draw a map of Namibia and label some of its geographic features.

Persia became Iran in 1935.

United Nations designates today as the International Day for the Elimination of Racial Discrimination.

Bertrand Piccard and Brian Jones in 1999 became the first people to circle the Earth in a hot air balloon. Their 26,000-mile trip took 19 days, 21 hours, and 55 minutes.

Aries the Ram is the astrological sign for March 21 through April 19.

Birthdays

Johann Sebastian Bach (born Eisenach, Germany, 1685; died Leipzig, Germany, July 28, 1750) was a composer of Baroque music. His work is very complex, and it was not popular during his lifetime. He became famous after his death. He created several hundred compositions, including almost 300 cantatas.

Play some of his music and have students compare it to music of other composers.

Peter Catalanotto (born Long Island, New York, 1959) is a children's author and illustrator. One of his books is *Dylan's Day Out.* Visit a Web site at: http://www.ala.org/alsc/wisniew.html.

Francis Lewis (born Wales, 1713; died New York, New York, December 31, 1802) signed the Declaration of Independence. He represented New York.

Francis Lewis led a very exciting and at times dangerous life. Students could make a timeline of his life.

Rosie O'Donnell (born Commack, New York, 1962) is an actress and talk show host.

David Wisniewski (born Middlesex, England, 1953) is a children's author and illustrator. One of his books, *Golem,* won the 1997 Caldecott Medal. Visit a Web site at: http://www.ala. org/alsc/wisniew.html.

March

 22

Puerto Rico celebrates Emancipation Day.

United Nations declares today as World Day for Water.

Jordan celebrates Arab League Day.

Lawn sprinkler was patented by J. W. Smith in 1898.

LASER (Light Amplification by Stimulated Emission of Radiation) was patented in 1960 by Charles Towne and Arthur Schawlow.

Valery Polyakov in 1995 set a record for living in space for the longest time, 439 days, in the space station *Mir*.

International Day of the Seal was declared by Congress in 1982. Experts are concerned about the cruelty of seal hunts. They are also worried that the species will become extinct.

 Research the different types of seals. Which species are under threat of extinction?

Birthdays

Randolph Caldecott (born Chester, England, 1846; died St. Augustine, Florida, February 12, 1886) was a children's illustrator. The Caldecott Awards, for illustrations of children's literature, are named after him. At age fifteen he went to work in a bank. However, he always carried a sketchbook with him, and he became an artist in 1872. Two of his works are *Three Jovial Huntsmen* and *The House That Jack Built.* Bad health forced him to come to America, but he died shortly after his arrival.

 Students could read and study some of the Caldecott winners. They could look at new books and make recommendations for next year's winner.

Marcel Marceau (born Strasbourg, France, 1923) is a very famous mime.

 Students could produce their own mime acts, perhaps accompanied by Stephen Sondheim's music.

Stephen Sondheim (born New York, New York, 1930) is a composer.

Elvis Stojko (born Newmarket, Ontario, Canada, 1972) is a figure skater.

Sir Anthony Van Dyck (born Antwerp, Belgium, 1599; died London, England, December 9, 1641) was a portrait painter. Visit a Web site at: http://www.vandyck.co.uk.

Andrew Lloyd Webber (born London, England, 1948) is a composer. His works include *Phantom of the Opera.*

arch

23 Tuscarora Indian War ended in 1713.

Handel's *Messiah* **premiered in London, England, in 1743.**

Pakistan celebrates Republic Day. The country's main religion is Islam. Islamabad is the capital of this mostly agricultural country.

 Two ancient settlements, Harappa and Mohenjo-Daro, are in Pakistan. Students could find out more about these places.

Lewis and Clark reached the Pacific Ocean in 1806.

White House had its first telephone installed in 1929.

United Nations declares today World Meteorological Day.

Patrick Henry gave his famous "Give me liberty or give me death" speech in Richmond, Virginia, in 1775.

Rivet was patented in 1794 by Josiah Pierson.

Near Miss Day happened in 1989. A fairly large meteor came within 500,000 miles of Earth. If the meteor had hit the Earth, the impact would have left a crater the size of Washington, DC.

 Students could find out more about meteors and meteorites.

Mir, **a Russian space station launched in 1986, returned to Earth in 2001.** Most of the station burned up on its reentry into the Earth's atmosphere.

Birthdays

Fannie Merritt Farmer (born Boston, Massachusetts, 1857; died Boston, Massachusetts, January 15, 1915) was a cooking expert. She standardized measurements so that cooking became much easier. She also wrote the *Boston Cooking School Cookbook.* This book, now known as *The Fannie Farmer Cookbook,* and its revisions have sold approximately four million copies.

Moses Malone (born Petersburg, Virginia, 1954) is a former basketball player.

Wernher von Braun (born Wirsitz, Germany, 1912; died Alexandria, Virginia, June 16, 1977) headed teams that developed space rockets.

 Have students research his life in Germany during World War II and his life in America after the war.

arch

24 **Rhode Island residents rejected the new Constitution in 1788.** The state eventually ratified the Constitution and the Bill of Rights in 1790.

 Students could find out why the people did not like the Constitution.

The Philippines celebrates its Independence Day. In 1934 the United States granted the Philippines its independence. The treaty took effect in 1946. The Philippines had been sold to the United States in 1898 for $20 million. Manila is the capital, and the country was named after Spain's King Philip II. Over 7,100 islands comprise the country.

Exxon *Valdez* in 1989 spilled about 11 million gallons of oil into Prince William Sound.

 Discuss how the oil was removed from the sound.

World TB Day commemorates this day in 1882, when Robert Koch discovered the cause of tuberculosis.

Birthdays

Lawrence Ferlinghetti (born Yonkers, New York, 1919) is a poet.

Harry Houdini (born Budapest, Hungary, 1874; died Detroit, Michigan, October 31, 1926) was a magician and escape artist.

Andrew W. Mellon (born Pittsburgh, Pennsylvania, 1855; died Southampton, New York, August 27, 1937) was a financier. He became very wealthy from investments made mostly in coal and oil. He was Secretary of the Treasury under three presidents. He donated his $25 million art collection and $15 million to create a new museum, the National Gallery of Art. Visit a Web site about the National Gallery of Art at: http://nga.gov.

 Have students find out how he reduced the national debt when he was Secretary of the Treasury.

John Wesley Powell (born Mt. Morris, New York, 1834; died Haven, Maine, September 23, 1902) was the second director of the United States Geological Survey. He also explored the Colorado River and made ethnological studies of the American Indians.

March

25 **Maryland was colonized by Lord Baltimore's group in 1634.**

 Students could learn how this colony differed from the others.

England abolished slavery in 1807.

Greece celebrates its Independence Day. It became free from Turkey's rule in 1821. The country is composed of a mainland and many small islands. Athens is the capital.

 Students could learn more about ancient Greece.

Pecan Day marks the day in 1775 when Thomas Jefferson gave George Washington several pecan trees. Jefferson had planted and grown quite a few pecan trees. Some of Washington's pecan trees are still alive.

 Find out more about the pecan tree and where it grows. The class could make pecan cookies.

Birthdays

John de la Mothe Gutzon Borglum (born Bear Lake, Idaho, 1867; died Chicago, Illinois, March 6, 1941) was an artist. In 1916 he sculpted Stone Mountain in Georgia, a memorial to the Confederate Army. He began to sculpt Mount Rushmore in 1927, but he died before it was completed.

Aretha Franklin (born Memphis, Tennessee, 1942) is a singer.

Elton John (born Reginald Kenneth Dwight in Pinner, England, 1947) is a singer and songwriter.

Arturo Toscanini (born Parma, Italy, 1867; died New York, New York, January 16, 1957) was a conductor.

arch

26

Bangladesh celebrates National Day. Dhaka is the capital. Farmers grow rice, jute, and tea in one of the rainiest climates in the world.

Joseph Francis of New York, New York, patented a lifeboat made from corrugated sheet iron in 1845.

 Hypothesize how this lifeboat worked.

Jonas Salk made known his discovery of the polio vaccine in 1953.

Spinach farmers in Crystal City, Texas, built a statue of Popeye in 1937.

 Children could discuss why they chose Popeye.

Fire extinguisher was patented by Thomas J. Martin in 1872.

Birthdays

Nathaniel Bowditch (born Salem, Massachusetts, 1773; died Boston, Massachusetts, March 16, 1838) was an astronomer and author. He wrote *The New American Practical Navigator* in 1802, and many of his ideas still apply today.

 Students could read Jean Lee Latham's *Carry On, Mr. Bowditch,* published in 1955. The book won the 1956 Newbery Medal.

Robert Lee Frost (born San Francisco, California, 1875; died Boston, Massachusetts, January 29, 1963) was a poet. He was awarded the Pulitzer Prize in 1924, 1931, 1937, and 1943. Students might enjoy reading and hearing some of his poetry. One of his most famous poems is *Stopping by Woods on a Snowy Evening.*

Sandra Day O'Connor (born El Paso, Texas, 1930) is a Supreme Court Associate Justice. She is the first woman to serve on the Supreme Court.

Diana Ross (born 1944) is a singer and an actress.

Tennessee Williams (born Columbus, Mississippi, 1911; died New York, New York, February 25, 1983) was a playwright. One of his plays was *The Glass Menagerie.*

arch

27

Shoelaces were invented in 1790.

Corkscrew was patented in 1860.

Luxembourg celebrates Osweiler. Horses, tractors, and automobiles are blessed.

Cherry trees were first planted in Washington, DC, in 1912. Helen Herron Taft and Viscountess Chinda (the Japanese ambassador's wife) planted the first of 3,000 trees.

Have students find out who donated the trees.

Alaska suffered a severe earthquake in 1964. Approximately 117 people died in the earthquake measuring 8.4 on the Richter scale.

Halley's Comet's thirty-second perihelion will occur in 2134.

Venera 8 **landed on Venus in 1972.** It was the first landing on Venus by a U.S. space probe.

President Truman and his family moved back into the White House in 1952 after major renovations had been completed.

Birthdays

Mariah Carey (Born New York, New York, 1970) is a singer.

Nathaniel Currier (born Roxbury, Massachusetts, 1813; died New York, New York, November 20, 1888) was a lithographer. He was part of the famous Currier and Ives partnership. Their lithographs answered a need for reasonably priced art. Now the originals are very expensive.

Wilhelm Konrad Roentgen (born Lennap, Prussia, 1845; died Munich, Germany, February 10, 1923) discovered X-rays. He won the Nobel Prize in 1901 for his work.

Edward Steichen (born Luxembourg, 1879; died West Redding, Connecticut, March 25, 1973) was a photographer.

 Steichen helped make photography an art. Students could look at some of his work. They could try their own hands at photographic art.

Sarah Vaughn (born Newark, New Jersey, 1924; died Los Angeles, California, April 3, 1990) was a famous jazz singer.

 Listen to a recording of her singing. She was known for her improvisation.

March

28 **J. A. Comenius published the first children's picture book in 1592.**

Nathaniel Briggs patented the washing machine in 1797.

 Students could speculate as to the appearance of this washing machine.

Child Labor Law was passed in Pennsylvania in 1848.

First world weightlifting championship was held in 1891.

Constantinople changed its name to Istanbul in 1930.

Robert Goddard used a gyroscope to control his rocket in 1935.

First national curling championships were held in 1957.

 Students could modify curling rules and create a curling contest.

Three Mile Island experienced a nuclear power plant disaster in 1979.

Birthdays

Marlin Perkins (born Carthage, Missouri, 1905; died 1986) was a zoo director and host of the television show "Wild Kingdom" from 1963 to 1985.

Reba McEntire (born McAlester, Oklahoma, 1955) is a country singer.

 She has won two Grammy Awards. Students could conduct their own Grammy Awards ceremony, honoring their musical peers.

March

29 Taiwan celebrates Youth Day.

Niagara Falls stopped flowing for one day in 1848. Ice had jammed the river.

Cheese, butter, and meat were rationed in 1943 as part of the effort to win World War II.

 Students could find out just how rationed the supplies were. How did people get their rations?

Dow Jones Industrial Average broke 10,000 for the first time in 1999.

Birthdays

Pearl Bailey (born Newport News, Virginia, 1918; died Philadelphia, Pennsylvania, August 17, 1990) was a singer. She was awarded the Presidential Medal of Freedom in 1988.

Lou Henry Hoover (born Waterloo, Iowa, 1875; died New York, New York, January 7, 1944) was the wife of Herbert Hoover, thirty-first president of the United States. She was a geology and mining major at Stanford University when they met. She was first lady during the Great Depression, and she often paid for White House social events with her own money. Visit a Web site at: http://www.whitehouse.gov/history/firstladies/lh31.html.

 Students could find out more about her life.

John Tyler (born Charles City County, Virginia, 1790; died Richmond, Virginia, January 18, 1862) was the tenth president (1841–1845) of the United States. He was the first president to become so from the death of his predecessor. Prior to being the president, he was a representative, a senator, and a governor. He was known as "His Accidency," and he was not a popular president. An impeachment proposal was defeated. After his presidency was over, he returned to the South. He was about to join the Confederate Congress, but he died before it convened. Visit a Web site at: http://www.whitehouse.gov/wh/glimpse/presidents/html/jt10.html.

 Children could find out why he was not well liked.

Denton True "Cy" Young (born Gilmore, Ohio, 1867; died Peoli, Ohio, November 4, 1955) was a very famous baseball pitcher.

 Examine with the class all his statistics. Does the Cy Young Award reflect his life?

March

30 Egg incubator was patented in 1843.

 Students could incubate some fertilized eggs. A local farmer might be able to provide the eggs.

Alaska was bought by the United States from Russia in 1867. The purchase was originally called Seward's Folly. William Seward, secretary of state, bought Alaska for $1.2 million. That averaged out to about two cents an acre.

The Fifteenth Amendment to the Constitution was adopted in 1870. A person's rights could not be denied on the basis of "race, color, or previous servitude."

Anesthesia was used for the first time in surgery in 1842. Dr. Crawford Long operated on a tumor on the neck of James Venable. The patient had been given ether. Long did not report the results of the surgery until 1849.

 Students could look up facts about the different types of anesthesia used today.

Pencil with eraser was patented in 1858 by Hyman Lipman of Philadelphia, Pennsylvania.

Texas in 1870 became the last Confederate state to be readmitted to the Union.

Queensboro Bridge, connecting Queens and Manhattan, was finished in 1909.

Birthdays

Vincent van Gogh (born Groot Zundert, Holland, 1853; died Auvers-sur-Oise, France, July 29, 1890) was an artist. He never received formal training. He often applied the paint with a palette knife. Visit a Web site at: http://www.oir.ucf.edu/wm/paint/auth/gogh.

 Students could compare and contrast the works of Goya and van Gogh.

Francisco José de Goya (born Aragon, Spain, 1756; died Bordeaux, France, April 16, 1828) was an artist. He produced more than 1,800 artworks. Visit a Web site at: http://www.oir.ucf.edu/wm/paint/auth/goya.

March

31 Virgin Islands celebrates Transfer Day. The United States bought the Virgin Islands from Denmark in 1917 for $25 million.

Eiffel Tower was finished in 1889. It was constructed for the 1889 Paris Exhibition. Alexandre Gustave Eiffel designed the structure.

 Students could compare its height to the heights of other tall constructions.

Daylight Saving Time came into effect for the first time in the United States in 1918.

Edward J. Dwight, Jr. became the first African American astronaut in 1962.

Birthdays

Robert Wilhelm Bunsen (born Gottingen, Germany, 1811; died Heidelberg, Germany, August 16, 1899) was a professor of chemistry. He invented the Bunsen burner.

Cesar Estrada Chavez (born Yuma, Arizona, 1927; died San Luis, Arizona, April 23, 1993) was a leader of the migrant workers. He founded the National Farm Workers Association in 1962 to improve migrant workers' working and living conditions.

René Descartes (born La Haye, Touraine, France, 1596; died Stockholm, Sweden, February 11, 1650) was a mathematician and a philosopher. He is famous for saying, "I think, therefore I am."

 Have students read about his philosophies more. Do they agree with him?

Albert Gore (born Washington, DC, 1948) was the forty-fifth vice president of the United States.

Franz Josef Haydn (born Rohrau, Austria-Hungary, 1732; died Vienna, Austria, May 31, 1809) was a composer. He composed over 100 symphonies, 12 operas, and hundreds of other pieces of music.

 Students could enjoy some of his music.

April is the fourth month of the year. Ancient Romans called the month *Aprilis*. This Roman name may have come from a word meaning "to open." Some people believe the month was named after Aphrodite, the Greek goddess of love. April's special flowers are the daisy and the sweet pea. The birthstone is the diamond.

Month-Long Activities

Alcohol Awareness Month increases awareness among adults of the problems of underage drinking. Contact: National Council on Alcoholism and Drug Dependence, Inc., Public Information Department, 20 Exchange Place, New York, New York 10005. Telephone: (212) 269-7797.

International Amateur Radio Month celebrates "hams," amateur radio operators around the world. Contact: International Society of Friendship and Goodwill, 8592 Roswell Road, Suite 434, Atlanta, Georgia 30350.

Keep America Beautiful Month reminds Americans to take responsibility for America's environment. Contact: Keep America Beautiful, Inc., 1010 Washington Boulevard, Stamford, Connecticut 06901. Visit a Web site at: http://www.kab.org.

Mathematics Education Month not only focuses on the role of mathematics in education and society, but also helps people know about the changes in mathematics education. Contact: National Council of Teachers of Mathematics, Communications Manager, 1906 Association Drive, Reston, Virginia 22901-1593. Telephone: (703) 620-9840. Visit a Web site at: http://www.nctm.org.

Prevention of Animal Cruelty Month aims to make the lives of animals better. Contact: American Society for the Prevention of Cruelty to Animals, 424 E. 92nd Street, New York, New York 10128. Telephone: (212) 876-7700. Visit a Web site at: http://www.aspca.org.

Sports Eye Safety Month encourages young athletes to wear eye/face protection. Contact: Prevent Blindness America, 500 E. Remington Road, Schaumburg, Illinois 60173. Telephone: (800) 331-2020.

ZAM! Zoo and Aquarium Month: 184 zoos and aquariums focus on education and conservation.

Special Weeks

National Library Week is for making Americans aware of all the services available to the public in the libraries. Contact: American Library Association, 50 East Huron Street, Chicago, Illinois 60611. Visit a Web site at: http://www.ala.org.

National Garden Week (second week) honors the efforts of 40 million Americans to beautify their properties and communities. Contact: National Garden Bureau, 1311 Butterfield Road, Suite 310, Downers Grove, Illinois 60515.

National Coin Week (third week) celebrates the history of numismatics and promotes coin collecting. Contact: American Numismatic Association, 818 N. Cascade Avenue, Colorado

Springs, Colorado 80903. Telephone: (719) 632-2646. Visit a Web site at: http://www.money.org.

National Science and Technology Week makes the public, especially children, aware of the impact of science and technology on their lives. Contact: Office of Legislative and Public Affairs, National Science Foundation, 4201 Wilson Blvd., Arlington, Virginia 22230.

Canada-United States Goodwill Week (week including April 28) marks the Rush-Bagot treaty of April 28, 1817. It defined armament arrangements for the Americans and the British in the Great Lakes. The week also educates Americans and Canadians about each other's lifestyles. Contact: Kiwanis International, Program Development Department, 3636 Woodview Trace, Indianapolis, Indiana 46268.

National Week of the Ocean focuses on the relationship of people and the ocean. Contact: National Week of the Ocean, Inc., PO Box 179, Fort Lauderdale, Florida 33302. Telephone: (305) 462-5573.

Reading Is Fun Week stresses the importance of reading. Contact: Reading Is Fundamental, Inc., 600 Maryland Avenue SW, Room 600, Washington, DC, 20024-2569. Telephone: (202) 287-3371.

Special Days

Daylight Saving Time becomes effective at 2:00 A.M. on the second Sunday in April.

Take Our Daughters and Sons to Work Day is the fourth Thursday in April.

National Arbor Day is the last Friday in April.

April

April Fool's Day: The custom of April Fool's Day may have begun in France in the 1500s. Before then, New Year's started on March 25 and ended April 1. People gave gifts on April 1 to mark the beginning of the new year. Then New Year was moved to January 1. Some people still gave gifts on April 1 as jokes. The custom spread to Britain in the eighteenth century and then to other countries.

San Marino National Day: San Marino has an area of only 24 square miles and a population of about 23,000 people. Surrounded by Italy, it is one of the oldest republics in the world.

 Locate San Marino on a map. Find its distance to the students' school. San Marino is known for its postage stamps. Students could research San Marino and design a new postage stamp.

Save the Rhino Day: At least five species of rhinoceros exist; all are endangered. People kill them for their horns. However, the horns are nothing but chunks of keratin, the material found in hair and nails. A rhino can grow to a length of 14 feet and weigh as much as four tons. These animals are shortsighted but have keen senses of smell and hearing. All rhinos are herbivores but will attack people if they feel especially threatened. Ancestors of present-day rhinos date back to prehistoric times. Their thick skins act as armor to protect them from enemies.

 Cut lengths of paper 14 feet long. Have students draw rhinos on the paper. Fill the paper with rhino facts students have gleaned from research. Display in the hall when finished.

St. Lasarus's Day is held in Bulgaria, celebrating young women and the goddess of spring and love.

Oliver Pollick created the dollar sign ($) in 1778.

Birthdays

Otto von Bismarck (born Schonhausen, Prussia, 1815; died Friedrichsruh, Germany, July 30, 1898) was a Prussian statesman nicknamed the "Iron Chancellor." He helped unite German states into one nation.

Lon Chaney (born Colorado Springs, Colorado, 1883; died New York, New York, August 26, 1930) was considered one of the finest actors during the silent film era. Nicknamed the "Man of a Thousand Faces," his films included *The Hunchback of Notre Dame* and *The Phantom of the Opera.*

William Harvey (born Folkestone, Kent, England, 1578; died London, England, June 3, 1657) discovered how blood circulated in mammals. Prior to his work, many scientists believed the liver changed food to blood and the body consumed that blood. Through experiments and observations, he found that the heart acts like a pump and that blood moves through veins and arteries, forming a closed system of circulation.

> Have students trace themselves on large paper. Using other resources, they can draw in their heart and circulatory system.

Sergei Vasilievich Rachmaninoff (born Semyonovo, Russia, 1873; died Beverly Hills, California, March 28, 1943) was a Russian composer, conductor, and pianist. He composed at least forty-five major works. He moved to the United States in order to escape the Bolshevik Revolution and eventually became an American citizen. Experts state his compositions reflect a romantic style influenced by his Russian heritage.

> Russians celebrate birthdays by making one-crust pies. Make a birthday pie. Eat pieces of the pie and listen to Rachmaninoff's music.

Jagjivan Ram (born Chandwa, Bihar, India, 1908; died New Delhi, India, July 6, 1986) worked closely with Gandhi and Nehru for India's independence. Ram was born into the "untouchable" caste. He was one of the first "untouchables" to graduate from college. He labored to eliminate the caste system and served in various cabinet positions in the new Indian government.

Libby Riddles (born Madison, Wisconsin, 1956) in 1985 was the first woman to win the 1,135-mile Iditarod.

Glenn Edward "Bo" Schembechler (born Barberton, Ohio, 1929) is a former football coach.

Rusty Staub (born New Orleans, Louisiana, 1944) is a former baseball player.

April

2

International Children's Book Day (in honor of Hans Christian Andersen's birthday)

> Have older children pick picture books and read them to younger children.

Ponce de Leon discovered Florida in 1513. Juan Ponce de Leon had been on Columbus's second voyage to the New World. Later he was commissioned by King Ferdinand to find Bimini, an island that held the legendary fountain of youth. At first Ponce de Leon thought Florida was an island. Because the area grew such lush vegetation, Ponce de Leon named it *Florida,* meaning "full of flowers." He was killed by natives in 1521 when he tried to return to Florida to establish a colony.

Students could make a map of Bimini and label the fountain of youth.

First U.S. mint was established in Philadelphia in 1792. It produced silver half-dismes and dismes (now spelled dimes). The mint is still active, and other mints are functioning in Denver and San Francisco. Visit a Web site at: http://www.usmint.gov/kids.

 Students could debate the idea of eliminating the production of the penny.

Nickelodeon, a children's television channel, premiered in 1979.

Birthdays

Hans Christian Andersen (born Odense, Denmark, 1805; died Copenhagen, Denmark, August 4, 1875) wrote 168 stories and fairy tales. Born the son of a poor shoemaker, he moved to Copenhagen when he was 14. He wrote his first story in 1835. Famous stories include *The Little Mermaid, The Emperor's New Clothes,* and *The Ugly Duckling.* He never married.

 In Denmark people celebrate birthdays by displaying banners. Students could make banners of Andersen's various stories.

Frederic Auguste Bartholdi (born Colmar, Alsace, 1834; died Paris, France, October 4, 1904) designed the Statue of Liberty and actively raised funds for its construction.

 Students could find out various facts about the Statue of Liberty and display them on posters.

Dana Carvey (born Missoula, Montana, 1955) is an actor.

Charlemagne (born 742; died Aauchen in what is now Germany, August 18, 814) became the ruler of the Franks in 768 and thus controlled Western Europe. Before he seized power, Europe was crumbling. "Charles the Great" restored the importance of education, arts, culture, law, and order.

Walter Chrysler (born Wamego, Kansas, 1875; died 1940) figured prominently in automobile manufacturing. He headed Buick Motor Company, General Motors Corporation, and Chrysler Corporation. He also financed construction of the Chrysler Building in New York, New York.

Buddy Ebsen (born Belleville, Illinois, 1908) is an actor.

Marvin Gaye (born Washington, DC, 1939; died Los Angeles, California, April 1, 1984) was a singer.

Emmylou Harris (born Birmingham, Alabama, 1947) is a singer.

Emile Zola (born Paris, France, 1840; died Paris, France, September 28, 1902) was a French novelist.

April

3

Johannes Gutenberg used movable type for the first time in 1451. Prior to his invention, monks and copyists copied books by hand. Therefore, books were rare and expensive. He cast his type from sand molds and adapted woodcut presses to hold his type. Gutenberg is most remembered for his forty-two-line Bibles, called such because each page was forty-two lines long. About forty such Bibles remain and are extremely valuable.

The Twenty-Third Amendment to the Constitution was adopted in 1961. It gave the residents of Washington, DC, the right to vote.

Pony Express had its first run in 1860. Prior to the Pony Express, a letter took three weeks to make its way across country. William Guin and William Russell started the Pony Express to speed up the delivery of mail. They hired 80 riders, bought 400 horses, and established 190 stations. The riders, mostly teenagers, had to be light weight and in excellent shape. They rode day and night and in all kinds of weather. They also faced hostile Indians at times. A letter carried via the Pony Express left St. Joseph, Missouri, and arrived in Sacramento, California (1,966 miles), in ten days. The Pony Express ended in October 26, 1861, two days after the telegraph started.

 Students could find and plot the exact route of the Pony Express. They could also write journals as if they were the riders. They could describe their adventures.

Microsoft Corporation was found to be a monopoly in 2000.

Birthdays

Marlon Brando (born Omaha, Nebraska, 1924) is an actor.

John Burroughs (born Roxbury, New York, 1837; died March 29, 1921) was a writer and naturalist. He wrote for 50 years on such topics as *Ways of Nature* and *The Breath of Life*.

Jane Goodall (born London, England, 1934) conducted long-term study of chimpanzees.

 Students could research chimpanzees and share their results.

Edward Everett Hale (born Boston, Massachusetts, 1822; died Boston, Massachusetts, June 10, 1909) was a clergyman and a writer. He is most famous for his story, *The Man Without a Country*. He also served as chaplain of the U.S. Senate from 1903 until he died.

Washington Irving (born New York, New York, 1783; died Tarrytown, New York, November 28, 1859) may have been one of the first great American writers and historians. His writings include *The Sketch Book* (containing "Rip van Winkle" and "The Legend of Sleepy Hollow"), *Tales of a Traveller, The Life of Washington,* and *The Alhambra*.

 Read portions of "Rip van Winkle." Students could then illustrate scenes from the story.

Henry Robinson Luce (born Denzhou, China, 1898; died Phoenix, Arizona, February 28, 1967) was a famous editor and publisher. Born the son of Presbyterian missionaries, he and Briton Hadden started *Time* magazine in 1923. He also started *Fortune* in 1930, *Life* in 1936, and *Sports Illustrated* in 1954. He married Clare Booth Luce, a diplomat and playwright.

Eddie Murphy (born Brooklyn, New York, 1961) is an actor.

Wayne Newton (born Norfolk, Virginia, 1942) is a singer.

April

4

Martin Luther King, Jr. was assassinated in 1968 in Memphis, Tennessee. James Earl Ray received a 99-year sentence for his action.

North American Treaty was signed in 1949. Twelve nations formed the original North American Treaty Organization: Belgium, Canada, Denmark, France, Great Britain, Iceland, Italy, Luxembourg, the Netherlands, Norway, Portugal, and the United States. Greece and Turkey became members in 1951, and West Germany joined in 1954. Spain became the last member in 1982. The main purpose of NATO is protection; an attack against one member is an attack against all members.

 Locate these countries on a world map. Decide whether all countries benefit equally from this treaty.

Senegal celebrates its Independence Day. France gave up custody of the country in 1960. Dakar is the capital. Plains cover most of the country, but some jungle grows in the southwestern portions.

Hungary celebrates a national holiday.

U.S. flag with thirteen stripes and a star for each state was adopted in 1818. Prior to this time, a star and stripe was added each time a state was admitted to the Union. By 1817 the flag had twenty stripes and twenty stars. The flag was becoming cumbersome. Samuel Chester Reid suggested the stripes remain at thirteen, and the number of stars change as new states joined the union.

 Research the history of the American flag. Make a poster showing some of the changes the flag has undergone.

Rhodes Scholarships were created in 1902. Cecil J. Rhodes, an English statesman, died, and his estate created the scholarships. The money allows over ninety students per year the opportunity to study at Oxford University.

Vitamin C was discovered by C. G. King in 1932. Vitamin C, also known as ascorbic acid, builds strong bones and teeth. It speeds up the healing process of wounds.

 Vitamin C is found in citrus fruits, tomatoes, potatoes, strawberries, cantaloupe, and cabbage. Make a fruit salad of strawberries, melon, and oranges. Discuss the benefits of vitamin C as children enjoy the treat.

Birthdays

Maya Angelou (born Saint Louis, Missouri, 1928) is an author and a poet.

Elmer Bernstein (born New York, New York, 1922) is a composer.

Dorothea Lynde Dix (born Hampden, Maine, 1802; died Trenton, New Jersey, July 17, 1887) fought for social reform, especially regarding jails, insane asylums, and orphanages.

Phoebe Gilman (born New York, New York, 1940) is a picture book author and illustrator. Her works include *Grandma and the Pirates,* 1990.

Edward Hicks (born Langhorne, Pennsylvania, 1780; died Newtown, Pennsylvania, August 23, 1849) was a self-taught artist known for his many Peaceable Kingdoms.

Elizabeth Levy (born 1942) is a children's author.

Muddy Waters (born McKinley Morganfield in Rolling Fork, Mississippi, 1915; died Westmont, Illinois, April 30, 1983) was a blues guitarist and singer.

Linus Yale (born 1821, Salsbury, New York; died New York, New York, December 25, 1868) was famous as a portrait painter and creator of Yale Infallible Bank Lock and inventor of the cylinder lock.

pril

 John Rolfe married Pocahontas in 1614. The two sailed to England in 1616, where Pocahontas was extremely popular. She died of smallpox in 1617.

 Decide whether she really saved John Smith when she was only twelve years old.

George Washington used his veto power for the first time in 1792.

Kareem Abdul-Jabbar became the highest scorer in the NBA in 1984. Born Ferdinand Lewis Alcindor, Jr., he scored 38,387 points in 1,560 games over twenty years.

 Create math problems regarding his basketball statistics. For example, find out his average number of points scored per game.

Cider mill was patented in 1906.

Birthdays

Bette Davis (born Lowell, Massachusetts, 1908; died Paris, France, October 7, 1989) was an actress.

Joseph Lister (born Upton, Essex, England, 1827; died Walmer, England, February 10, 1912) was a pioneer in performing antiseptic surgery.

Gregory Peck (born La Jolla, California, 1916; died Los Angeles, California, June 11, 2003) was an actor.

Richard Peck (born Decatur, Illinois, 1934) has written more than twenty books for children. *A Long Way from Chicago* was the 1999 Newbery Honor Book. *A Year Down Under* won the 2001 Newbery Medal.

Colin Powell (born Harlem, New York, 1937) is a former Chairman, Joint Chiefs of Staff of the Armed Forces of the United States. He has been active in politics, and he is the U.S. Secretary of State.

Judith A. Resnick (born Akron, Ohio, 1949) died in the *Challenger* explosion, January 28, 1986. In 1984 she became the second American woman to go into space.

Booker Tallaferro Washington (born a slave in Franklin County, Virginia, 1856; died Tuskegee, Alabama, November 14, 1915) was an important African American leader and educator. He founded the Tuskegee Institute, and he influenced presidents, governors, and members of Congress.

 Find out more about Washington's life. See if you agree with his philosophies and actions.

pril

 First modern Olympiad was held in Athens, Greece, in 1896. Women did not compete until 1900, and the first winter Olympics occurred in 1924.

 Hold a class-wide Olympiad. Include such events as reading and walking at the same time, spelling words associated with the Olympics, and conducting math problems related to sports statistics. Visit a Web site at: http://orama.com/athens1896.

United States declared war on Germany in 1917, bringing America into World War I.

South Africa celebrates Van Riebeeck Day, when Capetown was founded.

Ethiopia celebrates Victory Day.

Switzerland celebrates the Glarius Festival (1388).

Thailand celebrates Chakri Day. King Rama I (1782–1809) established the present dynasty and made Bangkok the capital city.

Robert E. Peary claimed in 1909 he was the first person to reach the North Pole. He, his assistant Matthew Henson, and four Eskimos traveled to within several miles of the North Pole. Peary rested for a few hours and then, with two Eskimos, finished the journey (according to his calculations).

 Many experts feel he did not actually reach the North Pole. Decide whether it matters if he was the first person to reach this destination. Celebrate the day by making and eating Eskimo pies.

Teflon was accidentally discovered in 1938 by Roy J. Plunkett, who worked for DuPont.

"Barney and Friends" premiered in 1992 on PBS.

Dow Jones Industrial Average in 1998 exceeded the 9,000 mark for the first time.

Birthdays

Graeme Base (born Amershame, England, 1958) is an author and illustrator. One of his most famous works is *Animalia,* published in 1986.

 Students could read and share *Animalia.* Then they could copy his style and make new *Animalia* pages.

Bert (Rik Albert) Blyleven (born Zeist, the Netherlands, 1951) is a former baseball player.

Andre Previn (born Berlin, Germany, 1929) is a pianist and composer.

Raphael Santi (Sanzio) (born Urbino, Italy, probably April 6, 1483; died Rome, Italy, April 6, 1520) was a painter and sculptor.

Rose Schneiderman (born Saven, Poland, 1882; died New York, New York, August 11, 1972) fought for better working conditions for women.

Lowell Thomas (born Woodington, Ohio, 1892; died Pawling, New York, August 29, 1981) was a reporter and radio newscaster.

James Watson (born Chicago, Illinois, 1928) created, with partner Francis H. C. Crick, a model for the structure of DNA. The two, along with Maurice H. F. Wilkins, received the 1962 Nobel Prize for physiology or medicine.

April

7 Metric system was born when France adopted the system in 1795.

United Nations World Health Day remembers the creation of the World Health Organization.

 Each child could make a poster of at least five healthy habits. Contact: United Nations, Department of Public Information, New York, New York 10017.

South Pacific **opened on Broadway in 1949.**

Birthdays

Jackie Chan (born Hong Kong, 1954) is an actor.

Tony Dorsett (born Aliquippa, Pennsylvania, 1954) is a former football player.

El Greco (born Domenikos Theotokopoulos in Iraklion, Crete, 1541?; died Toledo, Spain, April 7, 1614) was a great painter. He studied in Venice in 1559 or 1560. Looking for patrons, he moved to Toledo, Spain, in 1577. Named "The Greek" by the Spaniards, he spent the rest of his life in that country. His paintings, especially for the time, were fairly abstract. He used light and dark colors to his advantage, and he distorted figures to achieve an emotional impact. Visit a Web site at: http://www.artcyclopedia.com/artists/greco_el.html.

 Locate and display several prints of his work. Children could decide whether they like his style.

Billie Holiday (born Eleanora Fagan in Philadelphia, Pennsylvania, 1915; died New York, New York, July 17, 1959) was a singer.

Will Keith Kellogg (born Battle Creek, Michigan, 1860; died 1951) was a cereal manufacturer. Known as the King of the Corn Flakes, he started a cereal company in 1906 and made a $50 million fortune.

 Children could make a bar graph of favorite cereals.

John Oates (born New York, New York, 1948) is a songwriter of the team Hall and Oates.

Walter Winchell (born New York, New York, 1879; died Los Angeles, California, 1972) was a news commentator and writer. He created a very successful gossip column, and he was also popular on radio and television.

William Wordsworth (born Cockermouth, England, 1770; died Grasmere, England, April 23, 1850) may have been the most significant English Romantic poet. He wrote over 500 sonnets, and he collaborated with Samuel Taylor Coleridge to write *Lyrical Ballads*. Wordsworth actively supported the French Revolution.

April

Buddha was born in 563 B.C. He was the son of a wealthy Indian Prince. His original name was Siddhartha Gautama. When he was twenty-nine, he had a series of visions. He began to seek enlightenment. Sitting one day under a bo tree he found nirvana, a state of complete peace. He began to preach his ideas, including the idea of giving up all worldly possessions and desires. He died in 483 B.C. His followers, Buddhists, number 300 million and live for the most part in Japan, Sri Lanka, and Asia.

 Perhaps a Buddhist could come speak to the class.

Japan celebrates Flower Festival (Hana Matsuri) in honor of Buddha's birthday.

Poll tax was outlawed in 1966.

First synagogue in United States was built. The Spanish and Portuguese Synagogue (Shearith Israel) opened its doors in 1730.

Fire escape was patented in 1766. The system included a wicker basket on a series of pullies and chains.

Hank Aaron hit his 715th home run in 1974, breaking Babe Ruth's record set in 1935.

 Children could research the lives of both men. Did they meet each other? Create a dialogue between the two men.

Oleomargarine was patented in 1873.

Birthdays

Kofi Annan (born Kumasi, Ghana, 1938) is the United Nations Secretary General.

Gary Carter (born Culver City, California, 1954) is a former baseball player.

Elizabeth "Betty" Bloomer Ford (born Chicago, Illinois, 1918) is the wife of Gerald Ford, the thirty-eighth president of the United States. Visit a Web site at: http://www.whitehouse.gov/history/firstladies/ef38.html.

 Children could make a list of qualities the first lady should possess. Did Mrs. Ford have all those qualities?

John Havlicek (born 1940) is a basketball player honored in the Hall of Fame.

 Children could make a school hall of fame.

Trina Schart Hyman (born Philadelphia, Pennsylvania, 1939) is a picture book author and illustrator. She wrote, among other works, *Hershel and the Hanukkah Goblins* (Caldecott Honor Book, 1989).

Sonja Henie (born Oslo, Norway, 1912; died in an airplane crash en route to Oslo, October 12, 1969) was an ice skater and an actress.

Lewis Morris (born Westchester County, New York, 1726; died Westchester County, New York, January 22, 1798) signed the Declaration of Independence. He represented New York.

William Williams (born Lebanon, Connecticut, 1731; died Lebanon, Connecticut, August 2, 1811) signed the Declaration of Independence. He represented Connecticut.

April

9 **Civil War ended in 1865 when Robert E. Lee surrendered to Ulysses S. Grant at Appomattox, Virginia.** Over 600,000 soldiers died in the Civil War, more than all the wars the United States has ever fought combined. Because most of the war had been waged in the South, many of the southern states suffered severe damage. The war, however, ended slavery and reunited all the states.

 The Civil War changed ideas regarding battle. Research to find out what new machinery and which different strategies were used.

Civil Rights Bill of 1866 became law. Eventually most of the important parts of the bill were incorporated into a Constitutional amendment.

Tunisia celebrates Martyrs' Day.

Peterborough, New Hampshire, created the first free public library in the United States in 1833.

Philippines remembers Bataan Day (1942).

Sieur de la Salle found the Mississippi River in 1682 and claimed it and the waters draining into it for France. The Mississippi River, 2,348 miles long, is the longest river in the United States. It ranges in depth from 9 feet to 100 feet, and its drainage basin includes over one million square miles.

 Trace a map of the United States. Color the states whose rivers empty into the Mississippi. Add tributaries, such as the Missouri, Ohio, and Arkansas Rivers.

Samuel R. Percy patented dried milk in 1872.

First U.S. astronauts were appointed in 1959. All nine original astronauts were men, and they were all in the military. Visit a Web site at: http://mix.msfc.nasa.gov/abstracts/msfc-6413212.html.

 Investigate present astronaut requirements. Who are some of our present astronauts? How have ideas changed since the beginning of the program?

Valery Ryumin and Leonid Popov launched *Soyuz 35* **in 1980.** They docked at *Salyut 6* on April 10. They stayed in space 185 days, a record for that time, returning October 11, 1980.

Birthdays

W. C. Fields (born Claude William Dukenfield in Philadelphia, Pennsylvania, 1879; died Pasadena, California, December 25, 1946) was an actor and a comedian.

Paul Bustill Robeson (born Princeton, New Jersey, 1898; died Philadelphia, Pennsylvania, January 23, 1976) was a singer and an actor.

Carl Perkins (born Jackson, Tennessee, 1932) is a singer and a songwriter.

April

First U.S. patent law was formalized in 1790.

 Children could create a new invention and fill out a "patent application."

Safety pin was patented by Walter Hunt in 1849.

Synthetic rubber was first fabricated in 1930.

 Find out how Charles Goodyear accidentally created vulcanized rubber.

First three-dimensional movies opened in 1953.

Robert Gray became the first U.S. citizen to circumnavigate the world. He sailed from Boston in September 1787 and traded with the Northwest Coast Indians. He traveled to China before returning to the United States.

Birthdays

David Adler (born New York, New York, 1947) is an award-winning children's author. He has written over seventy books. One of his books is *Lou Gehrig, the Luckiest Man.* Visit a Web site at: http://www.davidaadler.com.

William Booth (born Nottingham, England, 1829; died London England, August 20, 1912) was the founder of the Salvation Army.

Commodore Matthew Calbraith Perry (born Newport, Rhode Island, 1794; died New York, New York, March 4, 1858) was the American officer who peacefully negotiated with the Japanese to open its harbors to world trade. He sailed into Tokyo Bay in July 1853. By combining diplomacy with a show of military power, he gained the trust of the Japanese. This agreement made Japan a world power by 1900.

John Madden (born Austin, New Mexico, 1936) is a sportscaster.

Don Meredith (born Mount Vernon, Texas, 1938) is a former sportscaster.

Frances Perkins (born Boston, Massachusetts, 1880; died New York, New York, May 14, 1965) was the first woman cabinet member, serving as Secretary of Labor for Franklin Delano Roosevelt from 1933 to 1945.

Joseph Pulitzer (born Budapest, Hungary, 1847; died Charleston, South Carolina, October 29, 1911) was a journalist and newspaper owner. He came to the United States to fight in the Civil War. After the war he was a reporter for a St. Louis newspaper. Later he became a part owner in the newspaper. For a while he served in the House of Representatives. He bought several newspapers and continued to be active in politics. His will provided money for the Pulitzer Prizes, including the areas of journalism, literature, drama, music, and public service.

 The Pulitzer Prizes have no special category for juvenile literature. Children could create their own prizes for their favorite books.

Omar Sharif (born Michael Shalhoub in Alexandria, Egypt, 1932) is an actor.

 # April

11 **Napoleon Bonaparte abdicated in 1814.** Born in 1769 on the island of Corsica, Bonaparte early showed a talent for the military. During the French Revolution he was a hero and became a major general. In 1804 the people voted him to be emperor. He expanded his kingdom to include most of Europe. However, he was unable to keep the kingdom intact. He was defeated in Russia and at Leipzig in the Battle of Nations. He abdicated in 1814 and was exiled to Elbe in the same year. He briefly returned to power before he was defeated at Waterloo. In 1815 he was exiled to St. Helena and died there in 1821.

 Research Napoleon's life more thoroughly. Was he thinking foremost about his new kingdom or about himself?

Harold Washington became the first African American mayor of Chicago in 1983. He was elected for a second term in 1987, but he died seven months later on November 25, 1987.

Halley's Comet made its closest approach to Earth yet in 1986. Edmund Halley discovered that certain similar comets had been seen in 1531, 1607, and 1682. He concluded the sightings were of the same comet. It was named in honor of him.

 The comet appears roughly every seventy-seven years. Figure out when it will be seen in the future.

Civil Rights Act of 1968 became law.

American Society for the Prevention of Cruelty to Animals was created in 1866.

Republic of Uganda celebrates Liberation Day. In 1979 the people overthrew dictator Idi Amin.

Apollo 13, **the nearly fatal space mission to the moon, was launched in 1970.** Astronauts John L. Swigert, Fred Haise, and James A. Lovell were on their way to the moon when an oxygen tank exploded. Their craft was severely damaged, and they had a great deal of difficulty returning home. The world held its breath until the craft fell safely into the Pacific Ocean on April 17.

Barbershop Quartet Day celebrates the founding of the Society for the Preservation and Encouragement of Barbershop Quartet Singing in America.

 Show a clip from the movie *The Music Man* where the town officials unwittingly organize a barbershop quartet. See if the children can create their own quartets.

Birthdays

Edward Everett (born Dorcester, Massachusetts, 1794; died Boston Massachusetts, January 15, 1865) was a famous politician and orator. He gave the main address at the dedication of the Gettysburg National Cemetery on November 19, 1863. His speech was very long. President Lincoln's now famous speech took less than two minutes. Afterward, Everett realized the greatness of Lincoln's speech and stated it would last for generations.

Joel Grey (born Joe Katz in Cleveland, Ohio, 1932) is an actor and a singer.

Charles Evans Hughes (born Glens Falls, New York, 1862; died Osterville, Massachusetts, August 27, 1948) was the eleventh chief justice of the Supreme Court.

 April

 12 **Civil War began in 1861 when Confederate troops attacked Fort Sumter near Charleston, South Carolina.** Visit a Web site at: http://civil-war.net.

 Have students color on a map the states that became the Confederacy, the states that remained in the Union, and the areas that were not states then.

Salk vaccine was allowed to be used for the first time in 1955. Dr. Jonas E. Salk produced the vaccine to prevent infantile paralysis, also known as poliomyelitis. Prior to the vaccination, polio was one of the worst diseases around. Salk started conducting research in 1947. He field-tested his vaccination in 1953, and it became available to the public in 1955.

Yuri Gagarin in 1961 was the first human to travel in space. A Soviet cosmonaut, Gagarin's voyage on *Vostok I* lasted 108 minutes.

Space shuttle's first flight occurred in 1981. Astronauts John Young and Robert Crippen guided the space shuttle *Columbia* around the Earth thirty-six times before landing the craft at Edwards Air Force Base in California on April 14. On February 1, 2003, *Columbia* disintegrated when it reentered the atmosphere at the end of a mission.

 Find out how the shuttle differed from the previous types of space exploration.

Jake Garn became the first senator to travel in space. He was a member of a *Discovery* crew that was launched in 1985.

Three important space travel events happened on this day. Children could make a timeline of significant space explorations.

Mount Washington, New Hampshire, recorded its strongest wind ever at 231 miles per hour in 1934.

James Tyng donned the first catcher's mask in 1877.

Birthdays

Henry Clay (born Hanover County, Virginia, 1777; died Washington, DC, June 29, 1852) was a politician. He was elected to the House of Representatives for six terms, and most of that time he was Speaker of the House. He also served in the Senate for almost twenty years. Clay wanted to be president, but he was never elected. He is remembered as saying, "I would rather be right than be president."

Beverly Cleary (born McMinnville, Oregon, 1916) is a children's author. She wrote, among other works, *Dear Mr. Henshaw* (Newbery Medal), 1984. Visit a Web site at: http://www. beverlycleary.com.

Lyman Hall (born Wallingford, Connecticut, 1724; died Burke County, Georgia, October 19, 1790) signed the Declaration of Independence. He represented Georgia. Visit a Web site at: http://www.virtualology.com/virtualmuseumofhistory/rebelswithavision.com/ lyman-hall.com.

David Letterman (born Indianapolis, Indiana, 1947) is a comedian and a talk show host.

 Letterman is known for his "top ten" lists. Students could make their own "top ten" homework excuses.

Scott Turow (born Chicago, Illinois, 1949) is a writer.

April

13

Metropolitan Museum of Art opened its doors for the first time in 1870. It contains over 200 galleries and possesses over three million pieces of art.

 Consider reading *From the Mixed-up Files of Mrs. Basil E. Frankweiler.* Two siblings run away to the museum. They solve a mystery, and readers learn a great deal about the museum.

Jefferson Memorial was dedicated in 1943. This date was picked in honor of Jefferson's birthday. Visit a Web site at: http://www.nps.gov/thje.

Rachel Carson's *Silent Spring* was first published in 1962. It helped create an awareness of Earth's fragility and pollution's hazards.

Birthdays

Samuel Becket (born Foxrock, County Dublin, Ireland, 1906; died Paris, France, December 22, 1989) wrote books and plays. During World War II he worked with a French resistance group. One of his most famous works is *Waiting for Godot.*

Alfred Butts (born Poughkeepsie, New York, 1899; died Rhinebeck, New York, April 4, 1993) invented the game *Scrabble*. He invented the game when he was out of a job during the Depression. After he sold the game to a company, he received three cents for each game sold.

 Bring in lots of Scrabble sets and have a tournament.

Lee Bennett Hopkins (born Scranton, Pennsylvania, 1938) is a poet and a novelist. His first career was as a teacher, and he found out how important poetry was to him and to children. One of his works is *Good Rhymes, Good Times*.

Butch Cassidy (born Robert Leroy Parker in Beaver, Utah, 1866; died? Bolivia, 1909) was the leader of the Wild Bunch. He and Harry Longabaugh (the Sundance Kid) were outlaws during the 1880s and 1890s in the West.

Thomas Jefferson (born Albermarle County, Virginia, 1743; died Charlottesville, Virginia, July 4, 1826) was the third president (1801–1808) of the United States. He hoped people would remember him for writing the Declaration of Independence, for writing the statute of Virginia for religious freedom, and for founding the University of Virginia. He also made possible the Louisiana Purchase of 1803. Visit a Web site at: http://whitehouse.gov/wh/glimpse/presidents/html/tj3/html.

 Jefferson invented several items that made life easier, including the swivel chair, a lap desk, and a decoding device. Students could evaluate his inventions and draw diagrams of them.

Frank Winfield Woolworth (born Rodman, New York, 1852; died Glen Cove, Long Island, New York, April 8, 1919) co-founded the F. W. Woolworth Company. While he was working in a store, he placed slower-moving items on sale for five cents. The idea was so successful that he opened the first five-and-ten-cent store. Before he died, he had created 1,000 stores, and the Woolworth Building in New York City was the world's tallest building then.

April

 The Society for the Relief of Free Negroes Unlawfully Held in Bondage was formed in Philadelphia, Pennsylvania, in 1775. This group was America's first abolition society.

Pan American Day is celebrated.

Honduras celebrates Día de las Americas (Pan American Day).

Abraham Lincoln was shot in 1865. He was at Ford's Theatre in Washington, DC, to see a performance of *Our American Cousin*. He died the next day.

 Students could decide how the future of America could have been different if Lincoln had not been assassinated.

Noah Webster's dictionary was copyrighted in 1828.

 Children can create their own picture dictionaries regarding a certain topic—for example, Spanish words or computer terms.

Birthdays

Sir John Gielgud (born London, England, 1904; died Buckinghamshire, England, May 21, 2000) was an actor and a director.

David Christopher Justice (born Cincinnati, Ohio, 1968) is a baseball player.

Loretta Lynn (born Butcher's Hollow, Kentucky, 1935) is a singer.

Gregory Alan Maddux (born San Angelo, Texas, 1966) is a baseball player.

Pete Rose (born Cincinnati, Ohio, 1941) is a former baseball player.

Anne Mansfield Sullivan (born Feeding Hills, Massachusetts, 1866; died Forest Hills, New York, October 20, 1936) was Helen Keller's teacher from 1887 until her death in 1936.

 Locate a copy of *The Miracle Worker.* Focus on the scene where they are next to the water pump. Helen realizes the movements Anne makes in Helen's hands are the word "water."

April

 15 Income Tax Day

Rubber Eraser Day is honored. Joseph Priestley accidentally invented the eraser in 1770 when he was experimenting with latex.

McDonald's opened its first franchise in Des Plaines, Illinois, in 1955. Hamburgers cost fifteen cents.

American School for the Deaf (originally called the Connecticut Asylum for the Education and Instruction of Deaf and Dumb Persons) was founded in Hartford, Connecticut. Thomas Hopkins Gallaudet and Laurent Clerc started the school in 1817.

"Unsinkable" *Titanic* sank in 1912 with 1,500 people on board. The luxury liner was on its maiden voyage from England to New York City when it hit an iceberg and sank three hours later. The ship did not provide enough lifeboats for all the crew and passengers. Over 700 people were rescued by the *Carpathia* when it reached the site. In 1985 Dr. Robert Ballard and his crew located the remains of the *Titanic* and photographed it.

 Debate whether the *Titanic* should be raised or not. Students may want to read Robert Ballard's *Exploring the Titanic,* published in 1988.

Insulin could be used by Americans for the first time in the year 1928. Diabetes can be controlled with insulin. In 1921 Dr. Frederick Grant Banting and his assistant, Charles Herbert Best, produced insulin from the pancreas of a dog. Later it was extracted from the pancreatic glands of butchered cows.

Birthdays

Thomas Hart Benton (born Neosho, Missouri, 1889; died Kansas City, Missouri, January 19, 1975) was an artist. His works of the American Midwest and South led to the development of artistic regionalism.

Roy Clark (born Meherrin, Virginia, 1933) is a singer.

Leonhard Euler (born Basel, Switzerland, 1707; died St. Petersburg, Russia, September 18, 1783) was a mathematician.

Henry James (born New York, New York, 1843; died London, England, February 28, 1916) was a prolific and noted American writer. He wrote over 110 stories, 20 novels, and 16 plays. Some of his most famous work includes *The Turn of the Screw* and *What Maisie Knew.*

Charles Willson Peale (Born Queen Anne County, Maryland, 1741; died Philadelphia, Pennsylvania, February 22, 1827) was a famous portrait painter during the Revolutionary period. He enjoyed painting famous Americans. He created at least sixty portraits of George Washington. His brother (James Peale), and four of his sons (Rembrandt, Rubens, Titian Ramsay, and Raphael) were also accomplished artists.

 Children can make a portrait of a fellow classmate. Hang the results in the "American Gallery."

Bessie Smith (born Chattanooga, Tennessee, 1894; died Clarksdale, Mississippi, September 26, 1937) was nicknamed the "Empress of the Blues." She combined spirituals with jazz, and some experts consider her one of the greatest singers in blues history.

Leonardo da Vinci (born Vinci, Italy, 1452; died Cloux, France, May 2, 1519) was a great artist and scientist. Famous works include *Mona Lisa, Saint John the Baptist,* and *The Last Supper.* His scientific interests ranged from plant studies to aviation.

 The Last Supper is a fresco; it is painted into the plaster on the wall. Fill disposable pie plates with wet plaster of paris. Children can paint right into the wet plaster surface. Let the plaster dry and display the results.

April

 Natural Bridges National Monument in Utah was dedicated in 1908. Visit a Web site at: http://www.nps.gov/nabr.

Apollo 16 **was launched in 1972.** John Young, Charles M. Duke, Jr., and Thomas K. Mattingly made the eleven-day trip, exploring the moon for seventy-one hours.

Birthdays

Kareem Abdul-Jabbar (born Lewis Alcindor, Jr., in New York, New York, 1947) is a former basketball player.

David M. Brown (born Arlington, Virginia, 1956; died in *Columbia* disaster, February 1, 2003) was an astronaut.

Charles Spencer "Charlie" Chaplin (born London, England, 1889; died Vevey, Switzerland, December 12, 1977) was a comedian best known for his character "The Little Tramp."

Queen Margrethe (born 1940) took the throne of Denmark in 1972. She and her husband, Prince Henrik, have two sons.

Henry Mancini (born Cleveland, Ohio, 1924; died Beverly Hills, California, June 14, 1994) was a composer. He wrote many movie scores and songs, winning twenty Grammies and four Oscars.

 Mancini wrote the theme of *The Pink Panther.* The children could watch a Pink Panther cartoon and see how the music adds to the humor.

Peter Ustinov (born London, England, 1921) is an actor.

Gertrude Chandler Warner (born Putnam, Connecticut, 1980; died Putnam, Connecticut, August 30, 1979) created the Boxcar Children series.

 Warner wrote only the first few books of the series. Now someone else writes the books. Check the cover of a Boxcar book to see if the author is really Warner. The children could propose a plot for a new Boxcar book.

Wilbur Wright (born Millville, Indiana, 1867; died Dayton, Ohio, May 30, 1912) invented, along with his brother Orville, the first airplane. The two were owners of a bicycle shop when they became interested in aviation. They first experimented with kites and then moved on to gliders. They often experienced failure as they tested idea after idea. On December 17, 1903, Orville flew their motorized airplane.

 Consider having a paper airplane contest. Encourage new designs rather than the standard plane. Have a contest for the longest flight, and have another contest for the most acrobatic plane.

April

 17

Richard the Lionhearted returned to England in 1194. He had been fighting in the Crusades.

Solidarity received legal status in Poland in 1989. Poland had for many years been run by the Communist Party, and the Communists tried to suppress Solidarity. Lech Walesa led Solidarity as it gained control of Poland's government.

Surveyor 3 **was launched in 1967.** It made a soft landing on the moon.

 Find a photograph of *Surveyor.* Find out how it worked and how it was able to land without sinking into the moon's dusty surface.

Syrian Arab Republic celebrates its Independence Day. Liberated from France in 1946, its capital is Damascus. Farmers grow cotton and grains on its arable land. Mountains and deserts form a good portion of its geography.

American Samoa celebrates the day in 1900 when it became an American territory. It was formerly Eastern Samoa.

Giovanni Verrazano discovered New York Harbor in 1524. An Italian, Verrazano was in France's employ when he found the harbor. He was trying to find the Northwest Passage to China.

Hershey sold its first Hershey bar in 1895.

Thank You School Librarian Day honors school librarians.

 Have the children make a banner to honor their school librarian.

Birthdays

Samuel Chase (born Somerset County, Maryland, 1741; died Baltimore, Maryland, June 19, 1811) signed the Declaration of Independence. He also served on the Supreme Court as an associate justice from 1796 until he died.

John Pierpont Morgan (born Hartford, Connecticut, 1837; died Rome, Italy, March 31, 1913) was a financier and corporate executive. He helped finance American Telegraph and Telephone, and he reorganized several railroads after a panic in 1893. He enjoyed collecting art, and his collections were often loaned to the Metropolitan Museum of Art.

 Children could brainstorm a list of famous paintings. Each could then create a fictional personal gallery of his/her favorites.

Thornton Wilder (born Madison, Wisconsin, 1897; died Hamden, Connecticut, December 7, 1975) was a playwright and novelist. He won a Pulitzer Prize in 1928 for his novel *The*

Bridge of San Luis Rey. He also won Pulitzers for his plays *Our Town* and *The Skin of Our Teeth.*

April

Canada celebrates Constitution Day. Queen Elizabeth II signed official documents at Parliament Hill, Ottawa, in 1982. These papers modified Canada's government from the rules set by the British North America Act of 1867.

 Most American children know very little about Canada. Have students draw or trace maps of Canada and add major cities, crops, industries, etc.

Paul Revere and William Dawes conducted their famous horse ride at 10:00 P.M. in 1775. They warned their fellow patriots that the British were marching to Lexington and Concord in Massachusetts.

 Read Henry Wadsworth Longfellow's account of the ride, *The Midnight Ride of Paul Revere.*

Zimbabwe celebrates its Independence Day. Great Britain gained control of Southern Rhodesia (now called Zimbabwe) by about 1895. Although most of the citizens were black, the leaders were white. The country experienced a great deal of turbulence until Zimbabwe became independent in 1980.

San Francisco suffered a severe earthquake in 1906. The quake and subsequent fires, occurring at 5:13 A.M., killed almost 4,000 people.

Yankee Stadium opened in 1923. Nicknamed "The House that Ruth Built," it hosted 74,000 fans. Babe Ruth made the day really special by hitting a three-run homer that won the game.

Yankee Stadium is still used today. Create some math problems about the stadium and its fans. For example, the stadium hosts about eighty home games a season. How many fans pass through its gates every year?

Grace Kelly married Prince Rainier Louis Henri Maxence Bertrand de Grimaldi, Prince of Monaco, in 1956.

Birthdays

Clarence Darrow (born Kinsman, Ohio, 1857; died Chicago, Illinois, March 13, 1938) was a lawyer. He defended John Scopes in the famous case of creationism versus evolution, sometimes known as "The Monkey Trial." That trial was the basis for the play and movie, *Inherit the Wind.*

Melissa Joan Hart (born Long Island, New York, 1976) is an actress.

April

Battle of Lexington, in 1775, marked the beginning of the American Revolutionary War. About 700 British troops were marching toward Lexington and Concord to destroy military supplies. Approximately seventy Minutemen met the redcoats in Lexington. Records do not indicate clearly who fired the first shot, but eight Minutemen died. Ten more Minutemen were injured. One British soldier was wounded. The British continued on to Concord and then turned back toward Boston. Along the way, patriots shot at the redcoats. British casualties came to 250, and American casualties numbered 90.

 Children could research the event a bit more and then write the story as if they were newspaper reporters.

Venezuela celebrates its Independence Day. Spain ruled Venezuela for around 300 years, but in 1811 the country declared itself independent.

 Students could find out what the word *Venezuela* means.

Sierra Leone became a republic in 1971. Prior to 1961, it was a British colony. From 1961 to 1971, the country struggled under various types of government.

 About half of all Sierra Leone's exports are diamonds. Children could find out how a diamond is made and cut.

Alfred P. Murrah Federal Building in Oklahoma City, Oklahoma, was bombed in 1995.

Birthdays

Lucretia Rudolph Garfield (born Hiram, Ohio, 1832; died South Pasadena, California, March 14, 1918) was the wife of James A. Garfield, twentieth president of the United States. Visit a Web site at: http://www.whitehouse.gov/history/firstladies/lg20.html.

Roger Sherman (born Newton, Massachusetts, 1721; died New Haven, Connecticut, July 23, 1793) was the only patriot to sign four of America's most valuable documents, The Articles of Association, the Declaration of Independence, the Articles of Confederation, and the Constitution. He also served in the House of Representatives from 1789 to 1791 and in the Senate from 1791 to 1793.

Al Unser (born Albuquerque, New Mexico, 1962) is an Indy Car national champion.

Frank Viola, Jr. (born Hempstead, New York, 1960) is a former baseball player.

April

20

Radium was isolated by Pierre and Marie Curie in 1902. Radium is a radioactive element and is harmful to people.

Ludlow Mine Incident happened in 1914 in Ludlow, Colorado. Striking miners were attacked by National Guardsmen. A number of people were shot to death, and more died in a fire.

Electron microscope was first shown in 1940.

 Children could compare the electron microscope with a traditional microscope.

Columbine High School shootings occurred in 1999 in Littleton, Colorado.

Taurus the Bull is the astrological sign for April 20 through May 20.

Birthdays

Daniel Chester French (born Exeter, New Hampshire, 1850; died Stockbridge, Massachusetts, October 7, 1931) was a sculptor. His most famous works include the *Minute Man* statue in Concord, Massachusetts, and the seated *Abraham Lincoln* in the Lincoln Memorial.

Don Mattingly (born Evansville, Indiana, 1962) is a former baseball player.

Joan Miró (born Barcelona, Spain, 1893; died Majorca, Spain, December 25, 1983) was a surrealistic painter. One of his famous works is *Dutch Interior,* painted in 1928.

 Obtain prints of some of Miró's works. See what the children think about his work.

John Paul Stevens (born Chicago, Illinois, 1920) is an associate justice of the Supreme Court. He was nominated by Gerald Ford in 1975.

 Children could research the process whereby a person becomes a Supreme Court justice. Is there a term limit for the justices? Should there be a term limit?

April

 21

Rome was founded in 753 B.C. Over two million people live in Rome. It is the home of numerous famous sites, including the Coliseum, the Fountain of Neptune, and the Pantheon.

 Students could prepare a travel brochure about Rome.

Brazil celebrates Tiradentes Day. Brazil's national hero was Jose da Silva Xavier, a dentist nicknamed Tiradentes (tooth puller). He was executed by Portuguese government officials when he led a revolt in 1789.

Brasilia was constructed as Brazil's capital in 1960.

Indonesia celebrates Kartini Day. Raden Adjeng Kartini was a champion of women's rights in the Republic of Indonesia.

Spanish-American War began in 1898. At that time Spain ruled Cuba, and many Americans had heard that the conditions on the island were intolerable. The United States sent the battleship *Maine* to protect Americans living there. In February the ship exploded, and 260 people on board died. "Remember the *Maine*" became a popular expression. War was declared, and battles occurred not only in and around Cuba but around the Philippines as well. Teddy Roosevelt became famous as one of the leaders of the Rough Riders.

Battle of San Jacinto occurred in 1836. General Antonio Lopez de Santa Anna and his 1,200 soldiers attacked General Sam Houston and his 910 men. The Texans retreated but then caught the Mexicans by surprise. In less than one half hour, the Texans won. As a result of this battle, Texas won its independence from Mexico.

"Red Baron" was killed. Baron Manfred von Richtofen had shot down more than eighty planes in less than two years before he was shot down in 1918. The German pilot was twenty-five years old when he died.

Birthdays

Charlotte Brontë (born Hartshead, Yorkshire, England, 1816; died Haworth, Yorkshire, England, March 31, 1855) was a novelist. She is best known for *Jane Eyre.* She wrote three other novels.

Tony Danza (born Brooklyn, New York, 1951) is an actor.

Queen Elizabeth II (born London, England, 1926) serves as the monarch over the United Kingdom.

Many people feel the British monarchy should be dissolved. Children could poll schoolmates regarding the issue.

Friedrich Froebel (born Oberweissbach, Thuringia, 1782; died Marienthal, Germany, June 21, 1852) was concerned with early education and created the first kindergarten.

 Children could visit a kindergarten and read books to the younger children.

John Muir (born Dunbar, Scotland, 1838; died Los Angeles, California, December 24, 1914) was a naturalist and writer. He helped establish Yosemite National Park and Sequoia National Park. He started the Sierra Club, and Muir Woods was dedicated to him in 1908.

Barbara Park (born Mount Holly, New Jersey, 1947) is a children's author. She is the author of the Junie B. Jones books. Visit a Web site at: http://www.randomhouse.com/kids/junieb/authorbio.html.

 April

 22

Brazil was discovered by Pedro Alvarez Cabral in 1500. Brazil was claimed for Portugal, and it is the only South American country where Portuguese is the principal language.

Roller skates were patented by James Plimpton in 1823.

Babe Ruth made his pitching debut in 1914 when the Baltimore Orioles defeated the Buffalo Bison 6–0.

Oklahoma Land Rush began at twelve noon 1889 when the government opened 1.9 million acres of land bought from the Creek and Seminole Indians. People raced to obtain the best plots of land. By evening 50,000 people had established home sites in the region.

 Children could research what a "sooner" was.

Girl Scout Leader's Day. Contact: Girl Scouts of the USA, Media Services, 420 Fifth Avenue, New York, New York 10018. Visit a Web site at: http://www.gsusa.org.

Earth Day was first celebrated in 1970. The original theme was "Give Earth a Chance." Earth Day celebrations differ locally and are often near the first day of spring.

 Children could plan an Earth Day event in their school. It could range from bringing in a speaker to creating a play.

Borge Ousland, a Norwegian explorer, became the first person to trek to the North Pole alone in 1994. He left Cape Atkticheskiy, Siberia, on March 2, 1994. He averaged about 19 miles a day over the 630-mile trip.

Birthdays

Paula Fox (born New York, New York, 1923) is an author. One of her books is *The Slave Dancer.*

S. E. Hinton (born Tulsa, Oklahoma, 1949) is a writer. One of her books is *The Outsiders.*

Nikolai Lenin (born Vladimir Ilyich Ulyanov in Simbirst, Russia, 1870; died Gorky, Russia, January 21, 1924) was a Russian revolutionist. His embalmed body is still encased in a glass coffin in Red Square.

Jack Nicholson (born Neptune, New Jersey, 1936) is an actor.

Yehudi Menuhin (born New York, New York, 1916; died Berlin, Germany, March 12, 1999) was a renowned violinist.

 Students could find out how a violin makes sounds.

April

 Saint George Feast Day remembers the death of the English martyr Saint George in the year 303. He killed the famous dragon that required daily sacrifice.

 The story of St. George and the Dragon has been written by several different authors. Find a version and read it to the class.

Spain celebrates Book Day and Lover's Day. This day remembers Saint George's death and the death in 1616 of Miguel de Cervantes Saavedra (author of *Don Quixote*). Women give men books, and men give women roses.

Top quark was discovered in 1994. This was the last of the six subatomic particles to be found. The other quarks are the bottom quark, strange quark, charm quark, up quark, and down quark. Combinations of these quarks form protons and neutrons.

Turkey celebrates National Sovereignty and Children's Day. The country remembers the Grand National Assembly's first meeting in 1923.

Smoking was banned on airplane flights lasting two hours or less in 1988.

Birthdays

Shirley Temple Black (born Santa Monica, California, 1928) starred in several movies as a child and served as an ambassador as an adult. Two of her movies were *Little Miss Marker* and *The Little Colonel.*

James Buchanan (born Cove Gap, Pennsylvania, 1791; died Lancaster, Pennsylvania, June 1, 1868) was the fifteenth president (1857–1861) of the United States. He was America's only unmarried president, and he was the only president born in Pennsylvania. Visit a Web site at: http://www.whitehouse.gov/history/presidents/jb15.html.

Phil Esposito (born Sault Saint Marie, Ontario, Canada, 1942) is a former hockey player.

Sergei Sergeyevich Prokofiev (born Sontsovka, Ukraine, 1891; died Moscow, Russia, March 5, 1953) was a famous pianist and composer.

 In 1934 Prokofiev composed the symphony *Peter and the Wolf.* Obtain a recording of the music and play it during class.

William Shakespeare (born Stratford-on-Avon, England, 1564; died Stratford-on-Avon, England, April 23, 1616) is one of the most famous poets and playwrights. His works are among the most quoted in the world. He wrote almost 40 plays and over 150 sonnets. Famous works include *Romeo and Juliet* and *Macbeth.*

 Find some of Shakespeare's works. Have the children put on a dramatic presentation.

Granville T. Woods (born Columbus, Ohio, 1856; died New York, New York, January 30, 1910) invented the Synchronous Multiplex Railway Telegraph, making possible communication between dispatchers and moving trains. This invention saved many lives. He held patents for many other inventions, including the trolley car.

April

24 **Library of Congress was created in 1800.** Today it houses more than 28 million books and pamphlets. It also contains the personal papers from President Washington to President Coolidge. Many other treasures are there, including a Gutenberg Bible and Mathew Brady's Civil War photographs. The Web site is http://www.loc.gov.

 Visit the school library. See if children can identify nonbook resources, such as the vertical file, videos, etc.

British burned the Capitol and the White House during the War of 1812.

 The White House earned that name only after the British burned it. Children could research the White House and draw its floor plans. The White House Web site is http://www.whitehouse.gov, and it contains excellent information.

Armenia remembers Martyrs' Day. Ottoman Turks massacred Armenians in 1915.

Birthdays

Edmund Cartwright (born Nottinghamshire, England, 1743; died Hastings, Sussex, England, October 30, 1823) was an inventor and a cleric. He created the power loom for weaving.

 Children could weave on a simple loom. They could then appreciate how the power loom made the production of textiles more efficient.

Evaline Ness (born Union City, Ohio, 1911; died New York, New York, August 12, 1986) was a children's book author and illustrator. *Sam, Bangs, and Moonshine* won the 1967 Caldecott Medal.

Barbra Streisand (born New York, New York, 1942) is an actress and a singer.

Robert Penn Warren (born Guthrie, Kentucky, 1905; died Stratton, Vermont, September 15, 1989) was a writer. He won the Pulitzer Prize for *All the King's Men*. In 1985 he became the first U.S. poet laureate.

April

25 **Egypt remembers Sinai Day, the day when Israel and Egypt agreed who controlled the Sinai.**

Macao marks the anniversary of its 1974 revolution.

Hubble Space Telescope was deployed in 1990. Sadly, the lenses were not working properly until a shuttle team repaired them in 1993. It was modified again in 1997. Because the telescope is beyond Earth's atmosphere, it can detect images seven to ten times better than any Earth scope.

 Children could find out how the Hubble differs from Earth-bound telescopes.

Martin Waldseemuller Remembrance Day. Martin Waldseemuller (born probably in Radolfzell, Germany, c. 1470; died probably St. Die, France, c. 1520) was an early cartographer. He gave the continents of North America and South America their names. He named them after Amerigo Vespucci, the person he thought had first discovered the land masses.

Students could speculate as to what Waldseemuller would have named the continents had he known Christopher Columbus explored the area first.

Anzac Day is remembered in Australia, New Zealand, and Western Samoa. ANZAC stands for the Australia and New Zealand Army Corps. World War I soldiers landed in Gallipoli, Turkey, in 1915.

Solar powered battery was invented in 1954.

Suez Canal began construction in 1859. The 118-mile canal connecting the Mediterranean Sea and the Red Sea began operations November 17, 1869. The canal has no locks because the two seas are fairly level.

St. Lawrence Seaway began operating in 1959. Construction began in September, 1954. Over 6,000 people had to be relocated because a reservoir would cover their land. Canada and the United States each operate a portion of the 450-mile seaway. It connects Lake Erie to Montreal.

 Children could study the Suez Canal and the St. Lawrence Seaway in more detail. How are the two alike? How are they different?

Birthdays

William Brennan (born Newark, New Jersey, 1906; died Virginia, July 25, 1997) was an associate justice for the Supreme Court.

Ella Fitzgerald (born Newport News, Virginia, 1918; died Beverly Hills, California, June 15, 1996) was a renowned jazz singer.

Meadowlark Lemon (born Lexington, South Carolina, 1932) is a former basketball player and star of the Harlem Globetrotters.

Guglielmo Marconi (born Bologna, Italy, 1874; died Rome, Italy, July 20, 1937) invented the wireless telegraph. He won the 1909 Nobel Prize in physics for his invention.

 April

26 **Chernobyl nuclear reactor disaster occurred in 1986 in the Ukraine.** An explosion destroyed the nuclear power plant, and more than 100,000 people had to leave the area.

Guernica Massacre happened in 1937. Nazi airplanes bombed Guernica, a small community in northern Spain. Pablo Picasso was so angered by the attack that he painted the famous *Guernica.*

 Obtain a print of *Guernica.* Look for the symbols and the way Picasso showed his outrage.

South Africa had its first multiracial elections from April 26 through April 29 in 1994.

Tanzania celebrates Union Day. In 1964 Tanganyika, Zanzibar, and Pemba united into one country, Tanzania.

Richter Scale Day honors the birth of Charles Francis Richter. Born in 1900 near Hamilton, Ohio, Richter developed the scale named after him that measures earthquake magnitude. He died in Pasadena, California on September 30, 1985.

 The Richter scale registers from one to nine, with nine being the highest. However, each number is ten times stronger than the one before it. For example, an earthquake measuring five is ten times stronger than one measuring four. Students could calculate how much stronger an earthquake of nine is compared to an earthquake of one. They could also make a chart of famous earthquakes and their numbers on the Richter scale.

United States Holocaust Museum opened in 1993.

Birthdays

John James Audubon (born Haiti, 1785; died New York, New York, January 27, 1851) was an ornithologist and an artist. One of his most famous works is *The Birds of America,* sketches of 1,065 birds. The National Audubon Society, a conservation group, was named in honor of him.

Carol Burnett (born San Antonio, Texas, 1936) is an actress and a comedian.

Patricia Reilly Giff (born Brooklyn, New York, 1935) is a children's author. One of her works is *Watch Out, Ronald Morgan!,* published in 1985.

Frederick Law Olmsted (born Hartford, Connecticut, 1822; died Waverly, Massachusetts, August 28, 1903) designed Central Park and other parks. He was also commissioner of Yosemite National Park.

 Children could design a new park that would fit into their community.

I(eoh) M(ing) Pei (born Guangzhou, China, 1917) is a prominent architect. He came to the United States in 1935 and studied at Massachusetts Institute of Technology and Harvard University. After becoming an American citizen in 1954, he started his own firm. Some of his designs include the John Hancock Tower, the East Building of the National Gallery of Art, and the new entrance to the Louvre in Paris.

April

27 **Netherlands celebrates flower parades.**

Togo celebrates its Independence Day. It became free from France in 1960. The small country is located on the southern coast of West Africa. Lome is the capital.

Afghanistan remembers Saur Revolution.

Thor Heyerdahl set sail on the Kon Tiki in 1947. He left Peru and arrived in Polynesia over 100 days later. Visit a Web site at: http://www.museumsnett.no/kon-tiki/expeditions.

Ferdinand Magellan was killed in 1721 near the Philippines. Only one of his five ships finished its trip around the world.

Sierra Leone celebrates its independence. In 1961 it broke away from the British government. Located on the western coast of Africa, this small country has many diamond deposits. Freetown is the capital.

Birthdays

Ludwig Bemelmans (born Meran, Austria, 1898; died New York, New York, October 1, 1962) was an author and illustrator. He came to the United States in 1914 and found work as a busboy. Later he wrote books for adults. However, he is most known for his children's books, including *Madeline* and all her adventures.

Ulysses Simpson Grant (born Point Pleasant, Ohio, 1822; died Mt. McGregor, New York, July 23, 1885) was the eighteenth president (1869–1877) of the United States. Visit a Web site at: http://www.whitehouse.gov/history/presidents/ug18.html.

 Grant was a famous Civil War general. Lee surrendered to him at Appomattox, Virginia, to end the war. Children could find out which other presidents were also military leaders. They could then decide whether a military leader made a good president.

Coretta Scott King (born Marion, Alabama, 1927) is a speaker and a writer. As the widow of Martin Luther King, Jr., she continues the work of the civil rights movement.

 Students could research and list Mrs. King's accomplishments.

Samuel Finley Breese Morse (born Charlestown, Massachusetts, 1791; died New York, New York, April 2, 1872) was an inventor and an artist. He invented the Morse code, and his first transmission, made on May 24, 1844, was, "What hath God wrought?"

 Children could learn about Morse code and send messages to each other.

pril

28 **Canada marks its National Day of Mourning.** This tradition, started in 1986, reminds Canadians that over one million people die or are injured in work-related accidents. The day reminds people to lobby for safer and healthier work conditions.

The *Bounty*'s crew mutinied in 1789. Visit a Web site at: http://www.lareau.org/bounty.html.

Yellow fever vaccine was reported in 1932.

Maryland became the seventh state in the United States by ratifying the Constitution in 1788. Maryland ranks forty-second in size and nineteenth in population. Annapolis is the state capital, and the state's nicknames include Old Line State and Free State. It is famous for crab cakes and its Chesapeake Bay Bridge. Contact: (410) 767-3400. Visit a Web site at: http://www.50states.com/maryland.htm.

 Children could find out how Maryland, Baltimore, and Annapolis got their names.

Air conditioner was patented by W. H. Carrier in 1914.

 Students could research how air conditioners work, and they could find out whether different types of coolant exist.

Birthdays

Lionel Barrymore (born Lionel Blythe in Philadelphia, Pennsylvania, 1878; died Van Nuys, California, November 15, 1954) was an actor.

Jay Leno (born New Rochelle, New York, 1950) is a comedian and a talk show host.

James Monroe (born Westmoreland County, Virginia, 1758; died New York, New York, July 4, 1831) was the fifth president (1817–1825) of the United States. He established the Monroe Doctrine, and he acquired Florida from Spain. Visit a Web site at: http://www.whitehouse.gov/history/presidents/jm5.html.

 Children could find out which capital city of an African country was named in honor of him.

April

29 **Italy celebrates St. Catherine of Siena Feast Day.** St. Catherine of Siena, the patron saint of Italy, was born in 1347. She died April 29, 1380.

Zipper was patented by Gideon Sundback of Hoboken, New Jersey, in 1913. However, it was not called a zipper until 1922, when the B. F. Goodrich Company used the term to describe fasteners on its galoshes.

 Children could make a list of nonclothing items that have zippers. For example, some binders have zippers.

Taiwan celebrates Cheng Cheng Kung Landing Day. In 1661 Cheng Cheng Kung of the Ming dynasty ousted Dutch colonists who had been there for thirty-seven years.

Birthdays

Edward Kennedy "Duke" Ellington (born Washington, DC, 1899; died New York, New York, May 24, 1974) was a jazz pianist, bandleader, and composer. He wrote over 2,000 compositions, including some for musicals, ballet, opera, and movies. He performed over 20,000 times in sixty-five countries with his jazz big band. One of his most famous pieces is *It Don't Mean a Thing (If It Ain't Got That Swing)*.

 Play some of Ellington's compositions.

Oliver Ellsworth (born Windsor, Connecticut, 1745; died Windsor, Connecticut, November 26, 1807) was the third chief justice of the Supreme Court.

William Randolph Hearst (born San Francisco, California, 1863; died Beverly Hills, California, August 14, 1951) became a media baron. At one time he owned twenty-five newspapers, several magazines, and a newsreel company. He is also remembered for building San Simeon, a huge estate in California. It had, among other luxuries, a zoo and an airport.

 San Simeon had just about every convenience possible. Children could draw their dream houses.

Zubin Mehta (born Bombay, India, 1936) is a renowned conductor. He received India's highest award, the Padma Bhusan (Order of the Lotus) in 1967.

Jerry Seinfeld (born Brooklyn, New York, 1954) is a comedian and actor.

April

30 **Louisiana became the eighteenth state of the United States in 1812.** It ranks thirty-first in area and twenty-first in population. The state was named after King Louis XIV of France, and Baton Rouge is the capital. Contact: (800) 33-GUMBO. Visit a Web site at: http://www.50states.com/louisian.htm.

 New Orleans, a major city in Louisiana, hosts Mardi Gras every year. Mardi Gras, meaning "Fat Tuesday," is a big tradition held the day before Ash Wednesday. Parades, parties, and feasts mark the day. Consider having a Mardi Gras celebration in the classroom.

Netherlands celebrates Queen Beatrix's birthday. She was born in 1938.

George Washington was inaugurated president in 1789 in New York City.

 Present presidents are inaugurated in January in Washington, DC. Children could try to figure out why George Washington's inauguration was so different.

Organization of American States was created in 1948. Some of its purposes were to promote peace, to further communication between countries, and to further economic development for all member countries.

Television began featuring regular programs in 1939.

 Children could interview parents and grandparents to find out what early television shows were like.

Sweden celebrates the Feast of Valborg. Known also as Walpurgis Night, people welcome spring by singing traditional songs.

Ashrita Furman somersaulted from Lexington, Massachusetts, to Boston, Massachusetts, in 1986. She somersaulted almost 9,000 times to travel the twelve miles.

Birthdays

Mary Scott Lord Dimmick Harrison (born Honesdale, Pennsylvania, 1858; died New York, New York, January 5, 1948) was the second wife of Benjamin Harrison, twenty-third president of the United States.

Michael J. Smith (born Beaufort, North Carolina, 1945; died January 28, 1986) was captain of the *Challenger,* the space shuttle that exploded in 1986.

Willie Nelson (born Abbott, Texas, 1933) is a singer and an actor.

MAY

May is likely named after Maia, the Roman goddess of spring. Her name relates to a Latin term meaning "growth" or "spring." The emerald is the birthstone for May. Lily of the valley and hawthorne are May's flowers.

Month-Long Activities

Asian Pacific Heritage Month has been honored by presidential proclamation every year since 1979.

National Bike Month stresses the importance of the bicycle for fun and physical fitness. Over five million people participate across the country. Contact: League of American Bicyclists, 1612 K Street, Suite 401, Washington, DC 20006. Telephone: (202) 822-1333.

Older Americans Month has been celebrated by presidential proclamation every year since 1963.

National Physical Fitness and Sports Month stresses the importance of exercise. Contact: President's Council on Physical Fitness and Sports, 701 Pennsylvania Avenue, Washington, DC 20004. Telephone: (202) 272-3421.

Special Weeks

Cartoon Appreciation Week is the first week in May. It reminds us that cartoons can both educate and amuse. Contact: Cartoon Art Museum, 814 Mission Street, Second Floor, San Francisco, California 94103.

 Students could bring in and discuss some of their favorite cartoons.

International Pickle Week is celebrated by Pickle Packers International, Inc., during the third week in May. Contact: DHM Group, Inc., PO Box 767, Holmdel, New Jersey 07733.

National Transportation Week has been observed by presidential proclamation since 1960. It is the week including the third Friday of May.

Police Week has been observed by presidential proclamation since 1962. It is the week that includes May 15.

Special Days

Kentucky Derby is the first Saturday in May.

Mother's Day is the second Sunday in May. It was first celebrated by Anna Jarvis of Philadelphia, Pennsylvania. She asked that her church hold a service in memory of all mothers. A presidential proclamation has been made every year since 1914, honoring the day.

Memorial Day is the last Monday in May. The first recorded Memorial Day was in 1865. The day honors the dead, especially those who died in battle.

National Teacher Appreciation Day is the Tuesday of the first full week of May.

National Spelling Bee Finals are held the Wednesday and Thursday of the week containing Memorial Day. Contact: Director, National Spelling Bee, Scripps-Howard, PO Box 5380, Cincinnati, Ohio 45201. Telephone: (513) 977-3028.

Armed Forces Day is the third Saturday in May. It has been remembered by presidential proclamation since 1936.

 May

May Day is celebrated throughout the world. Spring festivities occur in many parts of America.

 Children find maypole dancing to be fun.

Mother Goose Day reminds us of the pleasures of nursery rhymes. Contact: Mother Goose Society, 7303 Sharpless Road, Melrose Park, Pennsylvania 19027. Telephone: (215) 782-1059.

 Children could pantomime their favorite nursery rhymes.

Lei Day is celebrated in Hawaii. Leis are made, worn, and entered into competitions. The Lei Day Queen is crowned, and Hawaiian music, dance, and foods abound. The holiday was first celebrated in 1928.

Law Day educates people regarding the importance of the legal system. Contact: American Bar Association, 541 North Fairbanks Court, Chicago, Illinois 60611-3314. Telephone: (312) 988-5732.

Supernova was observed in 1006 by Chinese and Egyptian astronomers.

First wagon train left Independence, Missouri, for California in 1841. Most wagon trains left in the spring, because it took four or five months to reach their destination. The trains did not want to be isolated in the mountains during winter. The trains, perhaps as much as 100 wagons long, traveled about fifteen to twenty miles a day. The wagons were called prairie schooners because their white tops looked like billowing sails.

Children could view copies of Russell Freedman's *Children of the Wild West.*

Buffalo Bill premiered his Wild West Show in 1883.

Chicago began constructing the first skyscraper in 1884. It rose to a height of ten stories. The Home Insurance Company of New York owned the steel-framed building. It was finished by the fall of 1885, but two more floors were added at a later date.

Empire State Building was dedicated in 1931. For quite a long time it was the tallest building in the world. However, other buildings are now taller than it.

Italy celebrates Festival of St. Efisio.

Loyalty Day has been remembered by presidential proclamation since 1959.

Birthdays

Comte de Chardonnet (born Besançon, France, 1839; died Paris, France, March 25, 1924) invented rayon, one of the first synthetic fibers.

Mark Clark (born Madison Barracks, New York, 1896; died Charleston, South Carolina, April 17, 1984) was an American general who fought in both World War I and World War II.

Mary Harris "Mother" Jones (born Cork, Ireland, 1830; died Silver Spring, Maryland, November 30, 1930) was a famous labor leader. Her husband and four children died in a yellow fever epidemic. Then all her belongings were lost in the 1871 Chicago fire. After that, she worked tirelessly for the rights of factory workers.

Kathryn Elizabeth "Kate" Smith (born in Greenville, Virginia, 1909; died Raleigh, North Carolina, June 17, 1986) was a famous singer. She sang for the first time on radio on May 1, 1931. She recorded more than 3,000 songs and performed on radio more than 15,000 times. Irving Berlin wrote *God Bless America* especially for her. It became a theme song for both her and the country.

ay

Hudson Bay Company was organized in 1670.

William Herschel located the first binary star, Xi Ursae Majoris, in 1780.

U.S. government offered a reward of $100,000 for the capture of Jefferson Davis in 1865. The government charged Davis and his cabinet with conspiracy in the assassination of Abraham Lincoln. Davis and his advisors had fled to Abbeville, South Carolina. They disagreed about the future of the Confederacy.

 Students could find out what happened to the leadership of the Confederacy.

Oklahoma Territory was formed in 1890.

Diane Crump in 1970 became the first woman to ride in the Kentucky Derby.

 Students could read about how a person can become a jockey.

Birthdays

Catherine the Great (born Stettin, now Szczecin, Poland, 1729; died St. Petersburg, Russia, November 17, 1796) was Empress of Russia from 1762 to 1796. She is credited with making Russia into a modern state.

Harry Lillis "Bing" Crosby (born Tacoma, Washington, 1904; died Madrid, Spain, October 14, 1977) was a singer and an actor. For a time he and Bob Hope formed a famous comedy duo. One of his most famous recordings is *White Christmas.*

 Students could create their own comedy duos and produce short skits.

Elijah McCoy (born Colchester, Ontario, Canada, 1844; died Eloise, Michigan, October 10, 1929) was an inventor. The son of runaway slaves, his name is honored with the phrase, "the real McCoy." Visit a Web site at: http://www.princeton.edu/~mcbrown/display/mccoy.html.

Henry M. Robert (born Robertville, South Carolina, 1837; died Hornell, New York, May 11, 1923) was an American general. He also wrote *Robert's Rules of Order,* a guidebook regarding parliamentary procedure. See the guidebook at: http://www.bartleby.com/176.

 Children could check to see if their student council follows Robert's Rules.

May

3

Tuba Day celebrates the very large musical instrument.

 Someone could demonstrate how the tuba works.

Hong Kong celebrates Tin Hau Festival. Fisherman festoon their boats and hope for excellent fishing in the coming year.

Japan celebrates Constitution Memorial Day.

Mexico remembers the Day of the Holy Cross. Miners and construction workers are honored. Anyone who is building a structure must feed the workers. Crosses are displayed on all newly constructed buildings.

Corporation for Public Broadcasting began its commercial-free programming in 1971. Visit an Internet site at: http://www.pbs.org.

Poland celebrates Swieto Trzeciego Majo (Constitution Day). Its first constitution was ratified in 1794.

United Nations honors World Press Freedom Day.

Passenger air service began in 1919.

Dow Jones Industrial Average topped 11,000 for the first time in 1999.

New York State in 1904 became the first state to institute automobile speed limits. Cars could travel ten miles per hour in cities and twenty miles per hour in rural areas.

Birthdays

James Brown (born Augusta, Georgia, 1933) is a singer and a composer.

Golda (Mabovitz) Meir (born Kiev, Ukraine, 1898; died Jerusalem, Israel, December 8, 1978) moved to the United States in 1906. She left the United States for Palestine in 1921. It was divided into Israel and an Arab state in 1948. She served in various government capacities in Israel and was its prime minister from 1969 to 1974.

 Students could make a timeline of her life.

Jacob August Riis (born Ribe, Denmark, 1849; died Barre, Massachusetts, May 26, 1914) was a journalist and a photographer. He came to the United States in 1870 and found employment as a carpenter. He became a reporter and brought about changes in city housing, parks, and schools. He was one of the first photographers to use flash bulbs.

 Students could examine some of his photographs and discuss their impact.

Pete Seeger (born New York, New York, 1919) is a folksinger and songwriter.

May

4

Peter Minuit arrived in what is now Manhattan in 1626. Representing the Dutch government, he purchased Manhattan for goods worth sixty guilders (twenty-four dollars).

National Weather Observer's Day honors amateurs and experts who follow the weather. Visit a Web site at: http://www.weather.com.

China celebrates Youth Day. The day relates back to a demonstration in 1919 in Tiananmen Square.

Columbus discovered Jamaica in 1494.

 Columbus met the Arawak Indians, living on the island. Children could find out what happened to the Arawaks as more and more exploration and colonization took place.

Rhode Island celebrates Independence Day. In 1776 the colony broke all ties with England.

Atlantis, **an American shuttle spacecraft, was launched in 1989.** It successfully deployed *Magellan.* It traveled to Venus to map the planet's surface.

Birthdays

Horace Mann (born Franklin, Massachusetts, 1796; died Yellow Springs, Ohio, August 2, 1959) is known as the father of public education in the United States. He was the editor of the *Common School Journal.*

 Students could find out more about Mann and his ideas about education.

Julia Gardiner Tyler (born Gardiner's Island, New York, 1820; died Richmond, Virginia, July 10, 1889) was the second wife of John Tyler, tenth president of the United States. They were married while he was president. He died before the beginning of the Civil War, and the war left her penniless. Later, Congress voted to give her a pension. Visit a Web site at: http://www.whitehouse.gov/history/firstladies/jt10.html.

 Students could find out how the Civil War caused her to become destitute.

Virginia "Tammy" Wynette (Pugh) (born Red Bay, Mississippi, 1942) is a singer.

May

Cy Young in 1904 pitched baseball's first perfect game. He did not let any opposing player reach first base. The Cy Young Award for pitching was in honor of him.

Cinco de Mayo is celebrated in Mexico. The Battle of Puebla took place in 1862. General Ignacio Zaragoza led his Mexican army, outnumbered three to one, against Napoleon III's French forces. Zaragoza won. Speeches, festivals, and parades are held nation-wide.

 Children could have a Cinco de Mayo celebration. A piñata should be included.

Children's Day is celebrated in Japan and Korea.

Carnegie Hall had its first performance in 1891.

Alan Shepard, aboard *Freedom 7,* **became the first American and the second man to travel in space.** The year was 1961. He traveled about 115 miles into space at 5,000 miles per hour.

 Students could find out more about the purposes of this flight. Where and how did it land?

Thailand celebrates Coronation Day.

Gwendolyn Brooks was the first African American to win the Pulitzer Prize in 1950. Her book of poetry, *Annie Allen,* described the life of a black girl growing up during World War II.

Birthdays

Nellie Bly (born Elizabeth Cochrane Seaman in Armstrong County, Pennsylvania, 1867; died New York, New York, January 22, 1922) was perhaps the leading woman journalist of her time. She worked for the *Pittsburgh Dispatch,* reporting on working conditions, slum life, and other topics. She moved to New York and worked on Pulitzer's *New York World.* She pretended to be insane, and she was institutionalized. She then reported on the extreme conditions she found there. Perhaps her most exciting adventure came when she followed the route of Jules Verne's imaginary Phileas Fogg and traveled around the world in 72 days.

 Students could plan their own trip around the world.

Leo Lionni (born Amsterdam, Netherlands, 1910; died Chianti, Italy, October 11, 1999) was an author and illustrator of over thirty books. One of his books was *Swimmy.*

Karl Marx (born Treves, Germany, 1818; died London, England, March 14, 1883) was a writer and socialist. He created the ideas of communism.

 May

6 **The Philippines celebrates Araw Ng Kagitinan.**

Hindenburg **dirigible exploded in 1937 at 7:20 P.M.** Thirty-six of the ninety-seven passengers died. It was approaching its mooring mast at Lakehurst, New Jersey.

Roger Bannister was the first person to run a mile in less than four minutes in 1954.

The Chunnel, the tunnel between the United Kingdom and France, opened in 1994. It is thirty-one miles long, twenty-three of those miles under water. Visit a Web site at: http://www.raileurope.com/us/rail/eurostar/channel_tunnel.htm.

Birthdays

Sigmund Freud (born Freiberg, Moravia, 1856; died London, England, September 23, 1939) changed the field of psychiatry. He believed that most behavior was caused by unconscious parts of the brain.

 Children could read more about his theories. They could compare his ideas to those of other noted experts.

Willie Mays (born Westfield, Alabama, 1931) is a former baseball player. An outfielder, he hit 660 home runs during his career. He is remembered for making a spectacular catch during the 1954 World Series. He was inducted into the National Baseball Hall of Fame in 1979.

 Students could read a biography about him. They could write about the 1954 catch as if they were newspaper reporters.

Robert E. Peary (born Cresson, Pennsylvania, 1856; died Washington, DC, February 20, 1920) was an explorer. He led eight expeditions to the Arctic. He claimed he found the North Pole on April 6, 1909.

John Penn (born Caroline County, Virginia, 1740; died Williamsburg, North Carolina, September 14, 1788) signed the Declaration of Independence. He represented North Carolina.

 Students could read about a duel he almost fought.

Rabindranath Tagore (born Calcutta, India, 1861; died Calcutta, India, August 7, 1941) was a Hindu writer and composer. He received the Nobel Prize for literature in 1913.

Rudolph Valentino (born Castellaneta, Italy, 1895; died New York, New York, August 23, 1926) was a famous movie actor.

Orson Welles (born Kenosha, Wisconsin, 1915; died Los Angeles, California, October 10, 1985) was an actor and a director. His radio production of *The War of the Worlds* was so realistic that many people panicked. His *Citizen Kane* has been called one of the most creative movies ever made.

 Beethoven's Ninth Symphony in D Minor premiered in Vienna, Austria, in 1824. It is also called the *Choral* because of the added voices. Schiller's *Ode to Joy* was the inspiration for the composition. Beethoven was totally deaf when he composed this symphony.

 Students could enjoy listening to this symphony.

American Medical Association was created in 1847.

Beaufort Scale Day honors Sir Francis Beaufort, a British naval officer. He was born in Flower Hill, Heath, Ireland, in 1774. He died in Brighton, England, December 17, 1857. The Beaufort Scale measures wind velocity against simple items.

 Students could read about and illustrate the Beaufort Scale.

Fire escape ladder was patented in 1878 by Joseph R. Winters.

Lusitania **sank in 1915.** It was torpedoed by Germany, and 1,198 people died. The ship was traveling from New York to Liverpool, England. The United States protested the action, but Germany countered that the ship held munitions for England and was fair game.

A pearl weighing fourteen pounds was removed from a Philippine clam in 1934.

Birthdays

Johannes Brahms (born Hamburg, Germany, 1833; died Vienna, Austria, April 3, 1897) was a great classical composer of concertos, symphonies, and chamber music. Experts believe his strength was his ability to produce a theme and then to modify it as the music went on.

 Students could listen to some of his music and then compare it to that of Beethoven. Brahms cherished Beethoven's work.

Robert Browning (born near London, England, 1812; died Venice, Italy, December 12, 1889) was a famous poet. He was married to Elizabeth Barrett Browning. One of his works is *Pauline,* published in 1833. His works were not well known until he was about sixty years old.

Frank James "Gary" Cooper (born Helena, Montana, 1901; died Hollywood, California, May 13, 1961) was a famous movie actor. He won Academy Awards for his roles in *High Noon* and *Sergeant York.*

Nonny Hogrogian (born New York, New York, 1932) is an author and an illustrator. She has won two Caldecott Medals, one for *Always Room for One More* (1966) and one for *One Fine Day* (1972).

Edwin Herbert Land (born Bridgeport, Connecticut, 1909; died March 1, 1991) was an inventor and a scientist. He created the Polaroid Land camera, and he held more than 500 patents.

Peter Tchaikovsky (born Votinsk, Russia, 1840; died St. Petersburg, Russia, November 6, 1893) was a composer. He created six symphonies, three ballets, and eleven operas. Two of his ballets were *Swan Lake* and *The Nutcracker.*

Johnny Unitas (born Pittsburgh, Pennsylvania, 1933; died Timonium, Maryland, September 11, 2002) was a football player. A three-time NFL MVP, he was inducted into the Football Hall of Fame in 1979.

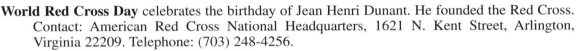

 8   **World Red Cross Day** celebrates the birthday of Jean Henri Dunant. He founded the Red Cross. Contact: American Red Cross National Headquarters, 1621 N. Kent Street, Arlington, Virginia 22209. Telephone: (703) 248-4256.

Students could investigate the various jobs of the Red Cross.

Hernando de Soto discovered the Mississippi River in 1541.

Captain George Vancouver located and named Mount Rainier in Washington in 1792.

John Styth Pemberton invented Coca-Cola in 1886 in Jacob's Pharmacy in Atlanta, Georgia. Visit a Web site at: http://www.geocities.com/heartland/4269/history.html.

Mount Pelée in Martinique erupted in 1902. In minutes 30,000 people died. Visit a Web site at: http://petibonom.tripod.com/mpelee/welcome.htm.

V-E Day was celebrated in 1945. Germany surrendered to the Allied Forces. A surrender document was signed at Reims and became effective one minute past midnight on May 9, 1945.

 Students could learn more about the last days of World War II in Europe. They could write about the surrender as if they were newspaper reporters.

First seawater conversion facility began operating in 1961. It desalinized water.

Birthdays

Louis Moreau Gottschalk (born New Orleans, Louisiana, 1829; died Rio de Janeiro, Brazil, December 18, 1869) was a famous pianist during the Civil War.

Enrique Iglesias (born Madrid, Spain, 1975) is a singer.

Harry Truman (born Lamar, Missouri, 1884; died Kansas City, Missouri, December 26, 1972) was the thirty-third president (1945–1953) of the United States. During World War I he served as an artilleryman. He was a senator before he was elected vice president. When Roosevelt died, Truman became president. Some of his actions were to join the United Nations, to accept Germany's surrender during World War II, and to drop the atomic bombs on Japan. Visit a Web site at: http://www.whitehouse.gov/history/presidents/ht33.html.

 Truman made an interesting statement: "The buck stops here." Students could discuss the statement and decide whether they agree with him.

May

 9

America's first political cartoon was printed in 1754 in Benjamin Franklin's *The Pennsylvania Gazeteer.* The cartoon depicted a snake cut into pieces. The caption was "Join or Die."

 Students could learn about the background of the cartoon. Students could then compose some of their own political cartoons.

Russia celebrates Victory Day of 1945. Twenty million Russians died during World War II. This day honors all those people.

Eye bank opened in New York, New York, in 1944.

 Students could find out more about the eye and how eye traumas can be treated.

Laser beam was bounced off the moon's surface successfully in 1962.

 Students could demonstrate how a laser works.

Lawn mower was patented by John Albert Burr in 1899.

Birthdays

J. M. Barrie (born Kirriemuir, Scotland, 1860; died London, England, June 19, 1937) was an author. One of his works was *Peter Pan.* Visit a Web site at: http://www.slainte.org.uk/scotauth/barridsw.htm.

Candice Bergen (born Beverly Hills, California, 1946) is an actress.

Belle Boyd (born Martinsburg, Virginia, 1843; died Kilbourne, Wisconsin, June 11, 1900) was a Confederate spy. After the Civil War, she was an actress and a speaker.

John Brown (born Torrington, Connecticut, 1800; died Charles Town, West Virginia, December 2, 1859) was an abolitionist. He led a raid on Harpers Ferry in the cause of abolition. He was caught and hanged.

Howard Carter (born Swaffham, England, 1873; died Kensington, England, March 2, 1939) was an archaeologist. He discovered King Tut's tomb.

Tony Gwynn (born Los Angeles, California, 1960) is a baseball player.

Billy Joel (born Hicksville, New York, 1949) is a singer and a composer.

Mike Wallace (born Brookline, Massachusetts, 1918) is a television journalist.

 May

10

Jefferson Davis and his cabinet were captured in Irwinville, Georgia, in 1865. They were taken to a prison in Nashville, Tennessee, and then to Richmond, Virginia.

 Students could discover the fate of these men.

Transcontinental railroad was finished in Promontory, Utah, in 1869. The Union Pacific Railroad and the Central Pacific Railroad met at Promontory Point. Leland Stanford drove in a golden spike to mark the completion of the rail lines. The spike was removed and preserved for history.

 Students could read more about the difficulties of the two train companies as they built the railroad lines. A good source of information is William Durbin's *The Journal of Sean Sullivan: A Transcontinental Railroad Worker.*

Adler Planetarium, the first U.S. planetarium, opened in Chicago in 1930.

 Students could change the classroom into a planetarium.

Nelson Mandela was inaugurated as president of South Africa in 1994.

Birthdays

Christopher Paul Curtis (born Flint, Michigan, 1954) is an author. His *Bud, Not Buddy* was awarded the 2000 Newbery Medal. Visit a Web site at: http://www.kidsreads.com/authors/au-curtis-christopher-paul.asp.

Judith Jamison (born Philadelphia, Pennsylvania, 1944) is a dancer and a choreographer.

George Ross (born New Castle, Delaware, 1730; died Philadelphia, Pennsylvania, July 14, 1779) signed the Declaration of Independence. A lawyer, he represented Pennsylvania.

May

11

Peter Stuyvesant became governor of New Amsterdam in 1647.

John Hart, one of the signers of the Declaration of Independence, died in 1779 in Hopewell, New Jersey. He was born around 1711 in Stonington, Connecticut. He represented New Jersey at the signing. When the British attacked New Jersey, Hart was forced to hide. When he was able to return to the farm, he found that his wife had died and that his children had moved.

Minnesota became the thirty-second state of the United States in 1858. Its name is derived from the Sioux word *minisota,* meaning "sky-tinted waters." It was settled by the French looking for furs. Its nicknames are the North Star State and the Gopher State. Minnesota has over 10,000 lakes, and the Mesabi Range produces about sixty percent of the country's iron ore. Contact: (800) 657-3700. Visit an Internet site at: http://www.50states.com/minnesot.htm.

 Students could plan a vacation through Minnesota.

Merrimac **was destroyed by the Confederate Navy in 1862.** Advancing Union troops could have possibly captured the ironclad, so it was sunk.

Glacier National Park was established in 1910. Located in northwest Montana on the United States-Canada border, the park encompasses a million acres. Visit an Internet site at: http://www.nps.gov/glac.

 Students could find out how glaciers and icebergs are formed.

WGY in Schenectady, New York, in 1928 became the first station to provide scheduled television broadcasts.

Battle of Hamburger Hill began in Vietnam in 1969.

Margaret A. Brewster in 1978 became the first woman Marine Corps general.

Birthdays

Irving Berlin (born Israel Isidore Baline in Tyumen, Russia, 1888; died New York, New York, September 22, 1989) was a songwriter. Although he could not read or write musical notation, he created many songs. Two of his most famous works are *God Bless America* and *White Christmas.*

 Students could sing some of his works.

Salvador Dalí (born Figueras, Spain, 1904; died Figueras, Spain, January 23, 1989) was a surrealist painter.

Martha Graham (born Allegheny, Pennsylvania, 1894; died New York, New York, April 1, 1991) was a dancer and a choreographer.

Peter Sis (born Brno, Moravia, Czechoslovakia, 1949) writes and illustrates books for children. One of his books is *Komodo!,* published in 1993. *Tibet Through the Red Box* was a 1999 Caldecott Medal winner. Visit a Web site at: http://www.petersis.com/index2.html.

 May

 12

Odometer was invented by William Clayton in 1847 while he was crossing the country in a wagon train.

 Children could research the different "-ometers," for example, the speedometer, tachometer, and odometer.

Portugal observes the Pilgrimage to Fatima.

New York, New York, passed a law against spitting in 1896.

Birthdays

Yogi Berra (born St. Louis, Missouri, 1925) is a former baseball player and manager. Visit a Web site at: http://www.yogi-berra.com.

Edward Lear (born Highgate, England, 1812; died San Remo, Italy, January 29, 1888) was a writer, artist, and ornithologist. He is famous for his limericks. Two of his works are *A Book of Nonsense,* printed in 1846) and *Nonsense Songs,* published in 1871.

 The children could write limericks. A limerick is a poem with five lines. The first, second, and fifth lines rhyme and have three metrical feet. The third and fourth lines rhyme and have two metrical feet.

Mildred McAfee (Parkville, Missouri, 1900; died Berlin, New Hampshire, September 2, 1994) was the first director of the WAVES (Women Accepted for Volunteer Emergency Service). She was appointed by President Franklin Roosevelt in 1942. Within three years her group had trained over 85,000 women. She was also president of Wellesley College.

Farley Mowat (born Belleville, Ontario, Canada, 1921) is an author. One of his books is *Owls in the Family.* Visit a Web site at: http://schwinger.harvard.edu/~terning/bios/mowat.html.

Florence Nightingale (born Florence, Italy, 1820; died London, England, August 13, 1910) elevated the status of nurses. During the Crimean War, she worked tirelessly for the wounded. She was known as the "Lady with the Lamp." She was the first woman to receive the British Order of Merit.

Students could interview a nurse and discuss the training of different kinds of nurses.

May

13 **United States declared war on Mexico in 1846.** However, General Zachary Taylor had crossed the border and had established a fort several months before.

 Students could investigate the reasons for the war.

Birthdays

Georges Braque (born Argenteuil, France, 1882; died Paris, France, August 31, 1963) was an artist. He and Picasso developed cubism. He also worked with collages.

 Students could look at some of his work. They could gather different fabrics, papers, yarn, etc. and make their own collages.

Joe Louis (born near Lafayette, Alabama, 1914; died Las Vegas, Nevada, April 12, 1981) was the heavyweight boxing champion from 1937 to 1949. Nicknamed the "Brown Bomber," he was buried in Arlington National Cemetery.

Sir Arthur Sullivan (born London, England, 1842; died London, England, November 22, 1900) was half of the Gilbert and Sullivan team. They wrote light operas. He also composed other songs, including *Onward, Christian Soldiers.*

 Students could listen to one of the team's operettas.

Stevie Wonder (born Steveland Morris Hardaway in Saginaw, Michigan, 1951) is a singer and a musician.

May

14 **Jamestown, Virginia, became the first permanent English colony in America in 1607.** Three ships, the *Susan Constant,* the *Godspeed,* and the *Discovery* brought Captain John Smith and others to American shores.

North Cape, Norway, receives sun twenty-four hours a day from this day until July 30.

 Students could brainstorm a list of advantages and disadvantages of so much sunlight.

Malawi celebrates Kamuzu Day.

The Philippines celebrates Carabao Festival.

Paraguay celebrates its Independence Days of May 14 and May 15. Paraguay became free of Spanish rule in 1811. The country, about the size of California, is located in South America. Asuncion is the capital, and it exports cotton and soybeans.

Lewis and Clark Expedition left St. Louis, Missouri, in 1804. They reached the Pacific Coast in 1805 and returned to St. Louis in 1806. Visit a Web site at: http://www.pbs.org/lewisand clark. A good book is Laurie Myers's *Lewis and Clark and Me: A Dog's Tale.*

John Philip Sousa's *The Stars and Stripes Forever* was performed for the first time. Philadelphia hosted the 1897 event when a statue of George Washington was dedicated.

Students could listen to the well-known music and perhaps even play it.

Israel became a nation in 1948. However, because the Jewish calendar is lunar, the day Israel celebrates varies from year to year.

 Students could make a timeline of Israel's history.

Birthdays

Gabriel Daniel Fahrenheit (born Danzig, Germany, 1686; died Amsterdam, Holland, September 16, 1736) was a scientist. The Fahrenheit temperature scale is named in honor of him. He was the first person to use mercury in thermometers.

Thomas Gainsborough (born Sudbury, Suffolk, England, 1727; died London, England, August 2, 1788) was an artist specializing in portraits and landscapes. One of his most famous works is *The Blue Boy.* Visit a Web site at: http://watt.emf.net/wm/paint/auth/gainsborough.

George Lucas (born Modesto, California, 1944) is a film producer. His works include the *Star Wars* movies.

George Selden (born Hartford, Connecticut, 1929; died New York, New York, December 5, 1989) was an author. One of his books is *The Cricket in Times Square.*

 May

15

Japan celebrates Aoi Matsuri, the Hollyhock Festival.

Mexico celebrates San Isidro Day. Farming areas honor San Isidro, the Plowman. People decorate livestock with flowers.

Ellen Church became the first flight attendant in 1930. The United Airlines employee flew from San Francisco, California, to Cheyenne, Wyoming.

Nylon stockings were first sold in 1940.

 Students could find out how nylon is made.

Peace Officer Memorial Day has been honored by presidential proclamation since 1963.

United Nations celebrates International Day of Families. The United Nations has been honoring this day since 1944.

Paraguay became free of Spanish rule in 1811. This landlocked country in South America lost land to Bolivia in the Chaco War. Asuncion is the capital.

Department of Agriculture was created in 1862. Visit a Web site at: http://www.usda.gov.

Birthdays

Lyman Frank Baum (born Chittenango, New York, 1856; died Hollywood, California, May 6, 1919) was an author and newspaper reporter. He is famous for his *Wizard of Oz* books.

 Students could read and enjoy some of his works.

Pierre Curie (born Paris, France, 1859; died Paris, France, April 19, 1906) was a physicist. He and his wife, Marie Curie, researched radioactivity. They and Antoine Henri Becquerrel received the 1903 Nobel Prize in physics for their work on the radioactivity of uranium.

Katherine Anne Porter (born Indian Creek, Texas, 1890; died Silver Spring, Maryland, September 18, 1980) was an author. One of her best-known novels is *Ship of Fools*. She was awarded the 1965 Pulitzer Prize and the National Book Award for *Collected Short Stories*.

Ellen Louise Axson Wilson (born Savannah, Georgia, 1860; died Washington, DC, August 6, 1914) was the first wife of Woodrow Wilson, twenty-eighth president of the United States. She worked to eliminate slum conditions. She died about one year after Wilson became president. Visit a Web site at: http://www.whitehouse.gov/history/firstladies/ew28-1.html.

 Two of Wilson's daughters were married in the White House. Children could learn about the children of the president. They could decide whether it would be fun to live in the White House.

Paul Zindel (born New York, New York, 1936) is a children's author. Two of his most popular books are *The Pigman* and *The Effect of Gamma Rays on Man-In-The-Moon Marigolds*.

ay

First nickel was minted in 1866.

Button Guinnett died following a duel near Savanna, Georgia, in 1777. A signer of the Declaration of Independence, he was born in England. His exact birthdate is unknown. Visit a Web site at: http://www.multied.com/bio/revoltbios/guinettbutton.html.

Andrew Johnson's impeachment trial ended in 1868 when the Senate failed by one vote to find him guilty of the charges.

American Horseshoe Pitchers Association was formed in 1914.

 Students could pitch some horseshoes on the playground.

Academy Awards, the Oscars, were awarded for the first time in 1929.

 The children could decide some Academy Award categories and pick some nominees. The class could vote to decide the winners.

Food stamps were used for the first time in 1939.

Gordon Cooper, an American astronaut, circled the Earth twenty-two times in 1963. His craft was the *Faith 7.*

First-class postage increased in 1971 from six cents to eight cents.

 Students could locate information about other postage price increases. They could graph the numbers.

Birthdays

Bruce Coville (born Syracuse, New York, 1950) is a children's author. One of his best-known books is *My Teacher Is an Alien,* published in 1989. Visit a Web site at: http://www.brucecoville.com/about.htm.

Margaret Rey (born Hamburg, Germany, 1906; died Cambridge, Massachusetts, December 21, 1966) was a children's author. She and her husband, H. A. Rey, created Curious George.

William Henry Seward (born Florida, New York, 1801; died Auburn, New York, October 10, 1872) was secretary of state for Abraham Lincoln and Andrew Johnson. He arranged the purchase of Alaska from Russia for $7.2 million. Many people called the deal "Seward's Folly."

ay

17   **World Telecommunications Day** is remembered by the United Nations. Contact: United Nations, Department of Public Information, New York, New York 10017.

Norway celebrates Uff Da Day. It gained its independence from Denmark in 1814. Parades mark the occasion.

Brown v. Board of Education **Supreme Court decision was announced in 1954.** The Supreme Court ruled against segregation in education.

New York Stock Exchange was created in 1792. Approximately twenty businessmen would meet under a buttonwood tree on Wall Street in New York City and trade stock. If the weather was bad, they met in a coffeehouse.

    Students could learn how the stock market works. They could pick several stocks and track the companies. Visit a Web site at: http://www.nyse.com.

Grain reaper was patented in 1834 by Cyrus McCormick.

Kentucky Derby was held for the first time at Churchill Downs in 1875. The winning horse was named Aristides.

    Students could find out how racing horses differ physically from other types of horses.

Birthdays

Mia Hamm (born Selma, Alabama, 1972) is a soccer player.

Edward Jenner (born Berkeley, Gloucestershire, England, 1749; died Berkeley, Gloucestershire, England, January 26, 1823) discovered the vaccine for smallpox. In 1980 health experts declared that the world was free from smallpox.

"Sugar" Ray Charles Leonard (born Washington, DC, 1956) is a former boxer.

Gary Paulsen (born Minneapolis, Minnesota, 1939) is a children's author. He wrote, among other works, *The Winter Room* (Newbery Honor Book), 1990.

    Students could read and enjoy some of his work. Visit a Web site at: http://www. garypaulsen.com.

ay

18   **The Twenty-Seventh Amendment to the Constitution was adopted in 1992.** It stated that senators and representatives can vote for a salary change. However, that change cannot go into effect until an election of representatives has taken place.

International Museum Day reminds us of the importance of museums. Contact: AAM/ICOM, 1575 I Street NW, Fourth Floor, Washington, DC 20005.

    Children could change a portion of the classroom into a museum and offer tours to other classes.

Haiti celebrates Flag and University Day.

Mount St. Helens erupted in 1980. The volcano, located in Washington, discharged debris and steam eleven miles into the air. The volcano had erupted previously in 1857.

 Students could learn more about what made Mount St. Helens erupt so violently.

Apollo 10 **was launched in 1969 and carried astronauts Thomas Stafford and Eugene Cernan.** The two traveled toward the moon and brought *Snoopy,* the lunar module, within nine miles of the moon. They circled the moon over thirty times and came back to Earth on May 26.

Union's first offensive engagement took place at Sewall's Point, Virginia, in 1861.

Gertrude Belle Elion became the first woman in 1991 to be inducted into the National Inventors Hall of Fame. In 1988 she was one of two people to win the Nobel Prize in medicine for her work finding antileukemia drugs.

 Students could find out where the National Inventors Hall of Fame is located. They could also research the other members.

Birthdays

Margot (Hookman) Fonteyn (born Reigate, Surrey, England, 1919; died Panama City, Panama, February 21, 1991) was a ballerina for forty-five years. She often performed with Rudolph Nureyev.

Lillian Hoban (born Philadelphia, Pennsylvania, 1924; died New York, New York, July 17, 1998) was an author and illustrator. Visit a Web site at: http://www.lillianhoban.com.

Pope John Paul II (born Karol Wojtyla in Wadowice, Poland, 1920) is the 264th leader of the Catholic Church. He was elected in 1978, and he is the first Polish pope.

Reggie Jackson (born Wyncote, Pennsylvania, 1946) is a former baseball player and a member of the National Baseball Hall of Fame.

May

19

Ringling Brothers Circus performed for the first time in 1884.

Turkey celebrates Youth and Sport Day. This holiday reminds the people of their drive for independence. Their leader was Mustafa Kemal Ataturk.

Simplon Tunnel from Iselle, Italy, to Brig, Switzerland, opened in 1898.

 Students could locate Italy and Switzerland on a map. They could find information about the tunnel.

Boys' Club of America was founded in 1906. It later became the Boys' and Girls' Club of America. Visit a Web site at: http://www.bgca.org.

Birthdays

Lorraine Hansberry (born Chicago, Illinois, 1930; died January 12, 1965) was a playwright. One of her most famous works is *A Raisin in the Sun.*

Bill Laimbeer, Jr. (Boston, Massachusetts, 1957) is a former basketball player.

Malcolm (Little) X (born Omaha, Nebraska, 1925; assassinated in New York, New York, February 21, 1965) was a civil rights activist.

Students could locate more information on Malcolm X. They could predict what might have happened if he had not been killed.

Sarah Miriam Peale (born Philadelphia, Pennsylvania, 1800; died Philadelphia, Pennsylvania, February 4, 1885) painted portraits. She was a member of the famous Peale family.

 Children could make a family tree of the Peales. Did any offspring of the next generation become artists?

Francis R. Scobee (born Cle Elum, West Virginia, 1939; died in *Challenger* explosion, January 28, 1986) was the commander of the *Challenger.*

ay

 Weights and Measures Day is the anniversary of a treaty signed in 1875. The document created the International Bureau of Weights and Measures.

Homestead Act was created by Congress in 1872. Any person over the age of twenty-one or who was the head of a family could procure 160 acres of public land. He/she had to be willing to live on it for five years and to make improvements on it. The act enticed between 400,000 and 600,000 families to the West.

Cameroon celebrates Republic Day. It was declared a republic in 1972.

Charles Lindbergh started his solo flight across the Atlantic in 1927. He left Long Island, New York, in the *Spirit of St. Louis* at 7:52 A.M. He arrived at Paris, France, 10:24 P.M. on May 21. "Lucky Lindbergh" won a $25,000 prize for his efforts. He instantly became a national hero.

 Students could read more about his life and the fame he faced.

Amelia Earhart started her first solo flight across the Atlantic in 1932. She was the first woman to fly alone over the Atlantic. She departed from Harbor Grace, Newfoundland. Thirteen and a half hours later she landed in Londonderry, Ireland.

Birthdays

Honore de Balzac (born Tours, France, 1799; died Paris, France, August 18, 1850) was a writer.

Dolley Payne Todd Madison (born Guilford County, North Carolina, 1768; died Washington, DC, July 12, 1849) was the wife of James Madison, the fourth president of the United States. She often served as hostess for the widower Thomas Jefferson when he was president. When her husband became president in 1809, she held the first inaugural ball. The British attacked and burned the White House during the War of 1812. She gathered up much of the building's treasures before the British arrived. Visit a Web site at: http://www.whitehouse.gov/history/firstladies/dm4.html.

 Students could research her life and then write about some of her adventures.

Mary Pope Osborne (born Fort Sill, Oklahoma, 1949) is an author. Her books include the Magic Treehouse series. Visit a Web site at: http://www.kidsreads.com/authors/au-osborne-mary-pope.asp.

Henri Julien Felix Rousseau (born Laval, Mayenne, France, 1844; died Paris, France, September 10, 1910) was an artist. Visit a Web site at: http://www.artcyclopedia.com/artists/rousseau_henri.html.

Rousseau was deemed a primitive painter because he had no formal training. Students could view some of his work and compare him to other painters.

Jimmy Stewart (born Indiana, Pennsylvania, 1908; died Beverly Hills, California, July 2, 1997) was an actor. One of his most popular movies was *It's a Wonderful Life.*

ay

21

Gemini the Twins is the astrological sign for May 21 through June 20.

Hundred Years' War began in 1369 and ended in 1453. The English and the French actually fought a number of different battles over the control of France.

 Students could find out who won the Hundred Years' War and what part Joan of Arc played in it.

American National Red Cross was created by Clara Barton in 1881. Over one million volunteers help in areas ranging from collecting donated blood to providing for disaster relief.

Pietà **was damaged in 1972 when Lazlo Toth attacked the sculpture.**

 Students could find out more about the *Pietà* and Michelangelo.

Birthdays

Albrecht Dürer (born Nuremberg, Germany, 1471; died Nuremberg, Germany, April 6, 1528) was a Renaissance artist. Visit a Web site at: http://www.artcyclopedia.com/artists/durer_albrecht.html.

 Dürer did a great deal of engraving. Children could research the process. They could make potato prints to get the feel of engraving.

Armand Hammer (born New York, New York, 1898; died Los Angeles, California, December 10, 1990) developed the Occidental Petroleum Company into a twenty-billion-dollar business. He donated millions of dollars to cancer research.

Andrei Dmitriyevich Sakharov (born Moscow, Russia, 1921; died Moscow, Russia, December 14, 1989) was a Soviet physicist and dissident. He developed the atomic bomb for the Soviets, but he later spoke out against the government. He was exiled to Gorky, Russia, for a number of years. He was appointed to the Soviet Congress of Peoples Deputies a few months before he died.

ay

22

National Maritime Day has been celebrated by presidential proclamation every year since 1933. The steamship *Savannah* departed this day in 1819 from Savannah, Georgia, and arrived in Liverpool, England. It was the first ship to successfully cross the Atlantic Ocean.

Yemen celebrates Unification Day. In 1990 North Yemen and South Yemen formed one country.

Aaron Burr was tried for treason starting this day in 1807.

Richard Nixon in 1972 became the first American president to visit Moscow.

Crater Lake National Park became America's fifth national park in 1902. Visit a Web site at: http://www.nps.gov/crla/home.htm.

Janet Guthrie in 1977 found out she was the first woman to qualify for the Indianapolis 500.

"Mister Rogers' Neighborhood" premiered in 1967.

Toothpaste tube was invented by Dr. Washington Sheffield in 1892.

Birthdays

Mary Cassatt (born Allegheny City, Pennsylvania, 1844; died Chateau de Beaufresne near Paris, France, June 14, 1926) was an artist. Most of her works were around the theme of children and families. Visit a Web site at: http://www.artcyclopedia.com/artists/cassatt_mary.html.

 She sometimes worked in pastels. Students could try this medium.

Sir Arthur Conan Doyle (born Edinburgh, Scotland, 1859; died Crowborough, Sussex, England, July 7, 1930) was a physician and a writer. He is most famous for his Sherlock Holmes stories.

 Students could read and share a favorite mystery book.

Arnold Lobel (born Los Angeles, California, 1933; died New York, New York, December 4, 1987) was a children's author and illustrator. He wrote, among other works, *Frog and Toad Together* (Newbery Honor Book), 1972. Visit a Web site at: http://www.carolhurst.com/authors/alobel.html.

 Readers could enjoy his books.

Richard Wagner (born Leipzig, Germany, 1813; died Venice, Italy, February 13, 1883) was a composer. One of his most famous works is *The Ring of the Nibelung.*

ay

23 Captain Kidd was hanged in 1701 relating to charges of piracy.

Bifocals were patented by Benjamin Franklin in 1785.

 Children could find out what bifocals are and how people use them.

South Carolina became the eighth state of the United States by ratifying the Constitution in 1788. It was named in honor of King Charles II. *Carolus* is Latin for Charles. Columbia is the state capital. Its nickname is the Palmetto State, and its leading sources of income are tobacco, rice, and textiles. Contact: (803) 734-0122. Visit an Internet site at: http://www.state.sc.us.

 Students could find out what a palmetto is.

Mount Everest was climbed for the first time by a woman, Junko Tabei, in 1975.

First nursery school in America was created in 1827.

First veterinary school in America was founded in 1879.

Nylon was invented in 1934 by Dr. Wallace H. Carothers of DuPont Laboratories. He called it *polymerble.*

World Turtle Day reminds people to protect tortoises and turtles. Visit a Web site at: http://www.tortoise.com.

Birthdays

Margaret Wise Brown (born New York, New York, 1910; died Nice, France, November 13, 1952) was a children's author. She wrote more than fifty books.

 Children could read one of her most famous books, *Goodnight Moon.*

Carolus Linnaeus (born near Kristianstad, Sweden, 1707; died Uppsala, Sweden, January 10, 1778) was a naturalist. He devised the classification system for living things. Every organism has a name where the first name is the genus and the second name is the species.

Scott O'Dell (born Los Angeles, California, 1898; died Santa Monica, California, October 15, 1989) was a children's author. He wrote, among other works, *Sing Down the Moon* (Newbery Honor Book), 1971.

May 24

Passenger train service began in 1830.

Brooklyn Bridge opened in 1883. The suspension bridge cost $16 million and took fourteen years to build.

 Students could research the Brooklyn Bridge and other bridges. The Brooklyn Bridge is 1,595 feet long. Where is the longest bridge?

First telegraph message was sent by Samuel F. B. Morse in 1844. The message, "What hath God wrought?" was sent from Washington, DC, to Baltimore, Maryland.

 Students could send messages to one another in Morse code.

First night baseball game was played in the major leagues. The Cincinnati Reds beat the Philadelphia Phillies in 1935. Over 20,000 baseball fans attended the game in Cincinnati, Ohio.

Eritrea celebrates its Independence Day. It broke away from Ethiopia in 1993. The country, bordering the Red Sea, was once under Italian and then British control. Asmara is the capital.

Scott Carpenter was launched into space in 1962. The second American to travel in space, he circled the Earth three times.

Birthdays

Bob Dylan (born Robert Zimmerman in Duluth, Minnesota, 1941) is a musician and a singer.

Emanuel Leutze (born Wurttenberg, Germany, 1816; died Washington, DC, July 18, 1868) came to America when he was nine years old. He started to paint at about age fifteen. Even though most people do not recognize his name, he painted some very famous pictures. They include *Washington Crossing the Delaware* and *Columbus Before the Queen.*

Frank Oz (born Hereford, England, 1944) is a puppeteer.

 Students could make puppets and put on a show.

African Freedom Day is celebrated by Chad, Equatorial Guinea, Liberia, Mauritania, and Zambia.

Constitutional Convention opened in Philadelphia, Pennsylvania, in 1787.

 Students could read Jean Fritz's *Shh! We're Writing the Constitution.*

Argentina celebrates its Independence Day. It became free of Spanish rule in 1810. Spaniards explored the area around 1515. Buenos Aires is the capital, and it is known for its large cattle herds.

Jordan celebrates its Independence Day. It became a country headed by a monarchy in 1946. Jordan's history is long. Crusaders invaded the country, followed by the Mongols in the thirteenth century. In 1517 Jordan became part of the Ottoman Empire. The British took control after World War I. Amman is the capital.

Students could find out about the relationship between Jordan and its neighbors.

National Tap Dance Day is held on the birthday of Bill "Bojangles" Robinson. Robinson was born in Richmond, Virginia, in 1878. He started his dancing career in vaudeville. He opened on Broadway in 1927. Robinson appeared in several movies with Shirley Temple, including *The Littlest Rebel* and *The Little Colonel.* He died in New York, New York, on November 25, 1949.

Disney's *Three Little Pigs* opened in 1933.

***Skylab 2* circled the Earth for twenty-eight days in 1973 while astronauts Pete Conrad and Paul Weitz conducted experiments.**

 Students could research the problems of weightlessness in space.

Gasoline engine was patented in 1844.

Birthdays

Miles Davis (born Alton, Illinois, 1926; died Santa Monica, California, September 28, 1991) was a jazz trumpeter. He experimented with different kinds of music.

Ralph Waldo Emerson (born Boston, Massachusetts, 1803; died Boston, Massachusetts, April 27, 1882) was a writer and a philosopher.

Ann McGovern (born New York, New York, year not disclosed) is a children's author. She has written more than fifty books. One of her most well-known books is *The Desert Beneath the Sea,* published in 1991.

Mike Myers (born Scarsborough, Ontario, Canada, 1963) is an actor.

Igor Sikorsky (born Kiev, Russia, 1889; died Easton, Connecticut, October 26, 1972) was an engineer. He created the first functioning helicopter in 1939.

Beverly Sills (born Brooklyn, New York, 1929) is a retired opera singer.

 Students could listen to some recordings of her singing.

Joyce Carol Thomas (born Ponca City, Oklahoma, 1938) is a children's author. She wrote *When the Nightingale Sings,* published in 1993.

ay

26

A solar eclipse ended a battle in 585 B.C. between the Lydians and the Medes.

Dow Jones Industrial Average was created in 1896.

 Students could find the list of stocks that comprise the Dow Jones. How were those stocks chosen?

Georgia declared its freedom from the Soviet Union in 1991. Located on the eastern coast of the Black Sea, Georgia has an area of about 27,000 square miles. Tbilisi is the capital.

Birthdays

Sally Kristen Ride (born Encino, California, 1951) was the first American woman to travel in space. Dr. Ride flew on a six-day *Challenger* mission that was launched June 24, 1983.

 Students could find out how Dr. Ride became interested in becoming an astronaut.

John Wayne (born Marion Michael Morrison in Winterset, Iowa, 1907; died Los Angeles, California, June 11, 1979) was an actor. He was known for his many westerns.

 John Wayne's walk and voice were often imitated. Students could attempt to impersonate John Wayne.

ay

27

Habeas Corpus Act was passed by England in 1679.

Golden Gate Bridge opened to pedestrian traffic in 1937. Visit a Web site at: http://www.thoma.com/thoma/ggbfacts.html.

 Children could find out why the bridge is named the Golden Gate.

Piano was invented in 1796.

 Children could look inside a piano to see how it works.

***Queen Mary* made its first voyage in 1936.** It traveled from Southampton, England, to New York, New York.

Cellophane tape was patented in 1930 by Richard Gurley Drew. Eventually 3M called the adhesive Scotch tape.

Birthdays

Amelia Jenks Bloomer (born Homer, New York, 1818; died Council Bluffs, Iowa, December, 1894) was a women's rights activist. Her name is associated with "bloomers."

Rachel Louise Carson (born Springdale, Pennsylvania, 1907; died Silver Springs, Maryland, April 14, 1964) was an environmentalist and an author. Her book *Silent Spring* sparked discussion over the use of pesticides.

Children could learn how pesticides work, their advantages, and their disadvantages.

James Butler "Wild Bill" Hickock (born Troy Grove, Illinois, 1837; died Deadwood, South Dakota, August 2, 1876) was a frontiersman and a lawman. He was killed while playing poker in a saloon.

Julia Ward Howe (born New York, New York, 1819; died Newport, Rhode Island, October 17, 1910) was a fervent abolitionist and women's suffragist. She wrote *The Battle Hymn of the Republic.*

Henry Kissinger (born Fuerth, Germany, 1923) is a former diplomat and member of the president's cabinet.

May

28   **Pure Food Law was enacted in 1881.**

First color and talking film was produced in 1929.

Sierra Club was organized in 1929. Visit a Web site at: http://www.sierraclub.org.

 Students could learn about the goals of the Sierra Club.

Azerbaijan celebrates its Independence Day. It withdrew from the Union of Soviet Socialist Republics in 1991. For most of its history, Azerbaijan's people were nomads. Today the country grows tea, tobacco, wheat, and other crops. Baku is the capital.

Dionne quintuplets were born in 1934 in Canada. The five girls' births caused quite an event. For a period of time the government took the girls away from their parents.

Birthdays

Ian Lancaster Fleming (born London, England, 1909; died 1964) was an author. In addition to his James Bond books, he wrote for children. One of the books is *Chitty Chitty Bang Bang,* published in 1964.

 Students could read parts of *Chitty Chitty Bang Bang.*

James Francis Thorpe (born Prague, Oklahoma, 1888; died Lomita, California, March 28, 1953) was an Olympic athlete, a baseball player, and a football player.

 Students could read about the controversy surrounding his athletic career. Was he an amateur or not when he competed in the Olympics?

May

29   **Constantinople fell in 1453.**

Rhode Island became the thirteenth state in the United States by ratifying the Constitution in 1790. Its name relates back to the island of Rhodes. It was the last of the original thirteen colonies to join the Union. The smallest of all the states, it manufactures jewelry, silver, and textiles. Providence is the state capital, and the state nicknames are the Ocean State and Little

Rhody. Contact: (800) 556-2484. Visit an Internet site at: http://www.50states.com/rdisland.htm.

 Students could find out how and why it separated from Massachusetts.

Wisconsin became the thirtieth state of the United States in 1848. Its nicknames include the Badger State and the Dairy State. Madison is the state capital. Its name dates back to an Ojibwa word, *wishkonsing,* meaning "place of the bearer." Contact: (800) 372-2737. Visit an Internet site at: http://www.50states.com/wisconsi.htm.

 Students could make cheese or yogurt.

President's Flag was officially adopted in 1916.

Birthdays

Patrick Henry (born Studley, Virginia, 1736; died near Brookneal, Virginia, June 6, 1799) was a patriot and a speaker.

Bob Hope (born Leslie Townes in Eltham, England, 1903) is a comedian.

John Fitzgerald Kennedy (born Brookline, Massachusetts, 1917; assassinated in Dallas, Texas, November 22, 1963) was the thirty-fifth president (1961–1963) of the United States. He graduated from Harvard University and was wounded during World War II. He was a member of Congress for three terms before he was elected to the Senate. He represented the state of Massachusetts. He was awarded the Pulitzer Prize for his *Profiles in Courage.* He beat Richard Nixon in the presidential race by only 118,000 votes. He was committed to the space program, and he sponsored the Peace Corps. He also increased America's involvement in Vietnam. Visit a Web site at: http://www.whitehouse.gov/history/presidents/jk35.html.

 Older children could read excerpts from his *Profiles in Courage.*

May

30 Ice cream maker was patented in 1842 by William Young.

Kansas and Nebraska Territories were created in 1854.

 Students could research these territories. They could draw on a map how far the territories extended.

Indianapolis 500 Road Race was held for the first time in 1911. Ray Harroun won the race with an average speed of seventy-five miles per hour.

 Students could record other winning speeds. They could predict future speeds.

Lincoln Memorial was dedicated in 1922. Daniel Chester French sculpted "Seated Lincoln."

Chicago Cubs traded Max Flack for St. Louis Cardinals player Cliff Heathcote between games in a doubleheader in 1922. Both Flack and Heathcote played for both teams the same day.

Croatia celebrates its Independence Day. It seceded from Yugoslavia in 1991. Zagreb is the capital.

Birthdays

Mel Blanc (born San Francisco, California, 1908; died Los Angeles, California, July 10, 1989) was the voice of many of the characters on Looney Tunes, including Bugs Bunny and Daffy Duck.

 Children could vote for their favorite Looney Tune characters.

Peter I (born Moscow, Russia, 1672; died St. Petersburg, Russia, January 28, 1725) was tsar and emperor of Russia. He wanted to make Russia more of a world power. He introduced Arabic numerals, and he simplified the Russian alphabet. He overhauled government and the military.

 ay

31 Copyright Law was established in 1790.

 Students could make a list of what can be copyrighted and what cannot.

First bicycle race was held in Paris, France, in 1868.

Madison Square Garden opened in 1879.

Flaked cereals were patented by Dr. John Harvey Kellogg in 1884. He developed the cereals as a healthy alternative to breakfasts of bacon and eggs.

The Seventeenth Amendment to the Constitution was adopted in 1913. It provided for the direct election of senators.

 Students could find out how senators were elected before this amendment.

South Africa celebrates Republic Day. The colonies unified in 1910 and became a republic in 1961.

Sesquicentennial Expo opened in Philadelphia, Pennsylvania, in 1926.

Birthdays

Clint Eastwood (born San Francisco, California, 1930) is an actor and a director.

Walt Whitman (born West Hills, Long Island, New York, 1819; died Camden, New Jersey, March 26, 1892) was a poet and a reporter. One of his most famous works is *Leaves of Grass*.

 Students could read and enjoy some of his poetry.

June

June was originally the fourth month of the calendar, and it had twenty-nine days. Its Latin name was *Junius*. Julius Caesar modified the calendar and made June the sixth month. He also added one day. June may have been named after Juno, the Roman goddess of marriage. The month's name may also have its roots in the Latin word *juniores*, meaning "young men." June's flower is the rose, and its birthstones are the pearl, alexandrite, and moonstone.

Month-Long Activities

Dairy Month reminds children of the importance of milk and milk products. Contact: Vice President, Public and Industry Affairs, Dairy Management, Inc., 10255 West Higgins Road, Suite 900, Rosemont, Illinois 60018. Telephone: (847) 803-2000.

National Fresh Fruit and Vegetable Month stresses the nutritional value of these foods. Contact: United Fresh Fruit and Vegetable Association, 727 North Washington Street, Alexandria, Virginia 22314. Telephone: (703) 836-3410.

National Skin Safety Month educates children about how to have fun safely in the sun. Contact: Skin Safety Council, 1650 Broadway, Suite 1400, New York, New York 10019.

Special Weeks

Amateur Radio Week recognizes the valuable services of the group. It is held annually, finishing with the fourth weekend in June. Contact: Public Relations Coordinator, American Radio Relay League, 225 Main Street, Newington, Connecticut 06111. Telephone: (860) 594-0328. E-mail: jhagy@arrl.org.

National Little League Week begins the second Monday in June. It has been recognized by presidential proclamation since 1959.

Principals Week is celebrated the week following Father's Day.

Special Days

Children's Day is the second Sunday of the month.

Father's Day is the third Sunday in June. Mrs. John B. Dodd proposed the idea of Father's Day in 1910. President Calvin Coolidge approved of the holiday in 1924, but it did not become an official presidential proclamation until 1966. Public Law 92-278 made it an official holiday in 1972.

June

 1

Kenya celebrates Madaraka Day (Self-rule Day).

People's Republic of China celebrates International Children's Day.

First recorded American earthquake occurred in Plymouth, Massachusetts, in 1638.

Soyuz 9, **a Soviet craft, set a space endurance record in 1970.** Cosmonauts Nikolayev and Sevastyanov stayed in space almost eighteen days.

Kentucky became the fifteenth state of the United States in 1792. It probably got its name from either the Iroquois word *kenta-ke,* meaning "meadowland," or the Wyandot word *kah-ten-tah-teh,* meaning "land of tomorrow." Its state song is *My Old Kentucky Home.* Tourist attractions include Mammoth Cave National Park. Contact: (800) 225-TRIP or (800) 225-PARK. Visit an Internet site at: http://www.50states.com/kentucky.htm.

 Children could compare and contrast Kentucky to their state.

Tennessee became the sixteenth state of the United States in 1796. Its nickname is the Volunteer State. Tennessee's name comes from *tenase,* meaning "main village of Cherokees." The Grand Ole Opry, located in Nashville, attracts many country music fans. Contact: (615) 741-2158. Visit an Internet site at: http://www.50states.com/tennesse.htm.

 Students could find out more about the Grand Ole Opry.

Lou Gehrig in 1925 played the first of 2,130 baseball games with the New York Yankees.

Superman comic was issued for the first time in 1938.

Birthdays

Alexi Lalas (born Detroit, Michigan, 1970) is a soccer player.

Jacques Marquette (born Laon, France, 1637; died near Ludington, Michigan, May 18, 1675) was a priest and an explorer. He arrived in the New World in 1666. He founded several missions before he met Louis Jolliet. The two, with five other people, started to explore the Mississippi River in 1673.

 Students could speculate on why a priest would become such an active explorer.

Marilyn Monroe (born Norma Jean Baker in Los Angeles, California, 1926; died Los Angeles, California, August 5, 1962) was an actress.

Doris Buchanan Smith (born Washington, DC, 1934; died August 28, 2002) wrote for children. Her *A Taste of Blackberries* was published in 1973.

Brigham Young (born Whittingham, Vermont, 1801; died Salt Lake City, Utah, August 29, 1877) was a Mormon church leader.

June

2

Bulgarians celebrate Hristo Botev Day. In 1876 Hristo Botev, writer and hero, died while fighting the Turks.

Grover Cleveland became the first president to wed in the White House when he married Francis Folsom, age 22, in 1886.

 Students might find out how Francis and Grover met.

Native Americans were given citizenship in 1924.

Queen Elizabeth II was crowned in 1953.

Birthdays

Charles "Pete" Conrad, Jr. (born Philadelphia, Pennsylvania, 1930; died near Ojai, California, July 8, 1999) was an astronaut. He participated in four space flights, and he was the third person to walk on the moon. Visit a Web site at: http://nauts.com/bios/nasa/conrad.html.

Paul Galdone (born Budapest, Hungary, 1914) is an author. One of his books is *The Little Red Hen.*

Jerry Mathers (born Sioux City, Iowa, 1948) is an actor. He is known for his television series "Leave It to Beaver."

John Randolph (born Prince George County, Virginia, 1773; died 1833) was a statesman. He was a descendant of Pocahontas and John Rolfe.

 Students could find out much more about his colorful life. He participated in an interesting duel.

Johnny Weissmuller (born Chicago, Illinois, 1904; died Acapulco, Mexico, January 20, 1984) was a famous swimmer and actor. He is known for his role as Tarzan.

 Students could research his swimming career.

June

3

Dutch West India Company was granted a charter in 1621.

Hernando de Soto claimed Florida for Spain in 1539.

New York Knickerbockers in 1851 became the first baseball team to wear uniforms. The uniform consisted of full-length blue pants, white shirts, and straw hats.

Corn harvester was patented by L. H. Jones in 1890.

Silver was no longer used in minting dimes and quarters as of 1965.

 Students could discover what kinds of metals are used in today's coins.

Major Edward H. White conducted the first American walk in space in 1965. White and his companion, Major McDivitt, orbited Earth sixty-six times in *Gemini 4.* White's walk lasted about twenty minutes.

Sally Jan Priesand became the first woman rabbi. She was ordained in 1972 and became assistant rabbi for a New York City congregation about two months later.

Casey at the Bat* was printed for the first time in 1888 in the *San Francisco Examiner. Although it was published anonymously, the author was Ernest L. Thayer.

 Students could read *Casey at the Bat* and put on a play for younger children.

Birthdays

Jefferson Davis (born Todd County, Kentucky, 1808; died New Orleans, Louisiana, December 6, 1889) was a U.S. senator until he became president of the Confederate States of America. He was held in prison for two years after the end of the Civil War, but he was never brought to trial. His citizenship was taken away until 1978, when President Jimmy Carter restored his rights posthumously and signed an amnesty bill.

Charles Richard Drew (born Washington, DC, 1904; died near Burlington, North Carolina, April 1, 1950) was a surgeon. His research found that plasma keeps safer and longer than whole blood. He created blood banks. In 1941 he became the first director of the American Red Cross Blood Bank. Visit a Web site at: http://www.lib.lsu.edu/lib/chem/display/charles_drew.html.

 Students could research the difference between plasma and whole blood. They could also find more information about blood banks.

Anita Lobel (born Kracow, Poland, 1934) is an author and an illustrator. One of her books is *No Pretty Pictures.* Visit a Web site at: http://www.anitalobel.com/biographical.htm.

June

 4

Jack Jouett became a hero on the night of June 3, 1781. He rode forty-five miles through the Virginia countryside to warn Thomas Jefferson and others that the British were coming. When the British arrived in Charlottesville, the Americans had escaped. Jouett was born in 1754 and died in 1822.

 Students could read more about Jouett's ride. They could compare it to Paul Revere's ride.

Tonga celebrates its Independence Day. It became independent from the United Kingdom in 1970. Tonga is composed of 172 islands and is located in the South Pacific. Its capital is Nuku'alofa. Captain James Cook explored the area in 1773. Today Tonga exports copra, bananas, and vanilla.

Finland celebrates Flag Day. The day marks the birth of Carl Gustav Mannerheim, born in 1867.

Roquefort Cheese Day celebrates the famous cheese, first made in 1070.

 Students could find out how Roquefort differs from other cheeses.

Henry Ford test drove his first car in 1896.

Minimum Wage Law was passed by Congress in 1912.

Pulitzer Prizes were awarded for the first time in 1917. Laura E. Richards and Maude H. Elliott, assisted by Florence H. Hall, won the biography award for *Julia Ward Howe.*

Bonnie Tiburzi became the first woman pilot for a U.S. airline in 1973.

Tiananmen Square Massacre occurred in 1989. Several thousand people were killed when Chinese troops opened fire on demonstrators. The protesters were demanding more freedom from the Chinese government. In the weeks following the massacre, thousands of demonstrators were imprisoned.

Personal Computer, Apple II, was introduced into stores in 1977.

Birthdays

George III (born London, England, 1738; died Windsor Castle, England, January 29, 1820) was the king of England during the American Revolution. He realized he was not a good political leader. His actions probably contributed to the start of the war. At one point he almost abdicated. He experienced periods of dementia, and from 1811 until his death the country was run by his son.

Read with the children Jean Fritz's *Can't You Make Them Behave, King George?*

June

5 **Hot air balloon was flown for the first time in 1783.** Joseph and Jacques Montgolfier launched their *globe aerostatique* in Annonay, France. It ascended 1,500 feet. The trip lasted ten minutes.

Denmark celebrates its Constitution Day. Its constitution was written in 1953, and the country is now a constitutional monarchy. Copenhagen is the capital.

Bananas were imported into the United States for the first time in 1876.

 Students could learn more about bananas. Then they could make banana pudding.

World Environment Day is observed by the United Nations. Contact: United Nations, Department of Public Information, New York, New York, 10017.

Birthdays

John Couch Adams (born Laneast, Cornwall, England, 1819; died Cambridge, England, January 21, 1892) discovered the planet Neptune.

Bill Moyers (born Hugo, Oklahoma, 1934) is a journalist.

Richard Scarry (born Boston, Massachusetts, 1919; died Gstaad, Switzerland, April 30, 1994) was a children's author and illustrator. He wrote more than 250 books, and over 100 million copies of his books were sold.

 Children could read and enjoy his works.

Socrates (born Athens, Greece, 469 B.C.; died Athens, Greece, 399 B.C.) was a philosopher and a teacher. One of his most famous sayings is "the unexamined life is not worth living."

 Students could find out more about the Socratic method of teaching.

June

6 **Cherokees started on the "Trail of Tears" in 1838.**

 Students could read more about the "Trail of Tears." A good book is Joseph Bruchac's *The Journal of Jesse Smoke: A Cherokee Boy, Trail of Tears, 1838.*

Susan B. Anthony was fined for voting in an 1872 election in Rochester, New York. She and a group of women tried to vote. They were arrested and sentenced to pay a fine. She would not pay the fine, but the judge freed her. He was afraid she might appeal the verdict to a higher court.

 Do students think she wanted to be arrested?

Sweden celebrates Flag Day. Gustavus I became the king of Sweden in 1523.

Korea observes Memorial Day, honoring those who died in wars.

First drive-in movie opened in 1933 in Camden, New Jersey. The drive-in could accommodate 500 cars.

YMCA began in London in 1944.

D day happened in 1944 when almost two million Allied soldiers and 2,000 ships landed on the shores of Normandy. Operation *Overlord* was very successful.

 Students could trace on a map the history of the D day operation.

David Stein in 1988 in New York City created a bubble fifty feet long.

 Students could make bubble solutions and see if they could beat his record.

Birthdays

Nathan Hale (born Coventry, Connecticut, 1755; hanged in Manhattan, New York, September 22, 1776) was an American patriot. He was famous for his quote, "I only regret that I have but one life to lose for my country."

Cynthia Rylant (born Hopewell, Virginia, 1954) is an author. She is known for her Henry and Mudge books. *Missing May* was the 1993 Newbery Medal winner. Visit a Web site at: http://www.eduplace.com/kids/hmr/mtai/rylant.html.

Peter Spier (born Amsterdam, Netherlands, 1927) is a children's author and illustrator. One of his best-known works is *Noah's Ark.* It won the 1977 Caldecott Medal.

June

 7

Vatican City became an independent country in 1929. Encompassing 108 acres, it is nestled in Rome, Italy. It is the smallest country in the world.

"The $64,000 Question" television game show premiered in 1955. Contestants answered questions about an area where they felt they were experts. If a contestant answered a question correctly, he/she could double the money won and move on to a more difficult question.

 Students could design and play a variation of *The $64,000 Question.*

Birthdays

Virginia Apgar (born Westfield, New Jersey 1909; died New York, New York, August 7, 1974) developed the Apgar score. Newborn babies receive the test, and doctors can then identify infants who need special attention.

Gwendolyn Elizabeth Brooks (born Topeka, Kansas, 1917; died Chicago, Illinois, December 3, 2000) was the first African American to win the Pulitzer Prize for poetry. Her book, *Annie Allen,* took the prize in 1950.

Paul Gauguin (born Paris, France, 1848; died Atoana, Hiva Ova, Marquesas, May 9, 1903) was an artist. He used bold colors and often painted landscapes. He was a stockbroker before he became a painter. He moved to Tahiti about three years after he became an artist. Visit a Web site at: http://www.artcyclopedia.com/artists/gauguin_paul.html.

 Students could view Gauguin's work. He and Vincent van Gogh shared a house for a while. They could compare the two artists' works.

Nikki Giovanni (born Knoxville, Tennessee, 1943) is a poet. Visit a Web site at: http://athena. english.vt.edu/giovanni/giovanni_biog.html.

 Students could read and enjoy some of her poetry.

Anna Kournikova (born Moscow, Russia, 1981) is a tennis player.

June

Laki Volcano began erupting in 1783 in southern Iceland. The eruption, lasting eight months, killed 10,000 people and caused weather changes all over the world.

James Madison suggested the Bill of Rights in 1789. The Bill of Rights added the first ten amendments to the Constitution.

 Students could find out why the Bill of Rights is so important.

George Wythe died in 1806 in Richmond, Virginia. He was born in Elizabeth City, Virginia, probably in the year 1726. The exact date of his birth is unknown. He was one of the signers of the Declaration of Independence.

First American-built steamship was launched in 1809.

Ives W. McGuffey patented the vacuum cleaner in 1869.

 Students could draw a vacuum cleaner and label its parts.

Birthdays

Tim Berners-Lee (born London, England, 1955) is credited with creating the World Wide Web.

Barbara Pierce Bush (born Rye, New York, 1925) is the wife of George Bush, forty-first president of the United States. Because her husband's occupations revolved around either the oil business or politics, they moved frequently. She counted twenty-nine moves. While she was first lady, she strove to improve literacy in America. Visit a Web site at: http://www.white house.gov/history/firstladies/bb41.html.

Francis Crick (born Northampton, England, 1916) discovered with James Watson the structure of DNA.

Ida Saxton McKinley (born Canton, Ohio, 1847; died Canton, Ohio, May 26, 1907) was the wife of William McKinley, twenty-fifth president of the United States. Visit a Web site at: http://www.whitehouse.gov/history/firstladies/im25.html.

Byron White (born Fort Collins, Colorado, 1917; died Denver, Colorado, April 15, 2002) was a Supreme Court justice. Before becoming a Supreme Court justice, he was a professional football player. In 1938 he was the highest paid player, earning $15,800 per year.

Frank Lloyd Wright (born Richland Center, Wisconsin, 1867; died Phoenix, Arizona, April 9, 1959) was a revolutionary architect. He believed a house and its surroundings should blend together. One of his most famous designs was *Falling Water* in western Pennsylvania. A house was designed around a small stream and waterfall.

 Students could look at some of his architectural designs. Do they like what they see?

June

9

Thomas Morton became America's first deported person in 1628. Massachusetts was the colony that deported him.

British leased Hong Kong from China in 1898. The lease was good for ninety-nine years. Hong Kong became part of China June 30, 1997.

 Students could find interesting facts about Hong Kong.

Charles Elmer Hires began selling his root beer in 1869.

 Students could find recipes for root beer.

Georgia Neese Clark in 1949 became the first woman treasurer of the United States.

Neptune was found in 1982 to have two faint rings.

Birthdays

Donald Duck (created 1934) is a cartoon character.

 Students could try to draw Donald Duck.

Amadeo Avogadro (born Turin, Italy, 1776; died Turin, Italy, July 9, 1856) was a chemist and a physicist. From 1820 until his death he was a professor at the University of Turin. His research led to Avogadro's Law: Two gases at the same pressure and temperature will have the same number of molecules.

Michael J. Fox (born Edmonton, Canada, 1961) is an actor.

Cole Porter (born Peru, Indiana, 1892; died Santa Monica, California, October 15, 1964) was a composer and a lyricist. He published his first song when he was ten years old. Two of his Broadway musicals were *Can Can* and *Kiss Me Kate*.

 Students could enjoy some of his music.

George Stephenson (born Newcastle, England, 1781; died Chesterfield, England, August 12, 1848) was an inventor. He worked on the steam locomotive.

June

10

Portugal celebrates a national holiday. The country's national poet, Luis Vas de Camoes, died on this day in 1580.

Dutch settlers arrived in Manhattan in 1610.

Continental Congress in 1776 organized a committee to write the Declaration of Independence.

 Students could research the members of the committee. Who did most of the writing?

Forest fire lookout stations, erected in Greenville, Maine, in 1905, were the first of their kind.

Students could find out more about the job of a lookout.

Alcoholics Anonymous was created in 1935 in Akron, Ohio.

Birthdays

Judy Garland (born Frances Gumm in Grand Rapids, Minnesota, 1922; died London, England, June 22, 1969) was an actress and singer. Her most famous movie was *The Wizard of Oz,* made in 1939. She also appeared on television and in concerts and nightclubs.

Maurice Sendak (born Brooklyn, New York, 1928) is a children's author and illustrator. He wrote, among other works, *Where the Wild Things Are* (Caldecott Medal), 1963. Visit a Web site at: http://www.pbs.org/wnet/americanmasters/database/sendak_m.html.

 Students could dramatize *Where the Wild Things Are.*

June

 Henry VIII married the first of his wives, Catherine of Aragon, in 1509.

Mount Pinatubo erupted in 1991 in the Philippines. The volcano, dormant for some time, disgorged ash and gas sixty miles into the air. Sulfuric acid droplets formed a layer in the Earth's atmosphere. It actually lowered the Earth's temperature by about one degree for several years.

King Kamehameha I Day is celebrated in Hawaii. King Kamehameha lived from 1737 to 1819.

Comstock Lode was discovered in Nevada in 1859. This time the metal was silver.

Player piano was patented by Joseph H. Dickenson in 1912.

Birthdays

Jacques-Yves Cousteau (born Saint-Andre-de-Cubzac, France, 1910; died Paris, France, June 25, 1997) was a famous oceanographer. He became interested in the ocean when he was a gunnery officer for the French Navy. He, along with Emile Gagnan, made the aqualung practical. He wrote more than fifty books and produced many films and documentaries about the ocean. He earned three Academy Awards for his films.

 Students could find out how the aqualung works.

Joe Montana (born New Eagle, Pennsylvania, 1956) is a former football player.

Robert Munsch (born Pittsburgh, Pennsylvania, 1945) is a children's author. He wrote, among other works, *Giant,* 1989.

 Students could read and enjoy some of his books.

Jeannette Rankin (born Missoula, Montana, 1880; died Carmel, New York, May 18, 1973) was the first woman elected to the House of Representatives.

Richard Georg Strauss (born Munich, Germany, 1864; died Garmisch-Partenkirchen, Germany, September 8, 1949) was a composer. One of his works is *Also Sprach Zarathustra,* composed in 1896.

Students could listen to recordings of his music.

June

 12

Philippines celebrates its independence from Spain in 1898.

Russia celebrates its Independence Day. It broke away from the USSR in 1991. Russia is almost double the size of the United States. Moscow is the capital.

 Students could find out more about the Russian language.

Bryan Allen became the first person to pedal an aircraft across the English Channel. He flew from Folkestone, England, to Cape Gris-Nez, France, in 1979. The trip took almost three hours.

Big Bend National Park was established in 1935. The park, encompassing over 800,000 acres, is located in the northern portion of the Chihuahuan Desert. Temperatures can reach 120 degrees Fahrenheit in the summer. However, temperatures can be extremely low in winter. Contact: Big Bend National Park, Texas, 79834. Visit a Web site at: http://www.nps.gov/bibe.

National Baseball Hall of Fame and Museum was established in 1939 in Cooperstown, New York. The first players to be honored included Ty Cobb and Babe Ruth.

Venera 4, **a Soviet space capsule, was launched in 1967.** It parachuted onto the surface of Venus on October 18, 1967.

Emily Powell in 1973 became the first woman hired to pilot passenger airplanes.

Little League in 1974 allowed girls to play in the league.

Birthdays

George Herbert Walker Bush (born Milton, Massachusetts, 1924) was the forty-first president (1989–1993) of the United States. During World War II he was a navy pilot. He was shot down during a flight over the Pacific Ocean. After the war, he went to Texas and found wealth in the oil fields. He was a congressman and a United Nations ambassador. During his presidency he approved Operation Desert Storm. Visit a Web site at: http://www.whitehouse.gov/history/presidents/gb41.html.

 Students could find out what former presidents do.

Anne Frank (born Frankfurt am Main, Germany, 1929; died in Belsen concentration camp, 1945) kept a diary during World War II. She and her family left Germany in 1933 because they were Jews. They sought sanctuary in Amsterdam. In July of 1942 they had to go into hiding. Anne began to record her thoughts and activities in a diary. In August of 1944 she and her family were found. She died the next year in a concentration camp. Her diary was found, and it was printed in 1947. In 1952 it was printed in the United States with the title *The Diary of a Young Girl.*

 Students could read and discuss her diary.

June

13 **Rhode Island in 1774 became the first colony to ban slave importation.**

Department of Labor was created by Congress in 1888. Visit a Web site at: http://www.dol.gov.

 Students could find more information about the Department of Labor.

Rawlins, Wyoming, experienced a two-foot snowfall in 1889.

Yukon became a Canadian Territory in 1898, and Dawson was the capital. Today Whitehorse is the territory's capital and largest city. The territory got its name from the Indian word *youcon,* meaning "big river." It is still known for its minerals and timber.

 Students could learn more about the climate and geography of the Yukon.

Supreme Court ruled in favor of Miranda in *Miranda v. Arizona* in 1966. As a result, police must inform people of their rights before they can be questioned.

Birthdays

Tim Allen (born Denver, Colorado, 1953) is an actor and a comedian.

Ashley Olsen (born Los Angeles, California, 1986) is an actress.

Mary-Kate Olsen (born Los Angeles, California, 1986) is an actress.

Winfield Scott (born Petersburg, Virginia, 1786; died West Point, New York, May 29, 1866) was an outstanding military leader. He also negotiated peace treaties with Indians. Twice he was nominated for president.

 Students could locate information about his military strategies.

June

14 **Flag Day** has been celebrated as a holiday since 1916. John Adams, in 1777, proposed the idea of a flag to the Continental Congress. He went on to describe its colors, stars, and stripes.

 Students could prepare a slide show of how our flag has changed over the years.

U.S. Army was created in 1775 by the second Continental Congress. The next day George Washington became commander of the new army.

Sandpaper was patented in 1834.

Warren G. Harding became the first president to communicate over the radio in 1922. He discussed the dedication of the Francis Scott Key Memorial in Baltimore, Maryland.

Hawaii became a territory in 1950.

Univac I was demonstrated for the first time in Philadelphia, Pennsylvania, in 1951. It was the first commercial computer.

 Students could research the Univac. How big was it? What could it do relative to today's computers? Where is it now?

Mariner 5 **was launched in 1967.** It flew by Venus on October 18, 1967. It determined that Venus's atmosphere is at least seventy percent carbon dioxide.

Birthdays

John Bartlett (born Plymouth, Massachusetts, 1820; died Cambridge, Massachusetts, December 3, 1905) was an editor and a publisher. He owned a bookstore. During his free time he produced *Familiar Quotations: Being an Attempt to Trace to Their Sources Passages and Phrases in Common Use.* It first appeared in 1855; and it has had numerous revisions since then. Visit an interesting Web site at: http://www.cc.columbia.edu/acis/bartleby/bartlett.

 Students could learn how to use *Bartlett's.* They could find quotes that interest them.

Margaret Bourke-White (born New York, New York, 1906; died Stamford, Connecticut, August 27, 1971) was a famous photojournalist. She photographed a number of World War II battles. When the Nazi concentration camps were opened, she photographed the horrors. She photographed Gandhi. One of her most famous books was *You Have Seen Their Faces,* photographs of southern poverty.

Bruce Degen (born Brooklyn, New York, 1945) is a children's book illustrator. He illustrated, among other works, the *Magic School Bus* series. Visit a Web site at: http://www.scholastic.com/magicschoolbus/books/authors.

 Students could read and enjoy some of the books he has illustrated.

Harriet Beecher Stowe (born Litchfield, Connecticut, 1811; died Hartford, Connecticut, July 1, 1896) was an author. She is best known for *Uncle Tom's Cabin.* The book greatly aided the abolitionist movement and may have been one of the main causes of the Civil War. Visit a Web site at: http://www.harrietbeecherstowe.org.

Laurence Yep (born San Francisco, 1948) writes for children. One of his most well-known works is a Newbery Honor Book, *Dragonwings,* published in 1975.

June

 15

Magna Carta was signed in 1215. Only four originals of the document still exist. King John I was forced to sign the document in Runnymede, England. It was the first English document to outline human rights. Visit a Web site at: http://www.bl.uk/collections/treasures/magna.html.

Arkansas became the twenty-fifth state of the United States in 1836. Hernando de Soto explored the area in 1541. Jacques Marquette and Louis Jolliet visited the region in 1673. Henri de Tonti built Arkansas Post in 1686. The capital is Little Rock, and the state's nickname is the Land of Opportunity. Its state gem is the diamond. Contact: (800) 643-8383. Visit an Internet site at: http://www.50states.com/arkansas.htm.

 Students could find out whether diamonds are found in Arkansas.

Great Smoky Mountains National Park was created in 1934. Because the park hovers on the border of Tennessee and North Carolina, it is close to large centers of population. Over eight million people visit the park each year. People lived in the area prior to its becoming a park. Over 6,000 tracts of land had to be purchased before the area could be declared a national park. Contact: Great Smoky Mountains National Park, Gatlinburg, Tennessee 37738. Visit a Web site at: http://www.nps.gov/grsm.

Ben Franklin flew his famous kite in 1752, and he demonstrated that lightning carries an electrical current.

 Franklin was lucky to survive the lightning. Students could locate more information on lightning and its dangers.

Vulcanized rubber was patented in 1844 by Charles Goodyear.

Diary of a Young Girl, **by Anne Frank, was published in the United States for the first time in 1952.**

Birthdays

Wade Boggs (born Omaha, Nebraska, 1954) is a former baseball player.

Edvard Grieg (born Bergen, Norway, 1843; died Bergen, Norway, September 4, 1907) was a composer and conductor. He was heavily influenced by Norwegian folk music. One of his most famous works is the *Peer Gynt Suite.*

 Students could enjoy hearing his music and listening to the tales behind the sounds.

Rachel Donelson Robards Jackson (born Halifax County, North Carolina, 1767; died Nashville, Tennessee, December 22, 1828) was the wife of Andrew Jackson, seventh president of the United States. She died after he was elected but before he was inaugurated. Visit a Web site at: http://www.whitehouse.gov/history/firstladies/rj7.html.

Brian Jacques (born Liverpool, England, 1939) is an author. He wrote the *Redwall* series.

June

Hammurabi the Great died in Babylon in 1686 B.C.

 Students could find out more about his accomplishments.

John Quincy Adams in 1838 began a three-week speech against the annexation of Texas.

Alaska gold rush began in 1897.

World Court was organized in 1920. It is located in the Peace Palace in The Hague, Netherlands.

 Students could investigate how the World Court works.

First helicopter flight took place in 1922. Henry Berline demonstrated the craft to the U.S. Bureau of Aeronautics.

Valentina Tereshkova became the first woman to travel in space in 1963. She was on the Soviet *Vostok VI.* She circled the Earth forty-eight times during the seventy-hour flight.

Birthdays

Cobi Jones (born Westlake Village, California, 1970) is a soccer player.

Stan Laurel (born Arthur Stanley Jefferson in Ulverston, Lanchashire, England, 1890; died Santa Monica, California, February 23, 1965) was half of the famous comedy team Laurel and Hardy. They pioneered in early films.

Students could watch clips of his work with Oliver Hardy. They could imitate the two.

June

17 **Germany celebrates Day of Unity.**

Marquette and Jolliet began exploring the Mississippi River area in 1673.

Iceland celebrates its Anniversary of the Establishment of the Republic. It gained its independence from Denmark in 1944. Vikings settled on the island in the ninth century A.D. Christianity arrived around A.D. 1000. Less than one percent of the land can be farmed. Reykjavik is the capital.

 Students could find out more about Iceland. Is Iceland covered with ice? How do the people of Iceland use geothermal energy?

Battle of Bunker Hill occurred in 1775.

National Spelling Bee was held for the first time in 1925.

Amelia Earhart in 1928 became the first woman to fly across the Atlantic Ocean.

Watergate Day happened in 1972 when five men were arrested for breaking into the Democratic National Committee headquarters.

 Students could make a timeline of events from this day until Nixon resigned.

Cape Hatteras Lighthouse in 1999 had to be moved because it was too close to the ocean. The 1,500-foot move was completed by August.

 The May 2000 issue of *National Geographic* describes the move. Students could research all the work that went into the move.

Birthdays

William Hooper (born Boston, Massachusetts, 1742; died Hillsboro, North Carolina, October 14, 1790) signed the Declaration of Independence. He represented North Carolina.

Igor Fyodorovich Stravinsky (born Oranienbaum, Russia, 1882; died New York, New York, April 6, 1971) was a Russian composer. Two of his most famous works are *The Firebird* and *The Rite of Spring*.

 Students could listen to some of his recordings.

Venus Williams (born Lynwood, California, 1980) is a tennis player.

June

18 **United States declared war against Great Britain, starting the War of 1812.**

Sally Ride became the first American woman in space in 1983. She and four other crew members were in the *Challenger* for six days.

 Students could find out more about the current roster of astronauts. How many are women?

Napoleon was defeated at Waterloo in 1815 by Wellington and Blucher.

Belmont Stakes was held for the first time in 1867.

Birthdays

Sammy Cahn (born Samuel Cohen in New York, New York, 1913; died Los Angeles, California, January 15, 1993) was a famous songwriter. He was nominated for an Academy Award twenty-six times. He won the award four times.

Pat Hutchins (born Yorkshire, England, 1942) is a picture book author and illustrator. She wrote, among other works, *The Doorbell Rang,* published in 1986.

 Students could read and enjoy some of her works.

George Leigh Mallory (born Moberley, Cheshire, England, 1886; died climbing Mt. Everest, June 8, 1924) was a mountain climber. He was asked why he wanted to climb the highest mountain in the world. His famous response was, "Because it is there."

Paul McCartney (born Liverpool, England, 1942) is a singer and composer. He was one of the Beatles.

Chris Van Allsburg (born Grand Rapids, Michigan, 1949) is a children's author and illustrator. He wrote, among other works, *Jumanji* (Caldecott Medal), 1981.

 Children could read and enjoy some of his works. Visit a Web site at: http://www. eduplace.com/rdg/author/cva/authorbio.html.

June

 National Juggling Day celebrates the old tradition of juggling.

 Students could try to juggle soft balls.

Statue of Liberty was received by the Americans from the French in 1885.

National Archives was created in 1934.

 Students could find out what is stored in the archives. Visit a Web site at: http://www. nara.gov.

Birthdays

Garfield the cat first appeared in 1978. Jim Davis created the comic strip character. Contact: Paws, Inc., 5440 East Co Road 450 North, Albany, Indiana 47320.

Henry Louis "Lou" Gehrig (born New York, New York, 1903; died New York, New York, June 2, 1941) was a baseball legend. He appeared in seven World Series. He died of amyotropic lateral sclerosis, which has become known as Lou Gehrig's disease.

 Students could track Gehrig's career and accomplishments.

Moe Howard (born Moses Horwitz in Bensonhurst, New York, 1897; died Hollywood, California, May 4, 1975) was one of the Three Stooges.

Blaise Pascal (born Clermont-Ferrand, France, 1623; died Paris, France, August 19, 1662) was a mathematician, a physicist, and a philosopher. At age sixteen he had developed Pascal's Theorem. In 1642 he invented the first adding machine. Along with Pierre de Fermat, he developed the mathematics of probability.

Elvira Woodruff (born Raritan, New Jersey, 1951) writes for children. One of her books is *George Washington's Socks.* Visit a Web site at: http://www.ewoodruff.com.

June

Congress adopted the Great Seal in 1782.

Last Great Buffalo Hunt occurred in 1882.

 Students could find out how the buffalo almost became extinct. Are there any free-ranging buffalo alive?

Caroline Willard Baldwin became the first woman to obtain a doctor of science degree in 1895. She graduated from Cornell University.

Alice Robertson became the first woman to officiate in the House of Representatives in 1921.

Ice cream soda was invented in Philadelphia in 1874 by Robert M. Greene. It was created to celebrate the fiftieth anniversary of the Franklin Institute.

 Students could make ice cream sodas.

West Virginia became the thirty-fifth state of the United States in 1863. It seceded from Virginia in 1861. Its nickname is the Mountain State, and the capital is Charleston. The state ranks forty-first in area and thirty-fifth in population. Today much of its income comes from coal and farming. Contact: (800) CALLWVW. It has a Web site at: http://www.50states. com/wvirgini.htm.

 Since Charleston is the capital, students could learn to dance the Charleston.

Birthdays

Audie Murphy (born Kingston, Texas, 1924; died in a plane crash near Roanoke, Virginia, May 28, 1971) was a World War II hero and an actor.

Ilan Ramon (born Tel Aviv, Israel, 1954; died in the *Columbia* disaster, February 1, 2003) was the first Israeli to enter space.

June

Cancer the Crab is the astrological sign for June 21 through July 22.

New Hampshire became the ninth state of the United States by ratifying the Constitution in 1788. It was named after the English county Hampshire. The capital is Concord, and its motto is "Live Free or Die." It ranks forty-fourth in area and forty-second in population. Mt. Washington is the tallest peak in New England. Martin Pring traveled its coast in 1603, and Samuel de Champlain explored the area in 1604. Contact: (603) 271-2666. Visit an Internet site at: http://www.50states.com/newhamps.htm.

 Students could make a list of famous people from New Hampshire.

Reaping machine was patented in 1834 by Cyrus Hall McCormick.

First long-playing record was demonstrated in 1948.

First day of summer is either June 21 or June 22. It marks the summer solstice in the Northern Hemisphere.

Birthdays

Henry Ossawa Tanner (born Pittsburgh, Pennsylvania, 1859; died Paris, France, May 25, 1937) was one of the first African American artists to have major exhibits.

 Students could view copies of his work. How does his style differ from that of other painters?

Martha Dandridge Custis Washington (born near Williamsburg, Virginia, 1731; died Mount Vernon, Virginia, May 22, 1802) was the wife of George Washington, the first president of the United States. Her first husband was Daniel Parke Custis; he died in 1757. She had to raise their two children alone. In 1759 she married George Washington. She never lived in the White House. The nation's capital moved from New York to Philadelphia while Washington was president. Visit a Web site at: http://www.whitehouse.gov/history/firstladies/mw1.html.

 Martha Washington entertained a great deal. Students could find out what was served at meals during those years.

Prince William (born London, England, 1982) is the son of Prince Charles. He will someday be king of England.

June

22 **Royal Greenwich Observatory was established in 1675 by order of Charles II.**

Doughnut was invented in 1847.

 Students could snack on small doughnuts.

British stormed aboard the USS _Chesapeake_ in 1807. This raid was one of the causes of the War of 1812.

V-Mail began in 1942. To conserve space on transport planes, letters were opened and photographed. A roll of film held 1,600 letters. The film was mailed overseas, and the letters were printed.

James Christy discovered Charon, Pluto's satellite, in 1978.

 Students could learn facts about Charon, including the origin of its name.

Mt. Didicus, an underwater volcano, erupted in 1991.

 Students could find out how many underwater volcanoes exist. Will Mt. Didicus ever rise above water level?

Birthdays

Anne Morrow Lindbergh (born Englewood, New Jersey, 1907; died Passumpsic, Vermont, February 7, 2001) was an author. She married Charles Lindbergh, and they had to face the fame he earned when he flew across the Atlantic.

June

 Luxembourg celebrates its independence and the official birthday of His Royal Highness Grand Duke Jean. It is a landlocked country smaller than Rhode Island. Luxembourg-Ville is the capital.

Students could locate Luxembourg on a map. How big is it?

Newfoundland celebrates Discovery Day.

William Penn signed a treaty with the Indians in 1683.

U.S. Government Printing Office was created by Congress in 1860.

U.S. Secret Service was established in 1861.

 Students could research the purposes of the Secret Service.

Typewriter was patented in 1868 by Christopher Latham Sholes.

 Students could find out how the typewriter has changed over the years.

Disney's *Lady and the Tramp* premiered in 1955.

Birthdays

Wilma Rudolph (born St. Bethlehem, Tennessee, 1940; died Brentwood, Tennessee, November 12, 1994) was the first American woman to win three gold medals in one Olympics. She specialized in track events.

Theodore Taylor (born Statesville, North Carolina, 1924) is an author. One of his books is *The Cay*.

Clarence Thomas (born Pinpoint, Georgia, 1948) is an associate justice on the Supreme Court.

June

Henry VIII was crowned in England in 1509.

 Students could learn about his many wives.

Matthew Thornton died in Newburyport, Massachusetts, in 1803. Representing New Hampshire, he signed the Declaration of Independence. His exact date of birth is unknown, but scholars know he was born in Ireland. Visit a Web site at: http://www.rebelswithavision. com/matthewthornton.net.

Coffee was first planted along the Kona coast of Hawaii in 1817.

Students could investigate the crops native to the area and the crops introduced into Hawaii.

National Football League was formed in 1922.

 Students could investigate today's various football leagues.

Berlin airlift began in 1948. After World War II, Germany was divided into four parts. The Soviet Union controlled the portion that held Berlin. Berlin itself had been divided into four parts. The Soviet Union denied access to the city. The United States, France, and Great Britain responded by airlifting food and other supplies into Berlin. The airlift lasted until May 12, 1949. Over 1.5 million tons of supplies were lifted in.

Macau celebrates Macau Day.

Birthdays

Kathryn Lasky (born Indianapolis, Indiana, 1944) is a children's author. *Sugaring Time,* published in 1983, was a Newbery Honor Book. Visit a Web site at: http://www.eduplace.com/kids/hmr/mtai/lasky.html.

Jean Marzollo (born Manchester, Connecticut, 1942) writes for children. Her books include the *I Spy* series. Visit a Web site at: http://www.jeanmarzollo.com/jeanbio.html.

Ellison Onizuka (born Kealakekua, Kona, Hawaii, 1946; died in the *Challenger* explosion, January 28, 1986) was an aerospace engineer aboard the *Challenger.*

June

 25

Virginia became the tenth state of the United States by ratifying the Constitution in 1788. It was named after Queen Elizabeth I, the Virgin Queen. Its nicknames include Old Dominion, Mother of Presidents, and Mother of States. The capital is Richmond. Virginia ranks thirty-sixth in area and twelfth in population. Jamestown was settled in 1607, and important landmarks include Arlington National Cemetery and Appomattox Courthouse National Park. Contact: (800) VISITVA. Visit an Internet site at: http://www.50states.com/virginia.htm.

 Students could find a list of birthplaces of presidents. Is Virginia truly the Mother of Presidents?

Custer's Last Stand took place in 1876 at Little Bighorn. Custer and his men attacked a camp of Sioux Indians. Custer had misjudged the number of Indian fighters, and all 200 soldiers were killed within two hours.

Minimum hourly wage was raised in 1938 from twenty-five cents to forty cents.

Korean War began in 1950. Soldiers from northern Korea attacked southern troops. The United States entered the conflict on June 30. The war ended July 27, 1953.

Mozambique celebrates a national holiday. It became independent from Portugal in 1975. Located on the east coast of Africa, it is almost double the size of California. Maputo is the capital.

Croatia and Slovenia declared their independence from Yugoslavia in 1991.

 Students could find a map of the old Yugoslavia. They could add the borders of the new countries.

Mir, **a Russian spacecraft, was damaged in a collision with an unmanned cargo ship in 1997.** The two Russian cosmonauts and one American astronaut were not injured. Repair supplies had to be sent up by rocket to the *Mir,* located 230 miles above the Earth.

Birthdays

Eric Carle (born Syracuse, New York, 1929) is a picture book author and illustrator. He wrote, among other works, *The Very Quiet Cricket,* 1990. Visit a Web site at: http://www. eric-carle.com.

 Students could read and enjoy some of his works.

George Orwell (born Eric Arthur Blair in Motihari, Bengal, 1903; died London, England, January 21, 1950) was a writer. Two of his most famous works are *1984* and *Animal Farm.*

June

 Madagascar celebrates its Independence Day. It became free from French rule in 1960. It is an island off the southeastern coast of Africa, and it is slightly smaller than Texas. It is the fourth largest island in the world. Antananarivo is the capital. It exports coffee, vanilla, and cloves.

United Nations Charter was signed by fifty nations in San Francisco, California, in 1945.

CN Tower was opened officially in 1976. Located in Toronto, Ontario, Canada, it stands 1,815 feet tall.

Universal Product Codes were put into practice in 1974.

Birthdays

Pearl Sydenstricker Buck (born Hillsboro, West Virginia, 1892; died Danby, Vermont, March 6, 1973) was an author. She won the Nobel Prize for *The Good Earth.*

 Older students could read passages from some of her books.

Abner Doubleday (born Ballston Spa, New York, 1819; died Mendham, New Jersey, January 26, 1893) was the "Father of Baseball." He fought in the Mexican War and in the Civil War. When the war ended, he had attained the rank of major general. He invented the game of baseball in 1839.

Arthur Middleston (born Charleston, South Carolina, 1742; died Goose Creek, South Carolina, January 1, 1787) signed the Declaration of Independence.

Roy Plunkett (born New Carlisle, Ohio, 1910; died Corpus Christi, Texas, May 12, 1994) worked for DuPont. He stumbled across polytetrafluoroethylene resin, now known as Teflon.

 Children could make a list of the uses for Teflon.

Nancy Willard (born Ann Arbor, Michigan, 1936) is an author. She wrote *A Visit to William Blake's Inn: Poems for Innocent and Experienced Travelers.* This book won the 1982 Newbery Medal and a Caldecott Honor Award.

Mildred Ella "Babe" Didrickson Zaharias (born Port Arthur, Texas, 1914; died Galveston, Texas, September 27, 1956) was a great athlete. She played for the women's All-American basketball team when she was sixteen years old. She won two gold medals during the 1932

Olympic Games in track events. She then went on to a string of championships in golf. She also enjoyed softball, swimming, and skating.

 Students could make a specific list of all her accomplishments.

Charlotte Zolotow (born Norfolk, Virginia, 1915) has written more than seventy books for children. Her *Mr. Rabbit and the Lovely Present,* illustrated by Maurice Sendak, was a Newbery Honor Book in 1962. Visit a Web site at: http://www.ipl.org/div/kidspace/askauthor/zolotow.html.

June

27

Djibouti celebrates a national holiday. It declared its independence from France in 1977. Located in northeastern Africa, the capital is named Djibouti as well.

Happy Birthday Song was created in 1859. Mildred J. Hill created the melody, and Patty Smith Hill wrote the lyrics. It was published in 1893. It is probably one of the most popular songs today. Mildred Hill died before it became so famous.

Newbery Medal was awarded for the first time to Hendrik Van Loon for *Story of Mankind* in 1922.

 Students could read and enjoy some of the past Newbery winners.

James Smithson, a British subject, died in Genoa, Italy, in 1829. He bequeathed his fortune to the United States, a country he had never visited. The Smithsonian Institute was created from his money and personal possessions. Visit a Web site at: http://www.si.edu.

 Students could find more information about the vast holdings of the Smithsonian.

Birthdays

James Lincoln Collier (born New York, New York, 1928) is an author. He wrote with his brother, Christopher Collier, *My Brother Sam Is Dead.* Visit a Web site at: http://www.edupaperback.org/authorbios/collier_jameslincoln.html.

Helen Adams Keller (born Tuscumbia, Alabama, 1880; died Westport, Connecticut, June 1, 1968) was a lecturer despite being deaf and blind. When she was nineteen months old, she became very sick and lost her sight and hearing. At age seven, she met Anne Sullivan. Anne taught her Braille; and she even learned how to speak. She graduated with honors from Radcliffe in 1904. She traveled and lectured for most of her adult life. The play *The Miracle Worker* was written in 1959. It became a movie in 1962.

 Students could wear blindfolds and earplugs. How hard is it to communicate?

Robert Keeshan (born Lynbrook, New York, 1927) is an actor. He is best known for his role of Captain Kangaroo.

H. Ross Perot (born Texarkana, Texas, 1930) is a businessman and former presidential candidate.

June

28

Molly Hays in 1778 carried pitchers of water to American soldiers during the Battle of Monmouth. She later became known as Molly Pitcher. Visit a Web site at: http://sill-www.army.mil/pao/pamolly.htm.

Archduke Ferdinand of Austria and his wife were assassinated in Bosnia in 1914. This event ignited the flames that would eventually become World War I.

Treaty of Versailles was signed in 1919, concluding World War I.

 Students could gather statistics on the war. They could also learn how the war changed military tactics.

Early Bird **satellite in 1965 made telephone calls from the United States to Europe more practical.**

 Students could find out how calls were made before the satellite and how the satellite worked.

Birthdays

Mel Brooks (born Melvyn Kaminsky in New York, New York, 1928) is a director and an actor.

Esther Forbes (born Westborough, Massachusetts, 1891; died Worcester, Massachusetts, August 12, 1967) was an author and illustrator. She won the 1943 Pulitzer for *Paul Revere and the World He Lived In.* In 1944 she won the Newbery Medal for *Johnny Tremain.* Visit a Web site at: http://www.edupaperback.org/authorbios/forbes_esther.html.

Bette Greene (born Parkin, Arkansas, 1934) is a children's author. She wrote *Summer of My German Soldier,* published in 1973.

Maria Goeppert Mayer (born Kattowitz, Germany, 1906; died San Diego, California, February 20, 1972) was part of the Manhattan Project team. She experimented with the separation of uranium isotopes. She became the first American woman to receive the Nobel Prize in physics when she shared it with J. Hans Daniel Jensen and Eugene Wigner in 1963.

Richard Rodgers (born Hammels Station, New York, 1902; died New York, New York, December 30, 1979) was a composer for musical theaters. He worked with two lyricists, Lorenz Hart and Oscar Hammerstein. Two of his works are *The King and I* and *The Sound of Music.* He won a Pulitzer Prize for drama for *South Pacific.*

Peter Paul Rubens (born Siegen, Westphalia, 1577; died Antwerp, Belgium, May 30, 1640) was an artist and a diplomat. By age twenty-one he had earned the status of master painter. He was also prolific in several languages. He became so busy that his shop was similar to a production line. He made the original sketches, his apprentices filled in the work, and he came along and completed the details. Visit a Web site at: http://www.artcyclopedia.com/artists/rubens_peter_paul.html.

 Students could look at some of his works. They could try his assembly line approach.

June

 Republic of Seychelles celebrates its Independence Day. It gained its freedom from the United Kingdom in 1976, but it remains a member of the commonwealth. The collection of about eighty islands lies in the western Indian Ocean. The area is slightly greater than twice the size of Washington, DC. Victoria is the capital. Its leading exports are coconuts and spices.

 Students could learn about the spices it exports.

Mesa Verde National Park was created in 1906. It is famous for its ancient Anasazi cliff dwellings. These farmers struggled constantly to cultivate their crops of corn and beans.

Contact: Mesa Verde National Park, Colorado 81330. Visit a Web site at: http://www.nps.gov/meve.

Olympic National Park was created in 1938. The park has fifty-seven miles of coastline and a temperate rain forest. It averages 145 inches of rain per year. Contact: Olympic National Park, 600 East Park Avenue, Port Angeles, Washington 98362. Visit a Web site at: http://www.nps.gov/olym.

 Students could research Mesa Verde National Park and Olympic National Park. They could compare and contrast the two parks. Which would they rather visit?

Combination milk bottle opener and milk bottle cover was patented in 1926 by R. B. Spikes.

Birthdays

George Washington Goethels (born Brooklyn, New York, 1858; died New York, New York, January 21, 1928) was the chief engineer and the first governor of the Panama Canal.

 Students could learn about the problems he faced as he built the Panama Canal.

Antoine de Saint-Exupery (born Lyons, France, 1900; died July 31, 1944) was an author. He wrote *The Little Prince*. Visit a Web site at: http://www.pbs.org/kcet/chasingthesun/innovators/aexupery.html.

June

Hong Kong was returned to the control of China in 1997.

Charles Blondin walked across Niagara Falls on a tightrope in 1859. Approximately 25,000 people watched the five-minute walk. On other occasions he walked across the falls on a tightrope pushing a wheelbarrow or on stilts.

 Students could draw a line on the playground. They could pretend the line was a tightrope. They could see if they could walk the line on stilts.

The Twenty-Sixth Amendment to the Constitution was adopted in 1971. It changed the voting age from twenty-one to eighteen.

 Students could find out why the voting age was changed. They could debate whether age eighteen is the right age to vote.

Gone with the Wind, **written by Margaret Mitchell, was published in 1936.**

Democratic Republic of Congo, formerly Zaire, celebrates its Independence Day. Belgium relinquished control in 1960. It is about one and a half times the size of Alaska. The capital is Kinshasa. Zaire is famous for its minerals and forest products.

Leap Second Adjustment Time can occur. The Bureau International de l'Heure in Paris, France, can decide whether to add or subtract a second to keep the clocks in line with the Earth's revolution.

Birthdays

Robert Ballard (born Wichita, Kansas, 1942) is an oceanographer and an explorer. He found and investigated the remains of the *Titanic*.

Elizabeth Kortright Monroe (born New York, New York, 1768; died Oak Hill, Virginia, September 23, 1830) was the wife of James Monroe, the fifth president of the United States. She was the daughter of a British soldier who decided to stay in America after the Revolutionary War. Since she and her husband had traveled so much during his career, she tried to model the White House functions after those of Europe. Visit a Web site at: http://www.whitehouse.gov/history/firstladies/em5.html.

 Students might see if they can find information on the fashions of her time. Did they dress fancily? Did they have extensive wardrobes?

July is the seventh month of the year. Originally it was the fifth month and was called *Quintilis,* meaning "five." Since Julius Caesar was born in that month, it was named in honor of him and became July. It also became thirty-one days long. July's birthstone is the ruby. The water lily is a flower associated with July.

Month-Long Activities

National Ice Cream Month honors that frozen favorite. Contact: International Ice Cream Association, 1250 H Street NW, Suite 900, Washington, DC 20005. Telephone: (202) 737-4332.

National Hot Dog Month celebrates one of America's favorite foods. More than 16 million hot dogs are eaten each year. Contact: Hot Dog & Sausage Council, 1700 North Moore Street, Suite 1600, Arlington, Virginia 22209. Telephone: (703) 841-2499. Visit a Web site at: http://www.hot-dog.org.

National Recreation and Parks Month reminds children to visit the outdoors. Contact: National Recreation and Parks Association, 22377 Belmont Ridge Road, Ashburn, Virginia 20148. Telephone: (703) 858-0784. Visit a Web site at: http://www.activeparks.org.

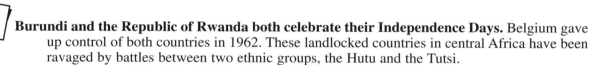

July

 1

Burundi and the Republic of Rwanda both celebrate their Independence Days. Belgium gave up control of both countries in 1962. These landlocked countries in central Africa have been ravaged by battles between two ethnic groups, the Hutu and the Tutsi.

Ghana celebrates Republic Day. Accra is the capital of Ghana, and its main crops include cocoa and coffee.

Philadelphia Zoological Society became the first U.S. zoo when it opened in 1874. Over 3,000 people came that first day. Admission was a quarter for adults and a dime for children. Visit a Web site at: http://www.phillyzoo.org.

 Children could list the animals found in zoos. They could draw up plans for a new zoo.

Canada celebrates Canada Day. Formerly called Dominion Day, the national holiday marks the 1867 union of Upper and Lower Canada and some Maritime Provinces.

 Students could locate the various parts of Canada on a map. Then they could develop a bingo game with questions about Canada's geography.

Battle of Gettysburg started in 1863. Many experts call this battle the turning point of the Civil War. Confederate General Robert E. Lee led his troops across the Mason-Dixon Line, heading for Harrisburg, Pennsylvania. However, the northern troops, led by General George Mead, met the Confederate troops at Gettysburg. The battle lasted for three days. On the last day of the battle, the rebel troops commenced Picket's Charge. Fifteen thousand troops tried to assail the Union's position. The northern troops held, and Lee lost the battle.

 Students could make a timeline of the battle. Michael Shaara's book, *Killer Angels,* offers in-depth looks at the people fighting on both sides.

Battle of San Juan Hill commenced in 1893.

Mammoth Cave National Park was created in 1941. Contact: Mammoth Cave National Park, Mammoth Cave, Kentucky 42259. Visit a Web site at: http://www.nps.gov/maca.

National Postal Worker Day honors all postal employees. Contact: United States Postal Service, 475 L'Enfant Plaza SW, Room 10653, Washington, DC 20260. Telephone: (202) 268-2158.

ZIP codes were introduced in 1963.

Kosmos 1383, **a cooperative space venture with the USSR, France, and the United States, was launched in 1982.** The deployed satellite was designed to receive distress signals from airplanes and ships.

Birthdays

Louis Bleriot (born Cambrai, France, 1872; died Paris, France, August 2, 1936) was an aviation pioneer. On July 25, 1909, he became the first person to fly across the English Channel.

Kalpana Chawla (born Karnal, India, 1961; died in *Columbia* disaster, February 1, 2003) was an astronaut.

Princess Diana (born Sandringham, Norfolk, England, 1961; died Paris, France, August 31, 1997) was the former wife of Price Charles. She was popular worldwide.

Cecil John Rhodes (born Bishop's Stortford, Hertfordshire, England, 1853; died Cape Town, South Africa, March 26, 1902) made a fortune from South Africa's diamond mines. He founded the Rhodes Scholarships for students attending Oxford University.

July

2

Halfway point of the year is marked at noon.

Declaration of Independence resolution was passed in 1776 by the Continental Congress. This step allowed for the adoption of the Declaration of Independence on July 4, 1776.

U.S. Constitution became the law in 1788. New Hampshire became the ninth state to ratify the Constitution, and plans were put into action to have the document become the law of the land.

 Students could examine a copy of the Constitution. They would probably be surprised at how brief it is.

Susan B. Anthony dollars were first issued in 1979.

Amelia Earhart, Fred Noonan, and their plane disappeared somewhere in the Pacific in 1937.

 Students could research the several theories about what happened to Earhart, Noonan, and the plane.

Birthdays

Jose Canseco (born Havana, Cuba, 1964) is a former baseball player.

Jean Craighead George (born Washington, DC, 1919) writes and illustrates books for children. *Julie of the Wolves,* published in 1972, won the Newbery Medal. Visit a Web site at: http://www.kidsreads.com/authors/au-george-jean-craighead.asp.

Thurgood Marshall (born Baltimore, Maryland, 1908; died Washington, DC, January 24, 1993) was the first African American to serve on the Supreme Court. For more than twenty years he directed the legal portion of the NAACP. He was victorious in the case of *Brown v. Board of Education,* ending "separate but equal" public schools. He was nominated to the Supreme Court by President Lyndon Johnson, and he was an associate justice twenty-four years.

 Students could read about some of the cases he heard while on the Supreme Court. Do they agree with his positions?

Richard Petty (born Randleman, North Carolina, 1937) is a former race car driver.

July

3 **Bank for Savings in New York, New York, became the first U.S. bank when it opened in 1819.**

 Students could learn about what happens to money when it is deposited in a bank.

Idaho became the forty-third state of the United States in 1890. Its name translates as "gem of the mountain." Boise is the state capital, and main sources of income are lumber, potatoes, and mining. Idaho was explored during the Louis and Clark expedition. It experienced a gold rush in 1860. Contact: (800) 635-7820. Visit an Internet site at: http://www.50states.com/idaho.htm.

 Idaho is known for its potatoes. Students could investigate why and how Idaho grows so many potatoes.

Birthdays

Samuel de Champlain (born Brouage, France, 1567; died Quebec, Canada, 1635) has been called the "Father of New France." He left France in 1603 to find the Northwest Passage. He did explore the St. Lawrence River and traveled as far as Niagara Falls. In 1608 he founded a fur trading post on the St. Lawrence River and named it Quebec. Over the years he explored more of the region and became good friends with the Algonquin and Huron Indians. He found Lake Champlain and named it after himself.

George M. Cohan (born Providence, Rhode Island, 1878; died New York, New York, November 5, 1942) was an important actor, writer, and producer of American theater. He wrote about forty plays and musicals. However, he is most famous for his songs, including "Give My Regards to Broadway" and "I'm a Yankee Doodle Dandy."

 Many of Cohan's songs are patriotic. Since this is a patriotic time of the year, the children could sing a medley of his songs.

Tom Cruise (born Syracuse, New York, 1962) is an actor.

Samuel Huntington (born Windham, Connecticut, 1731; died Norwich, Connecticut, January 5, 1796) was president of the Continental Congress and a signer of the Declaration of Independence. He was also the third governor of Connecticut.

July

Philippines celebrates its Independence Day. It gained its independence from the United States in 1946. The United States had acquired the country from Spain as part of the Spanish-American War settlement. The Philippines is an archipelago of more than 7,100 islands. Manila is the capital. Coconuts, bananas, and sugarcane are leading exports.

United States celebrates its Independence Day. It declared itself free of English rule in 1776. Interestingly, only two people signed the Declaration of Independence that day. Most people signed the document on August 2, 1776.

 Children could plan and carry out a Fourth of July parade.

"America the Beautiful" was published first in poem form in 1895 by Katherine Lee Bates, a professor at Wellesley College. Stories say she wrote the poem after visiting the top of Pikes Peak in Colorado.

James Monroe, John Adams, and Thomas Jefferson all died on this day. John Adams and Thomas Jefferson died miles apart but within hours of each other in 1826. James Monroe died in 1831.

 Students could find out what these three men thought of each other.

Statue of Liberty was given to the United States by France in 1884.

Pathfinder **landed on the surface of Mars in 1997.** The craft traveled for 211 days and 309 million miles to reach the surface of Mars. A small rover named *Sojourner* traveled about the surface and analyzed rocks and the surface of the planet.

Birthdays

Louis Armstrong stated he was born on July 4. However, records indicate he was born August 4, 1901.

Calvin Coolidge (born Plymouth, Vermont, 1872; died Northampton, Massachusetts, January 15, 1933) was the thirtieth president (1923–1929) of the United States. He was elected governor of Massachusetts in 1918 and was vice president when Harding died. Nicknamed "Silent Cal," he stressed respectability in government. The stock market went up, and he cut governmental costs. He was more concerned with matters within the country than with foreign affairs. He declined to run in 1928, even though he was popular. Visit a Web site at: http://www.whitehouse.gov/history/presidents/cc30.html.

Stephen Foster (born Lawrenceville, Pennsylvania, 1826; died New York, New York, January 13, 1864) was a songwriter. He composed almost 200 songs, including "Camptown Races" and "Swanee River."

Rube Goldberg (born San Francisco, California, 1883; died New York, New York, December 7, 1970) was a cartoonist. He created on paper intricate machines that would activate each other to perform one simple task.

 Students could see some of his cartoons and then draw their own Rube Goldbergs.

Nathaniel Hawthorne (born Nathaniel Hathorne in Salem, Massachusetts, 1804; died New Hampshire, May 18 or 19, 1864) was a writer. Two of his most famous works are *The Scarlet Letter* and *The House of Seven Gables*. He wrote at least 100 stories for magazines.

(Marvin) Neil Simon (born New York, New York, 1927) is a playwright. Two of his most admired works are *The Odd Couple* and *The Sunshine Boys.* He has also written scripts for movies.

July

5 **Algeria celebrates its Independence Day.** France relinquished control of the country in 1962. Algiers is the capital of this north African country. People have lived in the area that is now Algeria for 5,000 years.

Cape Verde celebrates its Independence Day. Portugal relinquished all claims to the country in 1975. The country is composed of fifteen islands. During the exploration period, the islands served as supply stations. During the last century, whaling became an important source of income.

 Students could find out what kinds of whales are located in that part of the Atlantic Ocean.

Venezuela celebrates its Independence Day. Spain gave up control of the country in 1821. The discovery of oil greatly changed this South American country. Caracas is the capital.

Birthdays

Phineas Taylor Barnum (born Bethel, Connecticut, 1810; died Bridgeport, Connecticut, April 7, 1891) created Barnum's American Museum in 1842. It featured unusual acts. He went on to highlight the talents of the singer, Jenny Lind. He opened "The Greatest Show on Earth" in 1871. Later he merged his business interests with J. A. Bailey and formed the Barnum and Bailey Circus.

 Students could create their own "Greatest Show on Earth."

David G. Farragut (born Knoxville, Tennessee, 1801; died Portsmouth, New Hampshire, August 14, 1870) was an admiral for the Union during the Civil War. During a battle at Mobile, Alabama, his fleet was in jeopardy. He cried, "Damn the torpedoes, full speed ahead!" The Union ships escaped, and Mobile gave in.

 Students could find out what happened to Farragut after the Civil War.

Sylvester Graham (born West Suffield, Connecticut, 1794; died September 11, 1855) invented the graham cracker.

July

6 **Antirabies inoculation was administered safely for the first time by Louis Pasteur in 1885.** He saved a child who had been bitten by a rabid dog.

Republican Party was formally created in 1854.

Comoros celebrates its Independence Day. This archipelago is located in the Mozambique Channel, and the country is smaller than Rhode Island. Moroni is the capital. Comoros declared its independence from France in 1975. Its major industry is perfume distillation.

Major League All-Star Game was held for the first time in 1933 in Comiskey Park, Chicago, Illinois.

Students could find out how players become a part of the All-Star Game. They could also find out which league has won the game most of the time.

Malawi celebrates its Independence Day. It received its independence from Great Britain in 1964. This landlocked country is located in central Africa. Lilongwe is the capital. Its major industries include the processing of tea, sugar, and tobacco.

Birthdays

George W. Bush (born New Haven, Connecticut, 1946) is the forty-third president (2001–) of the United States. He is a former governor of Texas. Visit a Web site at: http://www. whitehouse.gov/president/gwbbio.html.

John Paul Jones (born Kirkbean, Scotland, 1747; died Paris, France, July 18, 1792) was a Revolutionary War hero. His name was really John Paul, but he added the names Jones when he fled a murder charge in the Caribbean and came to the United States. He was captain of the *USS Bonhomme Richard* and battled the British *Serapis*. When the British captain asked him if he was ready to surrender, he replied, "Sir, I have not yet begun to fight."

Frida Kahlo (born Coyoacan, Mexico, 1907; died Coyoacan, Mexico, July 13, 1954) was a surrealist painter. She was the wife of Diego Rivera.

Helen Beatrix Potter (born London, England, 1866; died Sawrey, Lancashire, England, December 22, 1943) was a writer and illustrator. She is famous for her *Peter Rabbit* books. She wrote twenty-five books, featuring characters such as Squirrel Nutkin and Tom Kitten. She wrote the stories originally to please the children of a dear friend.

 Children could read and enjoy some of her works.

Nancy Davis Reagan (born Anne Francis Robbins in New York, New York, 1923) is the wife of Ronald Reagan, fortieth president of the United States. Her given name was Anne, but she was nicknamed Nancy as a small child. Her parents divorced, and her mother married Loyal Davis. He adopted Nancy. She became an actress and appeared in eleven movies. While she was first lady, she directed major changes to the second and third floors of the White House. Visit a Web site at: http://www.whitehouse.gov/history/firstladies/nr40.html.

 Students could find out how Nancy Reagan met her husband.

July

7 **Japan celebrates Tanabata.** The day remembers the meeting of two lovers, Shokujo, a princess, and Kenju, a shepherd.

 Students could find the full story and make a puppet play from it.

***The Adventures of Pinocchio* was created by Carlo Collodi, whose real name was Carl Lorenzini, in 1881.**

Solomon Islands celebrates its Independence Day. These islands in the Pacific became free from Great Britain in 1978. Honiara is the capital. The islands make money by selling the right to fish for tuna in their surrounding waters.

Birthdays

Jan Berenstain (born Philadelphia, Pennsylvania, 1923) is a children's author. She and her husband have created the Berenstain Bears series. Visit a Web site at: http://www.berenstainbears.com.

 Children could read and enjoy her works.

Marc Chagall (born Vitsyebsk, Russia [now Belarus], 1887; died St. Paul de Vence, France, March 28, 1965) was an artist. He went to France in 1923. His pictures contain elements of dreams and fantasy. Visit a Web site at: http://www.artcyclopedia.com/artists/chagall_marc.html.

 Students could view some prints of his work. They could check out how he uses color.

Patricia Coombs (born 1926) is a children's author. She wrote the Dorrie series.

Michelle Kwan (born Torrance, California, 1980) is a figure skater.

Leroy "Satchel" Paige (born Mobile, Alabama, 1906; died Kansas City, Missouri, June 8, 1982) was a baseball player. He moved from the Negro leagues to the major leagues. He played for the Cleveland Indians; they won the World Series in 1948.

Ringo Starr (born Richard Starkey in Liverpool, England, 1940) is a musician. He is one of the Beatles.

July

 8

Olive Branch Petition was signed by representatives from the Second Continental Congress in 1775. It was delivered to King George III as one last try to resolve the colonies' and the country's differences peacefully.

 Students could predict what would have happened if the king had not ignored the petition.

Declaration of Independence was read publicly for the first time in Philadelphia, Pennsylvania, in 1776 by Colonel John Nixon.

State Department issued the first passport in 1796.

 Students could see a passport and learn how they are issued.

Liberty Bell cracked in Philadelphia, Pennsylvania, for the second time in 1835. It was ringing to mark the funeral of Chief Justice John Marshall.

Dow Jones Industrial Average hit a low of 41.22 in 1932.

Birthdays

Kevin Bacon (born Philadelphia, Pennsylvania, 1958) is an actor.

Count Ferdinand von Zeppelin (born Constance, Baden, 1838; died Berlin, Germany, March 8, 1917) was a German scientist. He traveled to the United States during the Civil War. He went up in Union hot air balloons and realized the importance of air travel. He returned to Europe and developed lighter-than-air dirigibles. These dirigibles are sometimes called zeppelins.

Children could find out how we use dirigibles today and find out why we do not use them extensively.

July

9

Argentina celebrates its Independence Day. The country became free of Spanish control in 1816. About one-fourth the size of the United States, Argentina exports beef and wheat. Buenos Aires is the capital.

 Students might be interested in the music from *Evita.*

Doughnut cutter was patented by John Blondel in 1872.

 Students could make and eat doughnuts.

Corncob pipe was patented by Henry Tibbe in 1878.

Helicopter passenger service began in New York, New York, in 1953.

Dick Clark appeared for the first time in 1956 as the announcer on *American Bandstand.*

Birthdays

Tom Hanks (born Concord, California, 1956) is an actor. He won Oscars for his performances in *Forrest Gump* and *Philadelphia.*

Elias Howe (born Spencer, Massachusetts, 1890; died Brooklyn, New York, October 3, 1867) invented the sewing machine.

 Students could find out exactly how the sewing machine works.

Fred Savage (born Highland Park, Illinois, 1976) is an actor.

July

10

The Bahamas celebrates its Independence Day. Almost 700 islands make up the country. It became free of British rule in 1973, although it is still part of the British Commonwealth. Its capital is Nassau, and one of its major industries is tourism.

Wyoming became the forty-fourth state of the United States in 1890. The state is ninth in size, but it is fiftieth in population. Even Alaska has more people than Wyoming. Its name is derived from a Delaware phrase *maugh-wau-wa-ma,* meaning "great plains." Cheyenne is the state capital. Cattle ranching and uranium mining have provided considerable income to the state. Lately large reserves of petroleum and coal are helping the economy. Two tourist draws are Yellowstone National Park and Grand Teton National Park. Contact: (800) CALL-WYO. Visit an Internet site at: http://www.50states.com/wyoming.htm.

 Students could calculate the population density of various states. How does Wyoming compare to the other states?

Death Valley, California, noted a record-breaking temperature of 134 degrees Fahrenheit in 1913.

Birthdays

Mary McLeod Bethune (born Mayesville, South Carolina, 1875; died Daytona Beach, Florida, May 18, 1955) was born to a family of former slaves. She devoted her life to the improvement of conditions for African Americans. She served as an advisor to Franklin Roosevelt on minority rights.

David Brinkley (born Wilmington, North Carolina, 1920; died Houston, Texas, June 11, 2003) was a television journalist.

Arlo Guthrie (born Brooklyn, New York, 1947) is a singer.

Edmund Clerihew Bentley (born London, England, 1875; died London, England, March 30, 1956) created the clerihew. It is a poem composed of two rhymed couplets of different lengths.

 Students could read some clerihews and then create some.

James Abbott McNeill Whistler (born Lowell, Massachusetts, 1834; died London, England, July 17, 1903) was an artist. One of his best-known works is *Arrangement in Grey and Black: Portrait of the Painter's Mother.* Visit a Web site at: http://www.artcyclopedia.com/ artists/whistler_james_mcneill.html.

 Students could see some prints of his work. They could compare him to other artists.

July

11

Mongolia celebrates a national holiday. The people revolted against a feudal monarch in 1921.

Aaron Burr was killed by Alexander Hamilton in a duel in 1804.

James Smith, signer of the Declaration of Independence, died in 1806. He represented Pennsylvania. His exact date of birth is unknown, but he was born in Ireland around 1719. Visit a Web site at: http://www.ushistory.org/declaration/signers/smith.htm.

Skylab in 1979 reentered the Earth's atmosphere and broke apart. The pieces fell into the Indian Ocean and onto parts of Australia. Skylab had been launched May 14, 1973.

World Population Day marks this day in 1987 when the world's population reached five billion.

Birthdays

John Quincy Adams (born Braintree, Massachusetts, 1767; died Washington, DC, February 23, 1848) was the sixth president (1825–1829) of the United States. The first son of a president to become a president, he was a child during the Revolutionary War. He spoke at least seven languages. He was a senator before he beat Andrew Jackson for the presidency. After he was president, he served as a congressman for Massachusetts. Visit a Web site at: http://www.whitehouse.gov/history/presidents/ja6.html.

 Students could investigate the languages he spoke. They could learn a bit more about each of the languages.

Robert the Bruce (born Turnberry, Scotland, 1274; died Scotland, 1329) was an early king of Scotland. He spent most of his life trying to free Scotland from British control.

 His life was quite exciting. Students could read more about it.

Patricia Polacco (born Lansing, Michigan, 1944) is a writer and illustrator of books for children. One of her most well-known books is *The Bee Tree,* published in 1993.

E(lwynn) B(rooks) White (born in Mount Vernon, New York, 1899; died North Brooklyn, Maine, October 1, 1985) was a children's author. He wrote, among other works, *Charlotte's Web* (Newbery Honor Book), published in 1952, and *Stuart Little.*

 Children could read and enjoy some of White's work.

 July

 Kiribati celebrates its Independence Day. It became free of British rule in 1979. The thirty-three atolls, located in the Pacific Ocean, form a small country. Tarawa is the capital. Kiribati had been called the Gilbert Islands.

Birthdays

Bill Cosby (born Philadelphia, Pennsylvania, 1938) is an actor and a comedian.

George Eastman (born Waterville, New York, 1854; died Rochester, New York, March 14, 1932) founded Eastman Kodak. He invented the Kodak camera in 1888. The flexible film allowed anyone to take pictures.

 Children could find out how a camera works.

Buckminster Fuller (born Milton, Massachusetts, 1895; died Los Angeles, California, July 1, 1983) was an architect and an educator. He held more than 2,000 patents, and he wrote more than twenty-five books. One of his most well-known ideas is that of a geodesic dome. Visit a Web site at: http://www.pbs.org/wnet/bucky/film.html.

Oscar Greeley Clenening Hammerstein II (born New York, New York, 1895; died Doylestown, Pennsylvania, August 23, 1960) wrote lyrics and scripts for some of Broadway's biggest hits. He received a Pulitzer, along with Richard Rodgers, for *Oklahoma!* They earned another, along with Joshua Logan, for *South Pacific.*

 Children could produce a part of one of his musicals.

Rick D. Husband (born Amarillo, Texas, 1957; died in the *Columbia* disaster, February 1, 2003) was an astronaut.

Julius Caesar (born 102 B.C.; died March 15, 44 B.C.) was a Roman dictator. He conquered other territories. He is famous for the saying *Veni, vidi, vici* (I came, I saw, I conquered). He was assassinated by a group of aristocrats on the Ides of March.

Henry David Thoreau (born Concord, Massachusetts, 1817; died Concord, Massachusetts, May 6, 1862) was a writer and a philosopher. His *Civil Disobedience* influenced Gandhi and Martin Luther King, Jr.

Andrew Wyeth (born Chadds Ford, Pennsylvania, 1917) is an artist. His paintings often show isolated objects. His father, N. C. Wyeth, was a noted illustrator, and his son Jamie is also an artist.

 Wyeth often works in egg tempera. Children could try the medium and compare it to watercolors.

Kristi Tsuya Yamaguchi (born Hayward, California, 1971) is an Olympic gold medal figure skater.

July

13 **Northwest Ordinance was created in 1787.** It provided for the government of the territory north of the Ohio River. However, it was the foundation for all other territorial governments. It established how the territory could eventually become a state, and it guaranteed basic freedoms for its inhabitants.

 Students could find out how a territory became a state.

Source of Mississippi River was found by Henry Schoolcraft in 1832.

Radio was patented by Guglielmo Marconi in 1898.

 Students could find out how the radio works. They could show the difference between AM and FM.

Walter Poensich swam from Cuba to Florida, a distance of 128.6 miles, in 1978.

World Cup Soccer began in 1930. Fourteen teams competed in Montevideo, Uruguay.

Birthdays

Marcia Brown (born Rochester, New York, 1918) is an author and illustrator. She has created more than thirty books. She has received three Caldecott Medals: *Cinderella* in 1955, *Once a Mouse* in 1962, and *Shadow* in 1983.

Ashley Bryan (born New York, New York, 1923) is a picture book author and illustrator. He wrote, among other works, *Lion and Ostrich Chicks and Other African Folktales,* 1986.

 Students could read and enjoy some of Bryan's work.

Harrison Ford (born Chicago, Illinois, 1942) is an actor.

July

14 **Bastille Day** is celebrated in France. In 1789 the Bastille (a prison) fell to the rioting people. It marked the beginning of the French Revolution.

 Charles Dickens's *A Tale of Two Cities* gives great insight into the French Revolution.

Japan opened its doors to the West in 1853.

Matterhorn was conquered by Edward Whymper and group in 1865. Seven reached the top, but four were killed on descent.

Caves of Lascaux opened in France in 1948 to tourists.

Birthdays

Gerald Rudolph Ford (born Leslie Lynch King, Jr., in Omaha, Nebraska, 1913) was the thirty-eighth president (1974–1977) of the United States. Prior to being president, Ford was in the navy during World War II and was awarded ten battle stars. He was a congressman for thirteen terms. He was the only president not elected to either the presidency or the vice presidency. He was speaker of the House when Nixon resigned from office. Because the vice president had resigned earlier, Ford became president. Visit a Web site at: http://www. whitehouse.gov/history/presidents/gf38.html.

 Students could research the presidential line of succession.

Roosevelt "Rosie" Grier (born Cuthbert, Georgia, 1932) is an actor and a former football player.

Woodrow Wilson "Woody" Guthrie (born Okemah, Oklahoma, 1912; died New York, New York, October 3, 1967) was a singer and a songwriter. One of his most famous works is "This Land Is Your Land."

Laura Joffe Numeroff (born Brooklyn, New York, 1953) is an author. She wrote *If You Give a Mouse a Cookie*. Visit a Web site at: http://www.lauranumeroff.com.

Peggy Parish (born Manning, South Carolina, 1927; died Manning, South Carolina, November 19, 1988) was an author. She is known for her Amelia Bedelia series. Visit a Web site at: http://www.edupaperback.org/authorbios/parish_peggy.html.

Isaac Bashevis Singer (born Radymin, Poland, 1904; died Surfside, Florida, July 24, 1991) was a writer. He immigrated to the United States in 1935. He wrote in Yiddish, and he won the 1978 Nobel Prize for literature.

 Students could read some of the parts of *Stories for Children,* published in 1934.

July

 15

St. Swithin's Day is remembered in England. Swithin died in the year 862. Rain on this day means forty more days of rain.

Commodore Perry arrived in Japan in 1893.

Denmark beat Italy in the first women's soccer championship in 1970.

Apollo-Soyuz **mission was successful in 1975.** The American *Apollo 18* crew docked and worked with the Soviet *Soyuz 19* craft.

Birthdays

Thomas Bulfinch (born Newton, Massachusetts, 1798; died 1867) was a mythologist. He wrote *Bulfinch's Mythology*.

 Students could create some plays about some of the myths.

Clement Clarke Moore (born New York, New York, 1779; died Newport, Rhode Island, July 10, 1863) wrote *A Visit from Saint Nicholas*. It was published without his permission in a newspaper on December 23, 1823.

 Students could celebrate a little Christmas in July and read *A Visit from Saint Nicholas*.

Rembrandt Van Rijn (born Leiden, Netherlands, 1606; died Amsterdam, Netherlands, October 4, 1669) was a painter. He was a prolific artist. About 600 paintings and 1,400 drawings have survived. He created about 100 self-portraits, giving us a great deal of information about himself. Visit a Web site at: http://www.artcyclopedia.com/artists/rembrandt_van_rijn.html.

 Students could make self-portraits.

July

Joan of Arc led the French army in the Battle of Orleans in 1429.

Bolivia celebrates La Paz day. The capital city was founded in 1548.

Father Junipero Serra founded the first mission in California in 1769.

District of Columbia was formed in 1790 when President Washington authorized the construction of a new capital. The U.S. government continued to work from Philadelphia until 1800.

 Students could find out how the land was acquired for the District of Columbia.

Atomic test bomb was activated in 1945.

 Students could find out how nuclear bombs work.

Apollo 11 **was launched in 1969.** It landed on the moon's surface four days later.

Shoemaker-Levy, a comet, began crashing into Jupiter in 1994. The comet had broken apart into about twelve pieces, and scientists observed the explosions through telescopes, including the Hubble telescope.

Dow Jones Industrial Average exceeded 8,000 for the first time in 1997.

Birthdays

Roald Amundsen (born near Oslo, Norway, 1872; died near the Arctic, June 18, 1928) was an explorer. He was the first person to travel from the Atlantic Ocean to the Pacific Ocean through the Northwest Passage. He traveled to the South Pole in 1911 and soared over the North Pole in a dirigible in 1926. He was attempting to rescue another Arctic expedition when the plane and all its passengers went down.

Joshua Reynolds (born Plympton, Devon, England, 1723; died London, England, February 23, 1792) was an artist. He was known primarily for his portraits of English nobility.

 Students could compare the works of Reynolds and Rembrandt.

Ida B. Wells (born Holly Springs, Mississippi, 1862; died Chicago, Illinois, March 25, 1931) was a journalist. The daughter of slaves, she fought against lynchings. Visit a Web site at: http://www.cr.nps.gov/nr/travel/civilrights/il2.htm.

July

Spain turned Florida over to the United States in 1821.

 Children could find out why the land changed hands.

Harvard Observatory in 1850 took the first photographs of a star. The scientists chose Vega for their subject.

Douglas "Wrong Way" Corrigan started a flight from New York in 1938. His destination was Los Angeles, California, but the next day he landed in Ireland.

Students could calculate how many miles off target he was.

Disneyland opened in 1955. Visit a Web site at: http://www.disney.com.

Arco, Idaho, in 1955 became the first city to be powered by nuclear energy.

Jim Ryun broke the mile record by running it in three minutes, fifty-one seconds in 1966.

Sebastian Coe set a new mile record in 1979 at three minutes, forty-nine seconds in Oslo, Norway.

Birthdays

John Jacob Astor (born Waldorf, Germany, 1763; died 1848) moved to New York City when he was twenty years old. He made quite a bit of money from a fur trading business. He invested most of his money in real estate in Manhattan Island. He became very wealthy.

James Cagney (born New York, New York, 1904; died Stanfordville, New York, March 30, 1986) was a dancer and a film star. His credits include more than sixty movies.

Elbridge Gerry (born Marblehead, Massachusetts, 1744; died Washington, DC, November 23, 1814) signed the Declaration of Independence. He was also the fifth vice president of the United States.

 The term gerrymandering relates to some of Gerry's activities. Students could find out what the term means.

Karla Kuskin (born New York, New York, 1932) has written and illustrated over forty books for children. *Soap Soup and Other Verses* was published in 1992.

Rosa Jackson Lumpkin (born Georgia, 1876; died 1991) lived to be 115 years old.

 July _____

 Rome suffered a fire in A.D. **64.**

United States and Canada in 1932 agreed on a treaty to complete the St. Lawrence Seaway.

First successful helicopter trip flew near Stratford, Connecticut, in 1940.

 Students could investigate how a helicopter works.

India launched its first satellite, the *Rohini I,* in 1980.

Videotapes of the sunken *Titanic* were shown in 1986.

Birthdays

Felicia Bond (born Yokohama, Japan, 1954) is an illustrator. She illustrated *If You Give a Mouse a Cookie.* Visit a Web site at http://www.eduplace.com/kids/hmr/mtai/bond.html.

John Glenn (born Cambridge, Ohio, 1921) was the first American astronaut to circle the Earth. He traveled into space again in 1998 as a payload specialist on a shuttle mission. He is also a former senator from Ohio.

 Children could research the training Glenn experienced to get ready for his first mission. Visit a Web site at: http://www.jsc.nasa.gov/bios/htmlbios/glenn-j.html.

Nelson Rolihlahla Mandela (born Mbhashe, South Africa, 1918) was the son of a tribal chief. He became a lawyer and then joined the African National Congress. He was incarcerated for almost twenty-eight years because he spoke out against apartheid. He was released in 1990, and he became president of South Africa in 1994. In 1993 he won the Nobel Peace Prize.

 Students could make a timeline of his life.

Yevgeny Aleksandrovich Yevtushenko (born Zimma, USSR, 1933) is a poet.

July

 19 **Lady Jane Grey was deposed as queen of England in 1553.** The fifteen-year-old queen reigned for only nine days.

 Students could research the historical circumstance behind her short reign.

Franco-Prussian War started in 1870.

Women's Rights Convention was held in Seneca Falls, New York, in 1848. The atendees debated voting rights, property rights, and the laws regarding divorce.

Wimbledon tennis championships were held for the first time in 1877.

Prime Minister Winston Churchill started his "V for Victory" campaign in 1941.

TWA showed the first in-flight movie in 1961.

Geraldine Ferraro became in 1984 the first woman U.S. vice presidential nominee. She ran with Walter Mondale for the Democrats. They were defeated by Ronald Reagan.

Birthdays

Samuel Colt (born Hartford, Connecticut, 1814; died Hartford, Connecticut, January 20, 1862) perfected and manufactured the first repeating pistol. His company, after his death, produced the six-shooters popular in the Old West.

 Students could find out how the repeating pistol works.

Edgar Degas (born Paris, France, 1834; died Paris, France, September 26, 1917) was an Impressionist painter. Visit a Web site at: http://www.artcyclopedia.com/artists/degas_edgar.html.

 Students could view some of his prints. What do they think of his style?

John Newbery (born Waltham St. Lawrence, England, 1713; died London, England, December 22, 1767) was the first publisher to be concerned about children's literature. The Newbery Awards were created in his memory. Visit a Web site at: http://www.ala.org/alsc/newbery.html.

July

 20 **Colombia celebrates its Independence Day.** It declared its autonomy from Spain in 1810. Bogota is the capital of this country, located on the northwest coast of South America. It exports coffee, bananas, and petroleum.

Students could find out how bananas are grown and harvested. They could also make banana pudding.

Neil Armstrong and Edwin Eugene "Buzz" Aldrin landed the lunar module *Eagle* on the moon's surface in 1969. Armstrong walked on the moon first. The first human to do so, he stated, "That's one small step for a man, one giant leap for mankind." The two men walked on the moon for over two hours. Michael Collins stayed aboard the *Apollo XI*'s service module, *Columbia*.

 Students could try to figure out how Armstrong and Aldrin felt.

***Viking I* landed on Mars in 1976.**

Birthdays

Sir Edmund Percival Hillary (born Auckland, New Zealand, 1919) is an explorer. He and Tenzing Norgay on May 29, 1953, became the first people to reach the summit of Mount Everest.

 Students could determine what gear is necessary for such climbs.

July

21 **Gold was discovered in Alaska in 1902.**

Belgium celebrates National Day. Brussels is the capital of this country, located in northwestern Europe. It is about the size of the state of Maryland.

 Belgium's borders have shifted over the centuries. Students could make a series of maps showing the differences in the country.

Jesse James carried out his first bank robbery in 1873.

National Women's Hall of Fame opened in Seneca Falls, New York, in 1979. The site of the Women's Rights Convention in 1848, the hall honors many women.

 Students could find out who has been inducted. They could list future possible inductees. Visit a Web site at: http://www.greatwomen.org/home.php.

Birthdays

Frances Folsom Cleveland (born Buffalo, New York, 1864; died Baltimore, Maryland, October 29, 1947) was the wife of Grover Cleveland, the twenty-second and twenty-fourth president of the United States. She married him during his first term in office. He was twenty-eight years older than her. The Baby Ruth candy bar was named after their daughter. Cleveland died in 1908. The former first lady married Thomas J. Preston, Jr., in 1913. Visit a Web site at: http://www.whitehouse.gov/history/firstladies/fc2224.html.

 Children could eat small Baby Ruth candy bars and learn more about Frances Cleveland's life.

Ernest Hemingway (born Oak Park, Illinois, 1899; died Ketchum, Idaho, July 2, 1961) was a writer. Two of his most famous works are *The Old Man and the Sea* and *A Farewell to Arms*. He won the Nobel Prize for literature in 1954.

Isaac Stern (born Kreminiecz, USSR, 1920; died New York, New York, September 22, 2001) was a violinist.

Robin Williams (born Chicago, Illinois, 1952) is an actor and a comedian.

 July

 22 **Pied Piper of Hamelin, according to legend, piped the rats out of the town and into the river in 1376.** When the people refused to pay him, he piped the children out of town as well. The children were never seen again.

 Children could read one of the many versions of this tale.

Roanoke, North Carolina, colony was started in 1587.

Birthdays

Stephen Vincent Benet (born Bethlehem, Pennsylvania, 1898; did March 13, 1943) was a writer. He received a Pulitzer for *John Brown's Body,* a long poem published in 1928. He won another Pulitzer for *Western Star,* printed in 1943. He also wrote short stories and novels.

Margery Williams Bianco (born London, England, 1881; died New York, New York, September 4, 1944) was an author. She wrote, using the pen name Mary Williams, *The Velveteen Rabbit.*

Alexander Calder (born Philadelphia, Pennsylvania, 1898; died New York, New York, November 11, 1976) was an artist known for making enchanting mobiles.

 Students could make mobiles.

S. E. Hinton (born Tulsa, Oklahoma, 1948) is an author. One of her books is *The Outsiders.* Visit a Web site at: http://www.sehinton.com.

Emma Lazarus (born New York, New York, 1849; died New York, New York, November 19, 1887) wrote poetry. Part of her "The New Colossus" was written on the base of the Statue of Liberty.

Gregor Mendel (born Heinzendorf, Austria, 1822; died Brunn, Austria, January 6, 1884) was a monk who pioneered work in genetics. In 1856 he started experiments with pea plants in the monastery vegetable garden. He continued breeding and crossbreeding the plants for a number of years. He kept notes. His work was not seen until after his death.

Reverend William Archibald Spooner (born London, England, 1844; died Oxford, England, August 29, 1930) frequently confused parts of words. These led to spoonerisms. For example, he might say pony pest card, instead of penny post card.

 Children could make up their own spoonerisms. Visit a Web site at: http://www. fun-with-words.com/spoonerisms.html.

July

23 **Egypt celebrates its Anniversary of the Revolution.** In 1952 the military led a revolution against the monarchy and established a republic.

First swimming school was created in Boston, Massachusetts, in 1827. John Adams and John James Audubon were among its first pupils.

Leo the Lion is the astrological sign for July 23 through August 22.

Ice cream cone was invented by Charles Merchas in St. Louis, Missouri, in 1904.

 Students could enjoy small ice cream cones.

Eileen Collins became the first woman commander of a space vehicle, *Columbia,* in 1999. Visit a Web site at: http://www.jsc.nasa.gov/bios/htmlbios/collins.html.

Birthdays

Patricia Coombs (born Los Angeles, California, 1926) is an author. She writes the Dorrie series.

Don Drysdale (born Van Nuys, California, 1936; died Montreal, Canada, July 3, 1993) was a famous baseball pitcher and a broadcast announcer. He became a member of the Baseball Hall of Fame in 1984.

 Students could find out more about his baseball career.

Anthony M. Kennedy (born Sacramento, California, 1936) is an associate justice of the Supreme Court.

 Children could investigate the career of Kennedy before he became a Supreme Court justice.

Robert Quackenbush (born Hollywood, California, 1929) is an author and illustrator. He wrote the Miss Mallard series. Visit a Web site at: http://www.rquackenbush.com.

Haile Selassie (born Tafari Makonnen in Harer, Ethiopia, 1892; died August 27, 1975) was emperor of Ethiopia from 1930 until a military coup deposed him in 1974. He worked to improve conditions in his country.

July

 Cousins Day was created by Claudia A. Evart.

 Children could write postcards to their cousins.

Detroit was founded in 1701. Antoine de la Mothe Cadillac arrived at the site of present-day Detroit. Fort Pontchartrain du Detroit was the first construction at the site.

 Students could find out more about the city and then plan a tour of it.

Birthdays

Simon Bolivar (born Caracas, Venezuela, 1783; died Santa Marta, Colombia, December 17, 1830) was a South American patriot, often known as "The Liberator."

Barry Bonds (born Riverside, California, 1964) is a baseball player.

Alexandre Dumas (born Villers-Cotterets, France, 1802; died near Dieppe, France, December 5, 1870) wrote *The Count of Monte Cristo* and *The Three Musketeers.*

 Children could read portions of his works.

Amelia Earhart (born Atchison, Kansas, 1898; died 1937?) was a famous aviator. In 1932 she became the first woman to fly solo across the Atlantic Ocean. The trip took thirteen hours and thirty minutes. She flew from Hawaii to California in 1935.

July

25 **Louis Bleriot became the first person to fly a plane across the English Channel.** He left Les Baraques, France, in 1909 and landed in Dover, England.

 The Chunnel, a tunnel between England and France, opened not long ago. Children could find out more about the Chunnel.

Puerto Rico celebrates Constitution Day. Also called Commonwealth Day, the country adopted its constitution in 1952.

Andrea Doria **sank after colliding with a Swedish liner, the** *Stockholm,* **in 1956.** Visit a Web site at: http://www.andreadoria.org.

 Students could find out more about the ship and its passengers.

Vostok, Antarctica, experienced in 1983 the lowest temperature ever recorded, −128.6 degrees Fahrenheit.

Birthdays

Thomas Eakins (born Philadelphia, Pennsylvania, 1844; died Philadelphia, Pennsylvania, June 25, 1916) was a painter and a sculptor. His works were extremely realistic. Visit a Web site at: http://www.artcyclopedia.com/artists/eakins_thomas.html.

 Students could look at some of Eakins's work. Then they could try to draw an athletic event.

Anna Tuthill Symmes Harrison (born Morristown, New Jersey, 1775; died North Bend, Ohio, February 25, 1864) was the wife of William Henry Harrison, the ninth president of the United States. She never lived in the White House. She was too ill to be at his inauguration, and he contracted pneumonia at his swearing in ceremony. He died within a month of his inauguration. She outlived her husband by twenty-three years. Visit a Web site at: http://www.whitehouse.gov/history/firstladies/ah9.html.

Henry Knox (born Boston, Massachusetts, 1750; died October 25, 1806) was a general during the Revolutionary War. Knox was responsible for Washington's troops crossing the Delaware in 1776. Before the war he was a bookseller. After the war, Washington appointed Knox to be secretary of war.

July

26 **Netherlands celebrates its Independence Day of 1581.**

Cuba celebrates National Rebellion Day of 1953.

Liberia celebrates its Independence Day. In 1816 freed slaves settled in a town in Africa later named Monrovia. The colony grew and became the first republic in Africa in 1847.

Students could find out more about the development of Liberia.

Maldives celebrates its Independence Day. Great Britain gave up control of the coral islands in 1965. About 1,200 islands make up this country located in the Indian Ocean. Male is the capital.

Book printed in and about Esperanto was published for the first time in 1887. Visit a Web site at: http://ttt.esperanto.org.

 Students could find out more about Esperanto.

Apollo 15 **was launched in 1971.** Astronauts David Scott and James Irwin landed safely on the moon and used a four-wheeled vehicle, *Rover 1,* to travel across the surface. Alfred Worden remained in the command module, *Endeavor.*

New York became the eleventh state of the United States by ratifying the Constitution in 1788. Giovanni de Verrazano entered New York Bay in 1524. In 1609 Henry Hudson explored the area. Peter Minuit bought Manhattan Island from the Indians in 1625 and named the colony New Amsterdam. In 1664 the British attacked and won the territory. They renamed the land New York, after the Duke of York. He eventually became James II. The state's nickname is the Empire State, and the capital is Albany. New York, New York continues to be a leading power in commerce and industry. Contact: (800) 225-5697. Visit an Internet site at: http://www.50states.com/newyork.htm.

 Students could speculate as to what would have happened if New Amsterdam had remained under Dutch control.

Birthdays

George Catlin (born Wilkes-Barre, Pennsylvania, 1796; died Jersey City, New Jersey, December 23, 1872) was an artist. He is most known for his studies of Native Americans.

Aldous Huxley (born Godalming, Surrey, England, 1894; died Los Angeles, California, November 22, 1963) was a writer and a philosopher. One of his most well-known works is *Brave New World.*

George Bernard Shaw (born Dublin, Ireland, 1856; died Ayot St. Lawrence, England, November 2, 1950) was a playwright.

July

Department of State, under the name Department of Foreign Affairs, was created by Congress in 1789. Visit a Web site at: http://www.state.gov.

 Children could make a visual representation of what the State Department does.

Belarus celebrates its Independence Day. It left the Union of Soviet Socialist Republics in 1991. Minsk is the capital, and it exports chemicals and machinery. It has maintained close ties with Russia.

Korean War ended in 1953 when an armistice was signed in Panmunjon, Korea. Both sides claimed victory in a war that lasted for slightly over three years.

 Children could research the causes of the Korean War and what brought about its end.

Bugs Bunny appeared for the first time in a 1940 cartoon, "A Wild Hare."

Birthdays

Leo Durocher (born West Springfield, Massachusetts, 1906; died Palm Springs, California, October 7, 1991) was a famous baseball player and manager.

 Children could discuss his statement, "Nice guys finish last."

Peggy Gale Fleming (born San Jose, California, 1948) is an Olympic gold medal ice skater and a television commentator.

July

28 **Peru celebrates its Independence Day.** It gained its freedom from Spain in 1824. Lima is the capital of this fairly large country in South America.

 The Incas once controlled portions of what is now Peru. Children could find out more about the Incas and the Spanish conquistadors.

The Fourteenth Amendment to the Constitution was adopted in 1868. It settled issues regarding former slaves and the Civil War.

Ranger 7 **sent back over four thousand pictures of the moon in 1964.**

Oil was pumped through the Alaska Pipeline for the first time in 1977.

Birthdays

Natalie Babbitt (born Dayton, Ohio, 1932) is a children's author. She won the 1970 Newbery Honor Award for *Kneeknock Rise*. Visit a Web site at: http://www.ipl.org/youth/askauthor/babbitt.html.

 Children could read some of her work. *Tuck Everlasting* is excellent literature.

Bill Bradley (born Crystal City, Missouri, 1943) is a former basketball player and a former senator.

Jim Davis (born Marion, Indiana, 1945) is a cartoonist who created Garfield.

Thomas Heyward (born 1746; died March 6, 1809) signed the Declaration of Independence. He was captured by the British, and he was imprisoned until 1781.

Jacqueline Bouvier Kennedy Onassis (born Southampton, New York, 1929; died New York, New York, May 19, 1994) was the wife of John Kennedy, thirty-fourth president of the United States. She brought back an elegance to the White House, and she became very popular throughout the world. After Kennedy was assassinated, she and their two children moved to New York City. In 1968 she married Aristotle Onassis, a Greek shipping tycoon. He died in 1975. Visit a Web site at: http://www.whitehouse.gov/history/firstladies/jk35.html.

 Jacqueline Kennedy Onassis worked before her first marriage and after her second marriage. Children could investigate all her careers.

Beatrix Potter (born London, England, 1866; died Sawrey, Lancashire, England, December 22, 1943) was an author. She wrote the Peter Rabbit books.

July

29

Norway celebrates St. Olaf's Day. King Olaf died in battle at Stiklestad in 1030. He became the country's patron saint in 1164. Pageants and bonfires are part of the celebration.

Hurricane sank ten Spanish treasure galleons off the coast of Florida in 1715.

 Children could speculate as to the contents of those ships. They could find out whether those ships were ever salvaged.

Hawaii's first sugar plantation was started in 1835.

Transcontinental telephone link was connected in 1914 between New York City and San Francisco.

President Eisenhower signed the National Aeronautics and Space Administration (NASA) Act of 1958.

Pioneer 7 **sent back to Earth images of Saturn and its rings in 1978.**

Birthdays

Charles William Beebe (born Brooklyn, New York, 1877; died June 4, 1962) was a naturalist and an adventurer. He headed expeditions to the Galapagos Islands, Borneo, and other places. He wrote approximately 300 articles and books. One of the books was *Jungle Days,* published in 1925.

 Children could learn more about the Galapagos Islands.

Peter Jennings (born Toronto, Ontario, Canada, 1938) is a journalist.

Alice Hathaway Lee Roosevelt (born Chestnut Hill, Massachusetts, 1861; died February 14, 1884) was the first wife of Theodore Roosevelt, twenty-sixth president of the United States. They were married only about three years when she died shortly after giving birth to their daughter, Alice.

 The daughter, Alice, liked a particular color. It even carries her name. The children could discover the name of that color.

July

30

Vanuatu celebrates its Independence Day. It gained its freedom from France and Great Britain in 1980. This group of twelve larger islands and sixty smaller islands was called the New Hebrides. The country is located in the Pacific Ocean, and Port Vila is the capital. It retained membership in the British Commonwealth.

Children could find out Vanuatu's role during World War II.

WAVES (Women Accepted for Volunteer Emergency Service) was created in 1942. This organization was part of the navy. In 1948 women were incorporated into the navy, and the term WAVES was retired.

Birthdays

Emily Brontë (born Thornton, Yorkshire, England, 1818; died Haworth, Yorkshire, England, December 19, 1848) was an author. She wrote *Wuthering Heights.*

Henry Ford (born Dearborn Township, Michigan, 1863; died Dearborn Township, Michigan, April 7, 1947) created the assembly line for making cars. He became wealthy from selling so many cars.

Charles Dillon "Casey" Stengel (born Kansas City, Missouri, 1891; died Glendale, California, September 29, 1975) was a baseball player from 1912 to 1915. However, he is best known as being a colorful and successful baseball manager. He was elected to the Baseball Hall of Fame in 1966.

 Students could locate statistics on his success.

Vladimir Kosma Zworykin (born Murom, Russia, 1889; died July 29, 1982) came to the United States in 1919. In 1920 he headed a Westinghouse Electric Company team and developed the television camera and picture tube. He was also very important in research leading to the electron microscope.

 Children certainly enjoy television. They could record how much television they watch in a week.

 July

 31

England attacked the Spanish Armada in 1588.

Trinidad was sighted by Christopher Columbus in 1498.

Patent Office began operations in 1790. The first patent was granted to Samuel Hopkins for a potash process.

 Students could find out how patents are filed.

Arnette Hubbard became the first woman president of the American Bar Association in 1981.

 Students could interview a lawyer to understand more about the American Bar Association.

David R. Scott and James B. Irwin drove a vehicle on the moon in 1971.

U.S. men's gymnastics team won a gold medal in the 1984 Summer Olympics.

MTV debuted on cable television in 1981.

Birthdays

Lynne Reid Banks (born London, England, 1929) is a children's author. She wrote, among other works, *The Indian in the Cupboard,* published in 1980.

 Children could read and enjoy some of her work.

J(oanne) K(athleen) Rowling (born Bristol, England, 1965) is the author of the Harry Potter series. Harry Potter was also born on this day. Visit a Web site at: http://www.scholastic.com/harrypotter/home.asp.

August

August is the eighth month of the year. However, prior to Augustus, it was the sixth month. Romans called the month *Sixtilis,* meaning "sixth." However, it was given a new name to honor Augustus. The Romans also took away a day from February and gave it to August. Birthstones for August are the sardonyx and the peridot. August flowers are the gladiolus and the poppy.

Month-Long Activities

Children's Vision and Learning Month reminds children and adults to have their vision examined before the start of another school year. Contact: American Foundation for Vision Awareness, 243 North Lindbergh Boulevard, St. Louis, Missouri 63141. Telephone: (800) 927-AFVA.

Special Days

National Mustard Day is celebrated the first Saturday of August. Contact: Mount Horeb Mustard Museum, 109 East Main Street, Mount Horeb, Wisconsin 53572. Telephone: (608) 437-3986. E-mail: mustard1@ix.netcom.com.

August

1

Joseph Priestle discovered oxygen in 1774.

U.S. Customs was created in 1789.

Colorado became the thirty-eighth state of the United States in 1876. Its nickname is the Centennial State, because it became a part of the country 100 years after the revolution. Its name comes from a Spanish phrase meaning the color red. People were living in the Mesa Verde cliff dwellings around 1200. When gold was discovered in 1858, the local phrase became "Pike's Peak or Bust." Denver is the state capital, and tourism is one of the most important economic factors. Contact: (800) 433-2656. Visit an Internet site at: http://www.50states.com/colorado.htm.

 Students could examine Colorado's state flag and learn what the parts and colors mean.

Shredded wheat was patented in 1892.

Army Air Force was created in 1907.

Switzerland celebrates its Confederation Day of 1291. Parades and fireworks mark the day.

Trinidad and Tobago celebrate Emancipation Day. In 1834 Britain abolished slavery in all its colonies.

People's Republic of Benin celebrates a national day. The country announced its independence from France in 1960. Located on the western coast of Africa, the land was the site of a wealthy kingdom in the 1300s. Portuguese explorers came about 1485. In 1893 the French took control. Porto-Novo is the capital.

Hawaii Volcanoes National Park was established in 1916. The area includes the active volcanoes Kilauea and Mauna Loa. Contact: Hawaii Volcanoes National Park, Hawaii 96718. Visit a Web site at: http://www.nps.gov/havo.

Haleakala National Park was created in 1916. A vast, extinct volcano crater on Maui is the focus of this park. Contact: Haleakala National Park, PO Box 369, Makawao, Hawaii 96768. Visit a Web site at: http://www.nps.gov/hale.

Calamity Jane, born Martha Jane Cannary Burke, died in Terry, South Dakota in 1903. Her exact date of birth is not known.

 Students could check out her life and find out which stories were true and which were not.

Birthdays

William Clark (born Caroline County, Virginia, 1770; died St. Louis, Missouri, September 1, 1838) was an explorer. Meriwether Lewis and he headed the expedition into the Louisiana Purchase. They traveled from 1804 to 1806. Later he became governor of the Missouri Territory.

Gail Gibbons (born Oak Park, Illinois, 1944) is a children's author and illustrator. She has written over 100 books, including *Tell Me, Tree*. Visit a Web site at: http://www.gailgibbons.com.

Francis Scott Key (born Frederick County, Maryland, 1779; died Baltimore, Maryland, January 11, 1843) was a lawyer and a poet. He wrote *The Star-Spangled Banner* in 1814 after watching the British bombard Fort McHenry.

Herman Melville (born New York, New York, 1819; died New York, New York, September 28, 1891) was a novelist. One of his best-known works is *Moby Dick*.

 Students could read passages from *Moby Dick*.

Maria Mitchell (born Nantucket, Massachusetts, 1818; died Lynn, Massachusetts, June 28, 1889) was the first woman professional astronomer. She discovered a comet in 1847, and she became a professor of astronomy at Vassar College.

 August

2 **Census was taken in the United States for the first time in 1790.**

 Students could take a mock census in their classrooms.

Declaration of Independence was officially signed in 1776. Most people believe the Declaration was signed July 4; however, only John Hancock and Charles Thompson signed a draft then. Fifty delegates were at the official signing on August 2. Five more people signed the document before the end of the year. One more person signed it the next year.

William Still created the Underground Railroad in 1850.

 Students could trace the various routes of the Underground Railroad. They could learn about the stations and the risks everyone faced. Doreen Rappaport's *Escape from Slavery: Five Journeys to Freedom* is good reading.

Lincoln penny was issued in 1909.

Students could research numismatics.

Birthdays

James Arthur Baldwin (born New York, New York, 1924; died Saint Paul-de-Vence, France, November 30, 1987) was a noted writer. One of his most famous works is *Go Tell It on the Mountain.*

Holling C. Holling (born Holling Allison Clancy in Holling Corners, Michigan, died September 7, 1973) was a children's author and illustrator. One of his most famous books is *Minn of the Mississippi.*

James Howe (born Oneida, New York, 1946) is a children's author. He wrote the Bunnicula series and other books, including *There's a Monster Under My Bed.* Visit a Web site at: http://www.bcplonline.org/kidspage/kids_howe.html.

Pierre Charles L'Enfant (born Paris, France, 1754; died Prince Georges County, Maryland, June 14, 1825) was an American Revolution hero and an architect. He drew up the plans for Washington, DC.

Smokey Bear was "born" in 1944. The U.S. Forest Service created Smokey to teach children about preventing forest fires.

Augustust

3

Columbus left Palos, Spain, in 1492 with his three ships the *Nina,* the *Pinta,* and the *Santa Maria.* He commanded a crew of ninety men.

Robert de La Salle in 1678 built the *Griffon,* the first ship made in America.

Congress passed the first law limiting immigration in 1882.

 Students could locate and study today's laws regarding immigration.

Aerial crop dusting was achieved for the first time in 1921 in Troy, Ohio. Farmers were trying to get rid of caterpillars.

VTOL (vertical take-off and land) craft was demonstrated for the first time in 1954.

 Students could learn more about the VTOL.

Niger celebrates its Independence Day. France relinquished control of the country in 1960. The country is mostly covered with deserts and mountains. Niamey is the capital.

Birthdays

Margaret "Maggie" Kuhn (born Buffalo, New York, 1905; died Philadelphia, Pennsylvania, April 22, 1995) created the Gray Panthers. She did not want to retire at the age of sixty-five, but current laws gave her no choice. She founded the group to fight age discrimination. Laws regarding mandatory retirement changed as a result of her activities.

 Students could see if the Gray Panthers still exist today.

Elisha Graves Otis (born Halifax, Vermont, 1811; died Yonkers, New York, April 8, 1861) was an inventor. He created the first elevator with an automatic safety device. He showed the safety of the elevator in 1854, but elevators were not used extensively until skyscrapers were built.

Ernie Pyle (born Dana, Indiana, 1900; died Ie Shima, April 18, 1945) was a journalist and war correspondent. He won a Pulitzer Prize in 1944 for his reports on the bombings in London and other war-related stories. He was killed while reporting about the Pacific battles.

August

 4 **Coast Guard was founded in 1790.**

 Students could talk to a member of the Coast Guard. They could learn the purposes of the organization.

Virgin Islands were bought by the United States from Denmark in 1917.

 Students could find out why the islands were purchased.

Bahamas celebrates Emancipation Day.

Birthdays

Yasser Arafat (born Jerusalem, 1929) is president of the Palestinian National Authority.

Louis Armstrong (born New Orleans, Louisiana, 1901; died New York, New York, 1971) was an influential jazz musician. Also called Satchmo, he played the trumpet. He appeared in several movies, including *Hello, Dolly.*

 Children could listen to some of his music. They may want to read Patricia McKissack's *Louis Armstrong: Jazz Musician.*

Roger Clemens (born Dayton, Ohio, 1962) is a former baseball player.

Percy Bysshe Shelley (born Sussex, England, 1792; died near Leghorn, Italy, July 8, 1822) was a lyric poet. One of his best-known works is *Prometheus Unbound.*

Raoul Wallenberg (born Stockholm, Sweden, 1912; died 1947) was an architect. However, he is most remembered for saving 100,000 Jews from Nazi extermination during World War II. Wallenberg was arrested by the Soviets in Hungary in 1945. He died in prison on a day not officially disclosed.

August

 5 **Sir Humphrey Gilbert landed on Newfoundland in 1583 and claimed the land around St. John's harbor for England.** His ship, the *Squirrel,* sank in a storm near the Azores while he was trying to return to England.

 Students could figure out how historians know what he did if his ship sank before he reached England.

United States levied the first income tax in 1862. Any income over $800 was taxed at three percent.

 Students could convert $800 back then into today's dollars.

Joan Benoit in 1984 won the first Olympic gold medal for the United States in the women's marathon. Her time was two hours, twenty-four minutes, fifty-two seconds.

First traffic light in the United States was installed in Cleveland, Ohio, in 1914.

Birthdays

Neil Alden Armstrong (born Wapakoneta, Ohio, 1930) is a former astronaut and the first person to walk on the moon.

Thomas Lynch, Jr. (born Prince George's Parish, South Carolina, 1749; died 1779) signed the Declaration of Independence. He represented South Carolina. He was lost at sea with the exact date unknown.

Guy de Maupassant (born Normandy, France, 1850; died Paris, France, July 6, 1893) was a famous short story writer. He wrote at least 250 stories and several novels.

 Students could read and discuss *The Diamond Necklace.*

ugust

6 **Sandwich was invented in 1762 by John Montague, the fourth Earl of Sandwich.**

Constitutional Convention met from August 6 to September 10, 1787. This meeting was called the "Great Debate," and the purpose was to draft a constitution.

 Children could read *Shh! We're Writing the Constitution,* written by Jean Fritz.

Jamaica celebrates its Independence Day. It became free from Great Britain in 1962. The official day of celebration is the first Monday in August.

Bolivia celebrates its Independence Day. It gained its freedom from Spain in 1825. Bolivia is a landlocked country in South America. La Paz is the capital, and at one time the country was under Inca control. Although the country is presently bigger than the state of Texas, it was once much larger. Parts of the country were sold, and parts were given away as spoils of war. Its natural resources include silver, tin, oil, and natural gas.

Gertrude Ederle in 1926 became the first woman to swim the English Channel. She swam for fourteen hours and thirty-one minutes.

Atomic bomb was dropped on Hiroshima in 1945. The *Enola Gay,* a B-29 bomber, dropped the bomb that killed 70,000 to 80,000 people.

Voting Rights Act of 1965 was signed by President Lyndon Johnson. It outlawed any ways that might keep people from voting. Literacy tests were among the items made illegal.

Birthdays

Frank Asch (born Somerville, New Jersey, 1946) is a children's author and illustrator. He is known for his Moonbear series. Visit a Web site at: http://www.frankasch.com/about_asch.html.

Lucille Ball (born Celeron, New York, 1911; died Los Angeles, California, April 26, 1989) was an actress. She is famous for the series *I Love Lucy.*

 Children could compare and contrast *I Love Lucy* to today's comedy shows.

Barbara Cooney (born Brooklyn, New York, 1917; died Portland, Maine, March 14, 2000) was a children's author and illustrator. Her *Chanticleer and the Fox* won the 1959 Caldecott Medal, and her *Ox-cart Man* won the 1980 Caldecott Medal. Visit a Web site at: http://www.ortakales.com/illustrators/cooney.html.

Sir Alexander Fleming (born Lochfield, Scotland, 1881; died London, England, March 11, 1955) was a bacteriologist. He discovered penicillin and won a 1954 Nobel Prize.

Edith Kermit Carow Roosevelt (born Norwich, Connecticut, 1861; died Sagamore Hill, New York, September 30, 1948) was the second wife of Theodore Roosevelt, twenty-sixth president of the United States. They had five children, and he also had a daughter by his first marriage. Visit a Web site at: http://www.whitehouse.gov/history/firstladies/er26.html.

 Children could investigate what the Roosevelt children did while they were living in the White House. Did they really take a pony upstairs?

Alfred, Lord Tennyson (born Somersby, Lincolnshire, England, 1899; died Aldworth, England, October 6, 1892) was a poet.

August

7 | **Purple Heart was created by General George Washington in 1782 to be the Badge of Military Merit.** Experts believe only three were awarded during the Revolutionary War. The badge was made of purple cloth with silver braided trim.

U.S. War Department was created in 1789 by Congress. It was later renamed the Department of Defense.

Explorer VI **transmitted in 1959 the first photographs of Earth taken from space.**

Birthdays

Ralph Johnson Bunche (born Detroit, Michigan, 1904; died New York, New York, December 9, 1971) was a diplomat and United Nations representative. The grandson of a former slave, he joined the United Nations in 1947. He became an undersecretary in 1955. He won the 1950 Nobel Peace Prize for his work with Arabs and Jews.

 Students could learn about the work that earned him the Nobel Prize.

Betsy Byars (born Charlotte, North Carolina, 1928) is a children's author. She wrote, among other works, *Cracker Jackson,* 1985.

 Students could read and enjoy some of her work.

Nathaniel Greene (born Patowomut, Rhode Island, 1742; died Savannah, Georgia, June 19, 1786) was a general during the Revolutionary War.

Mata Hari (born Margaretha Gertrud Zelle in Leeuswarden, Netherlands, 1876; executed Vincennes, France, October 15, 1917) was a spy, perhaps a double agent, during World War I.

Rudolf C. Ising (born Kansas City, Missouri, 1903; died Newport Beach, California, July 18, 1992) created, along with Hugh Harmon, *Looney Tunes* and *Merrie Melodies.* He won an Academy Award for *Milky Way,* a cartoon about three kittens, in 1948.

 Students could make flip books.

Louis Seymour Bazett Leakey (born Kabete, Kenya, 1903; died 1972) was an anthropologist. He and his wife Mary devoted their lives to finding out more about early human life in eastern Africa.

Maia Wojciechowska (born Warsaw, Poland, 1927) is an author. She wrote *Shadow of a Bull,* the 1965 Newbery Medal winner.

August

 8

Mimeography was patented by Thomas Edison in 1876.

Refrigerator was patented in 1899.

 Students could conduct experiments to learn about the importance of refrigeration. They could leave certain foods, like milk, out of the refrigerator.

Venus 2 **was launched in 1978.** The spacecraft, carrying five probes, traveled to Venus.

Lynne Cox in 1897 became the first person to swim from the United States to Russia across the Bering Strait.

 Students could find out how far she had to swim. What were the conditions?

Genesis **was launched in 2001.** The space vehicle will travel toward the sun and gather particles on its way. A capsule will return in September 2004 with some of the samples.

Birthdays

Matthew A. Henson (born Charles County, Maryland, 1866; died New York, New York, March 9, 1955) was an explorer. He was hired to be Robert E. Peary's valet. The two explored the Arctic region. He described his adventures in *A Negro Explorer at the North Pole.*

 Students could learn more about Henson's life and why he chose to go to the Arctic.

Odie ("born" 1978) is Garfield (the Cat)'s friend. Visit a Web site at: http://www.garfield.com.

Esther Williams (born Los Angeles, California, 1923) is a former swimmer and actress.

August

 9

Webster-Ashburton Treaty was finalized in 1842. U.S. Secretary of State Daniel Webster and British representative Lord Ashburton negotiated the eastern border between the United States and Canada.

Stourbridge Lion was the first steam locomotive to run in 1829.

Escalator was patented in 1859.

Lassen Volcanic National Park was created in California in 1916. Lassen Peak and Cinder Cone National Monument, founded in 1907, and other lands were united to form one national park. The park contains all four types of volcanoes. Contact: Cinder Cone National Monument, Mineral, California 06063. Visit a Web site at: http://www.nps.gov/lavo.

 Students could illustrate the four kinds of volcanoes.

Atomic bomb was dropped on Nagasaki in 1945. Approximately 70,000 people died, and more than half of the city lay in ruins.

Richard Nixon resigned from office in 1974. He was about to be impeached for his part in the Watergate scandals.

Gerald Ford was sworn in as the thirty-eighth president in 1974.

Jesse Owens won four gold medals in the 1936 Olympic Games.

Singapore celebrates its Independence Day of 1965. It left Malaysia in 1963 to become its own country. Singapore is not quite four times the size of Washington, DC.

Birthdays

Jose Aruego (born 1932) is a children's author and illustrator.

 Students could read and enjoy some of his work, especially *Mitchel Is Moving.*

Whitney Houston (born Newark, New Jersey, 1963) is a singer.

Patricia McKissack (born Nashville, Tennessee, 1944) is a children's author. She wrote *The Dark-Thirty: Southern Tales of the Supernatural* in 1992. It was a Newbery Honor Book.

Seymour Simon (born New York, New York, 1931) is a children's author. He has written many nonfiction books about many different subjects. He books regarding space show thoughtful research.

 Students could read and enjoy some of his work.

P. L. Travers (born Maryborough, Queensland, Australia, 1899; died London, England, April 23, 1966) was an author. She wrote the Mary Poppins series.

ugust

10 **Ecuador celebrates its Independence Day.** It declared its autonomy from Spain in 1809. Quito is the capital.

"E Pluribus Unum" became the U.S. motto in 1776. It means "Out of many, one."

Missouri became the twenty-fourth state of the United States in 1821. Its name comes from the Iliniwek word *missouri,* meaning "owner of big canoes." The state's nickname is the "Show-Me State," and Jefferson City is the capital. It ranks nineteenth in area and sixteenth in population. St. Louis, a large Missouri city, was once the Gateway to the West. The Gateway Arch, a reminder of that role, was built in 1964 and stands 630 feet high. The Pony Express ran from Missouri to California. Contact: (800) 877-1234. Visit an Internet site at: http://www.50states.com/missouri.htm.

 Students could find out why Missouri is called the "Show-Me State."

Smithsonian Institute was created in 1846. Visit a Web site at: http://www.si.edu.

 Students could chart the various parts of the Smithsonian.

Japan surrendered unconditionally to the Allies in 1945.

Birthdays

Herbert Clark Hoover (born West Branch, Iowa, 1874; died New York, New York, October 20, 1964) was the thirty-first president (1929–1933) of the United States. His parents died when he was eight years old, and he was raised by Quaker relatives. He became a mining engineer and was a millionaire by age forty. During World War I he saved Americans remaining in Europe and distributed food to needy people in Belgium. His political slogan during his campaign was a "chicken in every pot." The Great Depression took place during his administration, but he felt government should not take responsibility for what was happening. People who lost their homes built shack cities and called them Hoovervilles. He was soundly defeated by Franklin Roosevelt and was not elected to a second term. He lived another thirty years after his presidency. Visit a Web site at: http://www.whitehouse.gov/history/presidents/hh31.html.

 Children could watch a portion of *Annie* to learn more about the conditions during the Depression.

August

 Chad celebrates its Independence Day from France. It became a sovereign country in 1962. It is a landlocked country in Africa, and N'Djamena is the capital. Its arid climate allows some farming and some pastoral activity. It has huge oil reserves.

 Students could make a map of Chad and its neighbors.

Babe Ruth hit his 500th home run in 1929.

Birthdays

David R. Atchison (born Frogtown, Kentucky, 1807; died Gower, Missouri, January 26, 1886) was president of the United States for one day, Sunday, March 4, 1849.

 Students could research the circumstances behind this unusual event. They could visit a Web site at: http://www.senate.gov/learning/min_2j.html.

Carrie Jacobs Bond (born Janesville, Wisconsin, 1862; died Hollywood, California, December 28, 1946) was a composer of songs and movie scores. One of her most famous songs is *I Love You Truly.*

Joanna Cole (born Newark, New Jersey, 1944) is a children's author. One of her enterprises is the Magic School Bus series.

 Students could dress like Ms. Frizzle.

Don Freeman (born San Diego, California, 1908; died February 1, 1978) was a children's author and illustrator. One of his books is *A Pocket for Corduroy*. Visit a Web site at: http://www.edupaperback.org/showauth.cfm?authid=28.

Alex Haley (born Ithaca, New York, 1921; died Seattle, Washington, February 13, 1992) was a novelist. One of his most famous works is *Roots*. The book, a Pulitzer Prize winner in 1975, has been translated into thirty-seven languages.

Gifford Pinchot (born Simsbury, Connecticut, 1865; died New York, New York, October 4, 1946) in 1905 headed the Division of Forestry, later called the Forest Service. He later became governor of Pennsylvania, serving from 1923 to 1927 and 1931 to 1935.

August

12 Police force was created in the American colonies in 1658.

Phonograph was invented by Thomas Edison in 1877.

Hawaii was annexed to the United States in 1898.

 Students could find out how the United States got Hawaii.

Echo I, a communications satellite, was launched in 1960.

 Students could report on how communications satellites work.

Enterprise, the first reusable space vehicle, was launched from a Boeing 747 in 1977.

Minimum wage went from seventy-five cents per hour to a dollar per hour in 1955.

Birthdays

George Wesley Bellows (born Columbus, Ohio, 1882; died New York, New York, January 8, 1925) was an artist.

Ann M. Martin (born Princeton, New Jersey, 1955) is a children's author. She has written many books, including The Baby-Sitters Club series. Visit a Web site at: http://www.scholastic.com/annmartin/bio.htm.

Christy Mathewson (born Factoryville, Pennsylvania, 1880; died Saranac Lake, New York, October 7, 1925) was a famous baseball player.

 Students could examine his baseball statistics, and they could find out whether he was inducted into the Baseball Hall of Fame.

Walter Dean Myers (born Martinsburg, West Virginia, 1937) is a children's author. He wrote *Darnell Rock Reporting*. Visit a Web site at: http://www.randomhouse.com/teachers/authors/myer.html.

August

13 Spanish conquered Aztecs in 1521.

Tunisia celebrates Women's Day.

Central African Republic became independent from France in 1960. It is a landlocked country a bit smaller than the state of Texas. Bangui is the capital.

Bambi premiered in 1942 at Radio City Music Hall.

International Lefthanders Day honors lefties. Contact: Lefthanders International, Box 8249, Topeka, Kansas 66608.

 Students could make a list of people who are left handed. Artworks might help. Children could examine portraits and seek subjects using their left hands to carry out activities. Visit a Web site at: http://www.channel21.com/lefties.html.

Berlin Wall was built in 1961. Before the wall was built, people from East Berlin were escaping to West Berlin. The wall was built to deter more immigration. It was torn down in November 1989.

 Students could find out more about East Berlin and West Berlin.

Birthdays

John Logie Baird (born Hellensburgh, Scotland, 1888; died Beyhill, England, June 14, 1946) was an early pioneer in television development.

Fidel Castro (born Mayari, Oriente Province, Cuba, 1927) is the leader of Cuba.

William Caxton (born Kent, England, 1422; died London, England, 1491) was the first printer to publish a book in English.

Alfred Hitchcock (born London, England, 1899; died Beverly Hills, California, April 29, 1980) was a movie director. He specialized in movies providing high suspense. Two of his most famous movies were *The Thirty-Nine Steps* and *The Birds*.

Annie Oakley (born Phoebe Ann Moses in Darke County, Ohio, 1860; died Greenville, Ohio, November 3, 1926) was a sharpshooter. She joined Buffalo Bill Cody's Wild West Show in 1885. She amazed audiences for years with her skills, including shooting the cigarette out of her husband's mouth.

 Students could find out how she got the last name Oakley. Students might want to read Robert Quackenbush's *Who's That Girl with the Gun?*

Lucy Stone (born West Brookfield, Massachusetts, 1818; died Greenville, Ohio, November 2, 1926) campaigned for women's rights. Her father did not believe women should have college educations. She had to work for nine years to earn the money to go to Oberlin College.

August

Cologne Cathedral completed construction in 1880. Rebuilding had started on August 14, 1248.

Social Security Act was approved by Congress in 1935.

 Students could learn more about social security and how it obtains its funds.

World War II ended in 1945. V-J Day was celebrated when President Truman proclaimed that the Japanese had surrendered. People rejoiced around the world. The official surrender took place on September 2, 1945, in Tokyo Bay aboard the USS *Missouri*.

 Students could make a timeline of World War II.

Wiffle ball was patented in 1953 by David Mullany.

Birthdays

Lynne Cheney (born Casper, Wyoming, 1941) is the wife of Vice President Richard Cheney. Visit a Web site at: http://www.whitehouse.gov/mrscheney.

Julia Child (born Pasadena, California, 1912) is an author and a television chef.

 Students could demonstrate to the class how to make simple foods.

Earvin "Magic" Johnson, Jr. (born Lansing, Michigan, 1959) is a basketball player.

Gary Larson (born Tacoma, Washington, 1950) is a cartoonist. He created *The Far Side.*

August

Korea celebrates Liberation Day of 1945. It became free of Japanese rule. Three years later, in 1948, Korea formally declared itself a republic.

Congo celebrates National Day. It became free from French control in 1960. Located on the western coast of Africa, this country exports sugarcane, coffee, and many other products. Brazzaville is the capital.

 Students could find out how sugarcane is grown and harvested.

Liechtenstein celebrates a national holiday. This tiny principality is located between Austria and Switzerland. Vaduz is the capital.

India celebrates its Independence Day. It became free from British rule in 1947. India has one of the oldest civilizations in the world. The country is actually on an Asian subcontinent, and New Delhi is the capital. Over eighty percent of the people are Hindi. One of its greatest natural resources is coal.

 Students could map India's very diverse geographic, climatic, and political regions.

Birthdays

Ben Affleck (born Berkeley, California, 1972) is an actor.

Napoleon Bonaparte (born Corsica, 1769; died St. Helena, May 5, 1821) was a French emperor.

Stephen G. Breyer (born San Francisco, California, 1938) is an associate justice of the Supreme Court.

Linda Ellerbee (born Bryan, Texas, 1944) is a writer and a reporter.

Edna Ferber (born Kalamazoo, Michigan, 1887; died New York, New York, April 16, 1968) was a novelist. *So Big* was very popular, and it won her a Pulitzer Prize.

Florence Kling Harding (born Marion, Ohio, 1860; died Marion, Ohio, November 21, 1924) was the wife of Warren Harding, twenty-ninth president of the United States. Visit a Web site at: http://www.whitehouse.gov/history/firstladies/fh29.html.

 One student could research Mrs. Harding's life and pretend to be her. The rest of the class could have a question and answer session with "Mrs. Harding."

Sir Walter Scott (born Edinburgh, Scotland, 1771; died Abbotsford, Scotland, September 21, 1832) was a famous poet.

August

Dominican Republic celebrates the restoration of the republic.

Battle of Bennington Day is celebrated in Vermont. The Green Mountain Boys defeated the British in 1777.

British soundly defeated the American troops in 1780 in the Battle of Camden in South Carolina.

 Students could read about the battle. Just how bad was the battle?

Bonanza Creek, Alaska, was where gold was found in 1896. Skookum Jim, Dawson Charlie, and others discovered gold in Rabbit Creek. It started the Klondike Gold Rush.

 Students could read about the Klondike Gold Rush. What problems did the prospectors face?

Sports Illustrated **appeared for the first time in 1954.**

Birthdays

Menachem Begin (born Brest-Litovsk, Poland, 1913; died March 9, 1992) was an important Israeli hero. He fought for Israel's freedom. He was elected Israel's prime minister in 1977 and signed the Camp David Accord in 1979. He and Anwar el-Sadat won the 1978 Nobel Peace Prize for their efforts.

Beverly Brodsky (born 1941) is a children's author and illustrator.

Matt Christopher (born Bath, Pennsylvania, 1917; died Charlotte, North Carolina, September 20, 1997) was a children's author. He is known for his novels about sports. Visit a Web site at: http://www.ipl.org/youth/askauthor/christopher.html.

 After reading one of Matt Christopher's sports books, children could make a list of new things they have learned about the sport.

Madonna (Louise Veronica Ciccone) (born Bay City, Michigan, 1958) is a singer and an actress.

 August

17 **Gabon celebrates its Independence Day.** It gained autonomy from France in 1960. The country, located on the western coast of Africa, is for the most part covered with rain forest. Libreville is the capital.

Indonesia celebrates its Independence Day. It became free from Dutch control in 1945. About 13,700 islands comprise this archipelago, located between Asia and Australia. Jakarta is the capital.

 Indonesia grows cassava. Students could find out more about this crop.

Clermont, **Robert Fulton's first steamboat, was operated for the first time in 1807.** It traveled between Albany and New York City. At first called "Fulton's Folly," the ship cruised the 150-mile stretch in thirty-two hours. However, Robert Fulton went into commercial service in 1808.

Wrench was patented in 1835 by Solyman Merrick.

Double Eagle II, **a balloon, landed in Miserey, France, in 1978.** The balloon and its crew, Larry Newman, Ben Abruzzo, and Max Anderson, had left Presque Island, Maine, on August 11, 1978. The balloon was the first of its kind to travel across the Atlantic Ocean.

 Students could list the difficulties the crew faced. For example, where would they sleep?

Birthdays

Davy Crockett (born Hawkins County, Tennessee, 1786; died at the Alamo, March 6, 1836) was an adventurer and a frontier fighter.

 Students could make a timeline of Davy Crockett's life.

Sean Penn (born Santa Monica, California, 1960) is an actor.

August

 18

Scientists discovered in 1686 a satellite circling Venus.

Condensed milk was patented by Gail Borden in 1853.

Birthdays

Rosalynn Smith Carter (born Plains, Georgia, 1927) is the wife of Jimmy Carter, thirty-ninth president of the United States. While she was first lady, she devoted much of her time to the performing arts. She also held a post of the President's Commission on Mental Health. Visit a Web site at: http://www.whitehouse.gov/history/firstladies/rc39.html.

 Students could find out whether the Secret Service protects former first ladies.

Roberto Clemente (born Carolina, Puerto Rico, 1934; died San Juan, Puerto Rico, December 31, 1972) was a baseball player. He joined the Pittsburgh Pirates and spent his entire career with them. He was killed in a plane crash while trying to deliver supplies to Nicaragua. An earthquake there had devastated parts of the country. He became a member of the Baseball Hall of Fame in 1973.

Virginia Dare (born Roanoke Island, 1587) was the first child of settlers to be born in the colonies. When a supply ship landed in Roanoke in 1591, the entire colony had disappeared.

 Students could speculate as to the colony's and Virginia Dare's fate.

Paula Danziger (born Washington, DC, 1944) is a children's author. She is well known for her Amber Brown series. Visit a Web site at: http://www.scholastic.com/titles/paula.

Meriwether Lewis (born Albemarle County, Virginia, 1774; died near Nashville, Tennessee, October 11, 1809) was half of the famous Lewis and Clark expedition. He later became governor of the Louisiana Territory.

 Older children might be able to solve the mystery surrounding Lewis's death.

August

 19

Indianapolis 500 Race Track was opened in 1909.

Sputnik 5 **was launched in 1960.** It carried two dogs, Strelka and Belka, into orbit. The dogs and the spacecraft were recovered.

Birthdays

Vicki Cobb (born 1938) is a children's author. Visit a Web site at: http://www.vickicobb.com.

 Students might enjoy trying some of her projects from *Science Experiments You Can Eat*.

William Jefferson "Bill" Clinton (born Hope, Arkansas, 1946) was the forty-second president (1993–2001) of the United States. Before he was president, he served first as Arkansas's state attorney general and then as its governor. Visit a Web site at: http://www.whitehouse.gov/history/presidents/bc42.html.

 Each student could decide whether he/she would like to be president.

Ogden Nash (born Rye, New York, 1902; died Baltimore, Maryland, May 19, 1971) was poet. He enjoyed writing humor.

 Children could read some of his poetry. Then they could write their own humorous verses.

Willie Shoemaker (born Fabens, Texas, 1931) is a former jockey.

Orville Wright (born Dayton, Ohio, 1871; died Dayton, Ohio, January 30, 1948) flew the first airplane on December 17, 1903. The day has been proclaimed National Aviation Day since 1939.

August

20

Hungary celebrates a national holiday. A landlocked country in eastern Europe, Hungary has been ruled by many other nations. Budapest is the capital.

Turkey celebrates Victory Day with parades and fireworks.

Plutonium was weighed for the first time in 1942 at the University of Chicago. Plutonium is the first manufactured element.

 Students could find out how plutonium is made.

Viking I **was launched in 1975.** It landed on the surface of Mars on July 20, 1976. It transmitted photographs and data regarding weather and atmosphere.

Voyager 2 **was launched in 1977.** It traveled near Jupiter in 1979, Saturn in 1981, Uranus in 1986, and Neptune in 1989. It transmitted photographs and data back to Earth.

Birthdays

Vitus Bering (born Horsens, Jutland, Denmark, 1680; died Bering Island, December 19, 1741) was an explorer. He confirmed that water separated Asia and North America. He also claimed land now known as Alaska for Russia. Heavy fogs forced him to land on Bering Island as he was trying to return to Russia. He died of scurvy on the island.

 Students now know that Bering Island is named after him. They could find out what other two geographic features bear his name.

Connie Chung (born Constance Yu-Hwa in Washington, DC, 1946) is a television journalist.

Benjamin Harrison (born North Bend, Ohio, 1833; died Indianapolis, Indiana, March 13, 1901) was the twenty-third president (1889–1893) of the United States. He was the grandson of William Henry Harrison. During the Civil War he was a brigadier general. He served in the U.S. Senate, representing Indiana. Although he lost the popular vote, he won the electoral vote and became president. He compared the White House to a jail. During his presidency, six new states were admitted to the Union. Visit a Web site at: http://www.whitehouse.gov/history/presidents/bh23.html.

 Students could find out which six states were added to the Union.

ugust

21 *Mona Lisa* **was stolen from the Louvre in 1911.** She was returned to the museum over two years later. Visit a Web site at: http://www.pbs.org/treasuresoftheworld/a_nav/mona_nav/main_monafrm.html.

Hawaii became the fiftieth state of the United States in 1959. Evidence indicates people lived on the islands as early as A.D. 500. James Cook first visited Hawaii in 1778, and he died there in 1779. Honolulu is the state capital, and the state's nickname is the Aloha State. Since the development of the jet airplane, the islands have become a popular tourist spot. It grows pineapples and sugarcane. Scientists are trying to channel the geothermal energy from the volcano Mauna Loa. The state fish is the humuhumunukunukuapuaa. Contact: (808) 923-1811. Visit an Internet site at: http://www.50states.com/hawaii.htm.

 Students could plan a simple luau.

Lincoln-Douglas debates began in 1858.

 Students could learn the fundamentals of debating. Then they could pick an issue and debate it.

William Clarke Quantrill and his band raided Lawrence, Kansas, in 1863. The Confederate leader's group killed at least 150 people.

American Bar Association was created in 1878.

Adding machine was patented in 1888 by W. S. Burroughs.

Gemini 5 **was launched into space in 1965.** For eight days astronauts Cooper and Conrad orbited the Earth 128 times, and they launched the first satellite from a manned craft.

Giant panda was born in 1999 in the San Diego Zoo.

Birthdays

William "Count" Basie (born Red Bank, New Jersey, 1904; died Hollywood, Florida, April 26, 1984) was a pianist and bandleader who influenced the development of jazz.

Wilt Chamberlain (born Philadelphia, Pennsylvania, 1936; died Los Angeles, California, October 12, 1999) was a famous basketball player. He was inducted into the Basketball Hall of Fame. He scored more than 4,000 points in one season.

 Students could find out more about his basketball career.

ugust

22 **Steamboat, invented by John Fitch, was successfully working in 1787.**

 Students could compare and contrast sailing vessels to steam-powered ships.

Liquid soap was patented in 1865.

Vietnam Conflict started in 1945 when Free French paratroopers entered Vietnam. Ho Chi Minh had staged a successful coup.

Birthdays

Ray Bradbury (born Waukegan, Illinois, 1920) is an author. One of his most famous works is *Fahrenheit 451.*

Claude Debussy (born St. Germain-en-Laye, France, 1862; died Paris, France, March 25, 1918) was a composer and a musician.

 Students could enjoy some of his music.

Norman Schwarzkopf (born Trenton, New Jersey, 1934) is a retired military general.

Archibald M. Willard (born Bedford, Ohio, 1836; died Cleveland, Ohio, October 11, 1918) was a painter. One of his most well-known works is *The Spirit of '76.*

 Students could analyze *The Spirit of '76* and some of his other works.

Carl Yastrzemski (born Southampton, New York, 1939) is a former baseball outfielder.

ugust

23 **Virgo is the astrological sign for August 23 through September 22.**

Horseshoes were patented by O. E. Brown in 1892.

 Students could find out how horseshoes are put on horses.

Bryan Allen became the first person in 1977 to produce human-powered flight. He pedaled the *Gossamer Condor* for one mile at a stipulated minimum altitude. This accomplishment, occurring in Schafter, California, earned him an award of 50,000 British pounds. The prize had been created by Henry Kremer, a British businessman.

 Students could find out how the *Gossamer Condor* worked.

Nicola Sacco and Bartolomeo Vanzetti were executed in 1927. They were convicted of robbing a shoe factory for its payroll. A guard was killed.

 Many experts believe the two were not involved at all in the robbery. Older students could investigate the case and give their opinions.

Dow Jones Industrial Average reached a high of 11,299.76 in 1999.

Birthdays

Kobe Bryant (born Philadelphia, Pennsylvania, 1978) is a basketball player.

Edgar Lee Masters (born Garnett, Kansas, 1869; died Melrose Park, Pennsylvania, March 5, 1950) was a writer. One of his most famous works is *Spoon River Anthology*.

Commodore Oliver Hazard Perry (born South Kingston, Rhode Island, 1785; died at sea on August 23, 1819) was a naval commander. During the Battle of Lake Erie in 1813, he stated, "We have met the enemy, and they are ours."

 ugust

24

Vesuvius in Italy erupted in A.D. **79.** It buried the cities of Pompeii and Herculaneum.

 The cities were buried and forgotten for centuries. Students could find out how and when Pompeii and Herculaneum were discovered.

Washington, DC, was burned in 1814 during the War of 1812. Many buildings, including the Capitol and the president's house, were burned. The president and other statesmen had left the city prior to the battle.

 Students could find out how the White House got its name.

Waffle iron was patented in 1869. It was invented by Cornelius Swarthout of Troy, New York.

Students could find out how a waffle iron works. Then they could make and eat some waffles.

Chef George Crum cooked the first potato chip in Saratoga Springs, New York, in 1853.

Ukraine celebrates its Independence Day. It seceded from the Union of Soviet Socialist Republics in 1991. The country has often been under the control of other nations, and its borders have changed. Kiev is the capital.

Birthdays

Steve Guttenberg (born Brooklyn, New York, 1958) is an actor.

Gregory Jarvis (born Detroit, Michigan, 1944; died in the *Challenger* explosion, January 28, 1986) was an astronaut.

Cal Ripken (born Havre de Grace, Maryland, 1960) is a baseball player.

Mason Williams (born Abilene, Texas, 1938) is a composer.

 ugust

25

Uruguay celebrates its Independence Day. It became free from Brazilian rule in 1828. Located on the southeastern coast of South America, the country raises a great deal of livestock. Montevideo is the capital.

National Park Service was created in 1916. Visit a Web site at: http://www.nps.gov.

Birthdays

Leonard Bernstein (born Lawrence, Massachusetts, 1918; died New York, New York, October 14, 1990) was a conductor and a composer. One of his musicals was *West Side Story.*

 Students could listen to some of Bernstein's music.

Sean Connery (born Edinburgh, Scotland, 1930) is an actor.

Althea Gibson (born Silver, South Carolina, 1927) is the first African American to win the women's singles tournament at Wimbledon. She won the tournament in 1957 and returned to a ticker tape parade in New York.

 Students could find out how one qualifies for Wimbledon.

Bret Francis Harte (born Albany, New York, 1836; died London, England, May 5, 1902) was a writer known especially for his tales of the American West. One of his most famous works is *The Outcasts of Poker Flats,* written in 1869. He completed *The Luck of Roaring Camp* in 1868.

 Students could read and enjoy some of his works.

Walt Kelly (born Philadelphia, Pennsylvania, 1913; died Hollywood, California, October 18, 1973) was a cartoonist. He is famous for his character, Pogo.

Lane Smith (born Tulsa, Oklahoma, 1959) writes and illustrates books for children. His *The Stinky Cheese Man and Other Fairly Stupid Tales,* published in 1992, was a Caldecott Honor Book.

August

26 **The Nineteenth Amendment to the Constitution was adopted in 1920.** It gave women the right to vote.

Women's Equality Day has been celebrated in the United States since 1973. A presidential proclamation in that year recognized women's right to vote.

Baseball games were televised for the first time in 1939. New York's WXBS broadcast a doubleheader between the Cincinnati Reds and the Brooklyn Dodgers. Red Barber was the announcer.

Krakatoa erupted in 1883, creating one of the biggest volcanic eruptions known. Over 36,000 people died in the ensuing tidal waves. Five cubic miles of the mountain were blown into the atmosphere, changing weather for years.

 Students could find out whether Krakatoa has been active since 1883. What happened to the island?

Birthdays

Macauley Culkin (born New York, New York, 1980) is an actor.

Lee DeForest (born Council Bluffs, Iowa, 1873; died Hollywood, California, June 30, 1961) was called the "Father of Radio." The owner of hundreds of patents, DeForest also worked with the photoelectric cell, talking films, and television.

 Students could find out why he was arrested.

Geraldine Ferraro (born Newburgh, New York, 1935) is the first woman to be nominated as vice president from a major political party. She had been voted into Congress in 1978 and was nominated for the vice presidency in July 1984.

Antoine-Laurent Lavoisier (born Paris, France, 1743; executed Paris, France, May 8, 1794) is known as the founder of modern chemistry. He studied the processes of combustion and also plant respiration. He established a method of naming chemicals that is still used today.

 Students could find out why he was executed.

Albert Bruce Sabin (born Bialystok, Poland, 1906; died Washington, DC, March 3, 1993) created an oral polio vaccine. It replaced the vaccine developed by Jonas Salk. Sabin's vaccine provided lifetime protection and could be swallowed. Jonas's vaccine had to be injected and had to be repeated. In 1971 Sabin received the U.S. National Medal of Science.

ugust

27 **First North American drama was performed in 1655 in Acoma, Virginia.** *Ye Bare and Ye Cubb* was written by Phillip A. Bruce. Virginia was one of the few colonies that did not prohibit production of plays.

Republic of Moldova celebrates its Independence Day. It broke away from the Union of Soviet Socialist Republics in 1991. Two of its boundaries are formed by the Dneister and Prut Rivers. The country's fertile soil allows for good agriculture. Kolonia is the capital.

First oil well was made in 1859. W. A. Smith found oil as he was sinking a shaft in Pennsylvania. The rig was soon producing twenty barrels of crude oil a day.

 Students could find out how oil rigs are dug and how oil is pumped.

Birthdays

Confucius (born Lu, China, 551? B.C.; died 479? B.C.) was a great philosopher. His philosophy stresses proper relationships with others and personal responsibility.

 Students could learn more about his beliefs and compare his ideas to theirs.

Lyndon Baines Johnson (born near Stonewall, Texas, 1908; died San Antonio, Texas, January 22, 1973) was the thirty-sixth president (1963–1969) of the United States. He fought during World War II and was awarded the Silver Star. After the war, he was elected first to the House of Representatives and then to the Senate. He represented the state of Texas. He soon became the Senate majority leader. He was John Kennedy's vice president and became president when Kennedy was assassinated. Important issues included poverty and the civil rights movement. The Vietnam War divided the country emotionally, and he did not seek another term in office. Visit a Web site at: http://www.whitehouse.gov/history/presidents/lj36.html.

 Students could research Johnson's War on Poverty.

Anne Rinaldi (born New York, New York, 1934) is a children's author. One of her books is *A Stitch in Time*. Visit a Web site at: http://scils.rutgers.edu/~kvander/rinaldi.html.

Mother Teresa (born Agnes Gonxha Bojaxhiu in Skopje, Yugoslavia, 1910; died Calcutta, India, September 5, 1997) was a missionary working with the poor in India. She received the Nobel Peace Prize in 1979.

August

 28 Spanish explorers first landed in Florida in 1565.

Henry Hudson in 1609 ventured into the Delaware Bay. He was exploring for the Dutch.

 Students could look at a map of Delaware Bay. They could find out how far upstream large ships can travel.

Ten women's rights campaigners were arrested in 1917 while picketing outside the White House.

Martin Luther King delivered his *I Have a Dream* speech in 1963 in front of the Lincoln Memorial in Washington, DC.

Birthdays

Roger Duvoisin (born Geneva, Switzerland, 1904, died Morristown, New Jersey, June 30, 1980) was a children's author and illustrator. One of his main characters in a series was Petunia. He won the 1948 Caldecott Medal for *White Snow, Bright Snow.*

 Children could read and enjoy some of his work.

Johann Wolfgang von Goethe (born Frankfurt am Main, Germany, 1749; died Weimar, Germany, March 22, 1832) was a philosopher, a scientist, and a writer. One of his greatest works is the verse play *Faust.*

Scott Hamilton (born Toledo, Ohio, 1958) is an ice skater. He is an Olympic gold medalist.

Lucy Ware Webb Hayes (born Chillicothe, Ohio, 1831; died Fremont, Ohio, June 25, 1889) was the wife of Rutherford B. Hayes, nineteenth president of the United States. She visited the Civil War battle sites to care for the wounded. She served as first lady of Ohio when her husband was elected governor. Because she believed in the temperance movement, alcohol was not served in the White House when she was first lady. Visit a Web site at: http://www. whitehouse.gov/history/firstladies/lh19.html.

 Students could research the temperance movement.

J. Brian Pinkney (born Boston, Massachusetts, 1961) is an author and illustrator. One of his books is *Cosmo and the Robot.* Visit a Web site at: http://www.eduplace.com/kids/hmr/ mtai/bpinkney.html.

August

29 **Shays' Rebellion started formally in 1786.** Farmers in debt were revolting against high taxes and their creditors. If people could not pay their debts, they were put in prison.

 Students could make a timeline of the rebellion and find out what happened to Daniel Shays.

The Philanthropist, **the first abolitionist newspaper, was printed in 1817.**

Gottlieb Daimler invented the motorcycle in 1885.

Birthdays

Karen Hesse (born Baltimore, Maryland, 1952) is a children's author. Her *Out of the Dust* won the 1998 Newbery Medal.

Oliver Wendell Holmes (born Cambridge, Massachusetts, 1809; died Boston, Massachusetts, October 7, 1894) was an author. He was famous for his charm and wit. One of his poems, *Old Ironsides,* saved the *Constitution* from being destroyed.

 Students could recite *Old Ironsides.*

John Locke (born Wrington, Somerset County, England, 1632; died Oates, England, October 28, 1704) was a philosopher. Thomas Jefferson was greatly influenced by Locke.

 Students could read more about Locke's philosophy. Then they could look for strands of that philosophy in the Declaration of Independence.

Charlie Parker (born Kansas City, Kansas, 1920; died Rochester, New York, March 12, 1955) was a jazz saxophonist.

August

 Direct telephone communication, nicknamed the Hotline, was completed between the White House and the Kremlin in 1963.

Discovery, **a space shuttle, made its first space voyage in 1984.** Launched from Kennedy Space Center, it manipulated a robot arm and launched three satellites.

 Students could locate more information on the robot arm.

Peru celebrates Saint Rose of Lima's Day.

Birthdays

Ellen Lewis Herndon Arthur (born Culpeper, Virginia, 1837; died New York, New York, January 11, 1880) was the wife of Chester A. Arthur, twenty-first president of the United States. She was the daughter of William Lewis Herndon, an explorer of the Amazon River. She died before Arthur was elected president. Visit a Web site at: http://www.whitehouse.gov/history/firstladies/ea21.html.

Virginia Lee Burton (born Newton Centre, Massachusetts, 1909; died Boston, Massachusetts, October 15, 1968) was a children's book illustrator. She won the 1943 Caldecott Medal for *The Little House.* She also wrote *Mike Mulligan and His Steam Shovel.* Visit a Web site at: http://libweb.uoregon.edu/speccoll/mss/childrenslit/vlburton.html.

Esther Cleveland (born Washington, DC, 1893; died New Hampshire, June 25, 1980) was the first president's baby to be born in the White House.

Donald Crews (born Newark, New Jersey, 1938) is a picture book author and illustrator. One of his works is *Flying,* published in 1986.

 Students could read and enjoy some of his works.

Mary Wollstonecraft Shelley (born London, England, 1797; died London, England, February 1, 1851) was an author. One of her most famous works is *Frankenstein.* She was married to poet Percy Bysshe Shelley, and she edited much of her husband's work after he died.

Students could read some of *Frankenstein* and compare it to some of today's adaptations of the monster.

Roy Wilkins (born St. Louis, Missouri, 1901; died new York, New York, September 8, 1981) was the grandson of a slave. A civil rights leader, he was a driving force in the NAACP.

Ted Williams (born San Diego, California, 1918; died Inverness, Florida, July 5, 2002) was a baseball player. An outfielder, he was inducted into the Baseball Hall of Fame.

August

Charleston, South Carolina, experienced a major earthquake (measuring 7.6 on the Richter scale) in 1886. The first major earthquake recorded in the eastern United States, it killed about one hundred people.

 Students could find out how and why earthquakes occur.

Klondike Eldorado was the site of a major gold discovery in 1896 in Alaska. Gold worth more than $30 million was mined from the claim in 1896. That gold today would be worth more than $600 million.

 Students could learn how gold is mined and processed.

Kyrgyzstan celebrates its Independence Day. Kyrgyzstan became free of Soviet rule in 1991. The country, located in eastern central Asia, has an area of about 76,000 square miles. Most of the country is covered with mountains. Bishkek is the capital.

Malaysia celebrates its Independence Day, granted from the United Kingdom in 1957. The country, located in Southeast Asia, covers an area of about 127,000 square miles and has a population of about 20 million people. The capital is Kuala Lumpur, the site of the world's two tallest buildings.

Trinidad and Tobago celebrate their Independence Day. The two islands located off the northeastern coast of South America became free of British rule in 1962. Over 1.2 million people live within the 200 square miles. Port of Spain is the capital. The islands export petroleum, cocoa, and sugar.

Birthdays

Alan Jay Lerner (born New York, New York, 1918; died New York, New York, June 14, 1986) was a lyricist. He teamed with Frederick Lowe on many musicals, including *My Fair Lady* and *Camelot.*

 Students could listen to the scores of some of his musicals.

Itzhak Perlman (born Tel Aviv, Israel, 1945) is a famous violinist.

September

September is the ninth month of the year. However, at one time it was the seventh month. Its name derives from the Latin *septem,* or "seven." When Julius Caesar made January the first month, September became the ninth month. Over the years September has had twenty-nine days or thirty-one days. Then Augustus changed the number of days to thirty. The sapphire is the gem for September. Its flower is the morning glory.

Month-Long Activities

National Hispanic Heritage Month is celebrated from September 15 through October 15 by presidential proclamation.

Children's Eye Health and Safety Month emphasizes the importance of eye care. Contact: Prevent Blindness America, 500 East Remington Road, Schaumburg, Illinois 60173. Telephone: (800) 331-2020. Visit a Web site at: http://www.preventblindness.org.

Library Card Sign-Up Month stresses the importance of libraries for children. Contact: American Library Association, 50 East Huron Street, Chicago, Illinois 60611. Visit a Web site at: http://www.ala.org.

 Children might want to read Jerry Spinelli's *The Library Card.* The book shows how four children's lives changed when library cards were issued to them.

National Honey Month lets us know that bees produce over 230 million pounds of honey a year. Contact: National Honey Board, 390 Lashley Street, Longmont, Colorado 80501. Telephone: (303) 776-2337. Visit a Web site at: http://www.honey.com.

Special Weeks

Constitution Week is celebrated from September 17 through September 23 by presidential proclamation since 1955.

Deaf Culture Week, the last full week in September, celebrates American Sign Language and deaf culture. Contact: National Association of the Deaf, 814 Thayer Avenue, Silver Spring, Maryland 20910-4500. Visit a Web site at: http://www.nad.org.

National Farm Safety Week is recognized by presidential proclamation for the third week in September.

Special Days

Labor Day occurs on the first Monday in September. The holiday was probably first observed in 1882 in New York City by the Carpenters and Joiners Union. The holiday grew in popularity, and over half the states were celebrating Labor Day by 1893. President Grover Cleveland made it a legal holiday in 1894.

Grandparents' Day is the first Sunday following Labor Day. It was made a holiday by presidential proclamation in 1979.

Native American Day is the fourth Sunday in September.

International Day of Peace is the third Tuesday in September. The United Nations General Assembly opens its session on this day. Contact: United Nations, Department of Public Information, New York, New York 10017.

National Hunting and Fishing Day has been celebrated on the fourth Saturday of September since 1979 as a result of a presidential proclamation.

September

Chop suey was invented in 1896.

Martha, the last passenger pigeon, died in 1914.

 Students could research more about the passenger pigeon and why it became extinct.

Japan honors Kanto Earthquake Memorial Day. In 1923 approximately 57,000 people died during Japan's most catastrophic earthquake.

Germany invaded Poland in 1939 and started World War II.

 Students could learn more about the events leading up to World War II.

Titanic **was found by Dr. Ballard in 1985.** The wreck was 500 miles off the coast of Newfoundland.

Slovakia celebrates the adoption of its constitution.

Uzbekistan celebrates its Independence Day. It withdrew from the Union of Soviet Socialist Republics in 1991. Steppe and deserts are major land features, and Tashkent is the capital.

Drug Abuse Resistance Education (D.A.R.E.) became available to schools in 1983. Today about seventy-five percent of all U.S. schools use D.A.R.E., and forty-four other countries are also trying it. Telephone: (800) 223-DARE. Visit a Web site at: http://www.dare-america. com.

Birthdays

Jim Arnosky (born New York, New York, 1946) is a children's book author and illustrator. He stresses animals, plants, and nature. One of his books is *Big Jim and the Whitelegged Moose.* Visit a Web site at: http://www.jimarnosky.com.

Engelbert Humperdinck (born Sieburg, Germany, 1854; died September 21, 1921) was a composer. He is famous for his opera *Hansel and Gretel.* He also wrote incidental music for plays, including several works by Shakespeare.

Edgar Rice Burroughs (born Chicago, Illinois, 1875; died Encino, California, March 19, 1950) was, at various times, a soldier, gold miner, cowboy, and policeman. He is famous for writing the *Tarzan* books. He wrote twenty novels. They have been translated into fifty languages, and over twenty million copies have been sold. The character was also featured in movies, comic strips, and television.

 Students could read passages from his *Tarzan* books. They could compare how Tarzan spoke in the books to how he spoke in the old movies.

September

2

Great Britain and the American colonies conducted a "Gregorian Correction" in 1752. The day after September 2 became September 14. Angry mobs protested in the streets because they felt they lost eleven days. The country also changed New Year's Day from March 25 to January 1.

Treasury Department was created by Congress in 1789. Visit a Web site at: http://www.treas.gov.

 Students could find out exactly what the treasury department does. Who is the current secretary of the treasury?

Anne Frank was found in her hiding place and sent to Auschwitz in 1944.

Wilma Rudolph, in 1960, became the first American woman to win three Olympic gold medals. Rome hosted the Olympics.

Birthdays

Eugene Field (born St. Louis, Missouri, 1850; died November 4, 1895) was a writer. He is most known for his poetry.

 Students might enjoy reading *The Gingham Dog and the Calico Cat,* published in 1894.

James Forten (born Philadelphia, Pennsylvania, 1766; died Philadelphia, Pennsylvania, March 4, 1842) was the son of free African Americans. He was almost sold into slavery during the Revolutionary War. Later he became a successful businessman and was active in the abolition movement.

 Students could read biographies about Forten. How did he help the antislavery movement?

Christa McAuliffe (born Concord, Massachusetts, 1948; died in the *Challenger* explosion, January 28, 1986) was a high school teacher. She was the first ordinary person chosen to travel in space. Six other crew members died with her.

Elizabeth De Trevino (born Bakersfield, California, 1904) was a children's author. One of her most popular works is *I, Juan de Pareja.*

September

3

Treaty of Paris was signed in 1783. Great Britain and the United States signed the treaty, formally ending the Revolutionary War.

 Students could find out why the treaty was signed in Paris.

Qatar celebrates its Independence Day. It declared its freedom from Great Britain in 1971. It is now ruled by a sheik. The country obtains most of its income from oil and banking. Doha is the capital.

Youngsters could locate Qatar on a map. They could label its major geographic features. Where is oil found?

San Marino celebrates a national day. The people honor Saint Marinus, the country's founder.

Labor Day was celebrated as a legal holiday for the first time in 1894.

First professional football game was played in 1895 in Latrobe, Pennsylvania.

Birthdays

Aliki Brandenberg (born Wildwood Crest, New Jersey, 1929) is a picture book author and illustrator. She wrote, among other works, *How a Book Is Made,* 1986.

 Children could read and enjoy her books.

Prudence Crandall (born Hopkinton, Rhode Island, 1803; died Elk Falls, Kansas, January 28, 1890) was a teacher. Her school was boycotted when the families found out she had included an African American girl. She then created a school for "young ladies and misses of colour."

September

 Romulus Augustulus was deposed in A.D. 476. Many experts believe this event marks the fall of the Roman Empire.

 Students could find maps of the Roman Empire. How far did its power reach?

Henry Hudson recorded in his log that he discovered Manhattan in 1609.

 Students could find out how the island has changed over the years.

Los Angeles, California, was created in 1781.

 Students could compare the age of Los Angeles to the ages of other cities.

Electricity was brought into several buildings on several streets in New York City in 1882.

First self-service restaurant opened in 1885.

George Eastman patented the roll film camera and the Kodak name in 1888.

Transcontinental television premiered in 1951.

Birthdays

Paul Harvey (born Tulsa, Oklahoma, 1918) is a broadcaster.

Syd Hoff (born New York, New York, 1912) is a children's author and illustrator. One of his books is *Danny and the Dinosaur.*

Sarah Childress Polk (born Murfreesboro, Tennessee, 1803; died Nashville, Tennessee, August 14, 1891) was the wife of James Polk, eleventh president of the United States. She was a very active first lady, serving as her husband's secretary. Visit a Web site at: http://www.whitehouse.gov/history/firstladies/sp11.html.

September

5 **First Continental Congress met secretly in 1774 in Philadelphia, Pennsylvania.** Peyton Randolph from Virginia was the president.

 Students could find out how people were chosen to attend the First Continental Congress.

Gasoline pump was operated for the first time in 1885. It was created by Sylvester F. Bowser of Fort Wayne, Indiana.

 Students could find out how the gas pump and all pumps work.

Voyager I **was launched in 1977.** It has traveled at least 6.5 million miles.

Western Samoa celebrates a national holiday.

St. Gotthard Automobile Tunnel opened in 1980. The tunnel connects Switzerland to more southern countries. It took ten years and over $400 million to construct.

Birthdays

Paul Fleischman (born Monterey, California, 1952) is a children's author. His father is Sid Fleischman.

 Students could read and enjoy some of his works. One of his books, *Bull Run,* describes the Civil War from various points of view.

Jesse James (born Centerville [now Kearney], Missouri, 1847; died St. Joseph, Missouri, April 3, 1882) was an outlaw of the Old West. He, his brother Frank, and eight other men began holding up banks and stagecoaches after the Civil War. They started robbing trains in 1873. The government in 1876 hunted the men down, but the James brothers eluded them. The two then formed another group in 1879. The Missouri governor put a bounty of $10,000 on them. One member of the gang, Robert Ford, shot James in the back of the head and claimed the reward.

Darryl F. Zanuck (born Wahoo, Nebraska, 1902; died Palm Springs, California, December 21, 1979) was a famous film producer. Among his credits were *The Jazz Singer* (the first sound picture) and *The Grapes of Wrath.*

September

6 **Nebuchadnezzar died in 1104 B.C.** He was one of the great Babylonian kings.

Swaziland celebrates Somhlolo, its independence day. Although it has remained part of the British Commonwealth, it became free of direct British rule in 1968. The country has its own monarch. This landlocked country in southern Africa exports sugar and asbestos. Mbabane is the capital.

 Students could find out the uses of asbestos.

Massachusetts Bay Colony was created in 1628.

Video tape recording on magnetic tape was made for the first time in 1958.

Oberlin Institute, now Oberlin College, opened its doors in 1837. It was the first co-educational college.

Baltic states of Latvia, Estonia, and Lithuania declared their independence from the Soviet Union in 1991. These three countries had been part of the Soviet Union for fifty-one years.

Birthdays

Jane Addams (born Cedarville, Illinois, 1860; died Chicago, Illinois, May 21, 1935) was an activist for social welfare and women's rights. She founded Hull House and was the co-winner of the Nobel Peace Prize in 1931. Visit a Web site at: http://www.uic.edu/jaddams/hull/ja_bio.html.

John Dalton (born Eaglesfield, England, 1766; died Manchester, England, July 27, 1844) was a scientist.

 Students could research his contributions to science.

Marquis de Lafayette (born Marie-Joseph-Paul-Yves-Roch-Gilbert du Motier in Chavaniac, France, 1757; died Paris, France, May 20, 1834) was called "The Hero of Two Worlds." He contributed to the American Revolution by convincing Louis XVI to send men to fight. He attained the rank of major-general and helped force Cornwallis to surrender at Yorktown. He returned to France and drafted "A Declaration of the Rights of Man and of the Citizen."

 Students could find out what happened to Lafayette after he returned to France. They could read Jean Fritz's *Why Not, Lafayette?*

September

Brazil celebrates its Independence Day. It became free from Portuguese rule in 1822. This South American country is only slightly smaller than the United States. Brasilia is the capital. It exports coffee and chemical products. The people speak Portuguese.

 Students could compare and contrast Portuguese with Spanish.

"Uncle Sam" symbol was used for the first time in 1813. It appeared in a Troy, New York, newspaper.

 Students could find out who Daniel Wilson was and what he was doing during the War of 1812.

Boulder Dam (now Hoover Dam) began operating in 1936.

Blitz on London began in 1940.

Raggedy Ann dolls were patented by John Gruelle in 1915.

Birthdays

Alexandra Day (born Cincinnati, Ohio, 1941) is a children's author and illustrator. One of her books is *Frank and Earnest.*

Elizabeth I (born Greenwich Palace, 1533; died Richmond, England, March 24, 1603) was queen of England from 1558 until her death. Her parents were Henry VIII and Anne Boleyn. During her reign England became a leading power.

Students could read from the Royal Diaries series, *Elizabeth I: Red Rose of the House of Tudor England,* by Kathryn Lasky.

Charles Harden "Buddy" Holly (born Lubbock, Texas, 1936; died near Mason City, Iowa, February 3, 1959) was a leader of rock 'n' roll. One of his most famous songs was "Peggy Sue."

Jacob Lawrence (born Atlantic City, New Jersey, 1917; died Seattle, Washington, June 9, 2000) was a painter and illustrator. He received the Spingarn Medal. Visit a Web site at: http://www.whitney.org/jacoblawrence.

J. P. Morgan, Jr. (born Irvington, New York, 1867; died 1943) was a banker and a philanthropist.

Anna Mary Robertson "Grandma" Moses (born Greenwich, New York, 1860; died Hoosick Falls, New York, December 13, 1961) was a contemporary primitive artist. She began painting when she was seventy-eight years old.

September

 Pledge of Allegiance was read publicly for the first time in 1892.

 Students could research who wrote the Pledge of Allegiance. Two people, James Upham and Francis Bellamy, are possibilities.

Margaret Gorman became the first Miss America in 1921 in Atlantic City, New Jersey.

Warsaw, Poland, was conquered by Nazis in 1939.

Italy surrendered in 1943. This event helped end World War II.

President Gerald Ford pardoned Richard Nixon in 1974.

United Nations observes International Literacy Day. Contact: United Nations, Department of Public Information, New York, New York 10017.

Department of Veterans Affairs was created in 1989.

"Star Trek" premiered in 1966. Only seventy-nine episodes were created for the original series. However, it has spawned movies, cartoons, and other series.

Mark McGwire hit his sixty-second home run of the 1998 season, breaking Roger Maris's thirty-seven-year-old record.

Birthdays

Antonin Dvorak (born Nelahozeves, Czechoslovakia, 1841; died Prague, Czechoslovakia, May 1, 1904) composed music. He wrote nine symphonies, plus numerous operas, chamber music, and cantatas. One of his most famous compositions is *Humoresque,* written for piano in 1894.

Jack Prelutsky (born Brooklyn, New York, 1940) writes poetry.

 Children really enjoy his work. They could try *The New Kid on the* Block, published in 1984. They could illustrate some of his poems.

Richard the Lionhearted (born Oxford, England, 1157; died 1199) ruled England from 1189 to 1199.

Students could find out more about his exciting life. He actually spent very little time in England.

Jon Scieszka (born Flint, Michigan, 1954) is a children's author. One of his books is *Math Curse.* Visit a Web site at: http://falcon.jmu.edu/~ramseyil/scieszka.htm.

Peter Stuyvesant (born Scherpenzeel, Netherlands, 1610; died New York, New York, February 1672) was the last governor of New Netherlands. The citizens did not like his harsh and cruel ways, so they did not support him when the British came into the harbor.

September

 9

Persia defeated Athens at the Battle of Marathon in 490 B.C.

 Students could learn about the concept of running a marathon.

"United States of America" became our country's official name in 1776.

California became the thirty-first state of the United States in 1850. It is about third in land area but first in population. It produces so many goods that it is about the sixth largest economy in the world. One of its concerns is that it lacks water to sustain both population growth and agricultural needs. Sacramento is the capital, and the nickname is the Golden State. The state motto is *Eureka,* meaning "I have found it." It has had eight major earthquakes since 1900. Contact: (800) 862-2543. Visit an Internet site at: http://www.50states.com/californ.htm.

 Children could learn more about one of its most famous places, Hollywood.

Tajikistan celebrates its Independence Day. It separated from the Union of Soviet Socialist Republics in 1991. Tajikistan, covered with mountains, is prone to earthquakes. Dushanbe is the capital.

 Students can find out what a qishlaq is.

Birthdays

Michael Keaton (born Michael Douglas in Pittsburgh, Pennsylvania, 1951) is an actor.

Leo Tolstoy (born south of Moscow, Russia, 1828; died Astapovo, Russia, November 20, 1910) was a novelist and a philosopher. He was concerned about the disparity between the "haves" and the "have nots." Two of his most famous novels are *War and Peace* and *Anna Karenina.*

September

 10

John Smith became the leader of Jamestown Colony Council in Virginia in 1608.

Belize celebrates Saint George's Caye Day.

Battle of Lake Erie took place in 1813.

Sewing machine was patented by Elias Howe in 1846.

Lincoln Highway, the first coast-to-coast highway, was finished in 1917.

 Students could try to find a map of this highway. Is any of it still being used?

Hot dog was invented in 1927.

 Students could find out how hot dogs are made.

TV dinner was produced by Swanson for the first time in 1953.

Birthdays

Carter Braxton (born Newington, Virginia, 1736; died Richmond, Virginia, October 10, 1797) signed the Declaration of Independence.

 Braxton actually staved off a possible battle in Virginia. Children could find out more about his abilities to make peace.

Charles Kuralt (born Wilmington, North Carolina, 1934; died New York, New York, July 4, 1997) was a television journalist. He was famous for his series "On the Road."

Roger Maris (born Hibbing, Minnesota, 1934; died Houston, Texas, December 14, 1985) was a baseball player. In 1961 he broke Babe Ruth's 1927 record of most home runs hit in a season.

Arnold Palmer (born Latrobe, Pennsylvania, 1929) is a professional golfer.

Mungo Park (born Selkirk, Scotland, 1771; died 1806) was an explorer of Africa. He was instrumental in mapping the Niger River.

eptember

11 **United States was attacked by Al Qaeda terrorists in 2001.** The terrorists commandeered four passenger planes. They crashed two of them into the World Trade Center in New York City and one plane into the Pentagon. The fourth airplane, destined for Washington, DC, crashed into western Pennsylvania. It appears the passengers tried to regain control of the aircraft. More than 3,000 people died in the attacks. The country responded by attacking possible Al Qaeda cells and other terrorist groups. Security within the country became more stringent.

Benjamin Franklin stated in 1773, "There never was a good war or a bad peace."

 Students could write a position paper regarding this statement.

Annapolis Convention was held from September 11 through September 14, 1786, in Annapolis, Maryland. Delegates from New York, Delaware, New Jersey, Pennsylvania, and Virginia met to discuss economic interests. They concluded the meeting by calling for another meeting of all the states. This new group became the Constitutional Convention.

ZR-1 (the largest functioning dirigible) flew over the Woolworth Tower (New York's tallest building) in 1923.

First giant panda was born in captivity in 1963 in China.

 Students could find out more about pandas.

Birthdays

William Sydney Porter (born Greensboro, North Carolina, 1862; died New York, New York, June 5, 1910) wrote under the pseudonym O. Henry. He is most known for his short stories, including "The Gift of the Magi" and "The Ransom of Red Chief."

 Students could read and enjoy his stories.

September

 12

Ethiopia celebrates its Revolution Day.

Guinea-Bissau celebrates Amilcar Cabral's birthday as a national holiday.

Canyonlands National Park was created in 1964. Contact: Canyonlands National Park, 125 W-2000 South, Moab, Utah 84532. Visit a Web site at: http://www.nps.gov/cany.

 Students could plan a trip through Canyonlands National Park.

"Lassie" premiered on television in 1954. The show ran for twenty-two years.

 Students could find out more about the series. How many different dogs played Lassie?

Luna 2, **a Soviet spacecraft, was launched in 1959 and became the first vehicle to land on the moon.**

Luna 16, **a Soviet spacecraft, was launched in 1970.** It was the first craft to land on the moon, collect samples, and return to Earth. It did not carry any people.

Birthdays

Richard Jordan Gatling (born Hertford County, North Carolina, 1818; died New York, New York, February 26, 1903) was an inventor. He invented mainly items to improve agriculture. However, he is famous for the Gatling gun, the first machine gun.

James Cleveland "Jesse" Owens (born Oakville, Alabama, 1913; died Tucson, Arizona, March 31, 1980) was an athlete. He won four gold medals at the 1936 Olympic games in Berlin, Germany. He established eleven world records in track and field.

 Students could make a timeline of his life.

Valerie Tripp (born Mt. Kisco, New York, 1951) is an author of the American Girls Series.

September

 13

U.S. capital was established in New York in 1788.

Star-Spangled Banner **was written by Francis Scott Key during an attack on Fort McHenry in 1814.** The melody was composed by John Stafford Smith, a British composer, for another song. The song became the national anthem by presidential decree in 1916 and adopted by Congress in 1931.

Rhinoceros was exhibited for the first time in the United States in 1826 in a New York zoo.

First national hog-calling contest was held in 1926.

Birthdays

Roald Dahl (born Llandaff, South Wales, Great Britain, 1916; died Oxford, England, November 23, 1990) was a children's author. He wrote, among other works, *James and the Giant Peach,* 1961.

 Students could read portions of some of his works.

Milton S. Hershey (born Derry Township, Pennsylvania, 1857; died Hershey, Pennsylvania, October 13, 1945) developed the Hershey chocolate bar. His career began in Chicago and New York. He made and sold caramels. In 1905 he concocted the idea of the Hershey bar and returned to Pennsylvania. There he built the factory.

 Students could eat little Hershey bars while they learn more about his life.

Carol Kendall (born Bucyrus, Ohio, 1917) is a children's author. One of her most famous books is *The Gammage Cup.*

John J. Pershing (born Laclede, Missouri, 1860; died Washington, DC, July 15, 1948) was a general who led the American Expeditionary Forces during World War I. He was very influential in the outcome of World War I.

Walter Reed (born Gloucester County, Virginia, 1851; died Washington, DC, November 22, 1902) was an army physician. He conducted important research regarding yellow fever.

Arnold Schoenberg (born Vienna, Austria, 1874; died Brentwood, California, July 13, 1951) was a composer. He wrote atonal music. Eventually he developed a twelve tone system.

 Students could listen to some recordings of his music. Can they tell the difference between his music and music of other composers?

Mildred D. Taylor (born Jackson, Mississippi, 1943) is a children's author. She wrote, among other works, *Roll of Thunder, Hear My Cry* (Newbery Medal), 1976.

September

 First U.S. lighthouse started operating in 1716.

 Students could plot the history of lighthouses.

United States took control of Mexico City in 1847 during its war with Mexico.

Joe W. Kittinger became the first person to cross the Atlantic in a hot-air balloon. He left Caribou, Maine, on September 14, 1984, and landed near Capbreton, France, September 17, 1984. He broke his ankle when he was thrown from the gondola during the stormy landing. The 3,535-mile trip also established a new record for solo distance.

Birthdays

William H. Armstrong (born Lexington, Virginia, 1914; died Kent, Connecticut, April 11, 1999) was a children's author. He wrote, among other works, *Sounder* (Newbery Medal), 1970.

Frederick Heinrich Alexander Von Humboldt (born Berlin, Germany, 1769; died 1859) was a geographer and scientist.

 Students could learn how Humboldt used isothermal lines on his maps.

John Steptoe (born Brooklyn, New York, 1950; died August 28, 1989) was a picture book author and illustrator. He wrote, among other works, *Mufaro's Beautiful Daughters* (Caldecott Honor Book), 1987.

 Students could read and enjoy some of Steptoe's work.

James Wilson (born Carskerdo, Scotland, 1742; died Edonton, North Carolina, August 21, 1798) signed the Declaration of Independence. A lawyer, he also signed the Constitution.

Elizabeth Winthrop (born Washington, DC, 1948) has written more than thirty books. One of her books is *The Castle in the Attic.* Visit a Web site at: http://www.ipl.org/div/kidspace/askauthor/winthrop.html.

September

15

The Central American countries of Costa Rica, El Salvador, Guatemala, Honduras, and Nicaragua declared their independence from Spain in 1821.

Mexico celebrates its Independence Day. It begins celebrating at 11:00 P.M. and continues through the next day.

National Weather Vane Day celebrates the world's largest weather vane. Located in Montague, Michigan, it weighs 3,500 pounds. It is forty-eight feet high, and the arrow is twenty-six feet long.

 Students could mark off on the playground the dimensions of this weathervane.

Japan celebrates Respect for the Aged Day.

Alexander Fleming discovered penicillin in 1928.

***Weekly Reader* was first published in 1928.**

Kirsten, Samantha, and Molly appeared for the first time in 1986. The American Girl dolls were followed by others. More than four million dolls have been bought.

Birthdays

Mabel Bragg (born Milford, Massachusetts, 1870; died 1945) wrote children's books. One of her most famous books is *The Little Engine That Could.*

Agatha Christie (born Torquay, England, 1890; died Wallingford, England, January 12, 1976) was a writer. She is best known for her mysteries.

James Fenimore Cooper (born Burlington, New Jersey, 1789; died Cooperstown, New York, September 14, 1851) was a writer and a historian. Two of his most famous works are *The Last of the Mohicans* and *The Pathfinder.*

Tomie dePaola (born Meriden, Connecticut, 1934) is a picture book author and illustrator. He wrote, among other works, *The Legend of the Bluebonnet: An Old Tale of Texas,* 1983.

Robert McCloskey (born Hamilton, Ohio, 1914; died 2001) was a children's author and illustrator. He wrote around 200 books, including *Make Way for Ducklings* (Caldecott Medal), published in 1941. Visit a Web site at: http://www.edupaperback.org/showauth.cfm?authid=35.

 Students could read and enjoy McCloskey's books and dePaola's books.

William Howard Taft (born Cincinnati, Ohio, 1857; died Washington, DC, March 8, 1930) was the twenty-seventh president (1909–1913) of the United States. He weighed over 300 pounds. In 1900 he was in charge of the Philippines. In 1904 Theodore Roosevelt made Taft Secretary of War. He was president of the country during a difficult period. He became a Supreme Court justice in 1921. Visit a Web site at: http://www.whitehouse.gov/history/presidents/wt27.html.

 Taft was the only president who also served on the Supreme Court. Students could locate more presidential facts and create a trivia game.

September

 United Nations declares today as International Day for the Preservation of the Ozone Level. Contact: United Nations, Department of Public Information, New York, New York 10017.

 Students could learn more about the ozone level and what they can do to save it.

Mayflower **set sail in 1620 with 102 passengers and a meager crew.** It encountered terrible storms. It arrived at Provincetown, Massachusetts, on November 21, 1620. The passengers went ashore at Plymouth, Massachusetts, on December 26, 1620.

Cherokee Strip Day occurred in 1893.

 Students could learn more about this run for land.

Mexican Independence Day starts the evening of September 15 and continues through today.

Papua New Guinea celebrates its Independence Day. The country became independent in 1975, but it remains part of the British Commonwealth. It is composed of the larger island of New Guinea, the second biggest island in the world, and 600 smaller islands. Port Moresby is the capital.

Birthdays

David Copperfield (born Metuchen, New Jersey, 1956) is an illusionist.

Orel Leonard Hershiser (born Buffalo, New York, September 16, 1958) is a baseball player.

H(ans) A(ugustus) Rey(ersbach) (born Hamburg, Germany, 1898; died Cambridge, Massachusetts, August 26, 1977) was a children's author. He is best known for his books featuring Curious George.

 Students could read and enjoy some of the *Curious George* books.

Robin Yount (born Danville, Illinois, 1955) is a former baseball player.

September

Citizenship Day recognizes all new citizens. Presidential proclamation has acknowledged this day since 1952.

 Students could interview someone who has become a U.S. citizen. How does someone become a citizen?

Constitutional Convention unanimously approved the Constitution in 1787 in Philadelphia, Pennsylvania. Almost all of the forty-two delegates signed the document. It then had to be ratified by nine of the thirteen states.

 Children could write a classroom constitution.

Battle of Antietam occurred in 1862. This Civil War battle was called America's bloodiest day because over 25,000 soldiers were killed on the shores of the Potomac River.

National Football League was created in Canton, Ohio, in 1920.

Dow Jones Industrial Average dropped 685 points, the biggest one-day drop in history, in 2001.

Birthdays

Andrew "Rube" Foster (born Calvert, Texas, 1879; died Kankakee, Illinois, December 9, 1930) was the "Father of Negro Baseball." He was a pitcher and manager of the Chicago Lelands and the Chicago American Giants before he organized the Negro National League. He was the League's president from its inception until his death.

Paul Goble (born Surrey, England, 1933) is a children's author and illustrator. His *The Girl Who Loved Wild Horses* received the 1978 Caldecott Medal.

Gail Carson Levine (born New York, New York, 1947) is a children's author. Her *Ella Enchanted* was a 1998 Newbery Honor Book. Visit a Web site at: http://www.harperchildrens.com/hch/author/author/levine.

David H. Souter (born Melrose, Massachusetts, 1939) is an associate justice for the Supreme Court.

 Students could read the Constitution and locate the requirements for being a Supreme Court justice.

Friedrich Wilhelm von Steuben (born Magdeburg, Prussia, 1730; died Remsen, New York, November 28, 1794) aided the American army during the Revolutionary War. General George Washington made him a major general. He was in charge of the army's training. He taught them how to march and to use muskets and bayonets.

Hank Williams (born Georgia, Alabama, 1923; died Oak Hill, Virginia, January 1, 1953) was a country and western singer. One of his most popular works is *Your Cheatin' Heart.*

September

Capitol building cornerstone in Washington, DC, was laid by President Washington in 1793.

The New York Times **printed its first issue in 1851.**

CBS made its first radio broadcast in 1927.

Air Force was created as an independent service in 1947. There has been an air force component of the army since 1907.

 Students could make a timeline of the Air Force's history.

Chile celebrates its Independence Day. It became free of Spanish rule in 1810. This long, narrow country is bordered to the west by the Pacific Ocean and to the east by the Andes Mountains. Gran Santiago is the capital. Copper is one of its major exports.

 Students could learn more about Chile's climate and seasons.

Birthdays

Jean Bernard Leon Foucault (born Paris, France, 1819; died Paris, France, February 11, 1868) was a scientist. He measured the speed of light through different materials. His experiments with pendulums proved that the Earth rotated on its axis.

 Students could make a simple pendulum and watch it work.

George Read (born Cecil County, Maryland, 1733; died New Castle, Delaware, September 21, 1798) signed the Declaration of Independence. He represented Delaware. He also signed the Constitution.

Ryne Sandberg (born Spokane, Washington, 1959) is a former baseball player.

September

Jamestown was burned by Nathaniel Bacon and his men in 1676. This action later became known as part of Bacon's Rebellion. They were rebelling against Governor Sir William Berkeley and his laws regarding control of Jamestown. Berkeley fled, and Bacon became the colony's leader. He died shortly after taking control. Berkeley regained control. However, he was replaced a year later, and rebellion became unnecessary.

 Students could find out why Berkeley was unpopular in the colonies.

President George Washington gave his farewell address to the nation in 1796.

 Obviously, Washington gave this speech before radio and television existed. Students could find out where and when he gave the speech. Who comprised the audience?

Carpet sweeper was patented in 1876.

St. Christopher (St. Kitts) and Nevis celebrate Independence Day. They became free of British rule in 1983, but they remain a part of the British Commonwealth. The two islands are located in the eastern portion of the Caribbean Sea. Basseterre is the capital.

 Students could research the islands. Then they could write a short informational article for a pretend newspaper travel section.

Steamboat Willie, **the first talking and animated cartoon, appeared in 1928.** Mickey Mouse was Steamboat Willie.

Mexico experienced two disastrous earthquakes in 1985. One measured 8.1, and the other measured 7.5 on the Richter scale. Almost 10,000 people died, and 100,000 houses were damaged or ruined.

Birthdays

Charles Carroll (born Annapolis, Maryland, 1737; died Baltimore, Maryland, November 14, 1832) signed the Declaration of Independence. He was the last surviving signer of the document.

Sir William Golding (born Columb Minor, Cornwall, England, 1911; died near Truro, Cornwall, England, June 19, 1993) was a writer. One of his most famous works is *Lord of the Flies*. He won a Nobel Prize in literature in 1983.

September

Ferdinand Magellan began the voyage that would take his ship around the world in 1519. He died before the voyage was over, but the ship *Victoria* did complete the journey.

 Students could read log entries from sailors to learn about the voyage's terrible conditions.

USS *Constitution*, nicknamed "Old Ironsides," had its maiden voyage in 1797.

New York Stock Exchange had to close in 1873 because of a banking crisis. Although most issues were resolved within a week, the crisis made a lasting impression on the nation.

Electric range was patented in 1859.

 Students could find out how an electric stove works.

Birthdays

Alexander the Great (born 356 B.C.; died 323 B.C.) was a famous military leader.

 Students could map his many military conquests.

Arnold "Red" Auerbach (born Brooklyn, New York, 1917) is a basketball coach. He is honored in the Basketball Hall of Fame.

Upton Sinclair (born Baltimore, Maryland, 1878; died Bound Brook, New Jersey, November 25, 1968) was a novelist. One of his most well-known books is *The Jungle*.

September

The Hobbit **was published in 1937.**

Armenia celebrates a national holiday. It broke away from the Union of Soviet Socialist Republics in 1991. Armenia's history dates back to the sixth century B.C. Yerevan is the capital.

 Students could locate more information about ancient Armenia.

Belize celebrates its Independence Day. It left British rule in 1981. This small country is located on the northeastern coast of South America. Belmopan is the capital.

First western movie, *Kit Carson,* appeared on screen in 1903. The movie lasted twenty minutes.

Birthdays

Cecil Fielder (born Los Angeles, California, 1963) is a former baseball player.

Stephen King (born Portland, Maine, 1947) is an author. Two of his most famous works are *The Shining* and *The Stand.*

Francis Hopkinson (born Philadelphia, Pennsylvania, 1737; died Philadelphia, Pennsylvania, May 9, 1791) signed the Declaration of Independence. He was a lawyer and a judge.

Louis Jolliet (born near Quebec City, New France, 1645; died 1700) was an explorer. He and Jacques Marquette traveled extensively through the upper Mississippi River region.

 Students could trace some of the routes the two explorers traveled.

Margaret MacKall Smith Taylor (born Calvert County, Maryland, 1788; died East Pascagoula, Mississippi, August 14, 1852) was the wife of Zachary Taylor, twelfth president of the United States. She lived in the White House for less than eighteen months because he died in office. Even while first lady, however, she relegated social functions to her daughter. Visit a Web site at: http://www.whitehouse.gov/history/firstladies/mt12.html.

Herbert George Wells (born Bromley, Kent, England, 1866; died London, England, August 13, 1946) was a writer. Two of his most famous works are *The War of the Worlds* and *The Invisible Man.*

 Students could read and enjoy some of his works.

eptember

22 **Tacy Richardson rode her horse, Fearnaught, in 1777 through perilous territory to warn General Washington of approaching British troops.**

 Students could write about Tacy's ride from her point of view.

U.S. Post Office and the office of postmaster general were created by Congress in 1789.

Ice cream cone mold patent was filed in 1903 by Italo Marchiony.

 Students could celebrate the day by eating ice cream cones.

Mali celebrates its Independence Day. It became free from France in 1960. It was called French Sudan. Bamako is the capital.

Women were allowed to attend military academies, per Congress, in 1975.

First day of autumn occurs either on September 22 or September 23. It marks the autumnal equinox, and the length of the day equals the length of the night.

Birthdays

Michael Faraday (born near London, England, 1791; died Hampton Court, England, August 25, 1867) was an important and famous scientist. He discovered electromagnetism. He also conducted experiments regarding valence.

 Students could make electromagnets.

Esphyr Slobodkina (born Cheliabinsk, Siberia, 1908; died July 21, 2002) was an author and illustrator. One of her books is *Caps for Sale.*

Chen Ning Yang (born Hefei, Anhui, China, 1922) is a physicist. He and Tsung Dao Lee won the 1957 Nobel Prize in physics for disproving the law of parity.

September

Libra the Scales is the astrological sign for September 23 through October 22.

Lewis and Clark finished their exploration in 1806. Their expedition lasted two years, four months, and ten days, ending in St. Louis, Missouri. Their journals described buffalo, grizzly bears, and many other animals.

 Students could write a newspaper interview of the two famous explorers.

Santa Fe Trail opened in 1822.

Baseball Rules Code was adopted in 1845.

Neptune was discovered in 1846. In 1841 John Couch Adams began work to find the planet. Urbain J. J. Leverrier, unknown to Adams, also began making calculations. Astronomer Johann G. Galle used their predictions and located the planet.

 Students could locate more information on Neptune.

Hearing aid was patented in 1879.

 Students could find out hearing aids work.

Saudi Arabia celebrates the 1932 Kingdom Unification.

Birthdays

Augustus Caesar (born 63 B.C.; died A.D. 14) was a ruler of ancient Rome.

Ray Charles (born Albany, Georgia, 1930) is a singer and composer. One of his most famous compositions is *Georgia on My Mind.*

Euripides (born Salamis, Greece, 480 B.C.; died 406 B.C.) was a dramatist. He wrote at least seventeen tragedies. One of his most famous works is *Media,* completed in 431 B.C.

William C. McCool (born San Diego, California; died in the *Columbia* disaster, February 1, 2003) was an astronaut.

William McGuffey (born Washington County, Pennsylvania, 1800; died Charlottesville, Virginia, May 4, 1873) was an educator and author. He penned the *McGuffey Readers.*

 Students could try to find copies of *McGuffey Readers.* How do they compare with instructional reading books today?

Victoria Chaflin Woodhull (born Homer, Ohio, 1838; died Norton Park, Bremmons, Worcestershire, England, June 10, 1927) was an advocate of women's rights. She was the first woman candidate for the presidency.

eptember

24 **Guinea-Bissau celebrates its Independence Day.** It gained its freedom from Portugal in 1973. Bissau is the capital of this African country.

Faneuil Hall opened in Boston, Massachusetts, in 1742.

 Students could find out why Faneuil Hall was built. Is it still standing today?

Office of attorney general was created by Congress in 1789.

 Students could find out the exact purposes of the office of the attorney general.

The Bullwinkle Show **appeared for the first time in 1961.**

Sixty Minutes **was televised for the first time in 1968.**

Birthdays

F. Scott Fitzgerald (born St. Paul, Minnesota, 1896; died Hollywood, California, December 21, 1940) was a writer. One of his most famous works was *The Great Gatsby.*

Jim Henson (born Greenville, Mississippi, 1936; died New York, New York, May 16, 1990) created the Muppets. He was very active in the production of *Sesame Street.* He also created several movies.

 Students could create puppets and produce their own plays.

John Marshall (born Germantown, Virginia, 1755; died Philadelphia, Pennsylvania, July 6, 1835) was a member of the House of Representatives and was John Adams's secretary of state. However, he is most remembered as the Supreme Court chief justice who really defined the court. He also gave the Supreme Court an important role within the framework of the Constitution.

Wilson Rawls (born Scraper, Oklahoma, 1913; died Cornell, Wisconsin, December 16, 1984) was a children's author. He wrote *Where the Red Fern Grows* and *Summer of the Monkeys.* Visit a Web site at: http://pac.eils.lib.id.us/rawls/bio.html.

eptember

25 **Christopher Columbus started his second voyage to the New World in 1493.**

Vasco Nunez de Balboa claimed the Pacific Ocean and "all shores washed by it" for Spain in 1513.

 Students could find out just how big a territory Balboa really did claim.

First printing press in America was assembled in 1639.

Students could find out how the early printing press worked.

First U.S. Congress met in 1787.

The Twelfth Amendment to the Constitution was adopted in 1804. Prior to the amendment, the presidential candidate with the most votes became president. The one with the next amount of votes became vice president. This did not always work well. The amendment changed the process so that the president and vice president became a team.

Sequoia National Park was created in 1890. Contact: Sequoia National Park, Three Rivers, California 93271. Visit a Web site at: http://www.nps.gov/seki.

 Students could compare the sequoia to other types of trees.

USS *Enterprise,* **the first atomic-powered submarine, was launched in 1960.**

Sandra Day O'Connor became the first woman Supreme Court justice when she was sworn in in 1981.

Birthdays

William Cuthbert Faulkner (born New Albany, Mississippi, 1897; died Byhalia, July 6, 1962) was an author. Two of his most famous works were *The Sound and the Fury* and *The Portable Faulkner.* He won the Nobel Prize for literature in 1949.

Marcus "Mark" Rothko(witz) (born Dvinsk, Russia, 1903; died New York, New York, February 25, 1970) was an artist.

Dmitri Shostakovich (born St. Petersburg, Russia, 1906; died Moscow, Russia, August 9, 1975) was a composer.

Shel Silverstein (born Chicago, Illinois, 1932; died Key West, Florida, May 10, 1999) was an author, illustrator, and songwriter.

Will Smith (born Philadelphia, Pennsylvania, 1968) is an actor.

Barbara Walters (born Boston, Massachusetts, 1931) is a television journalist.

September

 26

Francis Drake's ship circumnavigated the world in 1580.

Cement was patented in 1871.

 Students could find out how cement is made.

U.S. Mint in 1889 stopped producing one-dollar and three-dollar gold pieces.

George Washington established his first cabinet. Thomas Jefferson became secretary of state. John Jay was appointed the first chief justice of the Supreme Court. Samuel Osgood was the first postmaster, and Edmund J. Randolph was made attorney general.

John Philip Sousa conducted his first band performance in 1892.

Yemen Arab Republic celebrates the 1962 proclamation of the republic.

West Side Story, **a musical, premiered in 1957 in New York, New York.**

 Students could listen to some of the songs from the musical.

Nixon and Kennedy, presidential candidates, held the first of four televised debates in 1960.

"Gilligan's Island" appeared on television for the first time in 1964.

Birthdays

John Chapman "Johnny Appleseed" (born Leominster, Massachusetts, 1774; died Allen County, Indiana, March 11, 1845) is believed to have planted many orchards of apple trees. He was well regarded by both the Indians and the settlers. His death is remembered as Johnny Appleseed Day.

George Gershwin (born Brooklyn, New York, 1898; died Beverly Hills, California, July 11, 1937) was a composer. He often teamed with his brother, Ira. Two of his most famous works are *I Got Rhythm* and *The Man I Love.*

 Children could listen to one of his classics, *Rhapsody in Blue.*

Shamu (born Orlando, Florida, 1985) is the first killer whale born in captivity to survive to adulthood.

Serena Williams (born Saginaw, Michigan) is a tennis player.

September

 27 **Matchbooks were patented 1892 by Joshua Pusey of Lima, Pennsylvania.**

 Students could find out how matchbooks are assembled.

Birthdays

Samuel Adams (born Boston, Massachusetts, 1722; died Boston, Massachusetts, October 2, 1803) was a leader during the American Revolution. He attended the First and Second Continental Congresses. He signed the Declaration of Independence and the Articles of Confederation.

 Students could find out what he did after the Revolutionary War. They may also want to read Jean Fritz's *Why Don't You Get a Horse, Sam Adams?*

Paul Goble (born Haslemere, England, 1933) is an author and illustrator of children's books. *The Girl Who Loved Wild Horses* won the Caldecott Medal in 1978.

Thomas Nast (born Landau, Germany, 1840; died Guayaquil, Ecuador, December 7, 1902) was a political cartoonist. He created the symbols of the donkey and the elephant for the democratic and republican political parties.

Mike Schmidt (born Dayton, Ohio, 1949) is a former baseball player.

Bernard Weber (born Philadelphia, Pennsylvania, 1924) is a children's author and illustrator. He wrote, among other works, *Lyle, Lyle, Crocodile* (1965).

 Students could read and enjoy his works.

September

 28 **William the Conqueror arrived in England in 1066.**

 Students could find out where William was born and why he came to England.

Taiwan celebrates Confucius's birthday.

Juan Rodriguez Cabrillo discovered California in 1542. Cabrillo National Monument in San Diego Bay stands today. Visit a Web site at: http://www.nps.gov/cabr.

Siege of Yorktown commenced in 1781. It was the last major battle of the Revolutionary War.

 General Washington lost more battles than he won. The students could find out why Yorktown was so important.

Pokemon appeared in the United States in 1998.

Birthdays

Ed Sullivan (born New York, New York, 1902; died New York, New York, October 13, 1974) hosted the *Ed Sullivan Show,* airing on Sunday nights. He often featured new talent. He introduced the Beatles to America.

Kate Douglas Wiggin (born Philadelphia, Pennsylvania, 1856; died Harrow, England, August 24, 1923) established kindergartens in California. However, she is most known for being a children's author. One of her most famous works is *Rebecca of Sunnybrook Farm.*

 Students could read portions of her books.

September

29 **Scotland Yard began operating in 1829.**

 Students could find out why London police officers are called "bobbies."

Space shuttle *Discovery* was launched for the first time in 1988. It was the first American space flight since the *Challenger* disaster of 1986.

Washington National Cathedral was completed in 1990 after eighty-three years of construction.

 Students could find out how a cathedral differs from other types of churches.

Birthdays

Gene Autry (born Tioga, Texas, 1907; died Studio City, California, October 2, 1998) was an actor and a singer. He is most known for his roles in westerns.

Stan Berenstain (born Philadelphia, Pennsylvania, 1923) is a children's author. He and his wife have created the Berenstain Bears series.

Miguel de Cervantes Saavedra (born Alcala de Henares, Spain, 1547; died Madrid, Spain, April 23, 1616) was a writer. One of his most famous works is *Don Quixote.*

 Students could find out why Don Quixote fought windmills.

Enrico Fermi (born Rome, Italy, 1901; died Chicago, Illinois, November 28, 1954) was a physicist. He immigrated to the United States in 1938. He developed the first nuclear chain reaction. He was part of the team that developed the atomic bomb. He received the 1938 Nobel Prize in physics.

September

Babe Ruth hit his sixtieth home run for the season in 1927. That record stood until Roger Maris hit sixty-one home runs in 1961.

Botswana celebrates Botswana Day, its Independence Day. The United Kingdom gave up control of Botswana in 1966. This landlocked African country is fairly prosperous. It is a leading producer of diamonds. Gold has also been found in the country. Because large herds of game still roam the country, tourism also brings in a great deal of revenue.

Rayon was patented in 1902.

 Students could find out how rayon is different from nylon and other synthetic fabrics.

James Meredith enrolled as the first African American at the all-white University of Mississippi in 1962. President Kennedy sent federal troops to quell the riots. Three people died and fifty more were hurt.

Frisbee was patented in 1958 by Walter "Fred" Morrison.

 Students could find out the story behind the Frisbee. They could create a Frisbee course on the playground.

"The Flintstones" debuted on television in 1960.

Guadalupe Mountains National Park was established in 1972. Contact: Guadalupe Mountains National Park, HC 60, Box 400, Salt Flat, Texas 79847-9400. Visit a Web site at: http://www.nps.gov/gumo.

Birthdays

Edgar Parin D'Aulaire (born Munich, Germany, 1898; died May 1, 1986) was an author. One of his books was *D'Aulaire's Book of Greek Myths.*

Hans Wilhelm Geiger (born Neustadt, Germany, 1882; died Berlin, Germany, September 24, 1945) invented the Geiger counter.

 Students could find out how a Geiger counter works.

Elie Wiesel (born Sighet, Romania, 1928) is an author and a survivor of the Holocaust. He was awarded the 1986 Nobel Peace Prize for helping Holocaust victims.

OCTOBER

In early times October was the eighth month of the year. Its name is derived from the Latin word *octo,* meaning "eight." Julius Caesar changed the calendar and made October the tenth month. Since that time, the month has had thirty-one days. The calendula is October's flower. October birthstones are the opal and the tourmaline.

Month-Long Activities

Computer Learning Month shares new technology, new software, and new uses for computers. Contact: Computer Learning Foundation, Department CHS, PO Box 60007, Palo Alto, California 94306-0007. Telephone: (415) 327-3347. E-mail: clf@legal.com.

Family History Month stresses the importance of keeping and sharing family stories and traditions. Contact: Monmouth County Historical Association, 5 Hampton Court, Neptune, New Jersey 07753-5672. Visit a Web site at: http://nj5.injersey.com/kjshelly/mcgc.html.

 Children could make family trees.

National Popcorn Poppin' Month celebrates the nutritious snack. Contact: The Popcorn Institute, 401 North Michigan Avenue, Chicago, Illinois 60611-4267. Telephone: (312) 644-6610. Visit a Web site at: http://www.popcorn.org.

 Children could pop some popcorn and then enjoy it.

National Pizza Month honors one of America's favorite foods. A recipe contest is part of the month's celebrations. Contact: National Association of Pizza Operators, 137 East Market Street, New Albany, Indiana 47151. Telephone: (812) 949-0909.

Special Weeks

Fire Prevention Week educates children about what to do in case of fire. Presidential proclamation has declared the week to be the first or second week in October since 1925. Visit a Web site at: http://www.firepreventionweek.org or at: http://www.sparky.org.

 Perhaps a fireperson could visit the classroom and share fire safety information.

National Forest Products Week begins with the third Sunday in October. Presidential proclamations have been issued for National Forest Products Week since 1960.

National School Lunch Week is observed by presidential proclamation for the week beginning with the second Sunday in October. 1962 marked the first observance of this week.

 The school cafeteria manager could speak to the class on nutrition.

Special Days

Child Health Day is the first Monday in October. Presidential proclamations have been issued for this day since 1928.

Columbus Day is the second Monday in October.

Canada celebrates its Thanksgiving on the second Monday in October.

Daylight Saving Time ends at 2:00 A.M. on the last Sunday in October.

Supreme Court starts its new session on the first Monday in October.

October

Spain turned over control of Louisiana to France in 1800.

Yosemite National Park was established in 1864. Yosemite Valley and Mariposa Big Tree Grove combined to make the national park. Contact: Yosemite National Park, PO Box 577, Yosemite National Park, California 95389. Visit a Web site at: http://www.nps.gov/yose.

 Children could locate Yosemite National Park on the map. They could guide an imaginary bus driver from San Francisco to the park.

First postcard was produced in 1869.

Free delivery of rural mail began in 1896.

First issue of *National Geographic* magazine was published in 1864.

 Each student could examine an issue of *National Geographic* magazine. They could share interesting facts they learn.

Nigeria celebrates its Independence Day. In 1960 it became independent from the United Kingdom, and in 1963 it became a republic. The country is larger than Texas, and Niamey is the capital.

People's Republic of China celebrates its birthday; it came into being in 1949.

World Series held its first game in 1903.

Albert Einstein became a U.S. citizen in 1940.

Roger Maris in 1961 hit his sixty-first home run in the season, a new record breaking Babe Ruth's record of sixty home runs in 1927. Maris's record stood until 1998, when Mark McGuire hit sixty-two home runs.

Birthdays

Julie Andrews (born Walton-on-Thames, England, 1935) is a singer and an actress. She won an Oscar for *Mary Poppins.*

James Earl "Jimmy" Carter (born Plains, Georgia, 1924) is the thirty-ninth president (1977–1981) of the United States. He graduated from the United States Naval Academy. Later he became a Georgia state senator and eventually became the state's governor. During his presidency, he faced high inflation. He negotiated the Camp David Accord between Egypt and Israel. He was awarded the 2002 Nobel Peace Prize. Visit a Web site at: http://www.whitehouse.gov/history/presidents/jc39.html.

Mr. Carter has become very involved with Habitat for Humanity. The students could research the group's goals and how they are accomplished.

Caroline Lavinia Scott Harrison (born Oxford, Ohio, 1832; died Washington, DC, October 25, 1892) was the first wife of Benjamin Harrison, twenty-third president of the United States. She succumbed to tuberculosis during Harrison's fourth year as president. She helped create the Daughters of the American Revolution. Visit a Web site at: http://www.whitehouse.gov/history/firstladies/ch23.html.

Vladimir Horowitz (born Berdichev, Russia, 1904; died New York, New York, November 5, 1989) was a famous pianist. He performed in his first concert when he was sixteen years old. He became a U.S. citizen when he was forty-four years old. One of his most memorable recitals was when he returned to Russia on April 20, 1986.

Mark McGwire (born Pomona, California, 1963) is a former baseball player.

William Hubbs Rehnquist (born Milwaukee, Wisconsin, 1924) is the present chief justice of the Supreme Court.

Richard Stockton (born Princeton, New Jersey, 1730; died Princeton, New Jersey, February 8, 1781) was an attorney. He signed the Declaration of Independence.

October

First camel appeared in the United States in Boston in 1721.

Guinea celebrates its Independence Day. France relinquished control in 1958. Located in western Africa, the land was the site of ancient caravan routes. The country is slightly bigger than the state of Utah, and Conakrey is the capital.

Redwood National Park was created in 1968. Contact: Redwood National Park, 1111 Second Street, Crescent City, California 95531. Visit a Web site at: http://www.nps.gov/redw.

 Giant redwoods reside in this forest. Children could find some statistics about these trees. Even the pinecones are huge.

Thurgood Marshall was sworn into the Supreme Court in 1967. Marshall was the first African American Supreme Court justice. He retired on June 27, 1991.

 Students could find out how Supreme Court justices are appointed.

Birthdays

Charlie Brown and Snoopy ("born" 1950) are the creations of Charles Schultz. Their last comic strip was published on February 13, 2000.

Mohandas Karamchand "Mahatma" Gandhi (born Porbandar, India, 1869; died New Delhi, India, January 30, 1948) led India's fight for independence from Great Britain. Trained as a lawyer in England, Gandhi stressed the use of nonviolence. He was assassinated in his garden by a Hindu who resented Gandhi's views about Moslems.

 Children could find out more about Gandhi's philosophies. They could compare them to those of Martin Luther King, Jr.

Julius Henry "Groucho" Marx (born New York, New York, 1890; died Los Angeles, California, August 19, 1977) was an actor. He and his brothers formed the Marx Brothers. Two of their most famous movies are *Animal Crackers,* produced in 1930, and *Duck Soup,* premiering in 1933. He was also the host of an early television show, *You Bet Your Life.*

 October

 3 **Germany was reunified in 1990.** East Germany and West Germany had been two separate countries for forty-five years. When they combined, they took West Germany's name, The Federal Republic of Germany.

 Students could find out how and why Germany was divided in the first place.

Korea celebrates National Foundation Day. Tangun, a legendary hero, founded his kingdom of Chosun in 2333 B.C.

Honduras celebrates Francisco Morazan Day to honor the 1799 birth of Francisco Morazan, a national hero.

Netherlands marks Relief of Leiden Day. The city was liberated in 1574.

"Captain Kangaroo" premiered on television on CBS in 1955.

"Mickey Mouse Club" began its first season on ABC also in 1955.

Frank Robinson in 1974 became the first African American to be hired as a major league baseball team manager. He was the only player to be selected most valuable player by both the National League and the American League. He was hired to manage the Cleveland Indians.

 Sports fans could make a timeline of Robinson's life.

Rebecca L. Felton became the first female United States senator. In 1922 Georgia Governor Thomas Hardwick appointed Mrs. Felton to the seat vacated by the death of Thomas Watson.

Birthdays

James Alfred Wight Herriot (born Glasgow, Scotland, 1916; died Yorkshire, England, February 23, 1995) was a writer and a veterinarian. He wrote among other works *All Creatures Great and Small.*

Harvey Kurtzman (born Brooklyn, New York, 1902; died Mount Vernon, New York, February 21, 1993) founded *Mad* magazine (1952).

 Students could poll parents and teachers as to their attitudes toward *Mad* magazine.

Thomas Clayton Wolfe (born Asheville, North Carolina, 1900; died Baltimore, Maryland, September 15, 1938) was an author. One of his most well known works is *You Can't Go Home Again.*

October

4 **Gregorian calendar adjustment was made in 1582.** Earlier that year Pope Gregory XIII had announced that the day following October 4 would be October 15. The adjustment took place in most Catholic countries. Great Britain and the colonies did not change until 1752.

Crimean War started in 1853.

Jet passenger service began in 1958.

Sputnik I, **a Soviet spacecraft, was launched in 1957.** It was the first successful man-made satellite, weighing 184 pounds and remaining in space for twenty-one days.

 Sputnik marked the beginning of the space race. Children could read more about the space exploration competition between the United States and the former Soviet Union.

Luna 3 **was launched in 1959 by the Soviets.** It was the first spacecraft to photograph the moon's far side.

Lesotho celebrates Independence Day. It became free from British rule in 1966. The country, about the size of Maryland, is entirely surrounded by South Africa. Maseru is the capital. Tourism is its major industry.

Birthdays

Karen Cushman (born Chicago, Illinois, 1941) is a children's author. *Catherine, Called Birdie* was a 1995 Newbery Honor Book. *The Midwife's Apprentice* was the 1996 Newbery Medal winner. Visit a Web site at: http://www.eduplace.com/rdg/author/cushman.

Rutherford Birchard Hayes (born Delaware, Ohio, 1822; died Fremont, Ohio, January 17, 1893) was the nineteenth president (1877–1881) of the United States. He attended Harvard Law School. During the Civil War he was wounded five times. At the end of the war, he had attained the rank of general. He returned to Ohio and eventually became its governor. He ran for president. He lost the popular vote, but he won the electoral vote. He concerned himself with improving civil service, and he ended a major railroad strike. He chose to run for only one term. Visit a Web site at: http://www.whitehouse.gov/history/presidents/rh19.html.

Robert Lawson (born New York, New York, 1862; died Rabbit Hill, Westport, Connecticut, May 26, 1957) was a children's book author and illustrator. He won both a Newbery Medal and a Caldecott Medal. One of his books was *Rabbit Hill.* Visit a Web site at: http://www.friend.ly.net/scoop/biographies/lawsonrobert.

Eliza McCardle Johnson (born Leesburg, Tennessee, 1810; died Carter's Station, Tennessee, January 15, 1876) was the wife of Andrew Johnson, seventeenth president of the United States. She was frail and did not serve as hostess in the White House. Her daughter, Martha Johnson Patterson, took over the role for her. Visit a Web site at: http://www.whitehouse.gov/history/firstladies/ej17.html.

Frederic Remington (born Canton, New York, 1861; died Ridgefield, Connecticut, December 26, 1909) was an artist. He was particularly interested in the Old West. His paintings are filled with action and adventure. He is also famous for his bronze works.

Damon Runyon (born Manhattan, Kansas, 1884; died New York, New York, December 10, 1946) was an author and a reporter.

Donald Sobol (born New York, New York, 1924) is a children's author. He is best known for his Encyclopedia Brown series.

 Children could read some Encyclopedia Brown books and try to solve the mysteries.

Edward Stratemeyer (born Elizabeth, New Jersey, 1862; died Newark, New Jersey, May 10, 1930) developed the Stratemeyer Syndicate that wrote more than 800 books and produced such series as The Hardy Boys, Nancy Drew, and Tom Swift.

The Tom Swift series generated puns called Tom Swifties. Visit a Web site at: http://thinks.com/words/tomswift.htm. Students could enjoy the puns and create some of their own.

October

5 **Thomas Stone died in Alexandria, Virginia, in 1787.** He was born in Charles County, Maryland, sometime in 1743. He signed the Declaration of Independence.

President Harry Truman made the first telecast speech from the White House in 1947. He asked citizens of the United States to eat no meat on Tuesdays, no eggs or chickens on Thursdays, and to eat one slice of bread less per day so that food could be sent to Europe. The continent's food production had been greatly reduced because of World War II.

Isaac Bashevis Singer won the Nobel Prize for literature in 1978.

Barry Bonds in 2001 set a new record for most home runs in one season. He broke Mark McGuire's record of seventy home runs when he hit his seventy-first home run at Pacific Bell Park. Bonds finished the season with a total of seventy-three home runs.

Birthdays

Chester Alan Arthur (born Fairfield, Vermont, 1830; died New York, New York, November 18, 1886) was the twenty-first president (1881–1885) of the United States. During the Civil War, he received patronage jobs. He became president after James A. Garfield was killed. During his presidency, even his own party was not happy with him. He was not renominated in 1884. Visit a Web site at: http://www.whitehouse.gov/wh/glimpse/presidents/html/ca21.html.

 Students could find out why Arthur was not renominated.

Robert Hutchings Goddard (born Worcester, Massachusetts, 1882; died Baltimore, Maryland, August 10, 1945) is known as the Father of the Space Age. He was taunted because he thought space travel was a real possibility. He designed and launched a liquid fuel powered rocket in 1926.

 Students could find out how today's rockets are fueled.

Louise Fitzhugh (born Memphis, Tennessee, 1928; died Bridgewater, Connecticut, November 19, 1974) was a children's author. She wrote, among other works, *Harriet the Spy,* 1964.

 Children could read and share some of her books.

Bill Keane (born Philadelphia, Pennsylvania, 1922) is a cartoonist. He created "Family Circus."

October

6 **Self-winding clock was patented in 1783.**

American Library Association was founded in 1876 in Philadelphia, Pennsylvania.

Germany celebrates Erntedankfest, the potato harvest festival.

Students could examine different kinds of potatoes. They could find out how potatoes are grown and harvested.

National German-American Day is celebrated by presidential proclamation since 1987.

Albert Sabin in 1956 discovered an oral polio vaccine.

Birthdays

Thor Heyerdahl (born Larvik, Norway, 1914; died Colla Micheri, Italy, April 18, 2002) was an ethnologist and an adventurer. He built and sailed the *Kon-Tiki*. He and five others sailed from Peru to eastern Polynesia on the balsa raft to prove that natives of South America could have settled the islands.

Jenny Lind (born Stockholm, Sweden, 1820; died Malvern, England, November 2, 1887) was an opera singer. She was known as the Swedish Nightingale.

Florence Seibert (born Easton, Pennsylvania, 1897; died St. Petersburg, Florida, August 23, 1991) was a doctor. She developed a test for tuberculosis that is given worldwide.

 The school nurse could talk to the class about the importance of the tuberculosis test.

Ruben Angel Sierra (born Rio Piedras, Puerto Rico, 1965) is a baseball player.

Elizabeth Gray Vining (born Philadelphia, Pennsylvania, 1902; died Kennett Square, Pennsylvania, November 27, 1999) was a children's author. Using the pseudonym of Elizabeth Gray, she wrote *Adam of the Road,* the Newbery Medal winner of 1943.

George Westinghouse (born Central Bridge, New York, 1846; died New York, New York, March 12, 1914) was an inventor. He held over 400 patents, and he created Westinghouse Electric Company. At one time his company employed about 50,000 people.

 Students could list some of his inventions.

October

 7

Double-decked steamboat arrived in New Orleans for the first time in 1816.

 Students could trace the routes steamboats took.

Dow Jones Industrial Average was created in 1896 to give a snapshot of the overall trends of the stock market. Today thirty stocks comprise the Dow Jones Industrial Average. Visit a Web site at: http://www.cftech.com/brainbank/finance/dowjonesavgshist.html.

Birthdays

Niels Bohr (born Copenhagen, Denmark, 1885; died Copenhagen, Denmark, November 18, 1962) developed the theory of atomic structure. He received the 1922 Nobel Prize for physics. Later he studied the nucleus of atoms and quantum mechanics.

 Students could draw a model of an atom and learn about its various rings.

Yo-Yo Ma (born Paris, France, 1955) is a musician.

Vladimir Putin (born St, Petersburg, Russia, 1952) is the president of Russia.

James Whitcomb Riley (born Greenfield, Indiana, 1849?; died Indianapolis, Indiana, July 22, 1916) was known as the "Hoosier" poet.

 Students could read some of his poetry.

Caesar Rodney (born Dover, Delaware, 1728; died Dover, Delaware, June 26, 1784) signed the Declaration of Independence.

Desmond Tutu (born Klerksdrop, South Africa, 1931) is the archbishop of South Africa and a Nobel Peace Prize recipient.

October

Alvin C. York Day honors the sergeant who, when separated from his patrol, captured 132 enemy soldiers, thirty-five machine guns, and a hill in France in 1918. He also killed twenty of the enemy as well. York received the U.S. Medal of Honor and the French Croix de Guerre.

 Students could find out what happened to York after World War I.

Great Chicago Fire of 1871 burned for thirty hours. Legend states Mrs. O'Leary's cow kicked over a lantern and started a fire in her barn. Almost 100,000 people lost their homes, and over 200 people died.

 Students could list the reasons why this fire was so devastating.

Peshtigo Forest Fire started in 1871. Experts believe this to be one of the most damaging forest fires ever. The fire began in Peshtigo, Wisconsin, and spread across six counties. More than 1,100 people died.

Peru celebrates Day of the Navy.

First patent for what became the microwave oven was filed by Percy Le Baron Spencer in 1945.

Birthdays

Chevy Chase (born Cornelius Crane in New York, New York, 1943) is a comedian and an actor.

Barthe DeClements (born Seattle, Washington, 1920) is an author. One of her books is *Sixth Grade Can Really Kill You.*

Jesse Jackson (born Greenville, North Carolina, 1941) is a minister and a civil rights leader.

Edward Rickenbacker (born Columbus, Ohio, 1890; died Zurich, Switzerland, July 23, 1973) was an aviator and a war hero.

 Students could find out what Rickenbacker did to become such a hero.

Faith Ringgold (born Harlem, New York, 1930) writes and illustrates children's books. *Tar Beach* was a Caldecott Honor Book in 1991.

R. L. Stine (born Columbus, Ohio, 1943) is the author of the Goosebumps series.

October

 9 **Iceland and the United States celebrate Leif Erikson Day.** The Viking may have discovered North America in the year 1000.

 Students could research the evidence and decide which European found the Americas first.

Calliope was patented in 1855.

Uganda celebrates its Independence Day. This landlocked African country became free from British rule in 1962. The capital is Kampala. Although Uganda has large reserves of natural resources, it is one of the poorest countries in the world.

 Students could find out why Uganda does not have a strong economy.

American Humane Association was created in 1877.

Korea celebrates Alphabet Day, also known as Hangul. King Sejong in 1446 promoted Hangul, a twenty-four-letter phonetic alphabet.

 Students could learn more about the Korean alphabet.

Birthdays

Johanna Hurwitz (born New York, New York, 1937) is a children's author. One of her books is *Hurray for Ali Baba Bernstein,* published in 1989.

John Lennon (born Liverpool, England, 1940; assassinated in New York, New York, December 8, 1980) was a composer and a member of The Beatles.

Camille Saint-Saens (born Paris, France, 1835; died Algiers, France, December 16, 1921) was a composer. One of his compositions was *The Carnival of the Animals.*

October

 10 **Synthetic detergent was invented in 1933.**

 Students could find out how soap and detergent differ.

Spiro Agnew, Richard Nixon's vice president, resigned in 1973 after being fined $248,735 for violating the public trust.

Fiji celebrates its Independence Day. The United Kingdom gave up custody of the 300 islands in 1970. The islands, located in the South Pacific, depend on agriculture and tourism for income. Suva is the capital.

 Students could locate Fiji on a map. They could decide what kind of weather the islands would have.

Japan celebrates Health-Sports Day.

Double Tenth Day is celebrated in China. On October 10, 1911 (the tenth day of the tenth month), the people revolted against the Manchu Dynasty. This last dynasty fell.

Naval Academy opened in Annapolis, Maryland, in 1845.

Birthdays

James Marshall (born San Antonio, Texas, 1942; died New York, New York, October 13, 1992) was a children's author and illustrator. He wrote, among other works, the Miss Nelson books. He also created the George and Martha series.

 Children could read and enjoy some of his works.

Daniel San Souci (born San Francisco, California, 1948) is a children's book author and illustrator. One of his books is *Ice Bear and Little Fox*. Visit a Web site at: http://www. childrenspages.com/illustrators/dsansouci.htm.

Robert San Souci (born San Francisco, California, 1946) is a children's book author. He wrote *Fa Mulan*. Visit a Web site at: http://www.cbcbooks.org/html/robert_san_souci.html.

Giuseppe Verdi (born Le Roncole, Italy, 1813; died Milan, Italy, January 27, 1901) was a composer. His works include *Rigoletto* and *Aida*.

Ben Vereen (born Miami, Florida, 1946) is a singer, an actor, and a dancer.

Benjamin West (born near Springfield, Pennsylvania, 1738; died London, England, March 11, 1820) was a painter. Visit a Web site at: http://www.ibiblio.org/wm/paint/auth/west.

October

11

Space shuttle program in 2000 launched its one hundredth mission. Astronauts aboard *Discovery* helped build the International Space Station. Visit a Web site at: http://spaceflight. nasa.gov/station.

 Students could try to imagine what daily life would be on the International Space Station. They could write to the astronauts and ask them questions.

World population in 1999 reached six billion people. Visit a Web site at: http://www.census. gov/ipc/www/world.html.

General Pulaski Memorial Day is celebrated by presidential proclamation. The first proclamation was issued in 1929.

Comptmeter, the first accurate adding machine, was patented by Dorr Eugene Felt in 1887.

Dr. Kathryn D. Sullivan became the first American woman to walk in space. She was part of the 1984 *Challenger* crew. The mission was completed October 13, 1984.

Jimmy Carter was awarded the 2002 Nobel Peace Prize for his efforts to bring peace to various parts of the world.

Birthdays

Art Blakey (born Pittsburgh, Pennsylvania, 1919; died New York, New York, October 16, 1990) was a jazz drummer and a bandleader.

Russell Freedman (born San Francisco, California, 1929) has written more than thirty books for children. His *Lincoln: A Photobiography* won the 1987 Newbery Medal.

Jerome Robbins (born New York, New York, 1918) is a choreographer.

Roscoe Robinson, Jr. (Born St. Louis, Missouri, 1928; died Washington, DC, July 22, 1993) was the first African American to be a four-star general in the army.

Anna Eleanor Roosevelt (born New York, New York, 1884; died New York, New York, November 7, 1962) was wife of Franklin Delano Roosevelt, thirty-second president of the United States. She was probably one of the most influential first ladies, holding her own press conferences. She was also a writer and a diplomat. She represented the United States at the United Nations. Visit a Web site at: http://www.whitehouse.gov/history/firstladies/ar32.html.

 Students could read more about her life. They could dramatize a portion of her life. Children might want to read Russell Freedman's *Eleanor Roosevelt: A Life of Discovery.*

Parson Mason Locke Weems (born Anne Arundel County, Maryland, 1759; died Beaufort, South Carolina, May 23, 1825) was a minister and a bookseller. He is famous for his fiction that he presented as fact. One of his tales was the one in which George Washington chopped down the cherry tree.

 Students could take a real person and "Parson Weems" a story.

October

12 **Christopher Columbus landed at El Salvador in 1492.** His journey, filled with dangers, marked the beginning of the age of exploration.

 Students could find out more about the voyage. They could decide whether Columbus was just a fortune hunter or not.

Equatorial Guinea celebrates its Independence Day. It gained its independence from Spain in 1968. The country consists of a mainland portion of Africa and five islands. The country, slightly larger than the state of Maryland, exports cocoa beans and coffee. Malabo is the capital.

 Students could find out how Spain had gained control of Equatorial Guinea.

Birthdays

Kirk Cameron (born Panorama City, California, 1970) is an actor.

Luciano Pavarotti (born Modena, Italy, 1935) is an opera singer.

 Students could listen to a recording of his music.

October

13 **White House cornerstone was placed into position in 1792.** The building was completed in 1800. The White House contains more than 100 rooms.

 Students could visit the White House Web site at: http://www.whitehouse.gov and take a virtual tour of the building.

U.S. Navy was created in 1775.

B'nai B'rith was founded by Henry Jones and others in New York, New York, in 1843.

Garret A. Morgan, an inventor, patented a device for breathing in 1914 that would make mining safer.

 Students could investigate working conditions in mines. Why would such a breathing device be necessary?

Boston Red Sox won the first World Series in 1903.

Birthdays

Nancy Kerrigan (born Woburn, Massachusetts, 1969) is a figure skater.

Molly Pitcher (born Mary Hays McCauley near Trenton, New Jersey, 1754; died Carlisle, Pennsylvania, January 22, 1832) was a Revolutionary War hero. She was carrying pitchers of water to the men at the Battle of Monmouth on June 28, 1778. When her husband could no longer man the gun, she took over.

 Students could read more about women and their roles during the Revolutionary War.

Conrad Richter (born Pine Grove, Pennsylvania, 1890; died Pottsville, Pennsylvania, October 30, 1968) was an author. One of his books is *The Fields,* Pulitzer Prize winner for fiction in 1951.

Margaret Hilda Roberts Thatcher (born Grantham, England, 1925) is a former prime minister of England.

 Students could find out how prime ministers are determined in England.

Paul Simon (born Newark, New Jersey, 1941) is a singer and a songwriter. One of his most famous works is "The Sound of Silence."

Rudolf Virchow (born Schivelbain, Prussia, 1821; died Berlin, Germany, September 5, 1902) has been called the Father of Pathology. He conducted valuable research in leukemia, rickets, tuberculosis, and other diseases.

October

Elie Wiesel was awarded the Nobel Peace Prize in 1986.

Martin Luther King, Jr. was awarded the Nobel Peace Prize in 1964. The youngest person to receive the award, he contributed the award money to the civil rights movement.

Hawaii celebrates Discoverers' Day, honoring all such adventurers.

First flight faster than sound was made in 1947. Air Force Captain Chuck Yeager flew a *BellX-1* over Muroc Dry Lake Bed in California.

Birthdays

e. e. cummings (born Cambridge, Massachusetts, 1894; died North Conway, New Hampshire, September 2, 1962) was a poet.

 Students could check out how he used punctuation and capitalization.

Dwight David Eisenhower (born Denison, Texas, 1890; died Washington, DC, March 28, 1969) was the thirty-fourth president (1953–1961) of the United States. During World War I, he was a tank training instructor. By the end of World War II he was a five-star general and Supreme Allied Commander. He was a popular president. The country was experiencing prosperity. The Korean War ended during his presidency. He had to send in the military to end segregation in Little Rock, Arkansas. Visit a Web site at: http://www.whitehouse.gov/history/presidents/de34.html.

 Students could compile some statistics about the number of presidents who had previously been officers in the military.

Francis Lightfoot Lee (born Westmoreland County, Virginia, 1734; died Richmond, Virginia, January 11, 1797) signed the Declaration of Independence. One of his descendants was Robert E. Lee.

Lois Lenski (born Springfield, Illinois, 1893; died Tarpon Springs, Florida, September 11, 1974) was a children's author. She won a Newbery Medal for *Strawberry Girl*. She also wrote a series featuring Mr. Small and others.

 Children could read and enjoy her works.

William Penn (born London, England, 1644; died July 30, 1718) founded Pennsylvania. His father, an admiral, had lent money to England. The king could not easily repay the debt in money, so he offered a huge land grant instead to William Penn. A Quaker, Penn made sure all inhabitants had religious freedom. He also worked to keep friendly relations with the Native Americans. He spent very little time in his home on the Delaware River.

 Children could find out what the words "Pennsylvania" and "Philadelphia" mean.

October

 "I Love Lucy" premiered on television in 1951.

White Cane Safety Day is remembered by presidential proclamation. The year 1964 marked the first proclamation.

Nikita Khrushchev was removed from power in the Soviet Union in 1964.

 Students could find out why he was removed from power.

Birthdays

Lee A. Iacocca (born Allentown, Pennsylvania, 1924) is a former automobile company executive.

Penny Marshall (born New York, New York, 1942) is an actress and a film director. One of the movies she directed is *A League of Their Own*.

Virgil (born 70 B.C.; died 19 B.C.) was a poet who lived in ancient Rome. One of his most famous works is the epic *Aeneid*.

 An epic is a long poem. Students could attempt to read pieces of his epics.

Edith Bolling Galt Wilson (born Wytheville, Virginia, 1872; died Washington, DC, December 28, 1961) was the second wife of Woodrow Wilson, twenty-eighth president of the United States. She married him while he was president, a year after his first wife died. He suffered a severe stroke in 1919, and for some time she may have been making decisions regarding the presidency. Visit a Web site at: http://www.whitehouse.gov/history/firstladies/ew28-2.html.

Students could find more information regarding Wilson, his wife, and the presidency during his stroke.

October

 16

Dictionary Day honors Noah Webster's birth. Visit a Web site at: http://humanities.uchicago. edu/forms_unrest/webster.form.html.

 Students could participate in a Dictionary Olympics. One event could be the fastest finder of words. Another event could be the best user of guide words.

John Brown and his party raided the U.S. arsenal in Harper's Ferry, West Virginia in 1859. Within days he was captured, and he was hanged December 2, 1859.

 Students could find out how John Brown's raid related to the issue of slavery.

World Food Day marks the founding of the Food and Agriculture Organization in 1945. Contact: United Nations, Department of Public Information, New York, New York 10017.

Karol Wojtyla, a Polish cardinal, was elected Pope John Paul II in 1978.

 Students could find out how a pope is elected.

Yale University was created in 1701.

Million Man March occurred in 1995. African American men joined together in Washington, DC, for a "holy day of atonement and reconciliation."

Birthdays

Manute Bol (born Gogrial, Sudan, 1962) is a basketball player.

Joseph Bruchac (born Greenfield Center, New York) is a children's author. One of his books is *Between Earth and Sky.*

Eugene Gladstone O'Neill (born New York, New York, 1888; died Boston, Massachusetts, November 27, 1953) was an American playwright. He received the 1936 Nobel Prize for literature and four Pulitzer Prizes for his plays. One of those plays is *Long Day's Journey into Night.*

Noah Webster (born West Hartford, Connecticut, 1758; died New Haven, Connecticut, May 28, 1843) was a teacher and a writer. He was also a lexicographer, and he compiled one of the first American dictionaries.

Oscar Wilde (born Fingal O'Flahertie Wills Wilde in Dublin, Ireland, 1854; died Paris, France, November 30, 1900) was a playwright and a poet. One of his most important works was *The Importance of Being Earnest.*

October

 17

First professional golf tour was held in Scotland in 1860.

 Perhaps a golfer could come in and demonstrate a golf swing.

Albert Einstein left Germany and came to the United States in 1933.

Mother Teresa was awarded the Nobel Peace Prize in 1979.

Museum of Modern Art, in New York City, hung Matisse's *Le Bateau* **upside down in 1961.** The mistake was not found until December 3, 1961.

Department of Education was created in 1979.

San Francisco experienced a large earthquake in 1989. Measuring 7.1 on the Richter scale, the earthquake killed over sixty people. Most of these people were crushed when a double-deckered highway collapsed.

 Students could find out how buildings and highways are now made to withstand the effects of earthquakes.

International Day for the Eradication of Poverty is sponsored by the United Nations.

Birthdays

Jupiter Hammon (born probably Long Island, New York, 1711; died 1790) was the first African American to publish his poetry. Born into slavery, he learned to read. He published his first poem, "An Evening Thought," in 1760.

 Children could read and enjoy some of his poetry.

Mae Jemison (born Decatur, Alabama, 1956) is an astronaut and a scientist.

Arthur Miller (born New York, New York, 1915) is a playwright. One of his best-known works is *Death of a Salesman.*

October

Alaska became a U.S. territory in 1867. Russia sold the land to the United States.

 Children could find out why Russia sold the land to the United States.

Writing can be traced back to Mesopotamia in 4224 B.C.

Football rules were delineated in 1873.

James Watson, Francis Crick, and Maurice Wilkins shared the 1962 Nobel Prize for medicine and physiology for theorizing the double-helix structure of DNA.

Water Pollution Control Act was passed by Congress in 1972.

Azerbaijan declared its independence from the Soviet Union in 1991. This mostly Muslim country is located in southwestern Asia. Baku is the capital.

Birthdays

James David Brooks (born St. Louis, Missouri, 1906; died Brookhaven, New York, March 8, 1992) was an artist. He began his artistic career painting murals for the Federal Art Project of the Works Progress Administration. Later his works became more abstract.

 Students could investigate the purposes of the WPA.

Mike Ditka (born Carnegie, Pennsylvania, 1939) is a sportscaster and a former football coach and a player. He was elected to the Football Hall of Fame.

Wynton Marsalis (born New Orleans, Louisiana, 1961) is a jazz trumpeter. He has received Grammies for both classical and jazz albums.

 Students could listen to some recordings of his music.

October

 Yorktown Day marks the surrender of General Lord Cornwallis and his troops to George Washington in 1781. This virtually ended the Revolutionary War. No other major battles occurred, and the official peace agreement, the Treaty of Paris, was signed September 3, 1783.

Napoleon retreated from Moscow in 1812.

Dow Jones Industrial Average dropped 508 points in 1987. It was called Black Monday.

Birthdays

Ed Emberley (born Malden, Massachusetts, 1931) is a children's author and illustrator. He won the 1968 Caldecott Medal for his illustrations of *Drummer Hoff.* He is also known for his books about drawing, including his Thumbprint series.

 Students could make some thumbprint pictures after looking at his books.

Annie Smith Peck (born Providence, Rhode Island, 1850; died New York, New York, July 18, 1935) was a famous mountain climber. In 1895 she scaled the Matterhorn. Later she climbed the Peruvian mountain Huascaran, setting a record for the highest peak ever climbed by man or woman in the western hemisphere. When she was 61, she climbed Mt. Coropuna in Peru. At the 21,250-foot summit, she planted a banner stating "Votes for Women."

 Students could find out when women did get the right to vote.

Philip Pullman (born Norwich, England, 1946) is a children's author. He wrote *The Golden Compass, The Subtle Knife,* and *The Amber Spyglass.* Visit a Web site at: http://www. randomhouse.com/features/pullman/philippullman/index.html.

Martha Wayles Skelton Jefferson (born Charles City County, Virginia, 1748; died Monticello, Virginia, September 6, 1782) was the wife of Thomas Jefferson, third president of the United States. She died before Jefferson was elected president. They had six children, but only two lived to adulthood. These two daughters often filled the role of hostess at the White House. Visit a Web site at: http://www.whitehouse.gov/history/firstladies/mj3.html.

 Students could find out more about this accomplished woman.

October

 Guatemala celebrates Revolution Day.

Kenya celebrates Kenyatta Day. The day celebrates Jomo Kenyatta, the first president of Kenya.

Students could find out more about Kenya and what Kenyans do on Kenyatta Day.

The 49th Parallel in 1818 defined the border between Canada and the United States.

Birthdays

John Dewey (born Burlington, Vermont, 1859; died New York, New York, June 2, 1952) was an educator and a philosopher.

Mickey Mantle (born Spavinaw, Oklahoma, 1931; died Dallas, Texas, August 13, 1995) was a baseball player. From 1951 through 1968, he played for the New York Yankees. He hit 536 home runs in regular play. He was inducted into the Baseball Hall of Fame in 1974.

 Students could compare Mantle's baseball stats to those of some current players.

Crocket Johnson (born David Liesk in New York, New York, 1906; died July 11, 1975) was a children's author and illustrator. One of his books is *Harold and the Purple Crayon.*

Christopher Wren (born East Knoyle, Wiltshire, England, 1632; died London, England, February 25, 1723) was an architect, an astronomer, and a mathematician. He designed St. Paul's Cathedral in London. According to his son, Wren created over fifty inventions and theories.

 Students could locate some photographs of the buildings he designed. What materials were used? How are the buildings different from newer ones?

October

 Magellan and his ships entered the Straits of Magellan in 1520.

Battle of Trafalgar occurred in 1805.

Thomas Edison presented an incandescent lamp demonstration in 1879.

 Students could find out how light bulbs give off light.

United States Marine Mammal Protection Act was passed by Congress in 1972.

Americans received five Nobel Prizes in 1976.

 Students could find out the names of the winners and their accomplishments.

Titanic Memorial Maritime Act was created in 1986. No U.S. citizen can buy, sell, or own *Titanic* artifacts.

Birthdays

Caroline Carmichael McIntosh Fillmore (born Morristown, New Jersey, 1813; died New York, New York, August 11, 1881) was the second wife of Millard Fillmore, the thirteenth president of the United States. However, she was not married to Fillmore while he was president.

Edward "Whitey" Ford (born New York, New York, 1928) is a former baseball player. He was inducted into the Hall of Fame.

Alfred Bernhard Nobel (born Stockholm, Sweden, 1833; died San Remo, Italy, December 10, 1896) was a chemist. He invented dynamite and became wealthy. However, the invention of dynamite came with costs, including human lives. Nobel left his estate, about $9 million, to the Nobel Fund. The interest from the fund is used to reward individuals in five areas. The Nobel Prize is the most prestigious award in the world.

 Students could find out how dynamite works.

October

 Parachute jump was made for the first time in 1797.

 Since airplanes were not around in 1797, from what did the person jump? What was the construction of the parachute?

Cuban Missile Crisis began when President Kennedy in 1962 demanded that missiles placed in Cuba be removed. The United States also placed an embargo around the island to prevent other arms being placed in Cuba. On October 28 the Union of Soviet Socialist Republics started to remove the weapons.

Holy See (Vatican) celebrates a national holiday. The Vatican is a small country within the city of Rome, Italy. The country consists of thirteen buildings and has a land area of less than one-fourth square mile. The Pope lives and works within the Vatican. The Vatican has its own post office.

New York Metropolitan Opera House celebrated its opening in 1883 with a production of *Faust.*

Sam Houston was sworn in as the first president of the Republic of Texas in 1826.

Xerographic image was produced for the first time in 1938 by Chester Carlson.

Peyton Randolph, the president of the Continental Congress, died in Philadelphia, Pennsylvania, in 1775. He was born circa 1721.

Birthdays

George Beadle (born Wahoo, Nebraska, 1903; died Pomona, California, June 9, 1962) won the 1958 Nobel Prize for medicine for his genetic research. He discovered the relationship between genes and cell chemistry.

Brian Boitano (born Mountain View, California, 1963) is an Olympic gold medal skater.

Franz Liszt (born Raiding, Hungary, 1811; died Bayre, Bavaria, July 31, 1886) was a pianist and a composer. Probably his most celebrated works are his twenty Hungarian rhapsodies.

 Students could listen to some recordings of his compositions.

Robert Rauschenberg (born Port Arthur, Texas, 1925) is an artist. He uses a variety of materials on one canvas. Visit a Web site at: http://www.artcyclopedia.com/artists/rauschenberg_robert.html.

 Students could view some of his work. Then they could create their own assemblages.

N. C. Wyeth (born Needham, Massachusetts, 1882; died near Chadds Ford, Pennsylvania, October, 1945) was an artist and illustrator. Visit a Web site at: http://www.tfaoi.com/newsmu/nmus82e.htm.

ctober

 Scorpio the Scorpion is the astrological sign for October 23 through November 21.

Hungary celebrates its independence from Soviet rule in 1989.

National Mole Day marks the celebration of Avogadro's number. Visit a Web site at: http://www. moleday.org.

Swallows leave Capistrano for the winter. They will return March 19.

 Do scientists know why the swallows leave and return when they do?

Thailand celebrates Chulalongkorn Day. King Chulalongkorn the Great ruled Thailand for forty-two years and died on October 23, 1910. One of his accomplishments was the abolishment of slavery in Thailand.

Birthdays

Nicolas Appert (born Chalons-Sur-Marne, France, 1752; died Massy, France, June 3, 1841) is known as the father of canning. He invented ways of sealing and preserving food in containers.

 Students could find out all the ways we preserve food today.

Michael Crichton (born Chicago, Illinois, 1942) is a writer. One of his works is *Jurassic Park.*

Johnny Carson (born Corning, Iowa, 1925) is a comedian and a former talk show host.

Gertrude Caroline Ederle (born New York, New York, 1906) is a former swimmer. At one point she held twenty-nine national and world records. She won a gold medal in the 1924 Olympics for the 400-meter free style event. In 1926 she became the first woman to successfully swim the English Channel. Although the channel is twenty-one miles wide, a storm forced her to swim thirty-five miles. She returned to New York to a ticker tape parade.

 Children could compare her records to those standing today.

Doug Flutie (born Manchester, Maryland, 1962) is a football player.

Pele (born Edson Arantes do Nascimento in Tres Coracoes, Brazil, 1940) is a soccer player.

 ctober

24 **Florida was given to the United States by Spain in 1820.**

Friction match was patented in 1836.

 Students could find out why the friction match works.

Annie Decker in 1859 became the first person to go over Niagara Falls in a barrel. The teacher from Michigan sustained only minor injuries.

"Black Thursday" occurred in 1929 when the stock market declined in record levels.

United Nations Day celebrates the founding of the organization in 1945. Contact: United Nations, Department of Public Information, New York, New York 10017.

Students could chart the major purposes of the United Nations. They could find out how it gains its funds.

Minimum wage was instituted in 1940 at forty cents per hour, and the work week was defined as forty hours of work per week.

Zambia celebrates its Independence Day. It was declared free of British control in 1964. The country, larger than Texas, is located in southern central Africa. Lusaka is the capital. One of Zambia's major industries is copper mining and processing.

Birthdays

Sarah Josepha Buell Hale (born Newport, New Hampshire, 1788; died Philadelphia, Pennsylvania, April 30, 1879) was a writer and an editor. Her most famous poem is "Mary Had a Little Lamb."

Belva A. Bennett Lockwood (born Royalton, New York, 1830; died Washington, DC, May 19, 1917) was the first woman to argue before the Supreme Court. She championed women's rights. In 1884 she became the first woman to be nominated for president of the United States. She served on many boards, including the Nobel Peace Prize nominating committee.

Anton Van Leeuwenhoek (born Delft, Holland, 1632; died Delft, Holland, 1723) invented the microscope. He invented the microscope to examine cloth quality. However, he went on to observe bacteria. He called the organisms "animalcules." He also studied blood of various organisms.

 Students could use microscopes, and they could look at some animalcules.

October

25 **First woman FBI agents completed basic training.** In 1972 Susan Lynn Roley and Joanne E. Pierce graduated from Quantico, Virginia.

 Students could find out what the FBI does. They could write about its history.

Taiwan was returned to Chinese rule in 1945 after being controlled by the Japanese for fifty years.

Kazakhstan celebrates its 1991 independence from the Soviet Union. Islam and Russian Orthodox religions each control about half the population. Astana is the capital.

Birthdays

Richard Evelyn Byrd (born Winchester, Virginia, 1888; died Boston, Massachusetts, March 11, 1957) was an explorer. He made five treks to the Antarctic, and he was the first person to fly over both the North Pole and the South Pole.

Pablo Picasso (born Malaga, Spain, 1881; died Mougin, France, April 8, 1973) was an artist. He was probably one of the most important influences on the arts. He developed cubism, and he was a very prolific artist. Visit a Web site at: http://www.artcyclopedia.com/artists/picasso_pablo.html.

 Students could view a range of his works. They could decide which period they like best. They can try to draw a cubist work.

Johann Strauss (born Vienna, Austria, 1825; died 1899) was an Austrian composer. He was known as the Waltz King because he wrote almost 400 waltzes. He also composed marches, polkas, and operettas.

    Students could learn to waltz to some of his music.

October

 26

Austria celebrates a national day. Austria is a landlocked country in Europe. It is slightly smaller than the state of Maine, and Vienna is the capital. Oil reserves and tourism are major sources of income.

    Students could locate Austria on the map. They could find the large cities and other geographical features.

Erie Canal started operating in 1825. Construction began on July 4, 1817. It joined the Hudson River and Lake Erie.

    Students could plot on a map the Erie Canal and surround the map with facts about the canal. For example, how much did it cost? How many people helped build it?

New York Public Library opened in 1911. It shares with the public more than 3 million books.

Astronomers observed four new moons of Saturn in 2000.

Birthdays

Hillary Rodham Clinton (born Park Ridge, Illinois, 1947) is the wife of Bill Clinton, forty-second president of the United States. She graduated from Wellesley College and Yale Law School. She has worked for a national health care plan. She is currently a senator from New York. Visit a Web site at: http://www.whitehouse.gov/history/firstladies/hc42.html.

Mahalia Jackson (born New Orleans, Louisiana, 1911; died Evergreen Park, Illinois, January 27, 1972) was a gospel singer. Eight of her records sold more than one million copies each. She never sang where liquor was served.

Steven Kellogg (born Norwalk, Connecticut, 1941) is a children's author and illustrator. He wrote, among other works, *The Day Jimmy's Boa Ate the Wash,* 1980.

    Students could write sequels to *The Day Jimmy's Boa Ate the Wash.* For example, they could write *The Day Jimmy's Boa Played Soccer.*

Pat Sajak (born Chicago, Illinois, 1946) is a game show host.

October

 27

First essay of the *Federalist Papers* was published in 1787 in a New York City newspaper. John Jay, James Madison, and Alexander Hamilton wrote the essays to persuade people to adopt the new Constitution. The last of the eighty-five essays was published April 4, 1788.

New York City subway began operating in 1904. The mass transit system was the first in the world to be built underground.

Navy Day has been observed since 1922.

St. Vincent and the Grenadines celebrate their Independence Day. The one large island of St. Vincent and the fifty smaller islands gained their freedom from the United Kingdom in 1979. However, they are still part of the British Commonwealth. Kingstown is the capital of the Caribbean country.

Turkmenistan celebrates its Independence Day. It separated from the Union of Soviet Socialist Republics in 1991. Ashkhabad is the capital. One of its major industries is breeding camels.

Dow Jones Industrial Average plunged 554.26 points in 1997, its largest drop ever until 2001.

Birthdays

Enid Bagnold (born Rochester, Kent, England, 1889; died London, England, March 31, 1981) was a novelist and a playwright. One of her books is *National Velvet.*

James Cook (born Martin-in-Cleveland, near Whitby, Yorkshire, England, 1728; died Keala-kekwa Bay, Hawaii, February 14, 1779) was an explorer. He made three trips though the Pacific area. He sailed around the world twice. His last voyage was to locate the Northwest Passage. He was killed by natives when he went to investigate a boat theft.

 Cartographers could mark his various voyages on a map. They could find out what foods he brought back to Europe.

Roy Lichtenstein (born New York, New York, 1923; died New York, New York, September 29, 1997) was an artist. He is part of the pop art movement. Some of his works resembled comic strips.

 Students could view some of Lichtenstein's work and then create their own pop art.

Nicolo Paganini (born Genoa, Italy, 1782; died Nice, France, May 27, 1840) was a famed violin virtuoso. He also composed works for the violin.

Theodore Roosevelt (born New York, New York, 1858; died Oyster Bay, New York, January 6, 1919) was the twenty-sixth president (1901–1909) of the United States. He was a sickly child, often experiencing asthma attacks. He challenged himself as an adult. He even climbed the Matterhorn. He became a lawyer; but after the death of his first wife, he ran a cattle ranch in North Dakota. During the Spanish-American War, he led the Rough Riders up San Juan Hill. Later he became governor of New York and then vice president to William McKinley. When McKinley died, Roosevelt became the youngest president at age forty-two. During his presidency he established 150 million acres of national parks and forests. He authorized the building of the Panama Canal. He received the Nobel Peace Prize for helping to resolve the Russo-Japanese War. The teddy bear is named in honor of him. Visit a Web site at: http://www.whitehouse.gov/history/presidents/tr26.html.

 Students could read *Bully for You, Teddy Roosevelt* by Jean Fritz, and then make a timeline of Roosevelt's exciting life.

Dylan Thomas (born Swansea, Wales, 1914; died New York, New York, November 9, 1953) was a poet and a playwright.

ctober

28 **Czechoslovakia was created in 1918 after a revolution in Prague.** The Czechs and the Slovaks united to form one country. That country split back into two countries in 1993.

Students could make maps of the before, after, and next after for Czechoslovakia. They could research the reasons for new split.

Helen Eugenie Moore was the first woman to be appointed to an ambassadorship. Harry S Truman swore her in as ambassador to Denmark in 1949.

 Students could find out what ambassadors do and how one becomes an ambassador.

Harvard University was founded in Cambridge, Massachusetts, in 1636.

Statue of Liberty was dedicated in 1886. President Grover Cleveland, August Bartholdi, and other officials attended the ceremony.

 Students could research the recent restorations to the Statue of Liberty. A good source of information is Lynn Curlee's *Liberty.*

Greece celebrates Ohi Day. *Ohi* means "no," and the day marks the country's resistance to Italian troops during World War II.

Dow Jones Industrial Average in 1997 shot up 337.14 points, the largest increase in history until September 8, 1998. Over one billion shares, a record, were sold.

Birthdays

Desiderius Erasmus (born Rotterdam, probably 1467; died Basel, Switzerland, July 12, 1536) was a writer and a scholar.

Bill Gates (born Seattle, Washington, 1955) is a developer of computer software.

Jonas Salk (born New York, New York, 1914; died La Jolla, California, June 23, 1995) developed the Salk polio vaccine and announced his results in 1953.

ctober

29 **Stock market crashed in 1929.** Four days of panic sent stock prices plummeting. Billions of dollars were lost. This crash heralded the beginning of the Great Depression.

 Students could compare the 1929 stock market with today's market.

Turkey celebrates the 1923 creation of the republic.

 Students could investigate Turkey's complex history.

National Organization for Women was founded in 1966.

John Glenn in 1998 traveled on the space shuttle *Discovery.* At seventy-seven years old, he was the oldest person to travel in space. The shuttle returned to Earth on November 7, 1998. He had been one of the original seven astronauts and had orbited the Earth in 1962.

Internet was used for the first time in 1969. Charley Kline of UCLA tried to send information to another university. The system crashed, but the idea was viable.

Birthdays

Daniel Decatur Emmett (born Mount Vernon, Ohio, 1815; died Mount Vernon, Ohio, June 28, 1904) wrote the words and the music of *Dixie*.

 Students could play *Dixie* on tissue paper-covered combs.

October

 Orson Welles presented a radio broadcast of H. G. Wells's *War of the Worlds* in 1938. Many people had not tuned in at the beginning, so they believed there was a real Martian invasion.

 Students could listen to a recording of the broadcast. They will probably understand how the original listening audience panicked.

Quebec citizens in 1995 voted to remain part of Canada.

 Students could investigate why the vote took place.

Birthdays

John Adams (born Braintree, Massachusetts, 1735; died Quincy, Massachusetts, July 4, 1826) was the second president (1797–1801) of the United States. He was a direct descendant of a *Mayflower* voyager. Before the Revolutionary War, he helped establish the Sons of Liberty. He was George Washington's vice president, but he felt the position was useless. Visit a Web site at: http://www.whitehouse.gov/history/presidents/ja2.html.

 Students could make a list of all his accomplishments.

Emily Price Post (born Baltimore, Maryland, 1872; died New York, New York, September 25, 1960) was a writer. She wrote several books on proper etiquette. For a time she wrote a syndicated column that appeared daily in about 200 newspapers.

Diego Maradona (born Lanus, Argentina, 1960) is a former soccer player.

October

 Halloween is celebrated by trick-or-treaters all over the country.

 Students could turn a portion of the classroom into a haunted hut.

UNICEF Day has been observed by presidential proclamation since 1967.

National Magic Day is celebrated today in memory of Harry Houdini, who died this day in 1926.

Martin Luther in 1517 nailed his 95 Theses to the church door in Wittenburg, Germany. His actions and the actions of others started the Reformation.

Earl Lloyd in 1950 became the first African American to play for the NBA. He played for the Washington Capitols, and the game was held in Rochester, New York.

Nevada became the thirty-sixth state of the United States in 1864. Its name comes from a Spanish phrase meaning "snow-covered." Its nicknames are the Sagebrush State and the Silver State. Carson City is the state capital. It was explored in 1776, but the first settlement was not built until 1849. In 1859 the Comstock Lode was discovered, and mining fever took over. In 1931 gambling became legal. Contact: (800) NEVADA. Visit an Internet site at: http://www.50states.com/nevada.htm.

 Students could pretend they were miners in old Nevada. What materials would they need to buy before they could amble on out to their stake?

Mount Rushmore was completed in 1941. The project, depicting likenesses of George Washington, Abraham Lincoln, Thomas Jefferson, and Theodore Roosevelt, took fourteen years to complete. Visit a Web site at: http://www.nps.gov/moru.

Birthdays

Chiang Kai-Shek (born Chekiang, China, 1887; died Taipei, Taiwan, April 5, 1975) was a military leader. He led the Nationalist forces against the Communist troops. Ultimately, he brought his army to Taiwan.

John Keats (born London, England, 1795; died Rome, Italy, February 23, 1821) was a great English poet.

Juliette Magill Kinzie Gordon Low (born Savannah, Georgia, 1860; died Savannah, Georgia, January 17, 1927) created the American Girl Scouts. When she was traveling in Europe, she became friends with Robert Baden-Powell, the founder of the Boy Scouts. When she returned to the United States in 1912, she organized the first group of Girl Guides. In 1915 the organization's name was changed to the Girl Scouts.

 Perhaps a Girl Scout could speak to the group.

William Paca (born Abingdon, Maryland, 1740; died Talbot County, Maryland, October 13, 1799) signed the Declaration of Independence. After the Revolutionary War, he became a U.S. district justice.

Katherine Paterson (born Qing Jiang, Jiansi, China, 1932) is a children's author. She wrote, among other works, *Jacob Have I Loved* (Newbery Medal), published in 1980.

Jane Pauley (born Indianapolis, Indiana, 1950) is a television journalist.

Dan Rather (born Wharton, Texas, 1931) is a television journalist.

Jan Vermeer (born 1632; died December 1675) was a Dutch painter. Experts believe he painted only thirty-five or thirty-six works. Visit a Web site at: http://www.artcyclopedia.com/artists/vermeer_jan.html.

NOVEMBER

November

November is now the eleventh month of the year. Before Julius Caesar, however, it was the ninth month. It obtained its name from the Latin *novem,* meaning "nine." Then Julius Caesar changed the calendar and made November the ninth month. The number of days in November has varied from twenty-nine to thirty-one. Augustus established the number of days at thirty. The chrysanthemum is November's flower. Topaz is the birthstone.

Month-Long Activities

Child Safety Month reminds adults to take good care of the children. Contact: National PTA, 330 N. Wabash Avenue, Suite 2100, Chicago, Illinois 60611-3690. Telephone: (312) 670-6782. Visit a Web site at: http://www.pta.org.

International Drum Month celebrates the popularity of drums. It also educates the public as to the wide variety of drums. Contact: Percussion Marketing Counsel, 12665 Kling Street, Studio City, California 91604.

Aviation History Month celebrates the experiments conducted by Joseph Michel Montgolfier and Jacques Etienne Montgolfier in November of 1782. The brothers were intrigued with the writings of Joseph Priestly. He had written about the relationships of various gases and temperature. They tried various types of bags with hot air and ultimately developed the hot-air balloon.

Peanut Butter Lovers' Month reminds us of the nation's favorite sandwich filling. Contact: Peanut Advisory Board, 1025 Sugar Pike Way, Canton, Georgia 30115.

 Children enjoy making peanut butter. Visit a Web site at: http://www.peanut butterlovers.com.

Special Weeks

American Education Week is the first full week before the fourth Thursday in November. Contact: National Education Association, 1201 16th Street NW, Washington, DC 20036. Visit a Web site at: http://www.nea.org.

Geography Awareness Week stresses the importance of local and global geography. It is sponsored by the Geography Education Program, National Geographic Society, PO Box 37138, Washington, DC 20013-7138.

Children's Book Week is the week before Thanksgiving. The week celebrates children's books and encourages children to read them. Visit a Web site at: http://www.cbc.books.org/htm/book_week.html.

Special Days

Thanksgiving Day is the fourth Thursday in November.

Election Day is the first Tuesday after the first Monday in November.

National Educational Support Personnel Day is the Wednesday of American Education Week. The day honors all school support employees. Contact: National Education Association, 1201 16th Street NW, Washington, DC 20036. Visit a Web site at: http://www.nea.org.

Great American Smokeout hopes to persuade smokers to quit. It is the third Thursday in November. Contact: American Cancer Society, 1599 Clifton Road NE, Atlanta, Georgia 30329. Telephone: (404) 320-3333. Visit a Web site at: http://www.cancer.org.

November

Stamp Act was imposed on the colonies by the British in 1765.

National Authors' Day honors all the country's authors. The custom dates back to 1929.

 Each child could pick out his/her favorite author and present a small biography about that person. Children could also read Eileen Christelou's *What Do Authors Do?*

Algeria celebrates the Anniversary of the Revolution.

White House was ready for occupancy in 1800. Visit a Web site at: http://www.whitehouse.gov.

 Children could find out how and when the White House has been modernized. Is there really a bowling alley in the basement?

Boston Female Medical School opened in 1848 as the first school to train women who wished to be doctors. The first student class numbered twelve. It merged with Boston University in 1874 to become one of the first coeducational medical schools in the country.

U.S. Weather Bureau began recording weather observations in 1870.

 Children could make daily weather observations and record them in charts.

Hockey mask was invented by Jacques Plante in 1959. The Montreal Canadiens goalie created the mask from plastic and resin after he had been injured numerous times.

Mexico observes Day of the Dead. People visit the graves of ancestors. However, the day is filled with happiness and music rather than with sadness.

Antigua and Barbuda celebrate their Independence Day. The two islands gained their independence from the United Kingdom in 1981. The islands are located in the Caribbean, southeast of Puerto Rico.

Prime Meridian was formally agreed to in 1884. Twenty-five countries met to establish uniform lines of longitude and resulting time zones.

Birthdays

Stephen Crane (born Newark, New Jersey, 1871; died Badenweiler, Germany, June 5, 1900) was an author. He is especially known for his short stories. His *The Red Badge of Courage* was written about the Civil War. He died at an early age from tuberculosis, made more serious by a bout of malaria fever.

Crawford Williamson Long (born Danielsville, Georgia, 1815; died Athens, Georgia, June 16, 1878) was the first doctor to use ether in an operation performed in 1842.

Fernando Valenzuela (born Navojoa, Sonora, Mexico, 1960) is a former baseball player.

November

2

Gaspar de Portola claimed San Francisco Bay for the Spanish in 1769.

Balfour Declaration was signed in 1917.

Radio broadcasting began in 1920 when station KDKA started its programs in Pittsburgh, Pennsylvania.

Newsreel theater was first opened in 1929.

North Dakota became the thirty-ninth state of the United States in 1889. The state ranks seventeenth in area and forty-seventh in population. Its nicknames include the Sioux State, the Peace Garden State, and the Flickertail State. Bismarck is the state capital. North Dakota is the nation's leading producer of wheat, and it has large reserves of lignite coal and natural gas. Contact: (800) 435-5663. Visit an Internet site at: http://www.50states.com/ndakota.htm.

South Dakota became the fortieth state of the United States in 1889. The two states' names stem from a Sioux word *dakota,* meaning "allies." People first came to South Dakota in search of gold. Then raising cattle became a means of living. Its nickname is the Coyote State, and Pierre is the state capital. Two important attractions are the Badlands National Park and Mount Rushmore National Monument. Contact: (800) 843-01930. Visit an Internet site at: http://www.50states.com/sdakota.htm.

 Do coyotes really live in the Coyote State? Children could find out whether the farmers and coyotes can exist side by side.

Spruce Goose **flew its first and only flight in 1947.** Howard Hughes designed and flew the $25 million plane made of wood. Originally called *Hercules,* the plane flew for about one mile at an altitude of seventy feet over Long Beach Harbor, California. It is now a tourist attraction in Long Beach, California.

 The words *Spruce Goose* make a *hink pink.* Children could make up some *hink pink* riddles. Visit a Web site at: http://www.uen.org/utahlink/activities/view_activity.cgi? activity_id = 5912.

Birthdays

Marie Antoinette (born Vienna, Austria, 1734; died October 16, 1793) was queen of France during the French Revolution. Daughter of the Emperor of Austria, she married the French dauphin when she was fifteen years old. The dauphin became king in 1774. The country was close to bankruptcy, and the court's extravagant life-style turned the people against them. Legend says that when she heard that the poor had no bread to eat, she stated, "Let them eat cake." The king and queen tried to escape the country, but they were discovered and imprisoned. He was beheaded in January of 1793. She, too, died at the guillotine.

George Boole (born Lincolnshire, England, 1815; died Ballintemple, Ireland, December 8, 1864) developed Boolean logic.

Daniel Boone (born Berks County, Pennsylvania, 1734; died St. Charles County, Missouri, September 26, 1820) was a pioneer, explorer, and army officer. His life has inspired many stories. He was captured by the Indians, but he later escaped. The British also seized him, but he got away soon after. He spent his life in the rugged frontier.

Warren Gamaliel Harding (born Corsica, Ohio, 1865; died San Francisco, California, August 2, 1923) was the twenty-ninth president (1921–1923) of the United States. Before he became president, he served as a state senator, a lieutenant governor, and a U.S. senator. He felt high tariffs and low taxes would help America. Unfortunately, some of his appointees were dishonest, and his administration was marred. He died of an embolism while in office. After his death, his wife destroyed many of his letters. Visit a Web site at: http://www.whitehouse.gov/history/presidents/wh29.html.

James Knox Polk (born Mecklenburg County, North Carolina, 1795; died Nashville, Tennessee, June 15, 1849) was the eleventh president (1845–1849) of the United States. He served in the House of Representatives for seven terms. At one point he was speaker of the House. He became Tennessee's governor, and then he felt his political career was over. However, in 1844 he became the dark-horse candidate and won the election. During his administration, over one million square miles of territory were added to the United States. He did not run for a second term. He died three months after leaving the White House. Visit a Web site at: http://www.whitehouse.gov/history/presidents/jp11.html.

 Students could find out what the term "dark horse" means. They could research whether any other dark horse candidates won.

November

 3 **Panama celebrates its Independence Day from Colombia.** This event happened in 1903.

Japan celebrates Culture Day.

Sputnik 2, **a Soviet spacecraft, was launched in 1957.** The Russian spacecraft carried the first animal into space, a dog named Laika. The dog died when the air supply ran out.

Micronesia celebrates its Independence Day. The archipelago, found in the western Pacific Ocean, gained its freedom from the United States and the United Nations in 1986. Kolonia is the capital.

 Students could discover how the United States gained control of Micronesia.

Birthdays

Stephen Fuller Austin (born Wythe County, Virginia, 1793; died Columbia, Texas, December 27, 1836) was a Texas hero. He founded a settlement in Texas in 1822 when the land belonged to Mexico. He was imprisoned when he pushed for Texas autonomy, but he was given his freedom in 1835. He ran against Sam Houston for the presidency of Texas, but he lost. The state capital is named in honor of him.

 Students could gather statistics on the city of Austin. How does it compare to other capitals?

Charles (Buchinsky) Bronson (born Ehrenfeld, Pennsylvania, 1922) is an actor.

William Cullen Bryant (born Cummington, Massachusetts, 1794; died New York, New York, June 12, 1878) was a poet.

Bette Bao Lord (born Shanghai, China, 1938) writes children's books. She wrote *In the Year of the Boar and Jackie Robinson,* published in 1984.

John Montague, Fourth Earl of Sandwich (born London, England, 1718; died London, England, April 30, 1792) invented the sandwich. He held many posts, including lord of the admiralty. Captain Cook named the Sandwich Islands in honor of him in 1778. According to legend, he created the sandwich as a way of saving time during a gambling party in 1762.

 Children could eat sandwiches at lunchtime and learn more about John Montague and the Sandwich Islands.

November

4 **King Tut's tomb was discovered in 1922.** Howard Carter had been looking for the tomb for a number of years. His expeditions had been financed by Lord Carnarvon. Tutankhamen had become pharaoh when he was nine years old. He died at approximately age nineteen. His tomb was one of the few that had never been plundered. The National Museum at Cairo retains the relics.

 Students could find out how bodies were mummified in ancient Egypt.

UNESCO (United Nations Educational, Scientific and Cultural Organization) was created in 1946.

Tonga celebrates Constitution Day. Of its 172 islands in the South Pacific, thirty-six are inhabited. It is a constitutional monarchy, and it still remains part of the British Commonwealth. Most of its income is derived from tourism and fishing.

Panama celebrates Flag Day.

Artificial leg was patented in 1846.

Cash register was patented in 1879 by James Ritty and John Ritty of Dayton, Ohio.

Refrigeration apparatus was patented by Thomas Elkins in 1879.

Birthdays

Laura Welch Bush (born Midland, Texas, 1946) is the wife of George W. Bush, the forty-third president of the United States. Visit a Web site at: http://www.whitehouse.gov/firstlady/flbio.html.

Walter Leland Cronkite (born St. Joseph, Missouri, 1916) is a journalist and former television anchorperson.

Gail Haley (born Charlotte, North Carolina, 1939) is a children's book author and illustrator. Her *A Story, A Story* was the 1971 Caldecott Medal winner.

Sterling North (born Edgerton, Wisconsin, 1906; died Whipanny, New Jersey, December 21, 1974) was a children's author. He wrote *Rascal.*

 Children could read and enjoy his work.

Will Rogers (born Oolagah, Indian Territory [now called Oklahoma], 1879; died near Point Barrow, Alaska, August 15, 1935) was a famous humorist, writer, and actor.

 Children could pick one of his witticisms. Do they agree or disagree with his point of view?

November

5 **Shirley Chisholm was the first African American woman to be elected to the House of Representatives.** She was elected in 1968, and she served until 1983.

Guy Fawkes Day is remembered in England. At least eleven people plotted to blow up Parliament and the house of King James I in 1605. They hid twenty barrels of gunpowder in the cellar of the Parliament building. The explosives were discovered the night before the intended detonation. The conspirators were tried, convicted, and beheaded. Guy Fawkes is the name most remembered among the guilty. During the evening of November 5, bonfires and fireworks light up the skies.

 Children could research why Guy Fawkes and his band were so angry with King James I.

Crossword puzzles were first published in 1889.

 Children could make a crossword puzzle.

George B. Selden patented the first gasoline-powered automobile in 1895.

 Students could make a timeline to show how cars have changed over the years.

Monopoly game, produced by Parker Brothers, premiered in 1935.

Mousetrap, **a play by Agatha Christie, opened in London in 1952.** Nightly performances of the play continue to this day.

Birthdays

Will Durant (born North Adams, Massachusetts, 1885; died Los Angeles, California, November 7, 1981) was an American historian.

Roy Rogers (born Leonard Slye in Cincinnati, Ohio, 1912; died Apple Valley, California, July 6, 1998) was a singer and an actor. He is famous for his cowboy roles in the early days of television.

Ida Minerva Tarbell (born Erie County, Pennsylvania, 1857; died Bethel, Connecticut, January 6, 1944) was a writer and historian. She meticulously researched her subjects, and she set a new standard for investigative reporting.

November

Rutgers beat Princeton in the first intercollegiate football game in 1869.

Gustavus Adolphus Day is remembered in Sweden. The king was killed in 1632.

"Meet the Press" premiered in 1947. It is the oldest running show on television. A panel of news reporters interviews a different guest, often a politician, each week.

 Students could view a tape of the show. Then they could create their own "Meet the Press" and interview the principal or a student council leader.

Birthdays

James Naismith (born Almonte, Ontario, Canada, 1861; died Lawrence, Kansas, November 28, 1939) invented basketball in 1891. He created the first hoop from a peach basket, and the first basketball was actually a soccer ball.

 Students could create a new indoor game that uses baskets and a soccer ball.

Adolphe Sax (born Dinant, Belgium, 1814; died Paris, France, February 7, 1894) invented the saxophone and the saxotromba. He became famous and wealthy. However, he lost his fortune and died in poverty.

A music teacher or saxophone student could demonstrate how the instrument works.

John Philip Sousa (born Washington, DC, 1854; died Reading, Pennsylvania, March 6, 1932) was a band conductor and a composer. He wrote, among other works, *The Stars and Stripes Forever.*

November

7 Battle of Tippecanoe took place in 1811.

Elephant was used for the first time to represent the Republican Party. *Harper's Weekly* published a Thomas Nast cartoon using the elephant in 1874.

 Children could decide whether the elephant is a good symbol for the Republican Party.

Russia remembers the October Revolution of 1917.

Jeannette Rankin was the first woman to be elected to the House of Representatives in 1916.

Museum of Modern Art in New York, New York, opened its doors in 1929.

L. Douglas Wilder in 1989 became the first elected African American governor of a state in the United States. He was governor of Virginia.

Birthdays

Albert Camus (born Mondavi, Algeria, 1913; died France, January 4, 1960) was a writer and a philosopher. He won the Nobel Prize for literature in 1957.

Marie Sklodowska Curie (born Warsaw, Poland, 1867; died Savoy, France, July 4, 1934) was a physicist. She and her husband, Pierre, worked on radioactive substances. They isolated two new elements, radium and polonium. She, her husband, and a third scientist received the 1903 Nobel Prize in physics. She won the 1911 Nobel Prize in chemistry for her extended work on radium.

 Radioactive elements are dangerous. Student scientists could find out how today's researchers protect themselves.

Isamu Noguchi (born Los Angeles, California, 1904; died 1988) was a sculptor. His works were very abstract, and he was interested in the relationship of mass and tension. He also designed furniture, gardens, bridges, and sets for ballets.

 Students could look at some photographs of his work. Then using odds and ends they could make their own free-form sculptures.

November

8 **Montezuma met Cortez in the Aztec capital in 1519.** Montezuma thought Cortez was a god and welcomed him into the country.

 Children could find out why Montezuma thought what he did.

Diego Bezerra de Mendoza discovered Lower California in 1533.

Montana became the forty-first state of the United States in 1889. Its name comes from the Spanish word *montana,* meaning "mountainous." Its nicknames are the Treasure State and Big Sky Country. Copper mining, lumbering, and tourism are major sources of income. The state's southeastern section has reserves of low-sulphur coal. Montana ranks fourth in area and forty-fourth in population. Contact: (800) 541-1447 or (800) 548-3390. Visit an Internet site at: http://www.50states.com/montana.htm.

 Students could draw a map of Montana and label its natural resources. Where do the tourists go?

Louvre opened in Paris, France, in 1793. Probably one of the most famous paintings in this museum is the *Mona Lisa.* Visit a Web site at: http://sunsite.unc.edu/louvre.

 The Louvre galleries measure eight miles in total, and the museum owns over one million pieces of art. Students could find out more about the Louvre and its new addition, designed by I. M. Pei.

X-rays were discovered by Dr. Wilhelm Roentgen in 1895.

 Children could view some X-rays and locate bones and other features.

Lewis and Clark reached the Pacific Ocean in 1805.

Birthdays

Christiaan Barnard (born Beaufort West, South Africa, 1922) performed the first successful heart transplant in 1967.

Edmund Halley (born London, England, 1656; died Greenwich, England, January 14, 1742) was an astronomer and mathematician. Halley's Comet is named in his honor. He first saw it in 1682. After conducting some research, he realized the comet returned approximately every seventy-six years. It has been sighted twenty-eight times. The first recorded sighting was in 240 B.C.

Margaret Mitchell (born Atlanta, Georgia, 1900; died Atlanta, Georgia, August 16, 1949) wrote *Gone with the Wind.* Although this was her only book, it has sold over ten million copies and has been translated into thirty languages.

November

Theodore Roosevelt traveled through the Panama Canal in 1906. This trip marked the first time an American president traveled to another country while in office.

 Children could make a chart of presidents and countries they have visited. Which president has traveled the most?

Kristallnacht transpired in Germany in 1938. Mobs of Germans demolished thousands of homes owned by Jews. Books and Torahs were burned. More than 30,000 Jews were arrested, and almost 100 people died. Kristallnacht, "crystal night," was given its name from the sound of window glass breaking.

Berlin Wall was opened in 1989. The almost twenty-eight-mile long wall was built in 1961 to separate East Berlin from West Berlin. People celebrated when they could freely walk from one part of the city to another.

Vietnam Veterans Memorial was unveiled in 1982 in Washington, DC. The memorial, designed by Maya Ying Lin, displays the names of the 58,000 Americans killed or missing in action during the Vietnam War.

 Children could see photographs of the memorial. They could discuss why it causes such strong emotions to visitors.

Cambodia celebrates its Independence Day. It broke from French rule in 1949. A good deal of this country's land is covered with forests. The capital is Phnom Penh.

Birthdays

Benjamin Banneker (born near Baltimore, Maryland, 1731; died Baltimore, Maryland, October 9, 1806) was known for his accomplishments in astronomy, surveying, and mathematics. During the years 1791 until 1796, Banneker recorded information regarding weather, astronomy, and the tides. He compiled this information into an almanac. Other prominent Americans, including Benjamin Rush, added their own essays. The works were published, and Thomas Jefferson received a copy of the first almanac.

 Students could compare and contrast various kinds of almanacs.

Pat Cummings (born Chicago, Illinois, 1950) is a writer and illustrator. One of her books is *Angel Baby*. Visit a Web site at: http://www.eduplace.com/kids/hmr/mtai/cummings.html.

Lois Ehlert (born Beaver Dam, Wisconsin, 1934) writes and illustrates children's books. Her *Color Zoo* was a Caldecott Honor Book in 1989.

Carl Sagan (born New York, New York, 1934; died Seattle, Washington, December 20, 1996) was a writer. One of his books was *The Dragons of Eden*. He wrote about science so that many people could understand the subject. He also was concerned with social issues.

Kay Thompson (born St. Louis, Missouri, 1908; died New York, New York, July 2, 1998) was an author. She wrote the Eloise series. Visit a Web site at: http://www.eloisewebsite.com.

November

 Marine Corps was created by the Continental Congress in 1775.

 Children could research the differences between the various branches of the armed services.

Motorcycle, invented by Gottlieb Daimler, was driven for the first time in 1885 by his son, Paul. The motorcycle had wooden wheels and iron tires.

Dial telephone service without using an operator was available coast to coast in 1951. This necessitated the use of area codes.

 Students could research the telephone's history. They could make a timeline of important dates.

Henry M. Stanley in 1871 found David Livingstone, the missing missionary, in Africa. He asked the famous question, "Dr. Livingstone, I presume?"

Great Wall of China was opened to tourists in 1970.

"Sesame Street" aired for the first time in 1969. It is still a favorite with young children.

 Each episode is sponsored by a number and a letter or two. Assign children to certain letters. Have them present new and unusual vocabulary words that begin with those letters.

Windshield wiper was patented in 1903 by Mary Anderson.

Birthdays

Martin Luther (born Eisleben, Saxony, 1483; died Eisleben, Saxony, February 18, 1546) was a priest who started the Protestant movement. He nailed his Ninety-Five Theses to the door of Wittenberg's castle church on October 31, 1517. He also was an accomplished musician. He was excommunicated from the Roman Catholic Church and married a former nun, Katherine von Bora.

November

 11

Veterans Day was celebrated for the first time in 1919. At one time the day was called Armistice Day, indicating the end of World War I. Today it honors all the people who fought in all the wars.

 Perhaps a veteran could be a guest speaker for the children.

Tomb of the Unknown Soldier was created in 1921.

Vietnam Women's Memorial was opened in Washington, DC, in 1993. The bronze sculpture honors the 11,500 women who served in the Vietnam War.

Washington became the forty-second state of the United States in 1889. Robert Gray traded sea otter pelts by 1792. Later farming and lumbering took over as chief occupations. Mountains split the state into two distinctive parts. The western portion receives abundant rainfall, while the eastern part is very dry. Its nickname is the Evergreen State, and Olympia is the capital. Attractions include Mount St. Helens National Monument and Mount Rainier National Park. Contact: (800) 544-1800. Visit an Internet site at: http://www.50states.com/washingt.htm.

 Washington is known for its apples. Consider bringing in various types of apples. Slice them, and have students compare the texture, sweetness, and taste.

Angola celebrates its Independence Day. Portugal relinquished its claims to Angola in 1975. The country, located in southwestern Africa, supports an economy that is about eighty-five percent agricultural. Luanda is the country's capital.

Birthdays

Abigail Smith Adams (born Weymouth, Massachusetts, 1744; died Quincy, Massachusetts, October 28, 1818) was the wife of John Adams, the second president of the United States. They moved into the partially completed White House just before Adams's term ended. Visit a Web site at: http://www.whitehouse.gov/history/firstladies/aa2.html.

Abigail was the wife of one president and the mother of another president. However, she could not even vote. Children could list possible frustrations Abigail Adams might have felt about the White House and the new country.

Leonardo DiCaprio (born Ridgewood, New Jersey, 1975) is an actor.

Fyodor Mikhailovich Dostoyevsky (born Moscow, Russia, 1821; died St. Petersburg, Russia, February 9, 1881) was a writer. Two of his most famous works were *Crime and Punishment* and *The Brothers Karamazov.*

George S. Patton, Jr. (born San Gabriel, California, 1885; died Heidelburg, Germany, December 21, 1945) was a military leader during World War I and World War II.

November

Abraham Lincoln in 1847 reported his election expenses as seventy-five cents for a barrel of cider.

Arches National Park in Utah was created in 1971. In 1929 the wind-eroded rock formations were declared a national monument. Then it became a national park. Contact: Arches National Park, PO Box 907, Moab, Utah 84532. Visit a Web site at: http://www.nps.gov/arch.

 Students could research what other factors in addition to wind were responsible for the arches.

National Cowboy Hall of Fame opened in 1965 in Oklahoma City, Oklahoma. Visit a Web site at: http://www.cowboyhalloffame.org.

Columbia STS-2 **was launched again in 1981.** It was the first space vehicle launched for a second time. *Columbia*, on February 1, 2003, disintegrated when it reentered the atmosphere at the end of a mission.

 We are reusing the shuttles. Students could make a list of things we throw away that perhaps could be re-used with some work.

Birthdays

Harry Blackmun (born Nashville, Illinois, 1908; died Arlington, Virginia, March 4, 1999) was a Supreme Court associate justice.

Grace Kelly (born Philadelphia, Pennsylvania, 1929; died Monte Carlo, Monaco, September 14, 1982) was an actress. She gave up her acting career to marry Prince Rainier III of Monaco in 1956.

Auguste Rodin (born Paris, France, 1840; died Meudon, France, November 17, 1917) was a very influential sculptor. He worked mostly with the human form, and one of his most famous pieces is *The Thinker.* Visit a Web site at: http://www.rodinmuseum.org.

 Students could mix one part vermiculite and one part plaster of paris with enough water to make a mixture the consistency of pudding. They can pour the mixture into milk cartons. The mixture will solidify. Students can remove the carton and carve the solid with spoons or other tools.

Marjorie Weinman Sharmat (born Portland, Maine, 1928) writes children's books. One of her books is *Nate the Great,* published in 1972.

Sammy Sosa (born San Pedro de Macoris, Dominican Republic, 1968) is a baseball player.

Elizabeth Cady Stanton (born Johnstown, New York, 1815; died New York, New York, October 26, 1902) worked for women's rights.

 Children would enjoy reading Jean Fritz's *You Want Women to Vote, Lizzie Stanton?*

Letitia Christian Tyler (born Cedar Grove, Virginia, 1790; died Washington, DC, September 10, 1842) was the first wife of John Tyler, tenth president of the United States. While Tyler was pursuing a political career, she took charge of their plantation. However, bad health won over, and she became an invalid. She died in the White House. Visit a Web site at: http://www.whitehouse.gov/history/firstladies/lt10.html.

Sun Yat-Sen (born Guangdong Province, China, 1866; died Peking, China, March 12, 1925) was the leader of China's 1911 rebellion.

November

13 **Holland Tunnel began operating in 1927.** The tunnel connects New Jersey and Manhattan, and it runs under the Hudson River. It was the first American underwater tunnel.

Disney's *Fantasia* was released in 1940.

 Children could perhaps see a portion of *Fantasia*. The film is, in a way, a series of music videos with classics as the background.

Peanut butter was invented in 1890.

 Students could make peanut butter and then enjoy it.

Birthdays

Louis Dembitz Brandeis (born Louisville, Kentucky, 1856; died Washington, DC, October 5, 1941) was a lawyer and respected Supreme Court Justice.

Whoopi Goldberg (born New York, New York, 1949) is an actress and comedian.

Robert Louis Stevenson (born Edinburgh, Scotland, 1850; died Samoa, December 3, 1894) was a writer. *Treasure Island,* first appearing in magazine installments, was published in 1883. He published *The Strange Case of Dr. Jekyll and Mr. Hyde* in 1886. *Kidnapped* was written in the same year. Another of his famous works was *A Child's Garden of Verses.*

 Children could dramatize scenes from his stories.

November

14 **First blood transfusion took place in 1666.**

Nellie Bly began a trip in 1889 to go around the world in eighty days. She was trying to copy the trip Jules Verne created for his character Phileas Fogg. She completed the trip in slightly over seventy-two days.

India celebrates Children's Day.

Apollo 12 **was launched in 1969.** The craft carried astronauts Gordon, Bean, and Conrad to the second landing on the moon's surface.

Dow Jones Industrial Average surpassed the 1,000 mark for the first time in 1972.

Moby Dick **by Herman Melville was published in 1851.**

Birthdays

Aaron Copland (born Brooklyn, New York, 1900; died North Tarrytown, New York, December 2, 1900) was a composer. Two of his most famous works are *Fanfare for the Common Man*, composed in 1942, and *Appalachian Spring*, composed in 1944.

Robert Fulton (born in what is now Fulton Township, Pennsylvania, 1765; died New York, New York, February 24, 1815) did not invent the steamboat, but he did make it practical.

Leo Hendrik Baekland (born Ghent, Belgium, 1863; died Beacon, New York, February 23, 1944) invented Bakelite, an early plastic.

 Today's children find plastic all around them. They could list ten items made of plastic and then try to find out what those items were made of before plastic was around.

Sir Frederick Grant Banting (born Alliston, Ontario, 1891; died near Newfoundland, 1941) discovered insulin.

Mamie Geneva Doud Eisenhower (born Boone, Iowa, 1896; died Gettysburg, Pennsylvania, November 1, 1979) was the wife of Dwight D. Eisenhower, thirty-fourth president of the United States. Because he was a military officer for many years, they lived in a variety of places. She enjoyed her years as first lady. Visit a Web site at: http://www.whitehouse.gov/history/firstladies/me34.html.

Astrid Lindgren (born Nas, Sweden, 1907; died Stockholm, Sweden, January 28, 2002) was a children's author. She is famous for *Pippi Longstocking*. Visit a Web site at: http://www.io.org/~wings/jane/a_lindgren/a_lindgren.html.

Claude Monet (born Paris, France, 1840; died Giverny, France, December 5, 1926) was a painter. One of his early paintings was entitled *Impression: Sunrise*. The painting conveyed his emotions regarding the scene. The title started the movement of impressionism. Visit a Web site at: http://www.artofmonet.com.

 Students could listen to Copland's music, and they could view prints of Monet's paintings. They could find out how both creative geniuses used emotion and feelings.

Jawaharlal Nehru (born Allahabad, India, 1889; died New Delhi, India, May 27, 1964) was India's first prime minister after it became an independent country.

William Steig (born New York, New York, 1907) is a children's author and illustrator. He wrote, among other works, *Doctor De Soto* (Newbery Honor Book), 1982. His *Sylvester and the Magic Pebble* won the 1970 Caldecott Medal.

 Students could read and enjoy some of his works. Visit a Web site at: http://www.williamsteig.com.

November

 Japan celebrates Shichi-Go-San. The day translates as "seven-five-three." Parents take their seven-year-old girls, five-year-old boys, and three-year-olds of either sex to the temples. They thank the guardian spirits for protecting the children and keeping them healthy.

Asser Levy became the first licensed kosher butcher in New Amsterdam in 1660. Later New Amsterdam's name was changed to New York City.

 Students could find out what a kosher butcher does.

Jeremiah Dixon and Charles Mason started to survey the Mason-Dixon Line in 1763. This line marked the border between Pennsylvania and Maryland. Later the line somewhat divided the country into the north and the south.

Zebulon Pike recorded seeing Pike's Peak in Colorado in 1806.

Birthdays

William Herschel (born Hanover, Germany, 1738; died Slough, England, August 25, 1822) was an astronomer. He discovered Uranus in 1781 and found that it rotated in a direction different from the other planets. He was also active in star astronomy, and he discovered infrared radiation.

 Students could research his life and then present the information in a talk show format.

Marianne Moore (born St. Louis, Missouri, 1887; died New York, New York, February 5, 1972) was a poet. Her *Collected Poems,* published in 1951, won a Pulitzer Prize.

Georgia O'Keefe (born Sun Prairie, Wisconsin, 1887; died Santa Fe, New Mexico, March 6, 1986) was an artist. Her works featured nature. She was married to photographer Alfred Stieglitz.

 Students could see prints of her work and discuss the influence of the desert on her art.

November

 Life preserver composed of cork was patented in 1841.

General Sherman and his army of about 60,000 soldiers started their "March to the Sea" in 1864.

Oklahoma became the forty-sixth state of the United States in 1907. French trappers visited the area around 1700. Several Native American groups were relocated to Oklahoma, only to be forced out later. Oil and gas were and still are important sources of income. The dust bowl of the 1930s forced many "Okies" to travel west. Its name can be traced to a Choctaw word *okla humma,* meaning "land of the red people." Its nickname is the Sooner State. Contact: (800) 652-6552. Visit an Internet site at: http://www.50states.com/oklahoma.htm.

 Oklahoma has a panhandle. Students could find out which other states also have panhandles.

Automobile traveled for the first time in excess of sixty miles per hour in 1901.

Chocolate chips were sold for the first time by Nestle Company in 1939.

Venera 3, **a Soviet unmanned space probe, was launched in 1965.** It crash landed on the surface of Venus on March 1, 1966. It was the first man-made object to travel to another planet.

Students could figure out how many days it took to get to Venus and the distance it traveled. They could make various math problems from those statistics.

Skylab 4, **with three astronauts, was launched in 1973.** The crew spent over eight days in space.

Birthdays

Jean Fritz (born Hankow, China, 1915) is a children's author. She wrote, among other works, *Homesick: My Own Story* (Newbery Honor Book), 1982.

 Students could read and enjoy her books.

W(illiam) C(hristopher) Handy (born Florence, Alabama, 1873; died New York, New York, March 28, 1958) was known as the father of the blues. One of his most famous works is *St. Louis Blues,* composed in 1914.

Robin McKinley (born Warren, Ohio, 1952) is a children's author. *The Hero and the Crown* won the Newbery Medal in 1984.

Barbara Reid (born Toronto, Canada, 1957) is a children's book illustrator. She illustrated, among other works, *Effie,* 1990.

 November

17 **Anne Hutchinson was exiled from Massachusetts in 1637 for speaking against the religious leaders.**

Homemade Bread Day is celebrated in America. Contact: Homemade Bread Day Committee, Box 3, Montague, Michigan 49437-0003.

 Children could make and enjoy bread.

Congress met in session for the first time in the Capitol building in 1800.

 Children could find floor plans of the building. They could find out where the Senate meets and where the House of Representatives meets.

Suez Canal began operating in 1869.

Birthdays

Indira Priyadarshini Gandhi (born Allahabad, India, 1917; died October 31, 1984) was the first woman prime minister of India. The only child of Jawaharlal Nehru, she served as prime minister from 1966 to 1977 and from 1980 until her assassination in 1984.

Robert "Bob" Mathias (born Tulare, California, 1930) is an Olympic decathlete and a former representative.

August Ferdinand Moebius (born Schulpforte, Germany, 1790; died Leipzig, Germany, September 26, 1868) was a mathematician. He was especially interested in topology, a branch of mathematics that involves space and surfaces.

 Children can participate in an interesting topology problem by seeing if they can peel an orange so that the peel stays in one piece.

November

 William Tell shot the famous apple from his son's head in 1307.

 Children could have an accuracy contest, but not with arrows and apples and heads. They could aim paper airplanes at a target.

Oman celebrates a national holiday. Located on the southeastern portion of the Arabian Peninsula, Oman exports a great deal of petroleum. Muscat is the capital.

United States established uniform time zones in 1883.

 The continental United States has four time zones. Students could find out how many time zones are added to account for Alaska and Hawaii. Then they could make up some good math problems about all those time zones.

Mickey Mouse appeared for the first time in 1928. The cartoon, *Steamboat Willie,* premiered in New York City's Colony Theater. It was the first animated talking production.

 Children could make Mickey Mouse ears and attach them to headbands.

Antarctica was discovered by Captain Nathaniel Palmer in 1820.

Teddy bear was created in 1902. The *Washington Evening Post* published cartoons of Teddy Roosevelt not shooting a bear cub.

Sacagawea golden dollar coins were minted in 1999.

Birthdays

Louis Jacques Mande Daguerre (born Cormeilles-en-Parisis, France, 1789; died near Paris, France, July 10, 1851) invented the first useful method of photography, the daguerreotype.

Johnny Mercer (born Savannah, Georgia, 1909; died Bel Air, California, June 25, 1976) was a singer, an actor, and a songwriter. Two of his most famous works are *Moon River* and *You Must Have Been a Beautiful Baby.*

Sir William Schwenck Gilbert (born London, England, 1836; died May 29, 1911) was half of the famous Gilbert and Sullivan creative force.

Students could listen to some of the Gilbert and Sullivan operettas, possibly *The Pirates of Penzance.*

Alan Shepard (born East Derry, New Hampshire, 1923; died Monterey, California, July 21, 1998) was an astronaut and the first U.S. citizen to travel in space. In addition, he commanded *Apollo 14* and spent thirty-three hours on the moon.

November

 Monaco celebrates a national holiday. Located between France and the Mediterranean Sea, the country covers only 1.21 square miles. More than 30,000 people live in Monaco. Its government is that of a constitutional monarchy. Most of the country's revenue comes from tourism.

Gettysburg Address was delivered by Abraham Lincoln in 1863. The Civil War battlefield was being dedicated as a national cemetery. While keynote speaker Edward Everett spoke for more than two hours, Lincoln's speech lasted just two minutes. However, the speech stands today as one of the best pieces of oration ever delivered. The Library of Congress stores the original written speeches.

 Children could read and discuss the Gettysburg Address.

Zion National Park was created in Utah in 1919. Contact: Zion National Park, Springdale, Utah 84767-1099. Visit a Web site at: http://www.nps.gov/zion.

 Many bats live in niches along Zion Canyon. Children could research bats and Zion National Park. Then they could make an "I am batty about Zion" commercial.

Puerto Rico was discovered by Columbus in 1493 when he made his second trip to the New World.

Birthdays

Roy Campanella (born Philadelphia, Pennsylvania, 1921; died Woodland Hills, California, June 26, 1993) was a great baseball player. One of the first African American major leaguers, he was the National League MVP in 1951, 1953, and 1955. He was paralyzed in a car accident in 1958. He became even more famous as a spokesperson for the handicapped. He entered the Baseball Hall of Fame in 1969.

George Rogers Clark (born Albemarle County, Virginia, 1752; died Louisville, Kentucky, February 13, 1818) was a frontiersman.

James Abram Garfield (born near Orange, Ohio, 1831; died Elberon, New Jersey, September 19, 1881) was the twentieth president (1881) of the United States. Born in a log cabin, he grew up to be a lawyer and a professor. At age thirty he was the youngest general of the Civil War. He was elected to Congress and became the dark horse candidate for the presidency. Garfield won by one-tenth of one percent of the votes. He was assassinated in office by Charles J. Guiteau, an unhappy person who had sought a job appointment from Garfield. Visit a Web site at: http://www.whitehouse.gov/history/presidents/jg20.html.

 Children could find out whether the Secret Service was around during Garfield's time. How is the president protected today?

Jack Schaefer (born Cleveland, Ohio, 1907; died Santa Fe, New Mexico, January 24, 1991) was an author. He wrote *Shane*. Visit a Web site at: http://www.aristos.org/schaefer/js-page.htm.

November

 Bill of Rights was ratified by New Jersey in 1789. It was the first state to approve the amendments.

Mexico celebrates its Revolution Day of 1910.

Universal Children's Day is observed by the United Nations. The day was first marked in 1953. Over 100 nations recognize this day.

 Children could propose ideas for a children's bill of rights.

Traffic light was patented in 1923 by Garrett Morgan.

Lincoln Borglum completed Mount Rushmore in 1941. His father, Gutzon Borglum, had started the project fourteen years earlier. The elder Borglum died March 6, 1941.

 The faces on Mount Rushmore are huge. For example, each head is sixty feet tall. Theodore Roosevelt's mustache is twenty feet across. The statues would be 465 feet tall if more than the heads were carved. Children could find other measurements. Then on the playground, they could lay out some of these numbers.

Peregrine White, born 1620, was the first child of Pilgrims born in the New World.

Birthdays

Chester Gould (born Pawnee, Oklahoma, 1900; died Woodstock, Illinois, May 11, 1985) was a cartoonist. His *Dick Tracy* first appeared in 1931 and was eventually syndicated in 1,000 newspapers.

Edwin Powell Hubble (born Marshfield, Missouri, 1889; died San Marino, California, September 28, 1953) was an astronomer. His theories on the expanding universe changed the course of astronomy. The Hubble Telescope was named after him.

 Older children could read more about his theories on the expanding universe.

Selma Lagerlof (born Varmland Province, Sweden, 1858; died Varmland Province, Sweden, March 16, 1940) was the first woman to win the Nobel Prize for literature. She received the 1909 prize for her collection of poems.

Oliver Wolcott (born Windsor, Connecticut, 1726; died East Windsor, Connecticut, December 1, 1797) signed the Declaration of Independence. He was also governor of Connecticut following the Revolutionary War.

November

 21

Mayflower **dropped anchor in Cape Cod, Massachusetts.** The Mayflower Compact was signed in 1620.

 The Mayflower Compact is very brief, but it was very important. The children could read and discuss the document.

North Carolina became the twelfth state of the United States by ratifying the Constitution in 1789. Its founders named the state after Charles I. *Carolus* means Charles in Latin. The state's nicknames are the Tar Heel State and Old North State. Raleigh is the state capital. In colonial times the state raised rice and tobacco. Leading sources of income today are tobacco, textiles, and furniture. The Wright Brothers flew their first airplane in Kitty Hawk, North Carolina. Contact: (800) VISITNC. Visit an Internet site at: http://www.50states.com/ncarolin.htm.

 Children could find out what a tar heel is.

Phonograph was invented in 1877 by Thomas Edison.

 The first phonograph certainly differs from today's compact disc players. Children could draw the different stages of development. They could also predict what the next stage will be.

Verrazano Narrows Bridge opened in 1964. The 4,260-foot suspension bridge connects Brooklyn and Staten Island. Visit a Web site at: http://www.mta.nyc.ny.us/bandt/html/veraz.htm.

Dow Jones Industrial Average exceeded 5,000 for the first time in 1995.

Birthdays

Troy Aikman (born West Covina, California, 1966) is a former football player.

Josiah Bartlett (born Amesbury, Massachusetts, 1729; died Kingston, New Hampshire, 1795) signed the Declaration of Independence. A physician, he represented New Hampshire.

Ken Griffey, Jr. (born Donora, Pennsylvania, 1969) is a baseball player.

Stanley "Stan the Man" Musial (born Donora, Pennsylvania, 1920) is a Baseball Hall of Fame outfielder and first baseman.

Elizabeth George Speare (born Melrose, Massachusetts, 1908; died Tucson, Arizona, November 15, 1994) was a children's author. She wrote, among other works, *The Sign of the Beaver* (Newbery Honor Book), published in 1983. She also wrote *The Witch of Blackbird Pond*.

Jean François Marie Voltaire (born Paris, France, 1694; died Paris, France, May 30, 1778) was a philosopher and a writer.

ovember

22 **SOS became the international distress signal in 1906.**

 Children could learn a bit about Morse code. They could practice sending SOS in Morse code.

Vasco da Gama rounded the Cape of Good Hope in 1497.

National Hockey League was founded in 1917.

 Sports enthusiasts could find out the names of the original teams of the NHL.

China Clipper, **a "flying boat," left San Francisco, California, and arrived in Manila about sixty hours later.** This 1935 flight started the first trans-Pacific mail delivery system.

 Children could learn how hydroplanes differ from airplanes.

Lebanon celebrates its Independence Day. It was under French control from the end of World War I until 1943. A bit smaller than Connecticut, the country has an ancient history. Beirut is the capital, and the country has experienced civil unrest for a number of years.

Sagittarius the Archer is the astrological sign for November 22 through December 21.

Birthdays

Sieur de La Salle (born Rouen, France, 1643; died in Texas, March 19, 1687) was an explorer. He traveled down the Mississippi River to the Gulf of Mexico. He claimed for France all the lands that emptied into the Mississippi River.

Guion S. Bluford, Jr. (born Philadelphia, 1942) was the first African American astronaut to travel in space. Visit a Web site at: http://www.nauts.com/bios/nasa/bluford.html.

Charles de Gaulle (born Lille, France, 1890; died Colombey-les-Deux-Eglises, France, November 19, 1970) was a French military leader during World War II. When the Germans occupied France, he became a source of inspiration for the French people. After the war, he became president of France. He led the country from 1958 to 1969.

George Eliot (born Mary Ann Evans in Chilvers Coton, Warwickshire, England, 1819; died Chelsea, England, December 22, 1880) was a writer. One of her most famous works is *Silas Marner.*

Wiley Post (born Grand Plain, Texas, 1898; died near Port Barrow, Alaska, August 15, 1935) was an early aviator and stunt parachutist. The self-taught pilot flew the *Winnie Mae.* He co-authored, along with his navigator Harold Gatty, *Around the World in Eight Days.* He and Will Rogers were traveling to the Orient when their plane crashed.

November

23 Japan celebrates Kinro-Kansha-No-Hi, Labor Thanksgiving Day.

Pencil sharpener was patented by J. L. Love in 1897.

 Students could take apart an old pencil sharpener to see how it works.

Andrew Jackson Beard patented his Jenny coupler in 1899. The inventor knew how dangerous it was to couple railroad cars. His invention allowed cars to join together by bumping into one another and saved many human hands and feet.

 Students could make a series of frames to show how the Jenny works.

Birthdays

Billy the Kid (born probably Henry McCarty in New York, New York, 1859; died Fort Sumner, New Mexico, July 14, 1881), also known as William H. Bonney, was an outlaw of the Old West.

Franklin Pierce (born Hillsboro, New Hampshire, 1804; died Concord, New Hampshire, October 8, 1869) was the fourteenth president (1853–1857) of the United States. He was a dark horse candidate, facing General Winfield Scott. One of his accomplishments was the Gadsden Purchase. Visit a Web site at: http://www.whitehouse.gov/history/presidents/fp14.html.

 Although Pierce was a Northerner, he espoused slavery. Older children could decide whether his presidential actions impacted ultimately on the Civil War.

Edward Rutledge (born Charleston, South Carolina, 1749; died Charleston, South Carolina, January 23, 1800) signed the Declaration of Independence. He also served as governor of South Carolina after the Revolutionary War.

November

24 **Barbed wire was patented in 1874 by Joseph Glidden.**

 Barbed wire really changed ranching in the West. Young historians could find out the advantages and disadvantages of barbed wire.

Birthdays

Frances Hodgson Burnett (born Cheetham Hill, Manchester, England, 1849; died Plandome, Long Island, New York, October 29, 1924) was a writer. Two of her most famous works are *Little Lord Fauntleroy,* published in 1886, and *The Secret Garden,* printed in 1910.

 Children could make before and after pictures of the secret garden.

Carlo (Lorenzini) Collodi (born Florence, Italy, 1826; died Florence, Italy, October 26, 1890) wrote *The Adventures of Pinocchio* in 1883.

Scott Joplin (born Texarkana, Texas, 1868; died New York, New York, April 1, 1917) was a musician and composer. He was known for his ragtime music.

Father Junipero Serra (born Majorca, Spain, 1713; died Mission San Carlos Borromeo, California, August 28, 1784) was a Franciscan priest who established the first mission, San Diego de Alcala, in California in 1769. He also created eight other missions in California.

Zachary Taylor (born Montebello, Virginia, 1784; died Washington, DC, July 9, 1850) was the twelfth president (1849–1850) of the United States. He was the son of a Revolutionary War hero. He was proud of being a professional soldier. He served in the military for forty years. He was elected to the presidency, although he had no political experience. Nicknamed Old Rough and Ready, he died in office after serving sixteen months. He was the last of the presidents to own slaves. Visit a Web site at: http://www.whitehouse.gov/history/presidents/zt12.html.

Henri de Toulouse-Lautrec (born Albi, France, 1864; died Malrome, France, September 9, 1901) was an impressionist painter. He often painted scenes about Paris's circuses, cabarets, and nightclubs.

 Toulouse-Lautrec also made lithographs. Children could view some of his work and find out how lithographs differ from paintings.

November

25 Delmonico's Restaurant in New York, New York, served a three-course meal for just twelve cents in 1834.

Evaporated milk was patented in 1884.

 Children could research the steps in making evaporated milk. They could also find out its uses.

Suriname celebrates its Independence Day. It became autonomous in 1975 from the Netherlands. It had been under Dutch control for the most part since 1667. Located on the northeastern coast of South America, the country exports bauxite and wood. Paramaribo is the capital.

Birthdays

Marc Brown (born Erie, Pennsylvania, 1946) is a children's author and illustrator. He is known for his Arthur books.

 Children could read and enjoy some of Brown's books.

Andrew Carnegie (born Dunfermline, Scotland, 1835; died Shadowbrook, Massachusetts, August 11, 1919) was an industrialist and a philanthropist. He came to America when he was twelve years old. He made a fortune in the steel industry. He donated about $350 million to charity, including moneys to 2,500 libraries. He built Carnegie Hall in New York City.

 Children could brainstorm what causes they would support if they had lots of extra money.

Joseph Paul "Joe" DiMaggio (born Martinez, California, 1914; died Hollywood, Florida, March 8, 1999) was an outfielder for the New York Yankees. He was nicknamed the Yankee Clipper and Joltin' Joe. He participated in ten World Series and eleven All-Star games. He entered the Baseball Hall of Fame in 1955.

Carrie Amelia Moore Nation (born Garrard County, Kentucky, 1846; died Leavenworth, Kansas, June 9, 1911) was a temperance leader. She felt that saloons were violating the law. Therefore, she and a few followers conceived of *hatchetation*. She would enter and destroy saloons with her hatchet.

ovember

26 **Thanksgiving Day was celebrated nationally for the first time in 1789.** President Washington issued a proclamation declaring that the day should be one of prayer and thanksgiving.

 Students could research what the first Thanksgiving meal was. How does it compare to what they eat on the holiday today?

Alice in Wonderland **was published in 1865.**

Mongolia celebrates Republic Day. It became a republic in 1924. Ulan Bator is the capital. The Gobi Desert occupies part of the country. Another part of the country is a high plateau.

Little Bighorn Battlefield National Monument was created from Custer Battlefield National Monument in 1991. A monument to the Native Americans who fought at Custer's Last Stand was also approved. Visit a Web site at: http://www.nps.gov/libi.

Sojourner Truth died in 1883 in Battle Creek, Michigan. She was born a slave in Alster County, New York, possibly in the year 1797. She became a free woman after the New York Emancipation Act of 1827. She became an itinerant preacher, speaking for the cause of abolition. She became famous for her speaking, and she met Abraham Lincoln in the White House in 1864. After the Civil War, she campaigned for women's rights.

 Students could read portions of the book *Sojourner Truth: Ain't I a Woman?* by Patricia McKissack.

Birthdays

Charles Schultz (born Minneapolis, Minnesota, 1922; died Santa Rosa, California, February 12, 2000) was a cartoonist and the creator of *Peanuts.*

 Students could read and discuss some of the *Peanuts* cartoons. They could try to draw their own cartoons.

November

 Williamsburg, Virginia, began restoration processes in 1926.

 Children could locate Williamsburg on a map. They could research the community. Was it important during the colonial period?

Gordie Howe played his thousandth game in the National Hockey League in 1960. He was the first player in the National Hockey League to do so.

 Students could find out how many years it took to play those thousand games. How many games did he play in his entire professional career?

Birthdays

Anders Celsius (born Uppsala, Sweden, 1701; died Uppsala, Sweden, April 25, 1744) invented the Celsius temperature scale. He was also an astronomer.

 Children could compare and contrast the Fahrenheit scale with the Celsius scale. They could also research where these scales are used.

Kevin Henkes (born Racine, Wisconsin, 1960) is a children's author and illustrator. One of his books is *Lilly's Purple Plastic Purse.*

Bruce Lee (born San Francisco, California, 1940; died July 20, 1973) was a movie star and an expert in martial arts.

Robert R. Livingston (born New York, New York, 1746; died Clermont, New York, February 26, 1813) was a patriot, a member of the Continental Congress, and a diplomat. He delivered the presidential oath to Washington at the inauguration in 1789.

Bat Masterson (born Henryville, Quebec, Canada, 1853; died New York, New York, October 25, 1921) was a gambler and a lawman of the Old West.

Bill Nye (born Washington, DC, 1955) hosts "Bill Nye, the Science Guy."

November

First automobile race in the United States took place in 1895. Six cars participated in the fifty-five mile race. The winner averaged seven miles per hour.

 Automobiles certainly travel much faster today. Children could locate and present statistics regarding various vehicles' speeds.

Lady Astor became the first woman to be elected to the British Parliament. Born in the United States, Lady Astor was elected in 1919.

 Children could find out how British Parliament elections differ from American elections.

Admiral Richard E. Byrd made the first ever flight over the South Pole in 1929.

Pablo Picasso's *Acrobat and Harlequin* **sold in 1988 for more than $38 million.**

Mauritania celebrates its Independence Day. It gained its freedom from France in 1960. The country, located in northwestern Africa, is larger than the state of Texas. The capital is Nouakchott. The country still depends on France for economic aid. Most of its income comes from livestock, iron ore, and gypsum.

Albania celebrates Liberation Day. Turkey gave up control of Albania in 1912. Located in southeastern Europe, the country is a bit bigger than the state of Maryland. Tirana is the capital. Its major industries are food processing and textiles.

Birthdays

Ed Young (born Tientsin, China, 1931) is a children's author and illustrator. He wrote, among other works, *Lon Po Po: A Red-Riding-Hood Story from China* (Caldecott Medal), published in 1989.

 Children could read and enjoy some of his work.

November

29 New York hosted the first performance of an Italian opera, *The Barber of Seville*, in 1825.

 Students could listen to a portion of the opera.

First Army-Navy football game was played in 1890 at West Point. Navy won.

First open heart surgery was performed in 1944 at Johns Hopkins.

Dale Cummings did 14,118 sit-ups in 1965.

Birthdays

Louisa May Alcott (born Philadelphia, Pennsylvania, 1832; died Boston, Massachusetts, March 6, 1888) was a novelist. One of her most famous works is *Little Women.*

Christian Johann Doppler (born Salzburg, Austria, 1803; died Venice, Italy, March 17, 1853) was an Austrian physicist. He proposed the Doppler effect.

 Children could read more about the Doppler effect regarding sound and set up experiments to verify Doppler's findings.

Madeleine L'Engle (born New York, New York, 1918) is a children's author. She wrote, among other works, *A Wrinkle in Time* (Newbery Medal), 1962. Visit a Web site at: http://www.vms. utexas.edu/%7eeithlan/lengle.html.

C(live) S(taples) Lewis (born Belfast, Ireland, 1898; died Oxford, England, November 22, 1963) was a writer and a professor of medieval literature. He wrote for both adults and children. His most famous work in children's literature is a series of seven books, *The Chronicles of Narnia.*

 Children could read and enjoy parts of the Narnia series.

Nellie Tayloe Ross (born St. Joseph, Missouri, 1876; died Washington, DC, December 20, 1977) was the first woman governor in the United States. After her husband, the governor of Wyoming, died, she completed his term. Then she campaigned and won her term. She was not reelected, but she became director of the U.S. Mint in 1933. She remained at that post for twenty years.

Charles Thomson (born Machera, County Derry, Ireland, 1729; died Lower Merion, Pennsylvania, August 16, 1824) was secretary for the First Continental Congress. He recorded government proceedings for the next fifteen years and collected thousands of documents. He gave all the records to the government in 1789.

November

 Articles of Peace between Great Britain and the United States were formally signed in Paris, France, in 1782. This officially ended the Revolutionary War.

Statue of Ramses II was uncovered in 1991 in Akhimim, Egypt.

 Children could investigate the life of Ramses II. They could make "artifacts" of his life and construct a small museum.

Barbados celebrates its Independence Day. It became free from Great Britain in 1966. This easternmost island in the Caribbean is 166 square miles. Bridgetown is the capital.

Yemen celebrates its Independence Day. It became free of the Ottoman Empire in 1918. During ancient times the area provided a caravan route for spices and precious goods. Today San'a is the capital.

Birthdays

Shirley Chisholm (born Brooklyn, New York, 1924) is a former member of the House of Representatives.

Sir Winston Leonard Spencer Churchill (born Oxfordshire, England, 1874; died London, England, January 24, 1965) was the Prime Minister of England during World War II.

 Children could read more about Churchill. How did he keep England functioning during the war?

Dick Clark (born Mt. Vernon, New York, 1924) is a television personality. He hosted "American Bandstand."

Lucy Maud Montgomery (born New London, Prince Edward Island, Canada, 1874; died Toronto, Canada, April 24, 1952) was an author. She wrote *Anne of Green Gables.*

Jonathan Swift (born Dublin, Ireland, 1667; died Dublin, Ireland, October 19, 1745) was an author and a satirist. One of his most famous works is *Gulliver's Travels,* published in 1726.

Mark Twain (born Samuel Langhorne Clemens in Florida, Missouri, 1835; died Redding, Connecticut, April 21, 1910) was a writer. His works include *The Adventures of Tom Sawyer* and *The Prince and the Pauper.*

His birth and death coincide with an astronomical event. Students could see if they can find the event.

Margot Zemach (born Los Angeles, California, 1931; died May 21, 1989) was an illustrator. She won the Caldecott Medal for *Duffy and the Devil.*

December is now the twelfth month of the year. However, until 46 B.C., it was the tenth month, and it had only twenty-nine days. December gets its name from the Latin word *decem,* meaning "ten." Julius Caesar changed the calendar and added two more days to December. Turquoise and zircon are December birthstones. Poinsettias, holly, and narcissus are December flowers.

Month-Long Activities

Bingo's Birthday Month celebrates the invention of the game. Edwin S. Lowe created Bingo in 1929. Now over five billion dollars are raised for charity each year through Bingo. Contact: Bingo Bugle, Inc., Box 527, Vashon, Washington 98070. Telephone: (800) 327-6437.

 Bingo can be an educational game. Develop a Bingo game around a theme. For example, use math facts or chemical elements.

International Calendar Awareness Month gets children ready for the coming year. Contact: Calendar Marketing Association, 621 East Park Avenue, Libertyville, Illinois 60048. Telephone: (800) 828-8225.

Universal Human Rights Month is remembered by the International Society of Friendship and Good Will.

December

1

Portugal became independent of Spain in 1640.

Washington, DC, became the capital of the United States in 1800. Parts of Virginia and Maryland were combined to make the new capital. Charles L'Enfant created the architectural plan for the city. The federal government is the largest employer, and printing is the biggest industry. Over seventeen million tourists visit the nation's capital every year. Contact: (202) 789-7000. Visit an Internet site at: http://www.dcpages.ari.net.

 Children could locate some of the many important buildings on a map of Washington, DC.

Father Flanagan created Boys' Town in 1917 in the state of Nebraska.

Romania celebrates National Day. Romania, a country in southeastern Europe, is slightly bigger than Utah. Bucharest is the capital.

Rosa Parks was arrested in 1955 in Montgomery, Alabama, because she did not give up her seat in a municipal bus. The African American's actions led to a boycott of the Montgomery bus system. Many experts believe this event triggered the civil rights movement.

 Students could relate the Montgomery boycott to the boycotts led by Gandhi in India.

Antarctica Treaty was signed by twelve nations in 1959. The continent will be kept as a scientific preserve. No nation can colonize it.

GATT Treaty (General Agreement of Tariffs and Trade) was approved by the Senate in 1994.

Birthdays

Jan Brett (born Hingham, Massachusetts, 1949) is an author and illustrator. She wrote *Hedgie's Surprise*. Visit a Web site at: http://www.janbrett.com.

Mary Martin (born Weatherford, Texas, 1913; died Rancho Mirage, California, November 3, 1990) was a stage and television star. She was known for her roles in *Peter Pan* and *South Pacific*.

 Peter Pan includes the Lost Boys. Children could draw house plans for the Lost Boys' residence.

Bette Midler (born Honolulu, Hawaii, 1945) is a singer and an actress.

December

 2

John Brown was hanged in 1859 for leading the abolitionist raid on Harper's Ferry.

Barney Clark was the first person to receive an artificial heart. The operation took place in 1982, and he lived almost 112 days after the surgery.

Denali National Park and Preserve was created in 1980. It contains Mount McKinley, the highest mountain in North America at 20,320 feet. Contact: Denali National Park and Preserve, PO Box 9, McKinley Park, Alaska 99755. Visit a Web site at: http://www.nps.gov/dena.

 Denali is home to many kinds of animals. Children could research Denali and its inhabitants. Each child could make a postcard, featuring an animal, from the national park.

Glacier Bay National Park and Preserve was formed in 1980. Visitors can view tidewater glaciers and both brown and black bears. Contact: Glacier Bay National Park and Preserve, Bartlett Cove, Gustavus, Alaska 99826. Visit a Web site at: http://www.nps.gov/glba.

United Arab Emirates was formed in 1971 when seven sheikdoms united and formed one country. The country gained its independence from the United Kingdom on the same day. The country's area is slightly larger than the state of South Carolina. Abu Dhabi is the capital, and it is known for its petroleum reserves.

Pan American Health Day has been celebrated by presidential proclamation since 1940.

Monroe Doctrine was established in 1823 in James Monroe's address to Congress. He stated that the American continents were not to be further colonized by European nations.

Safety razor was patented in 1901 by King C. Gillette.

First controlled, self-sustaining nuclear reaction occurred at the University of Chicago in 1942. Enrico Fermi and his scientific team were pleased with the outcome. The laboratory had been built below the stands of the football stadium.

Birthdays

Peter Carl Goldmark (born Budapest, Hungary, 1906; died Westchester, New York, December 7, 1977) invented long-playing records and color television.

David Macaulay (born Burton-on-Trent, England, 1946) is a children's author and illustrator. He wrote, among other works, *Black and White* (Caldecott Medal), 1990.

 Macaulay's *Motel of the Mysteries* is great fun to read. He makes fun of archaeology. Enjoy the book with the children. Then see if they can think of other "artifacts" and their meanings.

Monica Seles (born Novidad, Yugoslavia, 1973) is a tennis player.

Georges Pierre Seurat (born Paris, France, 1859; died Paris, France, March 29, 1891) was a painter. He developed *pointillism.* Rather than painting with brush strokes, Seurat made dots of paint side by side. When the viewer steps away from the artwork, images appear. One of his most famous works is *Sunday Afternoon on the Island of the Grand Jatte,* painted in 1886. Visit a Web site at: http://www.artcyclopedia.com/artists/seurat_georges.html.

 Children can make great pointillism works. Markers seem to work best.

Britney Spears (born Kentwood, Louisiana, 1981) is a singer.

December

Lao People's Democratic Republic celebrates a national holiday. This landlocked country in Southeast Asia is about the size of Utah. It was under French control from 1893 until 1946. It exports coffee and tin.

United Nations declares today as the International Day of Disabled Persons.

Illinois became the twenty-first state of the United States in 1818. Its name derives from the word *iliniwek,* meaning "tribe of the superior men." The state's nickname is the Prairie State. Although Springfield is the state capital, Chicago is a very large transportation center for rail, air, and water. Springfield was the site for the famous Lincoln-Douglas debates. Illinois still grows large amounts of corn and soybeans, but it also has deposits of coal and gas. The monarch butterfly is the state insect. Contact: (800) 223-0121. Visit an Internet site at: http://www.50states.com/illinois.htm.

 Monarch butterflies make annual migrations to winter in trees in Mexico, California, and Florida. Students could find out more about the monarch butterfly and its migration patterns.

Frederick Douglass in 1847 printed the first issue of *North Star,* an abolitionist newspaper.

Dr. Christiaan Barnard conducted the first successful heart transplant in Cape Town, South Africa, in 1967.

Birthdays

Joseph Conrad (born Jozef Teodor Konrad Nalecz Kozeniowski in Poland, 1857; died Bishopsbourne, Kent, England, August 3, 1924) was a writer. He came to England when he was sixteen; he could not speak English. He worked for the British Navy for sixteen years and perfected his English. Most of his works relate to the sea. One of his most famous works is *Lord Jim,* published in 1900.

Carlos Montoya (born Madrid, Spain, 1903; died Wainscott, New York, March 3, 1993) was a composer and guitarist. He is especially known for his flamenco rhythms and arrangements. Interestingly, he never learned to read music.

 Find a recording of Montoya's music and play it for the class.

Gilbert Charles Stuart (born Narragansett, Rhode Island, 1755; died Boston, Massachusetts, July 9, 1828) was an artist, known particularly for his portraits.

 Stuart is known for a painting of George Washington that he never completed. He actually made copies of that portrait and sold them. Students could generate reasons why he never completed the project.

December

 4

First Thanksgiving in North America was held in 1619 on Berkeley Plantation in Virginia.

George Washington said goodbye to his troops in 1783.

 Children could try to write his farewell speech.

Manila paper was invented in 1843.

National Grange was started in 1786. Visit a Web site at: http://www.grange.org.

 The Grange is still active today. Children could see if a local chapter exists nearby. Perhaps a member of the Grange could speak to the children.

Birthdays

Munro Wilbur Leaf (born Hamilton, Maryland, 1905; died Garrett Park, Maryland, December 21, 1976) was a children's author. One of his works is *The Story of Ferdinand.*

 Older children could read the classic *The Story of Ferdinand* to younger children.

December

 5

Haiti was discovered by Christopher Columbus in 1492.

Montgomery Bus Boycott began in 1955. Following Rosa Parks's arrest on December 1, 1955, buses were boycotted until December 20, 1956. A Supreme Court ruling forced the integration of the bus system.

The Twenty-first Amendment to the Constitution was adopted in 1933, repealing the Eighteenth Amendment and ending Prohibition.

United Nations declares today as International Volunteer Day for Economic and Social Development.

 The children could volunteer to help around the school. Consider picking up litter or building bird feeders.

Pipe wrench was patented in 1876.

Birthdays

George Armstrong Custer (born New Rumley, Ohio, 1839; died Little Bighorn, Montana Territory, June 25, 1876) was an army officer. He became famous during the Civil War for being fearless. After the war, he joined a regiment fighting the Indians in Montana Territory.

On June 25, 1876, he found an Indian village that he thought housed about 1,000 warriors. However, the number of warriors probably exceeded 2,000. Custer and about 210 soldiers attacked immediately. Every soldier was killed, and the battle became known as "Custer's Last Stand."

Walt(er Elias) Disney (born Chicago, Illinois, 1901; died Los Angeles, California, December 15, 1966) was a cartoonist and an empire builder. He invented Mickey Mouse and all the animal's friends. Disney produced a number of animated movies, including *Snow White and the Seven Dwarfs* (1937) and *Bambi* (1942). He also produced live action movies and television programs. Disneyland opened in 1955, and Disney World began operations in 1971.

 Children could have a Disney Day at school. They could wear Disney shirts and share Disney books.

Bill Picket (born Jenks-Branch, Texas, 1870; died Ponca City, Oklahoma, April 2, 1932) was a cowboy and rodeo star.

Otto Preminger (born Vienna, Austria, 1906; died 1986) was a film actor, director, and producer. He came to the United States in 1935. Two of his most famous works are *Laura* (1944) and *Exodus* (1960).

Christina Georgina Rossetti (born London, England, 1830; died London, England, December 29, 1894) was a poet. One of her most well-known collections appropriate for children is *Goblin Market and Other Poems,* published in 1872.

Martin Van Buren (born Kinderhook, New York, 1782; died Kinderhook, New York, July 24, 1862) was the eighth president (1837–1841) of the United States. The first president not to live during the Revolutionary War, he was nicknamed the "Little Magician." He was a lawyer and Andrew Jackson's vice president before he was elected president. Van Buren's presidency had quite a few conflicts. The North disliked his views regarding slavery. The South was not happy when he would not annex Texas. The Panic of 1837 caused a severe depression nationwide. Visit a Web site at: http://www.whitehouse.gov/history/presidents/mb8.html.

 Children could find out why he was called the "Little Magician."

December

 6 **Congress met for the first time in 1790 in Philadelphia, Pennsylvania.**

Encyclopedia Britannica **debuted in 1768 in Scotland.**

Everglades National Park was founded in 1947. The park contains over 1.5 million acres of land. It is the only place in the world where alligators and crocodiles coexist. Contact: Everglades National Park, PO Box 279, Homestead, Florida 33030. Visit a Web site at: http://www.nps.gov/ever.

 Children could use a Venn diagram to show the differences between alligators and crocodiles.

St. Nicholas Day is celebrated in Central and Northern Europe. Dutch children fill their shoes with hay the night before. Treats can be found in shoes the next day.

Columbus landed on the shores of Hispaniola in 1492.

Quito, Ecuador, was founded by the Spanish in 1534.

Finland celebrates its Independence Day. It became free from Russia in 1917. For centuries Sweden and Russia have fought over Finland. Russia took over the country in 1809. Today Helsinki is the capital. Over three-fourths of the land is covered with forests. It exports timber and wood pulp.

Birthdays

Dave Brubeck (born Concord, California, 1920) is a jazz musician.

Ira Gershwin (born New York, New York, 1896; died Beverly Hills, California, August 17, 1983) was a lyricist. He often worked with his brother, George. His Broadway hits include *Funny Face.*

Alfred Eisenstaedt (born Dirschau, Prussia, 1898; died Martha's Vineyard, Massachusetts, August 23, 1955) was a famous photojournalist. He was known for his photographs published by *Life* magazine. One of his most popular photographs was of a soldier kissing a nurse to celebrate the end of World War II.

 Collect some of his photographs and display them. See which ones interest the children. Let them peruse some of today's magazines. Have them evaluate some of the photographs.

Alfred Joyce Kilmer (born New Brunswick, New Jersey, 1886; died in battle near Ourcy, France, July 30, 1918) was a poet. One of his most famous poems is "Trees," published in 1913.

 The children could read "Trees" and evaluate it.

December

7 Cicero was murdered by Mark Antony in 43 B.C.

Cote d'Ivoire celebrates a national holiday. Located on the western coast of Africa, the country is a little bigger than the size of New Mexico. The country claims its capital is Yamoussoukro, but the United States recognizes Abidjan as the capital. It exports cocoa, cotton, and bananas.

Delaware became the first state of the United States by ratifying the Constitution in 1787. The state was named after Thomas West, Lord De La Warr. The Dutch arrived in 1631. The Swedes followed in 1638 and established the first permanent settlement, Wilmington, in the colony. Dover is the capital of this small state. Its nicknames are the First State and the Diamond State. The ladybug is Delaware's official state insect. Contact: (800) 441-8846. Visit an Internet site at: http://www.50states.com/delaware.htm.

 Children could research why Delaware is called the Diamond State. Are diamonds mined there?

Pearl Harbor, Hawaii, was attacked by the Japanese in 1941. President Roosevelt called the day "a date that will live in infamy." The Japanese airplanes attacked early in the morning. They destroyed almost the entire Pacific Fleet and approximately 200 airplanes. Almost 3,000 people were killed in the hour-long attack. This event brought about America's entrance into World War II.

Nationalist Party of China was exiled to Taiwan in 1949.

Apollo 17 **was launched into space in 1972.** The three-person crew landed on the moon and carried out research. It was the last manned trip to the moon.

Birthdays

Johnny Lee Bench (born Oklahoma City, Oklahoma, 1947) is a former baseball catcher. He is a member of the Baseball Hall of Fame.

Larry Bird (born West Badin, Indiana, 1956) is a former basketball player.

Willa Cather (born Winchester, Virginia, 1873; died New York, New York, April 24, 1947) is an author. One of her most famous works, published in 1913, is *O Pioneers!* She won the 1922 Pulitzer Prize for *One of Ours.*

Harry Chapin (born Greenwich Village, New York, 1942; died Long Island, New York, July 1981) was a folk singer and composer.

 Harry Chapin received the Special Congressional Medal of Honor for his concerns about world hunger. See if you can find recordings of his work. Play them. See if students would like to collect canned food for a local food bank.

Richard Warren Sears (born Stewartville, Minnesota, 1863; died Waukesha, Wisconsin, September 28, 1914) was working as a railroad station agent. He then began to sell watches via the mail. He formed a partnership with Alvah C. Roebuck, who repaired the watches. They created Sears, Roebuck and Company. At first it was strictly a mail order company. However, in 1925 they opened their first retail store.

 Sears and Roebuck formed a team. Children could list other famous teams (for example, Laurel and Hardy).

John Tunis (born Boston, Massachusetts, 1889; died Essex, Connecticut, February 4, 1975) was the author of sports books. Visit a Web site at: http://www.elliemik.com/tunis.html.

ecember

8 **Christmas cards were first produced in 1843.**

Guam celebrates Lady of Camarin Day.

United States declared war against Japan and thus entered World War II in 1941.

Union of Soviet Socialist Republics expired in 1991. Many portions of the Soviet Union broke away and formed their own countries. These countries include Russia, Ukraine, Georgia, and others.

 Children could find an old map showing the Soviet Union. They could compare and contrast it to a map showing all the new countries.

NAFTA (North America Free Trade Agreement) was signed in 1993. The agreement, reducing tariffs and cutting trade regulations, went into effect January 1, 1994.

Birthdays

Mary Azarian (born Washington, DC, 1940) is an illustrator. She won the 1999 Caldecott Medal for *Snowflake Bentley.* Visit a Web site at: http://www.maryazarian.com/bks.html.

Sammy Davis, Jr. (born New York, New York, 1925; died Los Angeles, California, May 16, 1990) was a singer and an actor.

Horace (born 65 B.C.; died 8 B.C.) was a great poet during ancient Roman times. Although his father had been a slave, Horace was well educated and a member of the army. Later, a wealthy friend recognized Horace's talents and supported him. Horace was free from financial worries and could write. One of his most famous works is *Odes.*

Diego Rivera (born Guanajuato, Mexico, 1886; died Mexico City, Mexico, November 25, 1957) was an artist known for his large murals. He worked in earth tones and celebrated the common people.

 Rivera made very large murals. Perhaps the children could plan and complete a very large but temporary mural in chalk on the playground.

Jean Sibelius (born Hameenlinna, Finland, 1865; died Jarvenpaa, Finland, September 20, 1957) was a composer and a conductor. His works seem to incorporate Finland's forests and waters. Among his most famous works is *Finlandia,* performed for the first time in 1900.

James Grover Thurber (born Columbus, Ohio, 1894; died New York, New York, November 2, 1961) was a writer and a cartoonist. Much of his work appeared in *The New Yorker* magazine. One of his most famous short stories is "The Secret Life of Walter Mitty."

 In "The Secret Life of Walter Mitty," Mitty daydreams about very exciting adventures. The children could create a thriller about getting to school.

Eli Whitney (born Westborough, Massachusetts, 1765; died New Haven, Connecticut, January 8, 1825) was an inventor. He invented the cotton gin in 1793. It could clean as much cotton as fifty people could clean. Even though he had patented the cotton gin, other manufacturers made copies of his work. He fought them in the courts over years of trials. He also made muskets for the U.S. military. In 1798 he made 10,000 guns. He believed that interchangeable parts really helped production. He may have invented machines to make interchangeable parts.

December

 9

Ball bearing roller skates were patented in 1884 by Levant Richardson.

Petrified Forest National Park was founded in 1962. In addition to the magnificent petrified forest, visitors can find Indian ruins and parts of the Painted Desert. Contact: Petrified Forest National Park, Arizona, 86028. Visit a Web site at: http://www.nps.gov/pefo.

 Share with children how petrified wood forms.

Computer mouse was invented in 1968, but it was not really used until 1984.

Birthdays

Clarence Birdseye (born Brooklyn, New York, 1886; died New York, New York, October 7, 1956) created a method of deep-freezing food. He, along with others, started General Foods Corporation.

Joan Blos (born New York, New York, 1928) writes books for children. *A Gathering of Days: A New England Girl's Journal, 1830–32* won the Newbery Medal in 1979.

Jean De Brunhoff (born Paris, France, 1899; died Switzerland, October 16, 1937) was a children's author. He is known for his books about *Babar the Elephant.*

 Children could read some of De Brunhoff's work.

Joel Chandler Harris (born Eatonton, Georgia, 1848; died Atlanta, Georgia, July 3, 1908) was an author. Among other works, he wrote the *Uncle Remus* stories.

Grace Brewster Murray Hopper (born New York, New York, 1906; died Arlington, Virginia, January 1, 1992) was a computer scientist and a mathematician. She was employed by the military for a good part of her life. She worked on the Mark I computer team. She coined the word "bug" for computer foul-ups when she found an insect in the Mark I's circuitry. She helped create COBOL, and she standardized the navy's computer languages. She retired from the military in 1986 as the oldest officer on active duty.

 Computers have created all kinds of new terms, such as RAM and Internet. Children could generate a list of new computer terms.

December

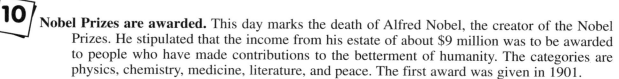

Nobel Prizes are awarded. This day marks the death of Alfred Nobel, the creator of the Nobel Prizes. He stipulated that the income from his estate of about $9 million was to be awarded to people who have made contributions to the betterment of humanity. The categories are physics, chemistry, medicine, literature, and peace. The first award was given in 1901.

 Children could go on the Internet and find the winners. The children could research the recipients and see whether they agree with the Nobel committee.

Thailand celebrates Constitution Day. Located in Southeast Asia, the country is larger than California. The capital is Bangkok, and the country was called Siam. Thailand is the world's second largest producer of tungsten and the third largest producer of tin.

United Nations celebrates Human Rights Day.

Mississippi became the twentieth state in the United States in 1817. Its nickname is the Magnolia State, and its name comes from an Ojibwa phrase, *misi sipi,* meaning "great river." Jackson is the state capital. The state ranks thirty-second in area and thirty-first in population. Hernando de Soto explored the area around 1540. The state water mammal is the porpoise. Contact: (800) 647-2290. Visit an Internet site at: http://www.50states.com/mississi.htm.

 Children love to spell Mississippi. Conduct a spelling bee, using states as the category.

Wyoming Territory in 1869 allowed women to vote and hold political office.

Treaty of Paris in 1898 ended the Spanish-American War.

Birthdays

Melvil Dewey (born Adams Center, New York, 1851; died Highlands County, Florida, December 26, 1931) created the Dewey decimal book classification system. He advocated the use of the metric system as well.

 Visit the library. Will the librarian discuss the advantages and disadvantages of the Dewey decimal book classification system?

Emily Elizabeth Dickinson (born Amherst, Massachusetts, 1830; died Amherst, Massachusetts, May 15, 1886) was a poet. A very shy individual, she rarely traveled. Only a few of her poems were published during her lifetime. After her death, her sister Lavinia found hundreds of poems among her effects. Lavinia was able to publish some of the poems. People appreciated Dickinson's work and more poems were issued. About 1,775 poems have been published, and Emily Dickinson is now regarded as one of the best American poets.

Thomas Gallaudet (born Philadelphia, Pennsylvania, 1787; died Hartford, Connecticut, September 9, 1851) created the Hartford School for the Deaf.

Mary Norton (born London, England, 1903; died Hartland, England, August 29, 1992) was a children's author. One of her most famous works is *Bedknobs and Broomsticks,* published in 1957. She also wrote the books about the Borrowers.

December

Edward VIII, the English monarch, abdicated in 1936 to marry the divorced American Wallis Warfield Simpson. His brother, George VI, became King of England.

United Nations International Children's Emergency Fund (UNICEF) was created in 1946. Contact: United Nations, Department of Public Information, New York, New York 10017.

Indiana became the nineteenth state of the United States in 1816. Indiana is the state capital, and the state's nickname is the Hoosier State. Mound builders lived in the area around A.D. 1000. It is about 36,185 miles square, placing it thirty-eighth in area. It ranks fourteenth in population. Farming is a leading source of employment in the north, and rich coal deposits can be found in the southern parts of the state. It is the leading U.S. producer of limestone. Contact: (800) 289-6646. Visit an Internet site at: http://www.50states.com/indiana.htm.

 The Indianapolis 500 has been running since 1911. Children could make a board game about Indiana. The board could be a speed track. The students who knew the most about Indiana would win the game.

Aurora borealis was documented in 1719.

Birthdays

Annie Jump Cannon (born Dover, Delaware, 1863; died Cambridge, Massachusetts, April 13, 1941) was an astronomer. She located several hundred new stars. However, she is best known for cataloging and classifying more than 225,000 stars.

 Children could find out how stars are classified.

Robert Koch (born Clausthal, Germany, 1843; died Baden-Baden, Germany, May 27, 1910) was an important bacteriologist. He discovered the specific bacteria that cause tuberculosis, anthrax, cholera, and other diseases. He also conducted experiments on sleeping sickness. He was awarded a Nobel Prize in 1905 for his studies on tuberculosis.

 Perhaps the school nurse could visit the class and discuss the importance of getting rid of bacteria.

Alexander Solzhenitsyn (born Kislovodsk, USSR, 1918) is an author. One of his best-known works is *One Day in the Life of Ivan Denisovich.*

December

Poinsettia Day marks the death of Dr. Joel Roberts Poinsett. He was the first person to bring the plant poinsettia from Central America to the United States. The plant was named in honor of him. He died in 1851 near Statesburg, South Carolina. Now the poinsettia is associated with the Christmas season.

 Students could draw a picture of the poinsettia flower and label its parts.

Pennsylvania became the second state of the United States by ratifying the Constitution in 1787. William Penn received a charter for the colony in 1681 and named it after his father. The name means, "Penn's Woods." The Constitution and the Declaration of Independence were both signed in Philadelphia. Harrisburg is the state capital, and its nickname is the Keystone State. In 1780 it was the first state to end slavery. It is a large transportation center, since it has access to both the Atlantic Ocean and Lake Erie. Contact: (800) VISITPA. Visit an Internet site at: http://www.50states.com/pennsylv.htm.

 Children could discover what a keystone is and how it relates to Pennsylvania's nickname.

Golf tee was patented by George Grant in 1899.

Guglielmo Marconi sent the first transoceanic radio signal from England to Newfoundland in 1901.

Kenya celebrates Jamhuri Day. It gained its independence from the United Kingdom in 1963. Today is also its Constitution Day. The country, slightly bigger than California, exports coffee, tea, and petroleum. Nairobi is the capital.

 Kenya's coffee is quite strong. Children could find out how coffee is grown and harvested.

Supreme Court ruled in favor of George W. Bush in 2000 regarding election results. Al Gore conceded the election, and Bush became president. Gore won the popular vote, but Bush won the electoral vote.

Birthdays

William Lloyd Garrison (born Newburyport, Massachusetts, 1805; died New York, New York, May 24, 1879) was an abolitionist and a writer.

John Jay (born New York, New York, 1745; died Bedford, New York, May 17, 1829) was a diplomat and a writer. He co-authored the *Federalist Papers* and was the first chief justice of the Supreme Court.

Frank Sinatra (born Hoboken, New Jersey, 1915; died Los Angeles, California, May 14, 1998) was a famous singer and actor.

December

 Santa Lucia Day is celebrated in Sweden. Girls wear white dresses and wake their families with coffee, Lucia buns (lussekatter), and music.

Abel Tasman discovered New Zealand in 1642.

 Tasmania was named after Tasman. Children could make a list of places named after people.

Sir Francis Drake, an English explorer, began his trip in 1577 that would eventually circumnavigate the world.

Actually Drake did not plan to sail around the world. He was a privateer intent on plundering Spanish ships. Children could check out his course and find out more about his "sea dog" years.

Birthdays

Mary Todd Lincoln (born Lexington, Kentucky, 1818; died Springfield, Illinois, July 16, 1882) was the wife of Abraham Lincoln, sixteenth president of the United States. She was the attractive daughter of a rich and prominent southern family. She married the impoverished Lincoln in 1842. They had four sons. Most of her life seemed riddled with agitation. While first lady, she was criticized for her extravagance. Her husband and three of her four sons died during her lifetime. Visit a Web site at: http://www.whitehouse.gov/history/firstladies/ml16.html.

 Children could investigate her life more. Since Lincoln was probably one of the best presidents, was she one of the best first ladies?

December

14 **Alabama became the twenty-second state of the United States in 1819.** People lived in the Russell Cave area around 6000 B.C. The Temple Mound culture moved into the Moundville location somewhere between 1200 and 1500. The state is named after the Alabama tribe. Montgomery is the capital, and its nicknames are the Yellowhammer State and the Heart of Dixie. The pecan is the state's official nut. Contact: (800) ALABAMA. Visit an Internet site at: http://www.50states.com/alabama.htm.

 The mound builders have left us fascinating artifacts. Children could learn more about these Native Americans.

Roald Amundsen found the South Pole in 1911. People had been trying to locate the South Pole for hundreds of years. He, four other adults, and over fifty sled dogs located the pole. All five men returned to base camp safely.

 Children could research why no country has ever claimed Antarctica.

Screw was patented in 1798.

Birthdays

James Harold Doolittle (born Alameda, California, 1896; died Pebble Beach, California, September 27, 1993) was an aviator and a military hero. As a young man, he was the first person to fly across North America in under a day. During World War II, he led the first aerial raid on five cities in Japan. He also spearheaded the Eighth Air Force for the Normandy invasion.

Margaret Madeline Chase Smith (born Skowhegan, Maine, 1897; died Skowhegan, Maine, May 29, 1995) was the first woman to be elected to both the House of Representatives (1941) and to the Senate (1949).

 Children could find out how the requirements for being a representative differ from those for being a senator.

December

15

Bill of Rights became a part of the Constitution in 1791. The first ten amendments became a part of the Constitution when Virginia ratified them. Presidential proclamations have marked this day from 1962.

 Children could examine some of the amendments and learn why each was so important at the time.

Vega I **was launched by the Soviet Union in 1984.** It was to make contact with Halley's Comet in March of 1986. It was to carry on scientific experiments.

Birthdays

Alexandre Gustave Eiffel (born Dijon, France, 1832; died Paris, France, December 23, 1923) designed the Eiffel Tower. He helped design the Statue of Liberty.

 The Eiffel Tower is a landmark for the city of Paris. Children could locate some facts about the tower and display them on a bulletin board.

John Paul Getty (born Minneapolis, Minnesota, 1892; died 1976) was one of the richest men in the world. He made a fortune of about $4 billion through petroleum. He earned his first million dollars by the age of twenty-three. He also enjoyed collecting art.

 Four billion is a very large number. To make the number more real to children, they could figure out how many years four billion seconds is.

Nero (born Antium, A.D. 37; died A.D. 68) was emperor of Rome from A.D. 54 until his death. Although his rule marked growth and relative peace for Rome, he was quite cruel. He executed those who disagreed with him, including at least two wives. The military leaders revolted in A.D. 68, and Nero killed himself within a short time.

December

16

Posadas is celebrated in Mexico. This event occurs nine days before Christmas. Families walk from house to house, seeking shelter for Mary and Joseph. At the last house, everyone enters. People feast and dance. A piñata is broken open. Diane Hoyt-Goldsmith's *Las Posadas: An Hispanic Christmas Celebration* gives great insights into this tradition.

Boston Tea Party was a protest against a duty placed on imported tea. In 1773 over 100 men, dressed as Indians and led by Samuel Adams, boarded three English ships moored in Boston's harbor. They dumped at least 300 chests of tea overboard. They did not want to pay the tax for the tea. The British retaliated by imposing the Intolerable Acts on the colonists. These acts led to further opposition on the part of the colonists and eventually the meeting of the First Continental Congress.

 Children could read more about the Boston Tea Party. Were the patriots right in what they did?

Electoral College meets during presidential election years to vote for the president and vice president.

Many people feel we should eliminate the Electoral College. Children could formally debate the issue.

Bahrain celebrates Independence Day. It broke away from Great Britain in 1971. These islands lie in the Persian Gulf. Manama is the capital.

Calabria, Italy, was the site of a massive earthquake in 1857. Over 10,000 people died.

Birthdays

Jane Austen (born Steventon, Hampshire, England, 1775; died Winchester, England, July 18, 1817) was a writer. Two of her most famous works are *Sense and Sensibility* and *Pride and Prejudice.*

Ludwig von Beethoven (born Bonn, Germany, 1770; died Vienna, Austria, March 26, 1827) was one of the greatest composers. He created nine symphonies, a number of overtures and chamber music, an opera, and about thirty-five sonatas. He grew deaf in his later years, but he still was able to compose.

 Children could listen to some of his music and perhaps perform simple melodies extracted from his work.

Bill Brittain (born Rochester, New York, 1930) is an author. One of his books is *All the Money in the World.*

Arthur Charles Clarke (born Minehead, England, 1917) is an author. He is best known for his science fiction, including *2001: A Space Odyssey.*

Margaret Mead (born Philadelphia, Pennsylvania, 1901; died New York, New York, November 15, 1978) was an anthropologist and a writer. *Coming of Age in Samoa,* published in 1928, showed her strong interest in other cultures. Her writings often compared and contrasted two cultures.

William "The Refrigerator" Perry (born Aiken, South Carolina, 1962) is a former football player.

George Santayana (born Madrid, Spain, 1863; died Rome, Italy, September 26, 1952) was a philosopher. One of his most famous quotes is, "Those who cannot remember the past are condemned to repeat it."

December

A Christmas Carol, **written by Charles Dickens, was published in 1843.**

 Children know this work quite well from all its dramatizations. They could write a simple script and produce a play.

Aztec stone calendar was discovered in Mexico City in 1790. The huge stone, weighing almost twenty-five tons and measuring over eleven feet in diameter, was probably carved around 1479. It was buried soon after the Spanish arrived. The stone demonstrated how the Aztec fifty-two-year calendar cycle worked.

Saturnalia was celebrated by the ancient Romans from December 17 through December 23. The festival was organized around the time of the winter solstice.

Bhutan celebrates a national holiday. It is a country about the size of Maryland and is located in the Himalayan Mountains. Ruled by a monarch, the country gained its independence from India in 1949. The capital is Timphu.

Wilbur and Orville Wright flew the first airplane in 1903 near Kitty Hawk, North Carolina. Orville piloted the first successful flight. Then Wilbur had his turn. Each flight lasted less than a minute. The flights were results of years of experimentation.

 Children could research the flights more and write a newspaper story with the facts. They could read Russell Freedman's *The Wright Brothers: How They Invented the Airplane.*

Birthdays

William Floyd (born Brookhaven, Long Island, New York, 1734; died Westernville, New York, August 4, 1821) signed the Declaration of Independence. A farmer, he was also a congressman after the Revolutionary War.

Deborah Sampson (born Plympton, Massachusetts, 1760; died Sharon, Massachusetts, April 29, 1827) fought during the Revolutionary War. Because women were not accepted into the army during the Revolutionary War, she disguised herself as a man. For over a year, she was a capable fighter. She was wounded and chose to dress the wound herself because she was afraid she would be discovered. She became very ill and had to seek medical attention. Her secret was discovered, and she was discharged from the army. She received a military pension for a number of years.

 Children might want to read Ann McGovern's *The Secret Soldier: The Story of Deborah Sampson,* published in 1987. Now women are part of the military. Children could interview a woman in the military. How is it different from the past?

John Greenleaf Whittier (born Haverhill, Massachusetts, 1807; died Hampton Fall, New Hampshire, September 7, 1892) was a poet. A Quaker, he was active in the antislavery movement. One of his most famous poems is "Ichabod," published in 1850. The poem criticizes the Compromise of 1850 and Daniel Webster.

Becember

 The Nutcracker, **created by Tchaikovksy, was performed for the first time in St. Petersburg, Russia, in 1892.**

New Jersey became the third state by ratifying the Constitution in 1787. It was named after an island in the English Channel. The state's nickname is the Garden State, and Trenton is the capital. During the American Revolution, at least 100 battles were fought in New Jersey. It is one of the most densely populated states. While it contains large cities, it also boasts about its shores. The honeybee is the state insect. Contact: (800) JERSEY7. Visit an Internet site at: http://www.50states.com/newjerse.htm.

 Children could locate on a map the sites of the Revolutionary War battles. They could find out why so many battles happened in New Jersey.

The Thirteenth Amendment to the Constitution was adopted in 1865, outlawing slavery.

Capitol Reef National Park was established in 1971. The park follows a 100-mile wrinkle in the Earth's crust. Visitors can view fossils, petrified trees, and Indian ruins. Contact: Capitol Reef National Park, Torrey, Utah 84775. Visit a Web site at: http://www.nps.gov/care.

Soyuz 13 **was launched in 1973.** Two Soviet cosmonauts orbited the Earth for eight days. They landed on Earth December 26.

Birthdays

Christina Aguilera (born Staten Island, New York, 1980) is a singer.

Ty(rus Raymond) Cobb (born Narrows, Georgia, 1886; died Atlanta, Georgia, July 17, 1961) was a famous baseball player. He played in more than 3,000 baseball games and had a batting average of .367.

Joseph Grimaldi (London, England, 1778; died London, England, May 31, 1837) was known as Joey the Clown. His antics added much to theater humor.

 Children could become clowns today and wear clown makeup. They could organize into small groups and create clown skits.

Paul Klee (born near Bern, Switzerland, 1879; died Muralto, Switzerland, June 29, 1940) was an artist. His paintings exude a dreamlike, fantasy quality. Visit a Web site at: http://www.artcyclopedia.com/artists/klee_paul.html.

Brad Pitt (born Shawnee, Oklahoma, 1964) is an actor.

Steven Spielberg (born Cincinnati, Ohio, 1947) is a film producer and director. Among his credits are *Jurassic Park* and *Close Encounters of the Third Kind.*

 Spielberg's movies are very popular. Students could investigate the revenues from the movies and show the results on a bar graph.

December

Valley Forge was the site of Washington's encampment during the winter of 1777 and 1778. The army of 10,000 soldiers had to make their own huts. Food and clothing were scarce. About one-fourth of the troops died, and a smallpox epidemic made matters worse. The British, on the other hand, had quite nice conditions in Philadelphia. The arrival of Baron von Steuben and his drilling techniques strengthened the army, and they experienced battle success by June.

 Read portions of *The Riddle of Penncroft Farm,* by Dorothea Jensen. It portrays the horrors of the Revolutionary War and the conditions of Valley Forge through the eyes of two adolescents.

Corrugated paper was patented in 1871 by Albert L. Jones of New York.

Birthdays

Eve Bunting (born Maghera, Northern Ireland, 1928) is a children's author. She has written more than 100 books, including *Fly Away Home.*

Richard E. Leakey (born Nairobi, Kenya, 1944) is an anthropologist.

 Children could find out what an anthropologist does. Does the career appeal to anyone in the group?

Kevin Edward McHale (born Hibbing, Minnesota, 1957) is a former basketball player.

Sir William Edward Parry (born Bath, England, 1790; died Ems, Germany, July 8, 1855) was an explorer. He led expeditions to the Arctic in search of the Northwest Passage.

 Children could explore the concept of the Northwest Passage. Why was it so important to the United Kingdom?

December

 Virginia Company left England in 1606 to establish the first colony, Jamestown, in America. Three ships, the *Godspeed,* the *Discovery,* and the *Susan Constant* carried approximately 120 people to their new land. The ships landed May 14, 1607.

Sacagawea died in 1812 at Fort Manuel on the Missouri River. Her exact birth date is unknown; most experts agree on the year 1787. Sacajawea was an interpreter for the Lewis and Clark Expedition. She was a Shoshone Indian who had been captured by enemies. She was sold as a slave to a French-Canadian trapper. She and the trapper joined the expedition.

 Many experts believe the expedition would have failed if she had not gone along. Students could investigate and list all that she accomplished.

Louisiana Purchase was finalized in 1803. The United States bought more than a million square miles of land from France for about twenty dollars a square mile.

 Students could find out why France sold the land to the United States. What is that land worth now?

Montgomery, Alabama, bus boycott ended in 1956. A Supreme Court decision forced the bus company to end segregation. The boycott had begun over a year before.

Marie Lago in 1986 became the first girl to join a boys' wrestling team.

Macao, a small region on the coast of China, which had been a Portuguese colony since 1557, reverted back to Chinese control in 1999.

Birthdays

Richard Atwater (born Chicago, Illinois, 1892; died August 21, 1938) was a children's author. He and his wife are famous for writing *Mr. Popper's Penguins.*

 Children could read *Mr. Popper's Penguins.* They could share it with younger children.

Lulu Delacre (born Puerto Rico, 1957) writes and illustrates books for children. She published *Arroz Con Leche: Popular Songs and Rhymes from Latin America* in 1989.

Harvey Samuel Firestone (born Columbiana, Ohio, 1868; died Miami Beach, Florida, February 7, 1938) created Firestone Tire & Rubber Company. At first he produced solid rubber tires. Then he experimented and developed air-filled tires. He, Thomas Edison, and Henry Ford sponsored joint projects regarding synthetic rubber.

December

 First day of winter occurs either on December 21 or on December 22. It marks the winter solstice in the Northern Hemisphere. This day has the least amount of daylight for the whole year.

Children might want to read *What Do Animals Do in Winter?* by Melvin and Gilda Berger.

Pilgrims reached Plymouth Rock in 1620.

 The Pilgrims did not intend to land in what is now Massachusetts. Why were they off course? Why did they land in December?

Phileas Fogg won his wager in 1872. The main character of Jules Verne's *Around the World in Eighty Days* returned to the Reform Club in London under the time limit. He acquired the bet of 20,000 pounds.

 Children could find out how much 20,000 pounds was in dollars in 1872.

Apollo 8 **was launched in 1968.** Colonel Frank Borman, Major William Anders, and Captain James Lovell orbited around the moon on December 24 and were on Earth December 27. One of their main goals was to view the dark side of the moon.

 Show the children why we never see the dark side of the moon.

Birthdays

Benjamin Disraeli (born London, England, 1804; died London, England, April 19, 1881) was an English politician and writer. He was elected to the House of Commons in 1837. He was the country's prime minister in 1868 and from 1874 to 1880.

Joseph Vissarionovich Stalin (born Gorgi, Georgia, 1879; died Moscow, USSR, March 5, 1953) was a dictator of the Soviet Union.

December

 Capricorn the Goat is the astrological sign for December 22 through January 19.

A coelacanth, a species of fish scientists thought had been extinct for 65 million years, was found off the shores of Africa in 1938.

Lincoln Tunnel opened in 1937.

Colo was the first gorilla born in captivity in 1956 at the Columbus, Ohio, zoo. He weighed a little more than three pounds.

 Children could make a timeline of a gorilla's growth. They could compare it to the growth of a human.

"Ding Dong School" debuted on television in 1952. It was one of the first shows dedicated to children.

Birthdays

William Ellery (born Newport, Rhode Island, 1727; died Newport, Rhode Island, February 15, 1820) signed the Declaration of Independence. He was a lawyer and a customs collector.

Steve Garvey (born Tampa, Florida, 1948) is a former baseball player.

Claudia Alta Taylor "Lady Bird" Johnson (born Karnack, Texas, 1912) is the widow of Lyndon Baines Johnson, thirty-sixth president of the United States. She helped establish the Head Start program for preschool children, and she advocated for the environment. Visit a Web site at: http://www.whitehouse.gov/history/firstladies/cj36.html.

 Mrs. Johnson wanted to eliminate many of the billboards along the highways. She felt the billboards detracted from nature's beauty. Children could decide whether the billboards are unsightly or whether they help consumers make decisions.

James Edward Oglethorpe (born London, England, 1696; died Cranham Hall, Essex, England, June 30, 1785) was one of the leading organizers of the Georgia colony.

Jerry Pinkney (born Philadelphia, Pennsylvania, 1939) is a children's illustrator. He illustrated, among other works, *The Talking Eggs* (Caldecott Honor Book), 1988. Visit a Web site at: http://www.friend.ly.net/scoop/biographies/pinkneyjerry.

 Children could have a Jerry Pinkney morning and read several of his works.

Giacomo Puccini (born Lucca, Italy, 1858; died Brussels, Belgium, November 29, 1924) was an opera composer. Two of his most famous operas are *Madame Butterfly,* completed in 1904, and *Tosca,* written in 1900.

Diane Sawyer (born Glasgow, Kentucky, 1946) is a television journalist.

December

 Maryland in 1788 donated ten square miles of land to the United States. This land became part of the District of Columbia.

Dick Rutan and Jeana Yeager made the first flight around the world without refueling. For 216 hours the *Voyager* flew almost 25,000 miles.

Transistor was invented in 1947 by John Bardeen, William Shockley, and Walter Brattain. They received the 1956 Nobel Prize in physics for their creation.

 Today's children have grown up with transistors. They could find out how transistors work and how the invention has changed technology and communication.

Jacquard loom was patented in 1801 by Joseph Marie Jacquard. This loom could easily weave very complex patterns.

 Jacquard used a series of punched cards to tell the loom what to do. This idea was adapted to instructions for early computers. Children could find some punched computer cards to see how instructions were delivered.

Birthdays

Avi (Wortis) (born New York, New York, 1937) is a children's author.

Jean-Francois Champollion (born Figeac, France, 1790; died Paris, France, March 4, 1832) solved the mystery of Egyptian hieroglyphics.

 Children could write coded messages to each other.

Keiki Kasza (born on a small island in the Sea of Japan, 1951) is a writer and illustrator. One of her books is *A Mother for Choco.*

December

24 **Christmas Eve** is celebrated by Christians.

War of 1812 ended in 1814 when a peace treaty was signed in Ghent, Belgium.

Libya broke away from Italy and gained its independence in 1951. Located on the Mediterranean coast of Africa, this country is mostly desert. Tripoli is the capital.

"Silent Night" was created in 1818. Franz Xavier Gruber developed the melody, and Joseph Mohr wrote the lyrics.

Birthdays

Christopher "Kit" Carson (born Madison County, Kentucky, 1809; died Fort Lyon, Colorado, May 23, 1868) was a frontiersman and an Indian agent.

 Children could read biographies of his life and make a trivia game.

James Prescott Joule (born Salford, Lancashire, England, 1818; died Cheshire, England, October 11, 1889) was a scientist. He formulated Joule's Law in 1840. An electrical conductor produces heat. The unit of energy is called a joule.

 Set up an experiment with a toaster to show how an electrical conductor carries heat. The children could enjoy the toast after the experiment.

Benjamin Rush (born Byberry, Pennsylvania, 1745; died Philadelphia, Pennsylvania, April 19, 1813) was an early American hero. He signed the Declaration of Independence. A physician, he was also called the father of psychiatry. He was the first doctor to label alcoholism as a disease.

 Rush was involved with all sorts of activities, ranging from the mint to abolition. Children could research his life and then compare him to Benjamin Franklin.

December

25 **Christmas** is celebrated by Christians worldwide.

General Washington and his army secretly crossed the Delaware River in 1776 and surprised the British troops in Trenton. The American victory was a milestone in the Revolutionary War.

 The trip across the river was filled with hazards. Children could investigate more about the battle.

Birthdays

Michael P. Anderson (born Plattsburg, New York, 1959; died in *Columbia* disaster, February 1, 2003) was an astronaut.

Clara Barton (born Oxford, Massachusetts, 1821; died Glen Echo, Maryland, April 12, 1912) was the founder of the American Red Cross. During the Civil War, she began helping the wounded. She also started a system to find missing soldiers. After the war, she traveled to

Europe. She observed the International Red Cross in action. She returned to the United States and in 1881 founded what was later known as the American Red Cross. She worked as its president until 1904.

Cab Calloway (born Rochester, New York, 1907; died Hosckessin, Delaware, November 18, 1994) was a jazz singer and bandleader. One of his most famous songs is "Minnie the Moocher."

Isaac Newton (born Woolsthorpe, Lincolnshire, England, 1642; died London, England, March 20, 1727) was a mathematician, a scientist, and a writer. He is remembered for three major contributions. He developed calculus, a branch of mathematics. He discovered relationships of light and color. He delineated theories of motion and gravity. All three of the accomplishments were made in an eighteen-month period.

 Children could eat Fig Newtons and carry out experiments with prisms.

Robert Ripley (born Santa Rosa, California, 1893; died 1949) was the creator of the *Believe It or Not* cartoons, books, and museums. The first *Believe It or Not* cartoon appeared in New York City's *Globe* December 19, 1918. Experts believe the peak readership for his work was about eighty million people.

 The class could create their own Believe It or Nots.

December

 Kwanzaa is celebrated in the United States. Lasting for seven days, the African American tradition began in 1966. Each day has a special theme. *Umoja* promotes unity. *Kujichagulia* stands for self-determination. *Ujima* provides for collective work and responsibility. *Ujamaa* works toward cooperative economics. *Nia* gives purpose. *Kuumba* develops creativity, and *Imani* means faith. Maulana Karenga started it.

 The class could celebrate Kwanzaa. The children could read *The Kwanzaa Contest* by Miriam Moore and Penny Taylor.

Bahamas celebrate Junkanoo. People in colorful costumes parade through towns to the sounds of homemade instruments.

Boxing Day is celebrated in Great Britain and Canada. Christmas boxes are given to people such as newspaper deliverers and postal workers.

 Wrap something small in a box. Children must list the attributes of the box contents without opening it. They can use all their senses. Then share what is in the box.

Coffee percolator was patented in 1865.

Austria celebrates St. Stephen's Day.

Shenandoah National Park was created in 1926. The park encompasses parts of the beautiful Blue Ridge Mountains in Virginia. Contact: Shenandoah National Park, Route 4, Box 348, Luray, Virginia 22835. Visit a Web site at: http://www.nps.gov/shen.

Birthdays

Charles Babbage (born Surrey County, England, 1792; died London, England, October 18, 1871) was a mathematician. He tried to develop two machines, the difference engine and the analytical engine. However, the time's technology would not permit either machine to be built. Both these machines were precursors to early computers.

 Children could take apart an old calculator to see how small the parts are today. They could compare the parts to an illustration of Babbage's work.

Laurent Clerc (born LaBalme, France, 1785; died July 18, 1869) worked with Thomas Hopkins Gallaudet to create the first school for the deaf. Clerc was probably the first deaf person to teach in the United States.

Thomas Nelson (born Yorktown, Virginia, 1738; died Hanover County, Virginia, January 4, 1789) signed the Declaration of Independence. He represented Virginia.

Mao Tse-Tung (born Hunan Province, China, 1893; died Beijing, China, September 9, 1976) was the Communist leader who ruled the People's Republic of China.

December

27 **World Bank was organized in 1945.**

"Howdy Doody" appeared on television for the first time in 1947. The extremely popular children's show featured a combination of people and puppets. Cartoons were also shown.

 Students could create a puppet show relating to the upcoming New Year's Eve.

Birthdays

Johannes Kepler (born Wurttemburg, Germany, 1871; died Regensburg, Germany, November 15, 1630) was the father of modern astronomy. He developed three laws that explain the motion of planets around the sun. Isaac Newton based his theories regarding motion and gravity on Kepler's work.

 Students could create models of Kepler's three laws of planetary motion.

Louis Pasteur (born Dole, Jura, France, 1822; died Villeneuve l'Etang, France, September 28, 1895) was a bacteriologist. He discovered a cure for rabies. The pasteurization process was named in honor of him.

 Children could discover how and why milk is pasteurized. Then they could make chocolate milk.

December

28 **Benjamin Franklin published** *Poor Richard's Almanack* **for the first time in 1732.** He wrote under the pseudonym Richard Saunders and published the almanac yearly through 1758. Here he penned some of his most famous lines, including, "A penny saved is a penny earned."

 Children could illustrate some of his famous sayings from the almanac.

Messina, Sicily, was hit by an earthquake in 1908. Almost 80,000 people died. The majority of the town was demolished.

Iowa became the twenty-ninth state of the United States in 1846. It was named after the Iowa Indian tribe. The area was originally part of the Louisiana Purchase. In 1838 it, along with parts of Minnesota, North Dakota, and South Dakota, was part of the Iowa Territory. Des Moines is the state capital, and its nickname is the Hawkeye State. It is still a leading producer of corn, cattle, and hogs. Contact: (800) 345-IOWA. Visit an Internet site at: http://www.50states.com/iowa.htm.

 Iowa has only four letters in its name. It and two other states have the shortest names. Students could arrange the states' names according to how many letters are in each name. What state has the longest name?

Chewing gum was patented in 1869 by F. W. Semple of Mount Vernon, Ohio.

 Children could see how gum is made. Then they could chew gum for part of the day.

Birthdays

Carol Ryrie Brink (born Moscow, Idaho, 1895; died August 15, 1981) was an author of more than thirty books. One of her books is *Caddie Woodlawn*. It received the 1936 Newbery Medal. Visit a Web site at: http://www.lib.usm.edu/%7edegrum/html/research/findaids/brink.htm.

Denzel Washington (born Mount Vernon, New York, 1954) is an actor.

Woodrow Wilson (born Staunton, Virginia, 1856; died Washington, DC, February 3, 1924) was the twenty-eighth president (1913–1921) of the United States. He was the first president from the South since the Civil War. Despite having learning disabilities, he earned a doctorate in political science. He became New Jersey's governor in 1910. During World War I, he tried to keep the United States neutral. Eventually America joined the war. After the war, he was instrumental in creating the League of Nations. However, Congress voted against joining the League. He won the 1919 Nobel Peace Prize. In that same year Wilson suffered a stroke, and his wife hid his condition from the country. Visit a Web site at: http://www.whitehouse.gov/history/presidents/ww28.html.

December

29 **Texas became the twenty-eighth state of the United States in 1845.** Its name derives from the Caddo *tavshas,* meaning "friends." Its nickname is the Lone Star State, and Austin is the capital. While it is the second largest state, more than three-fourths of the population live in cities. Houston, Dallas, and San Antonio are listed in America's ten largest cities. At one time Texas belonged to Spain. Then Mexico claimed ownership. For a while it was an independent country, and then it joined the United States. Oil is a major natural resource, and the state produces cotton and cattle. The state dish is chili. Contact: (800) 888-8TEX. Visit an Internet site at: http://www.50states.com/texas.htm.

 Children could make and eat chili.

Term "black hole" was created by Professor John Wheeler in 1967.

Birthdays

Molly Garrett Bang (born Princeton, New Jersey, 1943) is a picture book author and illustrator. She wrote, among other works, *Ten, Nine, Eight* (Caldecott Honor Book), 1984. Visit a Web site at: http://www.mollybang.com.

Children could read and enjoy some of her books.

Pablo Carlos Salvador Defillio de Casals (born Venrell, Spain, 1876; died Rio Pedros, Puerto Rico, October 22, 1973) was a famous cellist.

Charles Goodyear (born New Haven, Connecticut, 1800; died New York, New York, July 1, 1860) was an inventor. He was trying to develop a form of crude rubber. However, it cracked when it got cold. It stuck to other materials when it got hot. One day Goodyear accidentally dropped some rubber and sulfur on a hot stove. This vulcanization process made the rubber useful.

Andrew Johnson (born Raleigh, North Carolina, 1808; died Carter's Station, Tennessee, July 31, 1875) was the seventeenth president (1865–1869) of the United States. Johnson's father died when Andrew was three years old. Although he never went to school, he obviously had a great deal of common sense. He rose from being Greenville, Tennessee's mayor to state legislator. He was the governor of Tennessee before he was elected to the U.S. Senate. Since he remained loyal to the Union, he was almost hanged in Tennessee. He was Lincoln's vice president and became president when Lincoln was assassinated. He was impeached, but he was found not guilty by one vote. Visit a Web site at: http://www.whitehouse.gov/history/presidents/aj17.html.

 Children could make a flow chart of the steps of impeachment. Why was he impeached?

December

 30

USS *Monitor* sank in a storm off Cape Hatteras, North Carolina, in 1862. Sixteen crew members died.

 Students could find out why so many ships have sunk off Cape Hatteras.

Philippines remembers Rizal Day. Jose Rizal was executed by the Spanish in 1896.

Gadsden Purchase treaty was signed in 1953. The United States purchased from Mexico a strip of land south of the Gila River. James Gadsden, U.S. minister to Mexico, negotiated the deal with Antonio Lopez de Santa Anna, Mexico's leader. The United States paid $10 million for the area. The country gained almost 30,000 square miles of territory.

Birthdays

Simon Guggenheim (born Philadelphia, Pennsylvania, 1867; died November 2, 1941) was a businessman and a philanthropist.

Rudyard Kipling (born Bombay, India, 1865; died London, England, January 18, 1936) was a writer. He wrote more than 300 stories, and he is best known for his works about the India he loved. Among his most famous works are *The Jungle Book* and *Just So Stories*. He won the 1907 Nobel Prize for literature.

 Children could change one of his stories into a play, and then they could perform it.

Sandy Koufax (born Brooklyn, New York, 1935) is a former baseball pitcher and sports announcer.

Mercer Mayer (born Little Rock, Arkansas, 1943) is a children's author. He is known for his Little Critter character. Visit a Web site at: http://www.littlecritter.com.

Students could read some of his books.

Eldrick "Tiger" Woods (born Cypress, California, 1975) is a golfer.

December

 New Year's Eve is celebrated by many cultures around the world.

 Children could set up an early New Year's Eve celebration.

Leap Second may be added or subtracted, according to the Bureau International de l'Heure, located in Paris, France.

 Children could find out why and when the scientists choose to add a second.

Ghana celebrates its Revolution Day.

Hogmanay is celebrated in Scotland and Northern England.

Panama gained possession of the Panama Canal from the United States in 1999.

Birthdays

John Denver (born Henry John Deutschendorf in Roswell, New Mexico, 1943; died October 12, 1997) was a singer and composer.

George Catlett Marshall (born Uniontown, Pennsylvania, 1880; died Washington, DC, October 16, 1959) was chairman of the Joint Chiefs of Staff during World War II. Following the war, he was the country's secretary of state. He was the designer of the Marshall Plan, a way to help get war-torn Europe back on its feet.

Henri-Emile-Benoit Matisse (born Le Cateau, Picardy, France, 1869; died Nice, France, November 3, 1954) was an artist. He was a part of the *fauve* movement. He did not attempt to paint in a realistic style. He used bright colors and bold strokes. Visit a Web site at: http://www.artcyclopedia.com/artists/matisse_henri.html.

 Children could see some of his work, and they could try to imitate his style.

Allen, Judy, Earldene McNeill, and Velma Schmidt. *Cultural Awareness for Children.* New York: Addison-Wesley Publishing Company, 1992.

Chase's Calendar of Events: 2003. Chicago: Contemporary Publishing Company, 2003.

Douglas, George William. *The American Book of Days.* New York: H. W. Wilson Company, 1948.

Ferris, Robert G., ed. *Signers of the Declaration.* Washington, DC: U.S. Department of the Interior, National Park Service, 1973.

Haglund, Elaine J., and Marcia L. Harris. *On This Day: A Collection of Everyday Learning Events and Activities for the Media Center, Library and Classroom.* Littleton, CO: Libraries Unlimited, 1983.

Jacobson, Doranne. *Presidents and First Ladies of the United States.* New York: Smithmark Publishers, 1995.

Kovacs, Deborah, and James Preller. *Meet the Authors and Illustrators.* New York: Scholastic Professional Books, 1991.

Kovacs, Deborah, and James Preller. *Meet the Authors and Illustrators: Volume Two.* New York: Scholastic Professional Books, 1993.

Krythe, Maymie R. *All about the Months.* New York: Harper & Row, 1966.

Marks, Diana F. *Glues, Brews, and Goos: Recipes and Formulas for Almost Any Classroom Project.* Englewood, CO: Teacher Ideas Press, 1996.

McElmeel, Sharron L. *Adventures with Social Studies (Through Literature).* Englewood, CO: Teacher Ideas Press, 1991.

McGeveran, William A., ed. *The World Almanac and Book of Facts: 2003.* New York: World Almanac Books, 2003.

Miller, Anistatia R., and Jared M. Brown. *More On This Day in History.* Paramus, NJ: Prentice-Hall, 2002.

Milord, Susan. *Hands around the World: 365 Creative Ways to Build Cultural Awareness and Global Respect.* Charlotte, VT: Williamson Publishing, 1992.

Peoples Multicultural Almanac, The. Maywood, NJ: Peoples Publishing Group, 1994.

Pioch, Nicholas. *WebMuseum, Paris.* Available: http://www.oir.ucf.edu/wm/about/pioch.html (accessed December 28, 2002).

Scope Systems. 2002. *Historic Events and Birth-Dates.* Available: http://www.scopesys.com/today (accessed December 28, 2002).

Spinrad, Leonard, and Thelma Spinrad. *On This Day in History.* Paramus, NJ: Prentice-Hall, 1999.

Terzian, Alexandra M. *The Kids' Multicultural Art Book.* Charlotte, VT: Williamson Publishing, 1993.

Visit Your National Parks. 2003. Available: http://www.nps.gov/parks.html (accessed May 17, 2003).

Walker, H. Thomas, and Paula K. Montgomery. *Activities Almanac: Daily Ideas for Library Media Lessons.* Santa Barbara, CA: ABC-CLIO, 1990.

Webb, Lois Sinaiko. *Holidays of the World Cookbook for Students.* Phoenix, AZ: Oryx Press, 1995.

Webber, Ray. 2002. *50 States and Capitals.* Available: http://www.50states.com (accessed December 28, 2002).

Webster's Dictionary of American Women. New York: Smithmark Publishers, 1996.

Welcome to the White House. 2002. Available: http://www.whitehouse.gov (accessed December 28, 2002).

Whiteley, Sandy. *The Teacher's Calendar, 2002–2003: The Day-by-Day Directory to Holidays, Historic Events, Birthdays and Special Days, Weeks and Months.* Chicago, IL: Contemporary Publishing Company, 2002.

World Book Encyclopedia. 22 vols. Chicago: World Book, 2002.

Aaron, Henry Louis "Hank," Feb. 5, Apr. 8
Abdul-Jabbar, Kareem, Apr. 5, Apr. 16
Abernathy, Ralph, Mar. 11
Academy Awards were awarded for the first time in
    1929, May 16
accordion was patented in 1854, Jan. 13
Ada, Alma Flor, Jan. 3
Adams, Abigail Smith, Nov. 11
Adams, Ansel, Feb. 20
Adams, John, July 4, Oct. 30
Adams, John Couch, June 5
Adams, John Quincy, Feb. 12, June 16, July 11
Adams, Louisa Catherine Johnson, Feb. 12
Adams, Samuel, Sept. 27
Addams, Jane, Sept. 6
adding machine was patented in 1888, Aug. 21
adhesive postage stamps were used for the first time in
    1842, Feb. 15
Adler, David, Apr. 10
Adler Planetarium opened in Chicago in 1930, May 10
Adventures of Pinocchio was created in 1881, July 7
aerial crop dusting was achieved for the first time in
    1921, Aug. 3
Affleck, Ben, Aug. 15
Afghanistan remembers Saur Revolution, Apr. 27
African Freedom Day, May 25
Agnew, Spiro, resigned in 1973, Oct. 10
Aguilera, Christina, Dec. 18
Aiken, Howard Hathaway, Mar. 8
Aikman, Troy, Nov. 21
Ailey, Alvin, Jan. 5
air conditioner was patented in 1914, Apr. 28
Air Force was created as an independent service in 1947,
    Sept. 18
airplane landed for the first time on a ship in 1911, Jan. 18
Akers, Michelle, Feb. 1
Alabama became the twenty-second state in 1819, Dec. 14
Alamo fell to Mexico in 1836, Mar. 6
Alaska, Jan. 3, Mar. 27, Mar. 30, June 16, July 21, Aug.
    16, Aug. 31, Oct. 18
Alaskan Oil Pipeline, Mar. 9, July 28
Albania celebrates Liberation Day, Nov. 28
Alcohol Awareness Month, April
Alcoholics Anonymous was created in 1935, June 10
Alcott, Louisa May, Nov. 29
Aldrin, Edwin Eugene "Buzz," Jan. 20, July 20
Alexander, Lloyd, Jan. 30
Alexander the Great, Sept. 20
Alger, Horatio, Jr., Jan. 13
Algeria, July 5, Nov. 1
Ali, Muhammad, Jan. 17
Alice in Wonderland was published in 1865, Nov. 26
Allen, Bryan, June 12, Aug. 23
Allen, Ethan, Jan. 10
Allen, Tim, June 13

Alvin C. York Day, Oct. 8
Amateur Radio Week, June
American Bar Association was created in 1878, Aug. 21
American Baseball League and National Baseball League
    settled their differences in 1903, Jan. 9
American Education Week, November
American Girl dolls appeared for the first time in 1986,
    Sept. 15
American Heart Month, February
American Horseshoe Pitchers Association was formed in
    1914, Mar. 5
American Humane Association was created in 1877,
    Oct. 9
American League of Baseball was formed in 1900, Jan. 29
American Library Association was founded in 1876,
    Oct. 6
American Magazine was published for the first time in
    1741, Feb. 13
American Medical Association was created in 1847,
    May 7
American National Red Cross was created in 1881,
    May 21
American Red Cross Month, March
American Revolutionary War began in 1775, Apr. 19
American Revolution ended informally in 1783, Jan. 20
American Samoa became an American territory in 1900,
    Apr. 17
American School for the Deaf was founded, Apr. 15
American Society for the Prevention of Cruelty to
    Animals was created in 1866, Apr. 11
Americans received five Nobel Prizes in 1976, Oct. 21
America's first political cartoon was printed in 1754,
    May 9
"America the Beautiful" was published first in poem
    form in 1895, July 4
Amin, Idi, Apr. 11
Ampere, Andre, Jan. 22
Amundsen, Roald, July 16, Dec. 14
Andersen, Hans Christian, Apr. 2
Anderson, Marian, Feb. 27
Anderson, Michael P., Feb. 1, Dec. 25
Andrea Doria sank in 1956, July 25
Andretti, Mario, Feb. 28
Andrews, Julie, Oct. 1
anesthesia was used for the first time in surgery in 1842,
    Mar. 30
Angelou, Maya, Apr. 4
Angola celebrates its Independence Day, Nov. 11
Aniston, Jennifer, Feb. 11
Annan, Kofi, Apr. 8
Annapolis Convention was held in 1786, Sept. 11
Anno, Mitsumasa, Mar. 20
Antarctica Treaty was signed in 1959, Dec. 1
Antarctica was discovered by Captain Nathaniel Palmer
    in 1820, Nov. 18

Anthony, Susan B., Feb. 15, June 6

Antigua and Barbuda celebrate their Independence Day, Nov. 1

antirabies inoculation was administered safely for the first time in 1885, July 6

Anzac Day, Apr. 25

Apgar, Virginia, June 7

Apollo 1 fire in 1967, Jan. 27

Apollo 8 was launched in 1968, Dec. 21

Apollo 10 was launched in 1969, May 18

Apollo 11 was launched in 1969, July 16

Apollo 12 was launched in 1969, Nov. 14

Apollo 13 was launched in 1970, Apr. 11

Apollo 14, Feb. 6

Apollo 15 was launched in 1971, July 26

Apollo 16 was launched in 1972, Apr. 16

Apollo 17 was launched in 1972, Dec. 7

Apollo-Soyuz mission was successful in 1975, July 15

Appert, Nicolas, Oct. 23

Apple II personal computer was introduced into stores in 1977, June 4

apple parer was patented in 1803, Feb. 14

April Fool's Day, Apr. 1

Aquarius astrological sign, Jan. 20–Feb. 18

Arafat, Yasser, Feb. 9, Aug. 4

Archduke Ferdinand of Austria and his wife were assassinated in Bosnia in 1914, June 28

Arches National Park was created in 1971, Nov. 12

Archie comic books premiered in 1942, Feb. 11

Arco, Idaho, became the first city to be powered by nuclear energy in 1955, July 17

Argentina, May 25, July 9

Aries astrological sign, Mar. 21–Apr. 19

Arizona became the forty-eighth state in 1912, Feb. 14

Arkansas, Jan. 12, June 15

Armed Forces Day, May

Armenia, Apr. 24, Sept. 21

Armstrong, Louis, July 4, Aug. 4

Armstrong, Neil Alden, July 20, Aug. 5

Armstrong, William H., Sept. 14

Army Air Force was created in 1907, Aug. 1

Arnold, Benedict, Jan. 14

Arnosky, Jim, Sept. 1

Arthur, Chester Alan, Oct. 5

Arthur, Ellen Lewis Herndon, Aug. 30

Articles of Confederation were ratified in 1781, Mar. 1

Articles of Peace between Great Britain and the United States were signed in Paris in 1782, Nov. 30

artificial leg was patented in 1846, Nov. 4

Aruba celebrates Flag Day, Mar. 18

Aruego, Jose, Aug. 9

Asch, Frank, Aug. 6

Asian Pacific Heritage Month, May

Asimov, Isaac, Jan. 2

Astor, John Jacob, July 17

Astor, Lady, first woman to be elected to the British Parliament, Nov. 28

astronomers observed four new moons of Saturn in 2000, Oct. 26

Atchison, David R., Aug. 11

Atlantis space shuttle was launched in 1989, May 4

atomic bomb was dropped on Hiroshima in 1945, Aug. 6

atomic bomb was dropped on Nagasaki in 1945, Aug. 9

atomic test bomb was activated in 1945, July 16

Attucks, Crispus, Mar. 5

Atwater, Richard, Dec. 20

Audubon, John James, Apr. 26

Auerbach, Arnold "Red," Sept. 20

Augustus Caesar, Sept. 23

aurora borealis was documented in 1719, Dec. 11

Austen, Jane, Dec. 16

Austin, Stephen Fuller, Nov. 3

Australia, Jan. 26, Mar. 19

Austria, Oct. 26, Dec. 26

automobile driver's licenses became legal requirements in 1937, Jan. 21

automobile traveled for the first time in excess of sixty miles per hour in 1901, Nov. 16

automobile was driven faster than 100 miles per hour in 1905, Jan. 31

Autry, Gene, Sept. 29

Avi, Dec. 23

Aviation History Month, November

Avogadro, Amadeo, June 9

Azarian, Mary, Dec. 8

Azerbaijan, May 28, Oct. 18

Aztec stone calendar was discovered in 1790, Dec. 17

Babbage, Charles, Dec. 26

Babbitt, Natalie, July 28

Bach, Johann Sebastian, Mar. 21

Backus, Jim, Feb. 25

Backwards Day, Jan. 26

Bacon, Kevin, July 8

Bacon, Nathaniel, Jan. 2, Sept. 19

Baden-Powell, Robert, Feb. 22

Baekland, Leo Hendrik, Nov. 14

Bagley, Sarah G., first woman telegraph operator, Feb. 21

Bagnold, Enid, Oct. 27

Bahamas, July 10, Aug. 4, Dec. 26

Bahrain celebrates Independence Day, Dec. 16

Bailey, Pearl, Mar. 29

Baird, John Logie, Aug. 13

Balboa, Vasco Nunez de, claimed the Pacific Ocean and "all shores washed by it" for Spain in 1513, Sept. 25

Baldwin, Caroline Willard, first woman to obtain a doctor of science degree in 1895, June 20

Baldwin, James Arthur, Aug. 2

Balfour Declaration was signed in 1917, Nov. 2

Ball, Lucille, Aug. 6

Ballard, Robert, June 30

ball bearing roller skates were patented in 1884, Dec. 9

ballet performed for the first time in America in 1827, Feb. 7

Baltimore, Lord, Mar. 25

Baltimore, Maryland, first city to have its streetlights lit by hydrogen gas, Feb. 17

Balzac, Honore de, May 20

Bambi premiered in 1942, Aug. 13

bananas were imported into the United States for the first time in 1876, June 5

Bang, Molly Garrett, Dec. 29
Bangladesh celebrates National Day, Mar. 26
Banks, Lynne Reid, July 31
Banneker, Benjamin, Nov. 9
Bannister, Roger, first person to run a mile in less than four minutes in 1954, May 6
Banting, Sir Frederick Grant, Nov. 14
Barbados celebrates its Independence Day, Nov. 30
barbed wire was patented in 1874, Nov. 24
Barber, Walter Lanier "Red," Feb. 17
Barbershop Quartet Day, Apr. 11
Barbie doll premiered in 1959, Feb. 13
Barkley, Charles, Feb. 20
Barnard, Christiaan, Nov. 8, Dec. 3
"Barney and Friends" premiered in 1992, Apr. 6
Barnum, Phineas Taylor, July 5
Barrie, J. M., May 9
Barrymore, Lionel, Apr. 28
Bartholdi, Frederic Auguste, Apr. 2
Bartlett, John, June 14
Bartlett, Josiah, Nov. 21
Barton, Clara, May 21, Dec. 25
Base, Graeme, Apr. 6
baseball catcher's mask was patented in 1878, Feb. 12
baseball games were televised for the first time in 1939, Aug. 26
Baseball Rules Code was adopted in 1845, Sept. 23
baseball's first perfect game was pitched in 1904, May 5
Basie, William "Count," Aug. 21
Bastille Day, July 14
Batman and Robin appeared in newspaper comics in 1944, Feb. 20
"Battle Hymn of the Republic" was published in 1862, Feb. 1
Battle of Antietam occurred in 1862, Sept. 17
Battle of Bunker Hill occurred in 1775, June 17
Battle of Gettysburg started in 1863, July 1
Battle of Hamburger Hill began in Vietnam in 1969, May 11
Battle of Lake Erie took place in 1813, Sept. 10
Battle of Lexington in 1775, Apr. 19
Battle of New Orleans took place in 1815, Jan. 8
Battle of San Jacinto occurred in 1836, Apr. 21
Battle of San Juan Hill commenced in 1893, July 1
Battle of the Alamo started in 1836, Feb. 23
Battle of Tippecanoe took place in 1811, Nov. 7
Battle of Trafalgar occurred in 1805, Oct. 21
Baum, Lyman Frank, May 15
Beadle, George, Oct. 22
Beatles appeared for the first time on the "Ed Sullivan Show" in 1964, Feb. 9
Beaufort Scale Day, May 7
Becket, Samuel, Apr. 13
Beebe, Charles William, July 29
Beethoven, Ludwig van, Dec. 16
Beethoven's Ninth Symphony premiered in Vienna in 1824, May 7
Begay, Shonto, Feb. 7
Begin, Menachem, Aug. 16
Belarus celebrates its Independence Day, July 27
Belgium celebrates National Day, July 21

Belize, Mar. 8, Sept. 10, Sept. 21
Bell, Alexander Graham, Mar. 3, Mar. 10
Bellairs, John, Jan. 17
Bellows, George Wesley, Aug. 12
Belmont Stakes was held for the first time in 1867, June 18
Bemelmans, Ludwig, Apr. 27
Bench, Johnny Lee, Dec. 7
Benet, Stephen Vincent, July 22
Benin celebrates a national day, Aug. 1
Benny, Jack, Feb. 14
Benoit, Joan, won the first Olympic gold medal for the United States in the women's marathon, Aug. 5
Bentley, Edmund Clerihew, July 10
Benton, Thomas Hart, Apr. 15
Berenstain, Jan, July 7
Berenstain, Stan, Sept. 29
Bergen, Candice, May 9
Bering, Vitus, Aug. 20
Berlin, Irving, May 11
Berlin airlift began in 1948, June 24
Berlin Wall, Aug. 13, Nov. 9
Berners-Lee, Tim, June 8
Bernstein, Elmer, Apr. 4
Bernstein, Leonard, Aug. 25
Berra, Yogi, May 12
Bethune, Mary McLeod, July 10
Bezerra de Mendoza, Diego, discovered Lower California in 1533, Nov. 8
Bhutan celebrates a national holiday, Dec. 17
Bianco, Margery Williams, July 22
bifocals were patented by Benjamin Franklin in 1785, May 23
Big Bend National Park was established in 1935, June 12
Bill of Rights, Nov. 20, Dec. 15
Billy the Kid, Nov. 23
Bingo's Birthday Month, December
Bird, Larry, Dec. 7
Birdseye, Clarence, Dec. 9
Bismarck, Otto von, Apr. 1
Black, Shirley Temple, Apr. 23
Black History Month, February
"black hole" term was created in 1967, Dec. 29
Blackmun, Harry, Nov. 12
"Black Thursday" occurred in 1929, Oct. 24
Blackwell, Elizabeth, first woman to receive a medical doctor's degree in the United States, Feb. 3
Blair, Bonnie, Mar. 18
Blake, Eubie, Feb. 7
Blakey, Art, Oct. 11
Blanc, Mel, May 30
Blanchard, Jean-Pierre, Jan. 7, Jan. 9
Bledsoe, Drew, Feb. 14
Bleriot, Louis, July 1, July 25
Bliss, Sir Henry Edward Ernest Victor, Mar. 9
Blitz on London began in 1940, Sept. 7
Blondin, Charles, walked across Niagara Falls on a tightrope in 1859, June 30
blood bank was created in 1937, Mar. 15
Bloomer, Amelia Jenks, May 27
Blos, Joan, Dec. 9

Bluford, Guion S., Jr., Nov. 22
Blume, Judy, Feb. 12
Bly, Nellie, May 5, Nov. 14
Blyleven, Bert, Apr. 6
B'nai B'rith was founded in 1843, Oct. 13
Boggs, Wade, June 15
Bohr, Niels, Oct. 7
Boitano, Brian, Oct. 22
Bol, Manute, Oct. 16
Bolger, Ray, Jan. 10
Bolivar, Simon, July 24
Bolivia, July 16, Aug. 6
Bond, Carrie Jacobs, Aug. 11
Bond, Felicia, July 18
Bond, Michael, Jan. 13
Bonds, Barry, July 24, Oct. 5
book printed in and about Esperanto was published for
    the first time in 1887, July 26
Boole, George, Nov. 2
Boone, Daniel, Mar. 10, Nov. 2
Booth, William, Apr. 10
Borglum, John de la Mothe Gutzon, Mar. 25, Nov. 20
Borglum, Lincoln, Nov. 21
Borman, Frank, Mar. 14, Dec. 21
Boston Bicycle Club became America's first bicycle club
    in 1878, Feb. 11
Boston Female Medical School opened in 1848, Nov. 1
Boston Latin School opened its doors in 1635, Feb. 13
Boston Red Sox won the first World Series in 1903,
    Oct. 13
Boston Tea Party, Dec. 16
Botswana celebrates its Independence Day, Sept. 30
Boulder Dam began operating in 1936, Sept. 7
Bounty crew mutinied in 1789, Apr. 28
Bourke-White, Margaret, June 14
Bowditch, Nathaniel, Mar. 26
Boxing Day, Dec. 26
Boycott, Charles Cunningham, Mar. 12
Boyd, Belle, May 9
Boyle, Robert, Jan. 25
Boys' Club of America was formed in 1906, May 19
Boy Scouts of America was started in 1910, Feb. 8
Boys' Town created in 1917, Dec. 1
"Bozo the Clown" aired for the first time in 1959, Jan. 5
Bradbury, Ray, Aug. 22
Bradford, Andrew, Feb. 13
Bradford, William, Mar. 19
Bradley, Bill, July 28
Bragg, Mabel, Sept. 15
Brahms, Johannes, May 7
Braille, Louis, Jan. 4
Brandeis, Louis Dembitz, Jan. 28, Nov. 13
Brandenberg, Aliki, Sept. 3
Brando, Marlon, Apr. 3
Braque, Georges, May 13
Brasilia was constructed in 1960, Apr. 21
Braun, Wernher von, Mar. 23
Braxton, Carter, Sept. 10
Brazil, Jan. 20, Apr. 21, Apr. 22, Sept. 7
Brennan, William, Apr. 25
Brett, Jan, Dec. 1

Brewster, Margaret A., became the first woman Marine
    Corps general in 1978, May 11
Breyer, Stephen G., Aug. 15
Bridger, Jim, Mar. 17
Brink, Carol Ryrie, Dec. 28
Brinkley, David, July 10
British defeated American troops in the Battle of Camden
    in 1780, Aug. 16
British leased Hong Kong from China in 1898, June 9
British Parliament met for the first time in 1254, Feb. 11
British stormed aboard the USS *Chesapeake* in 1807,
    June 22
Brittain, Bill, Dec. 16
Brodsky, Beverly, Aug. 16
Brokaw, Tom, Feb. 6
Bronson, Charles, Nov. 3
Brontë, Charlotte, Apr. 21
Brontë, Emily, July 30
Brooklyn Bridge opened in 1883, May 24
Brooks, Garth, Feb. 7
Brooks, Gwendolyn Elizabeth, May 5, June 7
Brooks, James David, Oct. 18
Brooks, Mel, June 28
Brown, David M., Feb. 1, Apr. 16
Brown, James, May 3
Brown, John, May 9, Oct. 16, Dec. 2
Brown, Marc, Nov. 25
Brown, Marcia, July 13
Brown, Margaret Wise, May 23
Browning, Elizabeth Barrett, Mar. 6
Browning, Robert, May 7
Brubeck, Dave, Dec. 6
Bruchac, Joseph, Oct. 16
Brunei Darussalam celebrates a national holiday, Feb. 23
Brunhoff, Jean de, Dec. 9
Bryan, Ashley, July 13
Bryan, William Jennings, Mar. 19
Bryant, Kobe, Aug. 23
Bryant, William Cullen, Nov. 3
Buchanan, James, Apr. 23
Buck, Pearl Sydenstricker, June 26
Buddha was born, Apr. 8
Buffalo Bill, Feb. 26, May 1
Bugs Bunny appeared for the first time in a 1940 car-
    toon, July 27
Bulfinch, Thomas, July 15
Bulgaria, Jan. 14, June 2
Bulla, Clyde Robert, Jan. 9
"Bullwinkle Show" appeared for the first time in 1961,
    Sept. 24
Bunche, Ralph Johnson, Aug. 7
Bunsen, Robert Wilhelm, Mar. 31
Bunting, Eve, Dec. 19
Burbank, Luther, Mar. 7
Burnell, Jocelyn, discovered the first pulsar in 1968,
    Feb. 29
Burnett, Carol, Apr. 26
Burnett, Frances Hodgson, Nov. 24
Burns, George, Jan. 20
Burns, Robert, Jan. 25
Burr, Aaron, Feb. 6, May 22, July 11

Burroughs, Edgar Rice, Sept. 1
Burroughs, John, Apr. 3
Burton, Virginia Lee, Aug. 30
Burundi celebrates its Independence Day, July 1
Bush, Barbara Pierce, June 8
Bush, George Herbert Walker, June 12
Bush, George W., July 6, Dec. 12
Bush, Laura Welch, Nov. 4
Button, Dick, won his fifth consecutive world figure
    skating title in 1952, Feb. 29
Butts, Alfred, Apr. 13
Byars, Betsy, Aug. 7
Byrd, Richard Evelyn, Oct. 25, Nov. 28

cable car was patented in 1871, Jan. 17
Cabrillo, Juan Rodriguez, discovered California in 1542,
    Sept. 28
Caesar, Julius, Mar. 15, July 12
Cagney, James, July 17
Cahn, Sammy, June 18
Calabria, Italy, was the site of a massive earthquake in
    1857, Dec. 16
Calamity Jane died in 1903, Aug. 1
Caldecott, Randolph, Mar. 22
Calder, Alexander, July 22
Calhoun, John Caldwell, Mar. 18
California, Jan. 24, Sept. 9, Sept. 28
calliope was patented in 1855, Oct. 9
Calloway, Cab, Dec. 25
Cambodia celebrates its Independence Day, Nov. 9
Cameron, Kirk, Oct. 12
Cameroon celebrates Republic Day, May 20
Campanella, Roy, Nov. 19
Campfire Boys and Girls of America was created in
    1910, Mar. 17
Camus, Albert, Nov. 7
Canada, Apr. 18, Apr. 28, July 1, October
Canada and the United States began a joint project in
    1929 to protect Niagara Falls, Jan. 2
Canada-United States Goodwill Week, April
Cancer astrological sign, June 21–July 22
Cannon, Annie Jump, Dec. 11
Canseco, Jose, July 2
Canyonlands National Park was created in 1964, Sept. 12
Cape Hatteras Lighthouse was moved in 1999, June 17
Cape Verde celebrates its Independence Day, July 5
Capitol Reef National Park was established in 1971,
    Dec. 18
Capricorn astrological sign, Dec. 22–Jan. 19
"Captain Kangaroo" premiered on television in 1955,
    Oct. 3
Captain Kidd was hanged in 1701, May 23
Caraway, Hattie Wyatt, Jan. 12, Feb. 1
Carey, Mariah, Mar. 27
Carle, Eric, June 25
Carnegie, Andrew, Nov. 25
Carnegie Hall had its first performance in 1891, May 5
Carpenter, Scott, was launched into space in 1962, May 24
carpet sweeper was patented in 1876, Sept. 19
Carrey, Jim, Jan. 17
Carroll, Charles, Sept. 19

Carroll, Lewis, Jan. 27
Carson, Christopher "Kit," Dec. 24
Carson, Johnny, Oct. 23
Carson, Rachel Louise, Apr. 13, May 27
Carter, Gary, Apr. 8
Carter, Howard, May 9, Nov. 4
Carter, James Earl "Jimmy," Oct. 1, Oct. 11
Carter, Rosalynn Smith, Aug. 18
Cartoon Appreciation Week, May
Cartwright, Edmund, Apr. 24
Caruso, Enrico, Feb. 25
Carver, George Washington, Jan. 5
Carvey, Dana, Apr. 2
Casals, Pablo Carlos Salvador Defillio de, Dec. 29
Casey at the Bat was printed for the first time in 1888,
    June 3
Cash, Johnny, Feb. 26
cash register was patented in 1879, Nov. 4
Cassatt, Mary, May 22
Cassidy, Butch, Apr. 13
Castro, Fidel, Aug. 13
Catalanotto, Peter, Mar. 21
catcher's mask was first worn in 1877, Apr. 12
Cather, Willa, Dec. 7
Catherine the Great, May 2
Catlin, George, July 26
Catt, Carrie Lane Chapman, Jan. 9
Caxton, William, Mar. 8, Aug. 13
CBS made its first radio broadcast in 1927, Sept. 18
cellophane tape was patented in 1930, May 27
Celsius, Anders, Nov. 27
cement was patented in 1871, Sept. 26
census was taken in the United States for the first time in
    1790, Aug. 2
Central African Republic, Aug. 13
Cernan, Eugene, May 18
Cervantes de Saavedra, Miguel de, Apr. 23, Sept. 29
Cézanne, Paul, Jan. 19
Chad, May 25, Aug. 11
Chaffee, Roger, Jan. 27
Chagall, Marc, July 7
Challenger space shuttle, Jan. 28, Feb. 3, June 18, Oct. 11
Chamberlain, Wilt, Aug. 21
Champlain, Samuel de, July 3
Champollion, Jean-François, Dec. 23
Chan, Jackie, Apr. 7
Chaney, Lon, Apr. 1
Chapin, Harry, Dec. 7
Chaplin, Charles Spencer "Charlie," Apr. 16
Chapman, John "Johnny Appleseed," Mar. 11, Sept. 26
Chardonnet, Comte de, May 1
Charlemagne, Apr. 2
Charles, Ray, Sept. 23
Charleston, South Carolina, experienced a major earth-
    quake in 1886, Aug. 31
Charlie Brown, Oct. 2
Chase, Chevy, Oct. 8
Chase, Salmon Portland, Jan. 13
Chase, Samuel, Apr. 17
Chavez, Cesar Estrada, Mar. 31
Chawla, Kalpana, Feb. 1, July 1

cheese, butter, and meat were rationed in 1943, Mar. 29

Chekhov, Anton Pavlovich, Jan. 29

Cheney, Lynne, Aug. 14

Cheney, Richard, Jan. 30

Chernobyl nuclear reactor disaster occurred in 1986, Apr. 26

Cherokee Phoenix became the first Indian newspaper in 1828, Feb. 21

Cherokees started on the "Trail of Tears" in 1838, June 6

Cherokee Strip Day, Sept. 16

cherry trees were first planted in Washington, D.C. in 1912, Mar. 27

chewing gum was patented in 1869, Dec. 28

Chiang Kai-Shek, Oct. 31

Chicago began constructing the first skyscraper in 1884, May 1

Chicago Cubs traded a player between games in a doubleheader in 1922, May 30

Child, Julia, Aug. 14

Child Health Day, October

Children's Book Week, November

Children's Day, May 5, June

Children's Eye Health and Safety Month, September

Children's Vision and Learning Month, August

Child Safety Month, November

Chile celebrates its Independence Day, Sept. 18

China, May 4, June 1, Oct. 1, Oct. 10

China Clipper left San Francisco and arrived in Manila about sixty hours later in 1935, Nov. 22

Chisholm, Shirley, Nov. 5, Nov. 30

chocolate chips were sold for the first time in 1939, Nov. 16

Chopin, Frederick, Feb. 22

chop suey was invented in 1896, Sept. 1

Christie, Agatha, Sept. 15, Nov. 5

Christmas cards were first produced in 1843, Dec. 8

A Christmas Carol was published in 1843, Dec. 17

Christmas Eve is celebrated, Dec. 24

Christmas is celebrated, Jan. 6, Jan. 7, Dec. 25

Christopher, Matt, Aug. 16

Christy, James, discovered Charon, Pluto's satellite, in 1978, June 22

Chrysler, Walter, Apr. 2

Chung, Connie, Aug. 20

Chunnel opened in 1994, May 6

Church, Ellen, became the first flight attendant in 1930, May 15

Churchill, Sir Winston Leonard Spencer, July 19, Nov. 30

Cicero, Jan. 3, Dec. 7

cider mill was patented in 1906, Apr. 5

Cincinnati Red Socks became the first professional baseball team in the United States in 1869, Mar. 15

Citizenship Day, Sept. 17

Civil Rights Act of 1968 became law, Apr. 11

Civil Rights Bill of 1866 became law, Apr. 9

Civil War began in 1861, Apr. 12

Civil War ended in 1865, Apr. 9

clarinet was invented in Germany in 1690, Jan. 14

Clark, Abraham, Feb. 15

Clark, Barney, first person to receive an artificial heart, Dec. 2

Clark, Dick, July 9, Nov. 30

Clark, George Rogers, Nov. 19

Clark, Georgia Neese, first woman treasurer of the United States, June 9

Clark, Laurel Blair Salton, Feb. 1, Mar. 10

Clark, Mark, May 1

Clark, Roy, Apr. 15

Clark, William, Aug. 1

Clarke, Arthur Charles, Dec. 16

Clay, Henry, Apr. 12

Cleary, Beverly, Apr. 12

Clemens, Roger, Aug. 4

Clemente, Roberto, Aug. 18

Clerc, Laurent, Dec. 26

Clermont, Robert Fulton's first steamboat, was operated for the first time in 1807, Aug. 17

Cleveland, Esther, Aug. 30

Cleveland, Francis Folsom, June 2, July 21

Cleveland, Grover, Mar. 18, June 2

Clinton, Hillary Rodham, Oct. 26

Clinton, William Jefferson "Bill," Jan. 12, Feb. 12, Aug. 19

Clymer, George, Mar. 16

CN Tower was opened in 1976, June 26

Coast Guard, Jan. 28, Aug. 4

Cobb, Ty, Dec. 18

Cobb, Vicki, Aug. 19

Cody, William Frederic "Buffalo Bill," Feb. 26, May 1

Coe, Sebastian, set a new mile record in 1979, July 17

coelacanth was found off the shores of Africa in 1938, Dec. 22

coffee percolator was patented in 1865, Dec. 26

coffee was first planted along the Kona coast of Hawaii in 1817, June 24

Cohan, George M., July 3

Cole, Joanna, Aug. 11

Cole, Nat "King," Mar. 17

Coleman, Bessie, Jan. 26

Collier, James Lincoln, June 27

Collins, Eileen, first woman commander of a space vehicle, July 23

Collodi, Carlo, July 7, Nov. 24

Cologne Cathedral completed construction in 1880, Aug. 14

Colombia celebrates its Independence Day, July 20

Colorado, Feb. 28, Aug. 1

Colo was the first gorilla born in captivity in 1956, Dec. 22

Colt, Samuel, July 19

Columbia space shuttle, Feb. 1, Apr. 12, July 23, Nov. 12

Columbine High School shootings occurred in 1999, Apr. 20

Columbus, Christopher, Feb. 29, May 4, July 31, Aug. 3, Sept. 25, Oct. 12, Nov. 19, Dec. 5, Dec. 6

Columbus Day, October

Comenius, J. A., Mar. 28

Common Sense was published in 1776, Jan. 10

Comoros celebrates its Independence Day, July 6

comptmeter was patented in 1887, Oct. 11

Computer Learning Month, October

computer mouse was invented in 1968, Dec. 9

Comstock Lode was discovered in Nevada in 1859, June 11
Concorde flew for the first time in 1976, Jan. 21
condensed milk was patented in 1853, Aug. 18
Confederate States of America came into being in 1861, Feb. 4
Confucius, Aug. 27
Congo, June 30, Aug. 15
Congress convenes, Jan. 3
Congress first met, Sept. 25, Dec. 6
Congress met for the first time in the Capitol building in 1800, Nov. 17
Congress passed the first law limiting immigration in 1882, Aug. 3
Connecticut became the fifth state in 1788, Jan. 9
Connery, Sean, Aug. 25
Conrad, Charles, Jr. "Pete," May 25, June 2
Conrad, Joseph, Dec. 3
Constantinople, Mar. 28, May 29
Constitution
    became law in 1788, July 2
    11th Amendment adopted in 1798, Jan. 8
    12th Amendment adopted in 1804, Sept. 25
    13th Amendment adopted in 1865, Feb. 1, Dec. 18
    14th Amendment adopted in 1868, July 28
    15th Amendment adopted in 1870, Mar. 30
    16th Amendment adopted in 1913, Feb. 25
    17th Amendment adopted in 1913, Jan. 20
    18th Amendment adopted in 1919, Jan. 29
    19th Amendment adopted in 1920, Aug. 26
    20th Amendment adopted in 1933, Feb. 6
    21st Amendment adopted in 1933, Dec. 5
    22nd Amendment adopted in 1951, Feb. 26
    23rd Amendment adopted in 1961, Apr. 3
    24th Amendment adopted in 1964, Jan. 23
    25th Amendment adopted in 1967, Feb. 10
    26th Amendment adopted in 1971, June 30
    27th Amendment adopted in 1992, May 18
Constitutional Convention, May 25, Aug. 6, Sept. 17
Constitution Week, September
Cook, James, Jan. 17, Oct. 27
Coolidge, Calvin, July 4
Coolidge, Grace Anna Goodhue, Jan. 3
Coombs, Patricia, July 7, July 23
Cooney, Barbara, Aug. 6
Cooper, Frank James "Gary," May 7
Cooper, James Fenimore, Sept. 15
Cooper, L. Gordon, Mar. 6, May 16
Copernicus, Nicolaus, Feb. 19
Copland, Aaron, Nov. 14
Copperfield, David, Sept. 16
Copyright Law was established in 1790, May 31
corkscrew was patented in 1860, Mar. 27
Cormier, Robert, Jan. 17
corncob pipe was patented in 1878, July 9
corn harvester was patented in 1890, June 3
Corporation for Public Broadcasting began its programming in 1971, May 3
Corrigan, Douglas "Wrong Way," started a flight from New York in 1938, July 17
corrugated paper was patented in 1871, Dec. 19

Cosby, Bill, July 12
Costa Rica declared its independence from Spain in 1821, Sept. 15
Costner, Kevin, Jan. 18
Cote d'Ivoire celebrates a national holiday, Dec. 7
Cotton Bowl Classic, Jan. 1
cotton gin was patented in 1794, Mar. 14
Couric, Katie, Jan. 7
Cousins Day, July 24
Cousteau, Jacques-Yves, June 11
Coville, Bruce, May 16
Cox, Lynne, first person to swim across the Bering Strait, Aug. 8
Crandall, Prudence, Sept. 3
Crane, Stephen, Nov. 1
Crater Lake National Park became America's fifth national park in 1902, May 22
Crews, Donald, Aug. 30
Crichton, Michael, Oct. 23
Crick, Francis, June 8, Oct. 18
Crimean War started in 1853, Oct. 4
Crippen, Robert, Apr. 12
Croatia, May 30, June 25
Crockett, Davy, Aug. 17
Cronkite, Walter Leland, Nov. 4
Crosby, Harry Lillis "Bing," May 2
crossword puzzles were first published in 1889, Nov. 5
crown bottle cap was patented in 1892, Feb. 2
Cruise, Tom, July 3
Crum, George, cooked the first potato chip in 1853, Aug. 24
Crump, Diane, first woman to ride in the Kentucky Derby, May 2
Cuba, Jan. 1, July 26
Cuban Missile Crisis began in 1962, Oct. 22
Culkin, Macauley, Aug. 26
Cummings, Dale, did 14,118 sit-ups in 1965, Nov. 29
Cummings, E. E., Oct. 14
Cummings, Pat, Nov. 9
Curie, Marie Sklodowska, Apr. 20, Nov. 7
Curie, Pierre, Apr. 20, May 15
Currier, Nathaniel, Mar. 27
Curtis, Christopher Paul, May 10
Cushman, Karen, Oct. 4
Custer, George Armstrong, June 25, Dec. 5
Custer's Last Stand took place in 1876, June 25
Czechoslovakia, Jan. 1, Oct. 28

Daguerre, Louis Jacques Mande, Jan. 2, Nov. 18
Dahl, Roald, Sept. 13
Daimler, Gottlieb Wilhelm, Mar. 17, Aug. 29, Nov. 10
Dairy Month, June
Dalí, Salvador, May 11
Dalton, John, Sept. 6
Danza, Tony, Apr. 21
Danziger, Paula, Aug. 18
Dare, Virginia, Aug. 18
Darrow, Clarence, Apr. 18
Darwin, Charles, Feb. 12
D'Aulaire, Edgar Parin, Sept. 30
Davis, Bette, Apr. 5

Davis, Jefferson, Feb. 9, May 2, May 10, June 3
Davis, Jim, July 28
Davis, Miles, May 25
Davis, Sammy, Jr., Dec. 8
Dawes, William, Apr. 18
Day, Alexandra, Sept. 7
Daylight Saving Time, Mar. 31, April, October
D day happened in 1944, June 6
Deaf Culture Week, September
Dean, Jay Hanna "Dizzy," Jan. 16
de Angeli, Marguerite, Mar. 14
Death Valley, California, noted a record-breaking temperature of 134 degrees in 1913, July 10
Debussy, Claude, Aug. 22
Decatur, Stephen, Jan. 5
Decker, Annie, first person to go over Niagara Falls in a barrel, Oct. 24
Declaration of Independence, June 10, July 2, July 8, Aug. 2
DeClements, Barthe, Oct. 8
DeForest, Lee, Aug. 26
Degas, Edgar, July 19
de Gaulle, Charles, Nov. 22
Degen, Bruce, June 14
Delacre, Lulu, Dec. 20
de la Salle, Robert Cavelier, Sieur, Apr. 9, Aug. 3, Nov. 22
Delaware became the first state in 1787, Dec. 7
Delmonico's Restaurant in New York served a three-course meal for twelve cents in 1834, Nov. 25
Democratic Party used the donkey as its party emblem for the first time in 1870, Jan. 15
Denali National Park and Preserve was created in 1980, Dec. 2
Denmark beat Italy in the first women's soccer championship in 1970, July 15
Denmark celebrates its Constitution Day, June 5
Denver, Bob, Jan. 9
Denver, John, Dec. 31
dePaola, Tomie, Sept. 15
Descartes, René, Mar. 31
de Soto, Hernando, May 8, June 3
de Trevino, Elizabeth, Sept. 2
Detroit was founded in 1701, July 24
Dewey, John, Oct. 20
Dewey, Melvil, Dec. 10
dial telephone service without an operator was available coast to coast in 1951, Nov. 10
Diana, Princess, July 1
Diary of a Young Girl was published in the United States for the first time in 1952, June 12
DiCaprio, Leonardo, Nov. 11
Dickens, Charles, Feb. 7
Dickinson, Emily Elizabeth, Dec. 10
Dictionary Day, Oct. 15
Diesel, Rudolph, Mar. 18
Dillon, Diane, Mar. 13
Dillon, Leo, Mar. 2
DiMaggio, Joseph Paul "Joe," Nov. 25
"Ding Dong School" debuted on television in 1952, Dec. 22
Dionne quintuplets were born in 1934, May 28

direct telephone communication was completed between the White House and the Kremlin in 1963, Aug. 30
Discovery space shuttle, Feb. 20, Apr. 12, Aug. 30, Sept. 29, Oct. 29
Disney, Walt, Jan. 29, Dec. 5
Disneyland opened in 1955, July 17
Disney's *Fantasia* was released in 1940, Nov. 13
Disney's *Lady and the Tramp* premiered in 1955, June 23
Disney's *Sleeping Beauty* was released in 1959, Jan. 29
Disney's *Three Little Pigs* opened in 1933, May 25
Disraeli, Benjamin, Dec. 21
Distinguished Service Medal was created in 1918, Mar. 7
District of Columbia, July 16, Dec. 23
Ditka, Mike, Oct. 18
Dix, Dorothea Lynde, Apr. 4
Djibouti celebrates a national holiday, June 27
Dodge, Mary Elizabeth Mapes, Jan. 26
dollar sign was created in 1778, Apr. 1
Dolly the sheep was cloned in 1997, Feb. 23
Dominican Republic, Jan. 26, Feb. 27, Aug. 16
Donald Duck, June 9
Doolittle, James Harold, Dec. 14
Doppler, Christian Johann, Nov. 29
Dorsett, Tony, Apr. 7
Dostoyevsky, Fyodor Mikhailovich, Nov. 11
Doubleday, Abner, June 26
double-decked steamboat arrived in New Orleans for the first time in 1816, Oct. 7
Double Eagle II landed in Miserey, France, in 1978, Aug. 17
doughnut cutter was patented in 1872, July 9
doughnut was invented in 1847, June 22
Douglass, Frederick, Feb. 20, Dec. 3
Dow Jones Industrial Average, Jan. 8, Mar. 29, Apr. 6, May 3, May 26, July 8, July 16, Aug. 23, Sept. 17, Oct. 7, Oct. 19, Oct. 27, Oct. 28, Nov. 14, Nov. 21
Doyle, Sir Arthur Conan, May 22
Drake, Sir Francis, Sept. 26, Dec. 13
Drew, Charles, June 3
dried milk was patented in 1872, Apr. 9
drinking straw was patented in 1888, Jan. 3
Drug Abuse Resistance Education became available to schools in 1983, Sept. 1
Drysdale, Don, July 23
Duarte, Juan Pablo, Jan. 26
DuBois, W.E.B., Feb. 23
Duke, Charles M., Jr., Apr. 16
Dumas, Alexandre, July 24
Dunant, Jean Henri, May 8
Dunbar, Paul Laurence, Feb. 9
Durant, Will, Nov. 5
Durante, Jimmy, Feb. 10
Dürer, Albrecht, May 21
Durocher, Leo, July 27
Dutch settlers arrived in Manhattan in 1610, June 10
Dutch West India Company was granted a charter in 1621, June 3
Duvoisin, Roger, Aug. 28
Dvorak, Antonin, Sept. 8
Dwight, Edward J., Jr., first African American astronaut, Mar. 31

Dykstra, Leonard Kyle "Lenny," Feb. 10
Dylan, Bob, May 24

Eakins, Thomas, July 25
Earhart, Amelia, May 20, June 17, July 2, July 24
Early Bird satellite made telephone calls from the United States to Europe more practical, June 28
earmuffs were patented in 1877, Mar. 13
Earp, Wyatt, Mar. 19
Earth Day, Apr. 22
Eastman, George, July 12, Sept. 4
Eastwood, Clint, May 31
Ebsen, Buddy, Apr. 2
Echo I was launched in 1960, Aug. 12
Ecuador celebrates its Independence Day, Aug. 10
Ederle, Gertrude Caroline, Aug. 6, Oct. 23
Edison, Thomas Alva, Jan. 27, Feb. 11, Feb. 19, Aug. 8, Aug. 12, Oct. 21, Nov. 21
Edward VIII abdicated in 1936, Dec. 11
egg incubator was patented in 1843, Mar. 30
Egypt, Apr. 25, July 23
Ehlert, Lois, Nov. 9
Eiffel, Alexandre Gustave, Dec. 15
Eiffel Tower was finished in 1889, Mar. 31
Einstein, Albert, Mar. 14, Oct. 1, Oct. 17
Eisenhower, Dwight David, Oct. 14
Eisenhower, Mamie Geneva Doud, Nov. 14
Eisenstaedt, Alfred, Dec. 6
Eisner, Michael, Mar. 7
Election Day, November
Electoral College meets, Dec. 16
electric dental drill was patented in 1875, Jan. 26
electricity was brought into several buildings in New York City in 1882, Sept. 4
electric range was patented in 1859, Sept. 20
electric razor was patented in 1931, Mar. 18
electron microscope was first shown in 1940, Apr. 20
elephant was used for the first time to represent the Republican Party, Nov. 7
El Greco, Apr. 7
Elion, Gertrude Bell, first woman to be inducted into the National Inventors Hall of Fame, May 18
Eliot, George, Nov. 22
Elizabeth I, Jan. 13, Sept. 7
Elizabeth II, Feb. 6, Apr. 21, June 2
Ellerbee, Linda, Aug. 15
Ellery, William, Dec. 22
Ellington, Edward Kennedy "Duke," Apr. 29
Ellis Island opened its doors in 1892, Jan. 1
Ellsworth, Oliver, Apr. 29
El Salvador declared its independence from Spain in 1821, Sept. 15
Emancipation Proclamation was declared by Abraham Lincoln in 1863, Jan. 1
Emberley, Ed, Oct. 19
Emerson, Ralph Waldo, May 25
Emmett, Daniel Decatur, Oct. 29
Empire State Building was dedicated in 1931, May 1
Encyclopedia Britannica debuted in 1768, Dec. 6
Endangered Species Act became law in 1973, Feb. 3
England, Mar. 25, July 15, July 31, Nov. 5, Dec. 31

Enterprise was launched in 1977, Aug. 12
Epiphany is celebrated, Jan. 6
"E Pluribus Unum" became the U.S. motto in 1776, Aug. 10
Equatorial Guinea, May 25, Oct. 12
Erasmus, Desiderius, Oct. 28
Erie Canal started operating in 1825, Oct. 26
Eritrea celebrates its Independence Day, May 24
Erving, Julius Winfield "Dr. J," Feb. 22
escalator was patented in 1859, Aug. 9
Esposito, Phil, Apr. 23
Estonia, Feb. 24, Sept. 6
Ethiopia, Apr. 6, Sept. 12
Euler, Leonhard, Apr. 15
Euripides, Sept. 23
euro was introduced as the currency of many European nations in 1999, Jan. 1
evaporated milk was patented in 1884, Nov. 25
Everett, Edward, Apr. 11
Everglades National Park was formed in 1947, Dec. 6
Explorer I was launched in 1958, Jan. 31
Explorer VI transmitted the first photographs of Earth taken from space in 1959, Aug. 7
Exxon *Valdez* spilled oil into Prince William Sound in 1989, Mar. 24
eye bank opened in New York, New York, in 1944, May 9

Fahrenheit, Gabriel Daniel, May 14
false teeth were patented in 1822, Mar. 9
Family History Month, October
Faneuil Hall opened in Boston in 1742, Sept. 24
Faraday, Michael, Sept. 22
Farmer, Fannie Merritt, Mar. 23
Farragut, David G., July 5
Father's Day, June
Faulkner, William Cuthbert, Sept. 25
Federalist Papers, first essay published in 1787, Oct. 27
Feiffer, Jules, Jan. 26
Felton, Rebecca L., first female United States senator, Oct. 3
Ferber, Edna, Aug. 15
Ferlinghetti, Lawrence, Mar. 24
Fermi, Enrico, Sept. 29, Dec. 2
Ferraro, Geraldine, July 19, Aug. 26
Ferris, George Washington Gale, Feb. 14
Field, Eugene, Sept. 2
Fielder, Cecil, Sept. 21
Fields, W. C., Apr. 9
Fiji celebrates its Independence Day, Oct. 10
Fillmore, Abigail Powers, Mar. 13
Fillmore, Caroline Carmichael McIntosh, Oct. 21
Fillmore, Millard, Jan. 7
Finland, June 4, Dec. 6
fire engine was used in America for the first time in 1853, Jan. 1
fire escape ladder was patented in 1878, May 7
fire extinguisher was patented in 1863, Feb. 10
Fire Prevention Week, October
"fireside chats" were held for the first time in 1933, Mar. 12
Firestone, Harvey Samuel, Dec. 20
first airplane flight in 1903, Dec. 17

first American-built steamship was launched in 1809, June 8

first American cantilever bridge was finished in 1877, Feb. 20

first appendectomy was performed in 1885, Jan. 4

first Army-Navy football game was played in 1890, Nov. 29

first assembly-line production in 1914, Jan. 14

first automobile race in the United States took place in 1895, Nov. 28

first balloon flight across the English Channel in 1785, Jan. 7

first balloon flight in the United States in 1793, Jan. 9

first basketball game was played in 1892, Jan. 20

first bicycle race was held in Paris in 1868, May 31

first blood transfusion took place in 1666, Nov. 14

first camel appeared in the United States in 1721, Oct. 2

first children's picture book was published in 1592, Mar. 28

first Chinese newspaper in America was printed in 1900, Feb. 16

first-class postage increased to eight cents in 1971, May 16

first color and talking film was produced in 1929, May 28

first commercial airfield was built in 1907, Mar. 15

First Continental Congress met secretly in 1774, Sept. 5

first controlled, self-sustaining nuclear reaction occurred in 1942, Dec. 2

first cow to be milked while flying in an airplane, Feb. 18

first day of autumn, Sept. 22

first day of spring, Mar. 20

first day of summer, June 21

first day of winter, Dec. 21

first dental college in the United States opened its doors in 1840, Feb. 1

first drive-in movie opened in 1933, June 6

first flight faster than sound was made in 1947, Oct. 14

first free public library in the United States, Apr. 9

first fruit tree patent was granted in 1932, Feb. 16

first giant panda was born in captivity in 1963, Sept. 11

first glider flight occurred in 1894, Mar. 17

first helicopter flight took place in 1922, June 16

first hospital in the United States established in 1751, Feb. 11

first illustrated book published in England in 1481, Mar. 8

first killer whale was born in captivity in 1977, Feb. 28

first liquid-fueled rocket was fired in 1926, Mar. 16

first long-playing record was demonstrated in 1948, June 21

first mass inoculations of Salk antipolio vaccine took place in 1954, Feb. 23

first national curling championships were held in 1957, Mar. 28

first national hog-calling contest was held in 1926, Sept. 13

first nickel was minted in 1866, May 16

first night baseball game was played in the major leagues, May 24

first North American drama was performed in 1655, Aug. 27

first nursery school in America was created in 1827, May 23

first oil well was made in 1859, Aug. 27

first open heart surgery was performed in 1944, Nov. 29

first patent for what became the microwave oven was filed in 1945, Oct. 8

first postcard was produced in 1869, Oct. 1

first presidential press conference, Mar. 15

first printing press in America was assembled in 1639, Sept. 25

first professional football game was played in 1895, Sept. 3

first professional golf tour was held in 1860, Oct. 17

first radio in the White House was installed in 1922, Feb. 8

first railroad tunnel in the United States was completed in 1834, Mar. 18

first recorded American earthquake occurred in 1638, June 1

first recorded birth of quintuplets occurred in 1875, Feb. 13

first seawater conversion facility began operating in 1961, May 8

first self-service restaurant opened in 1885, Sept. 4

first submarine was launched in 1898, Mar. 17

first successful heart transplant, Jan. 2

first successful helicopter trip in 1940, July 18

first swimming school was created in Boston in 1827, July 23

first synagogue in the United States was built in 1730, Apr. 8

first telegraph message was sent in 1844, May 24

first telephone directory was published in 1878, Feb. 21

first televised basketball game occurred in 1940, Feb. 28

first Thanksgiving was held in 1619, Dec. 4

first three-dimensional movies opened in 1953, Apr. 10

first traffic light in the United States was installed in 1914, Aug. 5

first transoceanic radio signal was sent in 1901, Dec. 12

first U.S. astronauts were appointed in 1959, Apr. 9

first U.S. bank opened in New York in 1819, July 3

first U.S. commercial bank opened in Philadelphia in 1782, Jan. 7

first U.S. lighthouse started operating in 1716, Sept. 14

first U.S. mint was established in 1792, Apr. 2

first U.S. patent law was formalized in 1790, Apr. 10

first U.S. satellite was launched in 1958, Jan. 31

first U.S. subway began operating in 1870, Feb. 26

first veterinary school in America was founded in 1879, May 23

first wagon train left Independence, Missouri, for California in 1841, May 1

first western movie appeared on screen in 1903, Sept. 21

first woman FBI agents completed basic training, Oct. 25

first world weightlifting championship was held in 1891, Mar. 28

Fischer, Bobby, Mar. 9

Fitch, John, Jan. 21

Fitzgerald, Ella, Apr. 25

Fitzgerald, F. Scott, Sept. 24

Fitzhugh, Louise, Oct. 5

Flag Day, June 14

Flaherty, Robert Joseph, Feb. 16

flaked cereals were patented in 1884, May 31

Fleischman, Paul, Sept. 5

Fleischman, Sid, Mar. 16

Fleming, Sir Alexander, Aug. 6, Sept. 15

Fleming, Ian Lancaster, May 28

Fleming, Peggy Gale, July 27

"Flintstones" debuted on television in 1960, Sept. 30

Florida, Feb. 22, Mar. 3, Apr. 2, June 3, July 17, Aug. 28, Oct. 24

Florida Citrus Bowl, Jan. 1

Floyd, William, Dec. 17

fluoridation process was added to drinking water in 1945, Jan. 25

Flutie, Doug, Oct. 23

Fogg, Phileas, won his wager in 1872, Dec. 21

Fonteyn, Margot Hookman, May 18

food stamps were used for the first time in 1939, May 16

football rules were delineated in 1873, Oct. 18

Forbes, Esther, June 28

Ford, Edward "Whitey," Oct. 21

Ford, Elizabeth "Betty" Bloomer, Apr. 8

Ford, Gerald Rudolph, July 14, Aug. 9, Sept. 8

Ford, Harrison, July 13

Ford, Henry, Jan. 14, June 4, July 30

forest fire lookout stations were erected in Maine in 1905, June 10

Forten, James, Sept. 2

49th Parallel defined the border between Canada and the United States in 1818, Oct. 20

Foster, Andrew "Rube," Sept. 17

Foster, Stephen, Jan. 13, July 4

Foucault, Jean Bernard Leon, Sept. 18

fountain pen was patented in 1890, Jan. 7

Fox, Mem, Mar. 5

Fox, Michael J., June 9

Fox, Paula, Apr. 22

France, Feb. 6, July 14

Franco-Prussian War started in 1870, July 19

Frank, Anne, June 12, June 15, Sept. 2

Frankenstein was published in 1818, Mar. 11

Franklin, Aretha, Mar. 25

Franklin, Benjamin, Jan. 17, May 9, May 23, June 15, Sept. 11, Dec. 28

Frazier, Joe, Jan. 12

free delivery of rural mail began in 1896, Oct. 1

Freedman, Russell, Oct. 11

Freeman, Don, Aug. 11

French, Daniel Chester, Apr. 20

French and Indian War ended in 1763, Feb. 10

Freud, Sigmund, May 6

friction match was patented in 1836, Oct. 24

Friendship 7, Feb. 20

frisbee was patented in 1958, Sept. 30

Fritz, Jean, Nov. 16

Froebel, Friedrich, Apr. 21

Frost, Robert Lee, Mar. 26

Fuller, Buckminster, July 12

Furman, Ashrita, somersaulted from Lexington to Boston, Apr. 30

Gabon celebrates its Independence Day, Aug. 17

Gadsden Purchase treaty was signed in 1953, Dec. 30

Gagarin, Yuri Alexseyevich, Mar. 9, Apr. 12

Gainsborough, Thomas, May 14

Galdone, Paul, June 2

Galey, Gail, Nov. 4

Galileo, Jan. 28, Feb. 15

Gallaudet, Thomas, Dec. 10

Gama, Vasco da, Nov. 22

Gambia celebrates its Independence Day, Feb. 18

Gandhi, Indira Priyadarshini, Nov. 17

Gandhi, Mohandas Karamchand "Mahatma," Oct. 2

Garfield, James Abram, Nov. 19

Garfield, Lucretia Rudolph, Apr. 19

Garfield the cat, June 19

Garland, Judy, June 10

Garn, Jake, first senator to travel in space, Apr. 12

Garrison, William Lloyd, Dec. 12

Garvey, Steve, Dec. 22

gasoline engine was patented in 1844, May 25

gasoline-powered automobile was patented in 1895, Nov. 5

gasoline pump was operated for the first time in 1885, Sept. 5

Gates, Bill, Oct. 28

Gatling, Richard Jordan, Sept. 12

GATT Treaty was approved by the Senate in 1994, Dec. 1

Gauguin, Paul, June 7

Gaye, Marvin, Apr. 2

Gehrig, Henry Louis "Lou," June 1, June 19

Geiger, Hans Wilhelm, Sept. 30

Gemini 5 was launched in 1965, Aug. 21

Gemini 8, Mar. 16

Gemini astrological sign, May 21–June 20

General Pulaski Memorial Day, Oct. 11

Genesis was launched in 2001, Aug. 8

Geography Awareness Week, November

George, Jean Craighead, July 2

George III, June 4

Georgia (country), declared its freedom from the Soviet Union in 1991, May 26

Georgia (state), Jan. 2, Feb. 12

Germany, June 17, Sept. 1, Oct. 3, Oct. 6

Gerry, Elbridge, July 17

Gershwin, George, Sept. 26

Gershwin, Ira, Dec. 6

Getty, John Paul, Dec. 15

Gettysburg Address was delivered in 1863, Nov. 19

Ghana, Mar. 6, July 1, Dec. 31

giant panda was born in the San Diego Zoo in 1999, Aug. 21

Gibbons, Gail, Aug. 1

Gibson, Althea, Aug. 25

Gibson, Mel, Jan. 3

Gielgud, Sir John, Apr. 14

Giff, Patricia Reilly, Apr. 26

Gilbert, Sir Humphrey, landed on Newfoundland in 1583, Aug. 5

Gilbert, Sir William Schwenck, Nov. 18

"Gilligan's Island" appeared on television for the first time in 1964, Sept. 26

Gilman, Phoebe, Apr. 4

Gilmore, Lymon, built first commercial airfield, Mar. 15

Ginsburg, Ruth Bader, Mar. 15

Giovanni, Nikki, June 7

Girl Scout Leader's Day, Apr. 22

Girl Scouts of the United States of America was established in 1912, Mar. 12

Glacier Bay National Park and Preserve was formed in 1980, Dec. 2

Glacier National Park was established in 1910, May 11

Glenn, John, Feb. 20, July 18, Oct. 29

Goble, Paul, Sept. 17

Goddard, Robert Hutchings, Mar. 16, Mar. 28, Oct. 5

Goethe, Johann Wolfgang von, Aug. 28

Goethels, George Washington, June 29

Goldberg, Rube, July 4

Goldberg, Whoopi, Nov. 13

Golden Gate Bridge, Jan. 5, May 27

Golding, Sir William, Sept. 19

Goldmark, Peter Carl, Dec. 2

gold reached $1,000 per ounce in 1980, Jan. 18

gold standard became the law in 1900, Mar. 14

gold was discovered in Alaska in 1902, July 21

gold was found in Bonanza Creek, Alaska, Aug. 16

golf tee was patented in 1899, Dec. 12

Gone with the Wind was published in 1936, June 30

Goodall, Jane, Apr. 3

Goodyear, Charles, Dec. 29

Gore, Albert, Mar. 31, Dec. 12

Gorman, Margaret, first Miss America in 1921, Sept. 8

Gottschalk, Louis Moreau, May 8

Gould, Chester, Nov. 21

Goya, Francisco José de, Mar. 30

Graham, Martha, May 11

Graham, Sylvester, July 5

Grahame, Kenneth, Mar. 8

grain reaper was patented in 1834, May 17

Grammer, Kelsey, Feb. 21

gramophone was patented in 1878, Feb. 19

Grand Canyon National Park was created in 1919, Feb. 26

Grandparents' Day, September

Grant, Julia Dent, Jan. 26

Grant, Ulysses Simpson, Apr. 27

Gray, Robert, first U.S. citizen to circumnavigate the world, Apr. 10

Great American Smokeout, November

Great Britain and the United States signed a pact regarding seal hunting in 1812, Feb. 29

Great Chicago Fire of 1871, Oct. 8

Great Seal was adopted by Congress in 1782, June 20

Great Smoky Mountains National Park was created in 1934, June 15

Great Wall of China was opened to tourists in 1970, Nov. 10

Greece, Jan. 8, Mar. 25, Oct. 28

Greeley, Horace, Feb. 3

Greenaway, Kate, Mar. 17

Greene, Bette, June 28

Greene, Nathaniel, Aug. 7

Greenspan, Alan, Mar. 6

Gregorian calendar, Feb. 24, Sept. 2, Oct. 4

Grenada celebrates its Independence Day, Feb. 7

Grey, Lady Jane, was deposed as queen of England in 1553, July 19

Grey, Joel, Apr. 11

Grey, Zane, Jan. 31

Grieg, Edvard, June 15

Grier, Roosevelt "Rosie," July 14

Griffey, Ken, Jr., Nov. 21

Grimaldi, Joseph, Dec. 18

Grimaldi, Rainier de, Prince of Monaco, Apr. 18

Grimm, Jacob, Jan. 4

Grimm, Wilhelm Karl, Feb. 24

Grissom, Virgil, Jan. 27

Groening, Matt, Feb. 15

Groundhog Day, Feb. 2

Guadalupe Mountains National Park was established in 1972, Sept. 30

Guam, Mar. 6, Dec. 8

Guatemala, Sept. 15, Oct. 20

Guernica Massacre happened in 1937, Apr. 26

Guggenheim, Simon, Dec. 30

"Guiding Light" was broadcast for the first time in 1937, Jan. 25

Guinea-Bissau, Jan. 20, Sept. 12, Sept. 24

Guinea celebrates its Independence Day, Oct. 2

Guinnett, Button, died following a duel in 1777, May 16

Gulf War, Jan. 16, Feb. 27

Gutenberg, Johannes, Apr. 3

Guthrie, Arlo, July 10

Guthrie, Janet, Mar. 7, May 22

Guthrie, Woodrow Wilson "Woody," July 14

Guttenberg, Steve, Aug. 24

Guyana celebrates Republic Day, Feb. 23

Guy Fawkes Day, Nov. 5

Gwynn, Tony, May 9

gyroscope used by Robert Goddard to control rocket in 1935, Mar. 28

Habeas Corpus Act was passed by England in 1679, May 27

Haile Selassie, July 23

Haise, Fred, Apr. 11

Haiti, Jan. 1, Jan. 2, May 18, Dec. 5

Hale, Edward Everett, Apr. 3

Hale, Nathan, June 6

Hale, Sarah Josepha Buell, Oct. 24

Haleakala National Park was created in 1916, Aug. 1

Hale Telescope on Mount Palomar began operations in 1949, Feb. 1

Haley, Alex, Aug. 11

halfway point of the year is marked at noon, July 2

Hall, Lyman, Apr. 12

Halley, Edmund, Apr. 11, Nov. 8

Halley's Comet, Feb. 9, Feb. 16, Mar. 27, Apr. 11, Nov. 8

Halloween, Oct. 31

Hamilton, Alexander, Jan. 11, Feb. 6, July 11

Hamilton, Scott, Aug. 28

Hamilton, Virginia, Mar. 12

Hamm, Mia, May 17

Hammer, Armand, May 21

Hammerstein, Oscar Greeley Clenening, II, July 12

Hammon, Jupiter, Oct. 17

Hammurabi the Great, June 16

Hancock, John, Jan. 12

Handel, George Frederick, Feb. 23

Handel's *Messiah* premiered in 1743, Mar. 23

Handy, W. C., Nov. 16

Hanks, Tom, July 9
Hansberry, Lorraine, May 19
Happy Birthday song was created in 1859, June 27
Harding, Florence Kling, Aug. 15
Harding, Warren Gamaliel, June 14, Nov. 2
Harris, Emmylou, Apr. 2
Harris, Franco, Mar. 7
Harris, Joel Chandler, Dec. 9
Harrison, Anna Tuthill Symmes, July 25
Harrison, Benjamin, Aug. 20
Harrison, Caroline Lavinia Scott, Oct. 1
Harrison, George, Feb. 25
Harrison, Mary Scott Lord Dimmick, Apr. 30
Harrison, William Henry, Feb. 9
Hart, John, May 11
Hart, Melissa Joan, Apr. 18
Harte, Bret Francis, Aug. 25
Harvard Observatory took the first photographs of a star in 1850, July 17
Harvard University was founded in 1636, Oct. 28
Harvey, Paul, Sept. 4
Harvey, William, Apr. 1
Havlicek, John, Apr. 8
Hawaii, Jan. 21, June 11, June 14, June 24, July 29, Aug. 12, Aug. 21, Oct. 14, Dec. 7
Hawaii Volcanoes National Park was established in 1916, Aug. 1
Hawking, Stephen, Jan. 8
Hawthorne, Nathaniel, July 4
Haydn, Franz Josef, Mar. 31
Hayes, Lucy Ware Webb, Aug. 28
Hayes, Rutherford Birchard, Oct. 4
hearing aid was patented in 1879, Sept. 23
Hearst, William Randolph, Apr. 29
Heifetz, Jascha, Feb. 2
helicopter passenger service began in New York in 1953, July 9
Hello, Dolly! premiered on Broadway in 1964, Jan. 16
Hemingway, Ernest, July 21
Henie, Sonja, Apr. 8
Henkes, Kevin, Nov. 27
Henry, Patrick, Mar. 23, May 29
Henry the Navigator, Prince, Mar. 4
Henry VIII, Jan. 15, June 11, June 24
Henson, Jim, Sept. 24
Henson, Matthew A., Aug. 8
Herriot, James Alfred Wight, Oct. 3
Herschel, William, Jan. 11, Mar. 13, May 2, Nov. 15
Hershey, Milton S., Sept. 13
Hershey sold its first Hershey bar in 1895, Apr. 17
Hershiser, Orel Leonard, Sept. 16
Hesse, Karen, Aug. 29
Hewes, Joseph, Jan. 23
Heyerdahl, Thor, Apr. 27, Oct. 6
Heyward, Thomas, July 28
Hickock, James Butler "Wild Bill," May 27
Hicks, Edward, Apr. 4
Hillary, Sir Edmund Percival, July 20
Hindenburg dirigible exploded in 1937, May 6
Hitchcock, Alfred, Mar. 8
Hoban, Lillian, May 18

Hoban, Russell, Feb. 4
The Hobbit was published in 1937, Sept. 21
Hobbs, Lucy B., first woman dentist, Feb. 21
hockey mask was invented in 1959, Nov. 1
Hoff, Syd, Sept. 4
Hogmanay, Dec. 31
Hogrogian, Nonny, May 7
Holiday, Billie, Apr. 7
Holland, John Phillip, Feb. 29
Holland tunnel began operating in 1927, Nov. 13
Holling, Holling C., Aug. 2
Holly, Charles Harden "Buddy," Sept. 7
Holmes, Oliver Wendell, Aug. 29
Holmes, Oliver Wendell, Jr., Mar. 8
Holmes, Sherlock, Jan. 6
Homemade Bread Day, Nov. 17
Homer, Winslow, Feb. 24
Homestead Act was created by Congress in 1872, May 20
Honduras, Apr. 14, Sept. 15, Oct. 3
Hong Kong, May 3, June 9, June 30
Hooper, William, June 17
Hoover, Herbert Clark, Aug. 10
Hoover, J. Edgar, Jan. 1
Hoover, Lou Henry, Mar. 29
Hope, Bob, Mar. 23
Hopkins, Lee Bennett, Apr. 13
Hopkins, Stephen, Mar. 7
Hopkinson, Francis, Sept. 21
Hopper, Grace Brewster Murray, Dec. 9
Horace, Dec. 8
Horowitz, Vladimir, Oct. 1
horseless carriage was driven for the first time in 1896, Mar. 2
horseshoes were patented in 1892, Aug. 23
hot air balloon was flown for the first time in 1783, June 5
hot dog was invented in 1927, Sept. 10
Houdini, Harry, Mar. 24
Houston, Sam, Mar. 2, Oct. 22
Houston, Whitney, Aug. 9
Howard, Moe, June 19
Howard, Ron, Mar. 1
"Howdy Doody" appeared on television for the first time in 1947, Dec. 27
Howe, Elias, July 9
Howe, Gordie, Nov. 27
Howe, James, Aug. 2
Howe, Julia Ward, Feb. 1, May 27
Hubbard, Arnette, first woman president of the American Bar Association, July 31
Hubble, Edwin Powell, Nov. 21
Hubble Space Telescope was deployed in 1990, Apr. 25
Hudson, Henry, Aug. 28, Sept. 4
Hudson Bay Company was organized in 1670, May 2
Hughes, Charles Evans, Apr. 11
Hughes, Howard, Nov. 2
Hughes, Langston, Feb. 1
Hugo, Victor, Feb. 26
Hull, Bobby, Jan. 3
Human Rights Day, Dec. 10
Humboldt, Frederick Heinrich Alexander von, Sept. 14
Humperdinck, Engelbert, Sept. 1

Hundred Years' War began in 1369 and ended in 1453, May 21

Hungary, Apr. 4, Aug. 20, Oct. 23

Huntington, Samuel, July 3

hurricane sank ten Spanish treasure galleons off the coast of Florida in 1715, July 29

Hurwitz, Johanna, Oct. 9

Husband, Rick D., Feb. 1, July 12

Hutchins, Pat, June 18

Hutchinson, Anne, was exiled from Massachusetts in 1637, Nov. 17

Huxley, Aldous, July 26

Hyman, Trina Schart, Apr. 8

Iacocca, Lee A., Oct. 15

Ibsen, Henrik, Mar. 20

ice cream cone mold patent was filed in 1903, Sept. 22

ice cream cone was invented in 1904, July 23

ice cream maker was patented in 1842, May 30

ice cream soda was invented in 1874, June 20

Iceland celebrates its Anniversary of the Establishment of the Republic, June 17

Idaho became the forty-third state in 1890, July 3

Ides of March, Mar. 15

Iditarod sled dog race, Mar. 1, Apr. 1

Iglesias, Enrique, May 8

Illinois became the twenty-first state in 1818, Dec. 3

"I Love Lucy" premiered on television in 1951, Oct. 15

incandescent light bulb was patented in 1880, Jan. 27

Income Tax Day, Apr. 15

India, Jan. 26, July 18, Aug. 15, Nov. 14

Indiana became the nineteenth state in 1816, Dec. 11

Indianapolis 500 Race Track was opened in 1909, Aug. 19

Indianapolis 500 Road Race was held for the first time in 1911, May 30

Indonesia, Apr. 21, Aug. 17

insulin could be used by Americans for the first time in 1928, Apr. 15

International Amateur Radio Month, April

International Calendar Awareness Month, December

International Children's Book Day, Apr. 2

International Day for the Elimination of Racial Discrimination, Mar. 21

International Day for the Eradication of Poverty, Oct. 17

International Day for the Preservation of the Ozone Level, Sept. 16

International Day of Disabled Persons, Dec. 3

International Day of Families, May 15

International Day of Peace, September

International Day of the Seal, Mar. 22

International Drum Month, November

International Lefthanders Day, Aug. 13

International Literacy Day, Sept. 8

International Museum Day, May 18

International Pickle Week, May

International Volunteer Day for Economic and Social Development, Dec. 5

International Women's Day, Mar. 8

Internet was used for the first time in 1969, Oct. 29

Iowa became the twenty-ninth state in 1846, Dec. 28

Irving, Washington, Apr. 3

Irwin, James, July 26, July 31

Ising, Rudolf C., Aug. 7

Israel became a nation in 1948, May 14

Italy, Jan. 6, Apr. 29, May 1, Sept. 8

Ives, James Merritt, Mar. 5

Jackson, Andrew, Mar. 15

Jackson, Jesse, Oct. 8

Jackson, Mahalia, Oct. 26

Jackson, Rachel Donelson Robards, June 15

Jackson, Reggie, May 18

Jackson, Thomas Jonathan "Stonewall," Jan. 21

jacquard loom was patented in 1801, Dec. 23

Jacques, Brian, June 15

Jamaica celebrates its Independence Day, Aug. 6

James, Henry, Apr. 15

James, Jesse, July 21, Sept. 5

Jamestown colony, May 14, Sept. 10, Sept. 19, Dec. 20

Jamison, Judith, May 10

Japan, Jan. 7, Mar. 3, Apr. 8, May 3, May 5, May 15, July 7, July 14, July 15, Aug. 10, Sept. 1, Sept. 15, Oct. 10, Nov. 3, Nov. 15, Nov. 23

Japanese-American internment was ordered in 1942, Feb. 19

Jarvis, Gregory, Jan. 28, Aug. 24

Jay, John, Dec. 12

Jeffers, Robinson, Jan. 10

Jefferson, Martha Wayles Skelton, Oct. 19

Jefferson, Thomas, Jan. 30, Mar. 10, Mar. 25, Apr. 13, July 4

Jefferson Memorial was dedicated in 1943, Apr. 13

Jeffries, John, Jan. 7, Feb. 5

Jemison, Mae, Oct. 17

Jenner, Edward, May 17

Jennings, Peter, July 29

Jenny coupler was patented in 1899, Nov. 23

jet passenger service began in 1958, Oct. 4

Joan of Arc, Jan. 6, July 15

Jobs, Steven, Feb. 24

Joel, Billy, May 9

John, Elton, Mar. 25

Johnny Appleseed, Mar. 11, Sept. 26

Johnson, Andrew, Mar. 5, May 16, Dec. 29

Johnson, Claudia Alta Taylor "Lady Bird," Dec. 22

Johnson, Crocket, Oct. 20

Johnson, Earvin, Jr. "Magic," Aug. 14

Johnson, Eliza McCardle, Oct. 4

Johnson, Lyndon Baines, Aug. 27

Johnston, Tony, Jan. 30

Jolliet, Louis, June 15, June 17, Sept. 21

Jones, Brian, Mar. 21

Jones, Cobi, June 16

Jones, John Luther "Casey," Mar. 14

Jones, John Paul, July 6

Jones, Mary Harris "Mother," May 1

Joplin, Scott, Nov. 24

Jordan, Mar. 22, May 25

Jordan, Michael, Feb. 17

Jouett, Jack, June 4

Joule, James Prescott, Dec. 24

Joyce, James, Feb. 2

Joyner-Kersee, Jacqueline, Mar. 3
Julian calendar corrected, Feb. 24
Justice, David Christopher, Apr. 14

Kahlo, Frida, July 6
Kansas, Jan. 29, May 30
Kasza, Keiki, Dec. 23
Kaye, Danny, Jan. 18
Kazakhstan celebrates its 1991 independence from the
    Soviet Union, Oct. 25
Keane, Bill, Oct. 5
Keaton, Michael, Sept. 9
Keats, Ezra Jack, Mar. 11
Keats, John, Oct. 31
Keep America Beautiful Month, April
Keeshan, Robert, June 27
Keller, Helen Adams, June 27
Kelley, DeForest, Jan. 20
Kellogg, Steven, Oct. 26
Kellogg, Will Keith, Apr. 7
Kelly, Grace, Apr. 18, Nov. 12
Kelly, Walt, Aug. 25
Kendall, Carol, Sept. 13
Kennedy, Anthony M., July 23
Kennedy, John Fitzgerald, Mar. 1, May 29
Kentucky became the fifteenth state in 1792, June 1
Kentucky Derby, May, May 2, May 17
Kenya, June 1, Oct. 20, Dec. 12
Kepler, Johannes, Dec. 27
Kerrigan, Nancy, Oct. 13
Ketcham, Hank, Mar. 14
Key, Francis Scott, Aug. 1
Khrushchev, Nikita, Oct. 15
Kilmer, Alfred Joyce, Dec. 6
King, Coretta Scott, Apr. 27
King, Martin Luther, Jr., Jan. 15, Apr. 4, Aug. 28, Oct. 14
King, Stephen, Sept. 21
King Tut's tomb was discovered in 1922, Nov. 4
Kipling, Rudyard, Dec. 30
Kiribati celebrates its Independence Day, July 12
Kissinger, Henry, Feb. 1
Kittinger, Joe W., first person to cross the Atlantic in a
    hot-air balloon, Sept. 14
Klee, Paul, Dec. 18
Klondike Eldorado was the site of a major gold discov-
    ery in 1896, Aug. 31
Knox, Henry, July 25
Koch, Robert, Mar. 24, Dec. 11
Konigsburg, Elaine Lobl, Feb. 10
Kon Tiki set sail in 1947, Apr. 27
Korea, Mar. 1, May 5, June 6, Aug. 15, Oct. 3, Oct. 11
Korean War, June 25, July 27
Kosciuszko, Thaddeus, Feb. 4
Kosmos 1383 was launched in 1982, July 1
Koufax, Sandy, Dec. 30
Kournikova, Anna, June 7
Krakatoa erupted in 1883, Aug. 26
Kristallnacht transpired in Germany in 1938, Nov. 9
Kuhn, Margaret "Maggie," Aug. 3
Kuralt, Charles, Sept. 10
Kurtzman, Harvey, Oct. 3

Kuskin, Karla, July 17
Kuwait observes a national holiday, Feb. 25
Kwan, Michelle, July 7
Kwanzaa is celebrated in the United States, Dec. 26
Kyrgyzstan celebrates its Independence Day, Aug. 31

La Befana occurs in Italy, Jan. 6
Labor Day, September, Sept. 3
Laennec, René Theophile Hyacinthe, Feb. 17
Lafayette, Marquis de, Sept. 6
Lagerlof, Selma, Nov. 21
Lago, Marie, first girl to join a boys' wrestling team,
    Dec. 20
Laimbeer, Bill, Jr., May 19
Laki Volcano began erupting in Iceland in 1783, June 8
Lalas, Alexi, June 1
Land, Edwin Herbert, May 7
Lao People's Democratic Republic celebrates a national
    holiday, Dec. 3
largest diamond discovered in South Africa in 1905, Jan. 25
Larson, Gary, Aug. 14
Lascaux Caves opened to tourists in 1948, July 14
laser beam was bounced off moon's surface in 1962, May 9
laser was patented in 1960, Mar. 22
Lasky, Kathryn, June 24
Lassen Volcanic National Park was created in 1916, Aug. 9
"Lassie" premiered on television in 1954, Sept. 12
last Carolina parakeet died in 1918, Feb. 21
last Great Buffalo Hunt occurred in 1882, June 20
last passenger pigeon died in 1914, Sept. 1
Latvia declared its independence from the Soviet Union
    in 1991, Sept. 6
Laurel, Stan, June 16
Lavoisier, Antoine-Laurent, Aug. 26
Law Day, May 1
lawn mower was patented in 1899, May 9
lawn sprinkler was patented in 1898, Mar. 22
Lawrence, Jacob, Sept. 7
lawrencium was produced for the first time in 1961,
    Feb. 14
Lawson, Robert, Oct. 4
Lazarus, Emma, July 22
leaded gas was banned by the Environmental Protection
    Agency in 1985, Mar. 4
Leaf, Munro Wilbur, Dec. 4
League of Nations was formed in 1920, Jan. 10
League of Women Voters was organized in 1920, Feb. 14
Leakey, Louis Seymour Bazett, Aug. 7
Leakey, Richard E., Dec. 19
Leap Day, Feb. 29
Leap Second adjustment, June 30, Dec. 31
Lear, Edward, May 12
Lebanon celebrates its Independence Day, Nov. 22
Lee, Bruce, Nov. 27
Lee, Francis Lightfoot, Oct. 14
Lee, Rebecca, first African American woman to get a
    medical degree, Mar. 1
Lee, Richard Henry, Jan. 31
Lee, Robert E., Jan. 19
Leeuwenhoek, Anton van, Oct. 24
Lei Day, May 1

Leif Erikson Day, Oct. 9
Lemon, Meadowlark, Apr. 25
L'Enfant, Pierre Charles, Aug. 2
L'Engle, Madeleine, Nov. 29
Lenin, Nikolai, Apr. 22
Lennon, John, Oct. 9
Leno, Jay, Apr. 28
Lenski, Lois, Oct. 14
Leo astrological sign, July 23–Aug. 22
Leonard, "Sugar" Ray Charles, May 17
Leonardo da Vinci, Apr. 15
Leonov, Aleksei, first person to walk in space, Mar. 18
Lerner, Alan Jay, Aug. 31
Lesotho, Mar. 12, Mar. 21, Oct. 4
Letterman, David, Apr. 12
Leutze, Emanuel, May 24
Levine, Gail Carson, Sept. 17
Levy, Asser, first licensed kosher butcher in New
    Amsterdam in 1660, Nov. 15
Levy, Elizabeth, Apr. 4
Lewis, C. S., Nov. 29
Lewis, Francis, Mar. 21
Lewis, John Llewellyn, Feb. 12
Lewis, Meriwether, Aug. 18
Lewis, Shari, Jan. 17
Lewis, Sinclair, Feb. 7
Lewis and Clark expedition, Mar. 23, May 14, Aug. 1,
    Sept. 23, Nov. 8
Liberia, May 25, July 26
Liberty Bell cracked for the second time in 1835, July 8
Libra astrological sign, Sept. 23–Oct. 22
Library Card Sign-Up Month, September
Library of Congress, Jan. 30, Apr. 24
Libya gained its independence from Italy in 1951, Dec. 24
Lichtenstein, Roy, Jan. 17
Liechtenstein celebrates a national holiday, Aug. 15
lie detector was tested for the first time in 1935, Feb. 2
lifeboat made from corrugated sheet iron was patented in
    1845, Mar. 26
life preserver composed of cork was patented in 1841,
    Nov. 16
Lincoln, Abraham, Jan. 1, Feb. 1, Feb. 12, Apr. 14, Nov.
    12, Nov. 19
Lincoln, Mary Todd, Dec. 13
Lincoln-Douglas debates began in 1858, Aug. 21
Lincoln Highway was finished in 1917, Sept. 10
Lincoln Memorial was dedicated in 1922, May 30
Lincoln penny was issued in 1909, Aug. 2
Lincoln Tunnel opened in 1937, Dec. 22
Lind, Jenny, Oct. 6
Lindbergh, Anne Morrow, June 22
Lindbergh, Charles A., Feb. 4, May 20
Lindgren, Astrid, Nov. 14
Lindros, Eric, Feb. 28
Linnaeus, Carolus, May 23
Lionni, Leo, May 5
Lipman, Hyman, Mar. 30
liquid soap was patented in 1865, Aug. 22
Lister, Joseph, Apr. 5
Liszt, Franz, Oct. 22
Lithuania, Feb. 16, Sept. 6

Little Bighorn Battlefield National Monument was creat-
    ed in 1991, Nov. 26
Little League allowed girls to play in 1974, June 12
Livingston, Philip, Jan. 15
Livingston, Robert R., Nov. 27
Livingstone, David, Mar. 19, Nov. 10
Lloyd, Earl, first African American to play for the NBA,
    Oct. 31
Lobel, Anita, June 3
Lobel, Arnold, May 22
Locke, John, Aug. 29
Lockwood, Belva A. Bennett, Mar. 3, Oct. 24
Lofting, Hugh, Jan. 14
London, Jack, Jan. 12
London's first daily newspaper appeared in 1702, Mar. 11
"Lone Ranger" was broadcast for the first time in 1933,
    Jan. 30
Long, Crawford Williamson, Mar. 30, Nov. 1
Longfellow, Henry Wadsworth, Feb. 27
Lord, Bette Bao, Nov. 3
Los Angeles, California, was created in 1781, Sept. 4
Louis, Joe, May 13
Louisiana, Apr. 30, Oct. 1
Louisiana Purchase was finalized in 1803, Dec. 20
Louvre opened in Paris in 1793, Nov. 8
Lovell, James A., Apr. 11, Dec. 21
Low, Juliette Magill Kinzie Gordon, Oct. 31
Lowell, Amy, Feb. 9
Lowell, Percival, Mar. 13
Lowry, Lois, Mar. 20
Loyalty Day, May 1
Lucas, George, May 14
Luce, Clare Booth, Mar. 10
Luce, Henry Robinson, Apr. 3
Ludlow Mine Incident happened in 1914, Apr. 20
Lumpkin, Rosa Jackson, July 17
Luna 2 was launched in 1959, Sept. 12
Luna 3 was launched in 1959, Oct. 4
Luna 16 was launched in 1970, Sept. 12
Lusitania sank in 1915, May 7
Luther, Martin, Jan. 3, Oct. 31, Nov. 10
Luxembourg, Feb. 12, Mar. 27, June 23
Lynch, Thomas, Jr., Aug. 5
Lynn, Loretta, Apr. 14

Ma, Yo-Yo, Oct. 7
Macao, Apr. 25, June 24
MacArthur, Douglas, Jan. 26
Macaulay, David, Dec. 2
MacDonald, A. G., drove an automobile faster than 100
    miles per hour in 1905, Jan. 31
MacLachlan, Patricia, Mar. 3
Madagascar celebrates its Independence Day, June 26
Madden, John, Apr. 10
Maddux, Gregory Alan, Apr. 14
Madison, Dolley Payne Todd, May 20
Madison, James, Mar. 16, June 8
Madison Square Garden opened in 1879, May 31
Madonna, Aug. 16
Magellan, Ferdinand, Mar. 6, Apr. 27, Sept. 20, Oct. 21
Magna Carta was signed in 1215, June 15

magnetic tape recorder was invented in 1948, Jan. 27

Maine became the twenty-third state in 1820, Mar. 15

Major League All-Star Game was held for the first time in 1933, July 6

Malawi, Mar. 3, May 14, July 6

Malaysia celebrates its Independence Day, Aug. 31

Malcolm X, May 19

Maldives celebrates its Independence Day, July 26

Mali celebrates its Independence Day, Sept. 22

Mallory, George Leigh, June 18

Malone, Moses, Mar. 23

Mammoth Cave National Park was created in 1941, July 1

Mancini, Henry, Apr. 16

Mandela, Nelson Rolihlahla, Feb. 11, May 10, July 18

Manet, Edouard, Jan. 23

manila paper was invented in 1843, Dec. 4

Mann, Horace, May 4

Mantle, Mickey, Oct. 20

Mao Tse-Tung, Dec. 26

Maradona, Diego, Oct. 30

Marceau, Marcel, Mar. 22

Marconi, Guglielmo, Apr. 25, July 13, Dec. 12

Margrethe of Denmark, Apr. 16

Marie Antoinette, Nov. 2

Marine Corps was created by the Continental Congress in 1775, Nov. 10

Marine Mammal Protection Ace was passed in 1972, Oct. 21

Mariner 5 was launched in 1967, June 14

Maris, Roger, Sept. 10, Oct. 1

Marquette, Jacques, June 1, June 17

Marsalis, Wynton, Oct. 18

Marshall, George Catlett, Dec. 31

Marshall, James, Oct. 10

Marshall, John, Jan. 24, Sept. 24

Marshall, Penny, Oct. 15

Marshall, Thurgood, July 2, Oct. 2

Martin, Ann M., Aug. 12

Martin, Bill, Jr., Mar. 20

Martin, Mary, Dec. 1

Marx, Julius Henry "Groucho," Oct. 2

Marx, Karl, May 5

Maryland, Mar. 25, Apr. 28, Dec. 23

Marzollo, Jean, June 24

Mason-Dixon Line, Nov. 15

Massachusetts Bay Colony was created in 1628, Sept. 6

Massachusetts became the sixth state in 1788, Feb. 6

Massachusetts held a day of fasting to atone for punishing witches in 1699, Jan. 14

Masters, Edgar Lee, Aug. 23

Masterson, Bat, Nov. 27

Mata Hari, Aug. 7

matchbooks were patented in 1892, Sept. 27

Mathematics Education Month, April

Mathers, Jerry, June 2

Mathewson, Christy, Aug. 12

Mathias, Robert "Bob," Nov. 17

Matisse, Henri, Dec. 31

Matterhorn was conquered in 1865, July 14

Mattingly, Don, Apr. 20

Mattingly, Thomas K., Apr. 16

Maupassant, Guy de, Aug. 5

Mauritania, May 25, Nov. 28

Mauritius celebrates Independence Day, Mar. 12

May Day, May 1

Mayer, Maria Goeppert, June 28

Mayer, Mercer, Dec. 30

Mayflower, Sept. 16, Nov. 21

Mays, Willie, May 6

McAfee, Mildred, May 12

McAuliffe, Christa, Jan. 28, Sept. 2

McCartney, Paul, June 18

McCloskey, Robert, Sept. 15

McCool, William C., Feb. 1, Sept. 23

McCormick, Cyrus H., Feb. 15, May 17, June 21

McCovey, Willie "Stretch," Jan. 10

McCoy, Elijah, May 2

McDermott, Gerald, Jan. 31

McDonald's, Jan. 31, Apr. 15

McEntire, Reba, Mar. 28

McGovern, Ann, May 25

McGuffey, William, Sept. 23

McGwire, Mark, Sept. 8, Oct. 1

McHale, Kevin Edward, Dec. 19

McKean, Thomas, Mar. 19

McKinley, Ida Saxton, June 8

McKinley, Robin, Nov. 16

McKinley, William, Jan. 29

McKissack, Patricia, Aug. 9

McNair, Ronald, Jan. 28

Mead, Margaret, Dec. 16

"Meet the Press" premiered in 1947, Nov. 6

Mehta, Zubin, Apr. 29

Meir, Golda Mabovitz, May 3

Mellon, Andrew W., Mar. 24

Melville, Herman, Aug. 1

Memorial Day, May

Mendel, Gregor, July 22

Mendelssohn, Felix, Feb. 3

Menuhin, Yehudi, Apr. 22

Mercator, Gerhardus, Mar. 5

Mercer, Johnny, Nov. 18

Meredith, Don, Apr. 10

Meredith, James, enrolled as the first African American at the University of Mississippi, Sept. 30

Merrimac was destroyed by the Confederate Navy in 1862, May 11

Mesa Verde National Park was created in 1906, June 29

Messina, Sicily, was hit by an earthquake in 1908, Dec. 28

metric system was adopted in France in 1795, Apr. 7

Metropolitan Museum of Art opened its doors in 1870, Apr. 13

Mexico, Feb. 2, Feb. 5, May 3, May 5, May 15, Sept. 15, Sept. 16, Sept. 19, Nov. 1, Nov. 20, Dec. 16

Michelangelo Buonarroti, Mar. 6

Michener, James, Feb. 3

Michigan became the twenty-sixth state in 1837, Jan. 26

Mickey Mouse, Sept. 19, Nov. 18

"Mickey Mouse Club" began its first season in 1955, Oct. 3

Micronesia celebrates its Independence Day, Nov. 3

Microsoft Corporation was found to be a monopoly in 2000, Apr. 3

Middleston, Arthur, June 26

Midler, Bette, Dec. 1

milk bottle opener and cover was patented in 1926, June 29

milk was delivered in glass bottles for the first time in 1878, Jan. 11

Miller, Arthur, Oct. 17

Miller, Glenn, Mar. 1

Million Man March occurred in 1995, Oct. 16

Milne, A. A., Jan. 18

mimeography was patented in 1876, Aug. 8

minimum wage, June 4, June 25, Aug. 12, Oct. 24

Minnesota became the thirty-second state in 1858, May 11

Minuit, Peter, arrived in Manhattan in 1626, May 4

Miró, Joan, Apr. 20

Mir space station, Feb. 20, Mar. 22, Mar. 23, June 25

Mississippi became the twentieth state in 1817, Dec. 10

Mississippi River, Apr. 9, May 8, June 17, July 13

Missouri became the twenty-fourth state in 1821, Aug. 10

"Mister Rogers' Neighborhood" premiered in 1967, May 22

Mitchell, Margaret, Nov. 8

Mitchell, Maria, Aug. 1

Mix, Tom, Jan. 6

Moby Dick was published in 1851, Nov. 14

Moebius, August Ferdinand, Nov. 17

Moldova celebrates its Independence Day, Aug. 27

Molly Pitcher, June 28, Oct. 13

Monaco celebrates a national holiday, Nov. 19

Mona Lisa was stolen from the Louvre in 1911, Aug. 21

Mondrian, Piet, Mar. 7

Monet, Claude, Nov. 14

Mongolia, July 11, Nov. 26

Monitor and *Merrimac* battled in 1862, Mar. 9

Monopoly game premiered in 1935, Nov. 5

Monroe, Elizabeth Kortright, June 30

Monroe, James, Apr. 28, July 4, Dec. 2

Monroe, Marilyn, June 1

Monroe Doctrine was established in 1823, Dec. 2

Montague, John, Fourth Earl of Sandwich, Aug. 6, Nov. 3

Montana, Joe, June 11

Montana became the forty-first state in 1889, Nov. 8

Montezuma met Cortez in the Aztec capital in 1519, Nov. 8

Montgolfier, Jacques Etienne, Jan. 7, June 5

Montgolfier, Joseph, June 5

Montgomery, Lucy Maud, Nov. 30

Montgomery Bus Boycott, Dec. 5, Dec. 20

Montoya, Carlos, Dec. 3

Moore, Clement Clarke, July 15

Moore, Helen Eugenie, first woman to be appointed to an ambassadorship, Oct. 28

Moore, Marianne, Nov. 15

More, Sir Thomas, Feb. 7

Morgan, Garret A., patented a breathing device for miners in 1914, Oct. 13

Morgan, John Pierpont, Apr. 17

Morgan, J. P., Jr., Sept. 7

Morris, Gouverneur, Jan. 31

Morris, Lewis, Apr. 8

Morris, Robert, Jan. 31

Morrison, Toni, Feb. 18

Morse, Samuel Finley Breese, Apr. 27, May 24

Morton, Thomas, became America's first deported person in 1628, June 9

Moses, Anna Mary Robertson "Grandma," Sept. 7

Moss, Randy, Feb. 13

Mother Goose Day, May 1

Mother's Day, May

Mother Teresa, Aug. 27, Oct. 17

motorcycle was driven for the first time in 1885, Nov. 10

Mott, Lucretia Coffin, Jan. 3

Mt. Didicus, an underwater volcano, erupted in 1991, June 22

Mount Etna in Sicily erupted in 1693, Jan. 11

Mount Everest was climbed for the first time by a woman in 1975, May 23

Mt. Kilauea in Hawaii erupted in 1985, Feb. 23

Mount Pelée in Martinique erupted in 1902, May 8

Mount Pinatubo erupted in the Philippines in 1991, June 11

Mount Rushmore, Mar. 25, Oct. 31, Nov. 20

Mount St. Helens erupted in 1980, May 18

Mt. Vesuvius in Italy erupted in A.D. 62, Feb. 5

Mount Washington, New Hampshire, recorded its strongest wind ever in 1934, Apr. 12

Mousetrap, a play by Agatha Christie, opened in 1952, Nov. 5

movable type was used for the first time in 1451, Apr. 3

moving picture projector was patented in 1895, Feb. 13

Mowat, Farley, May 12

Moyers, Bill, June 5

Mozambique celebrates a national holiday, June 25

Mozart, Wolfgang Amadeus, Jan. 27

"Mr. Wizard" premiered on television in 1951, Mar. 3

MTV debuted on cable television in 1981, July 31

Muddy Waters, Apr. 4

Muir, John, Apr. 21

Munsch, Robert, June 11

Murphy, Audie, June 20

Murphy, Eddie, Apr. 3

Museum of Modern Art, New York, Oct. 17, Nov. 7

Musial, Stan, Nov. 21

Music in Our Schools Month, March

Myanmar celebrates its Independence Day, Jan. 4

Myers, Mike, May 25

Myers, Walter Dean, Aug. 12

Nader, Ralph, Feb. 27

NAFTA was signed in 1993, Dec. 8

Naismith, James, Nov. 6

Namibia celebrates its Independence Day, Mar. 21

Napoleon Bonaparte, Apr. 11, June 18, Aug. 15, Oct. 19

Nash, Ogden, Aug. 19

Nast, Thomas, Sept. 27

Nation, Carrie Amelia Moore, Jan. 21, Nov. 25

National Academy of Sciences was created in 1863, Mar. 3

National Aeronautics and Space Administration (NASA) Act of 1958 was signed, July 29

National Arbor Day, April

National Archives was created in 1934, June 19

National Audubon Society incorporated in 1905, Jan. 5

National Authors' Day, Nov. 1

National Baseball Hall of Fame, Jan. 29, June 12

National Bike Month, May

National Cherry Month, February

National Children's Dental Health Month, February

National Coin Week, April

National Cowboy Hall of Fame opened in 1965, Nov. 12

National Educational Support Personnel Day, November

National Farm Safety Week, September

National Football League, June 24, Sept. 17

National Forest Products Week, October

National Freedom Day, Feb. 1

National Fresh Fruit and Vegetable Month, June

National Gallery of Art opened in 1941, Mar. 17

National Garden Week, April

National Geographic Society was created in 1888, Jan. 13

National Geographic was first published in 1864, Oct. 1

National German-American Day, Oct. 6

National Grange was started in 1786, Dec. 4

National Handwriting Day, Jan. 23

National Hispanic Heritage Month, September

National Hockey League was formed in 1917, Nov. 22

National Honey Month, September

National Hot Dog Month, July

National Hunting and Fishing Day, September

National Ice Cream Month, July

Nationalist Party of China was exiled to Taiwan in 1949, Dec. 7

National Juggling Day, June 19

National League of Baseball was formed in 1876, Feb. 2

National Library Week, April

National Little League Week, June

National Magic Day, Oct. 31

National Maritime Day, May 22

National Mole Day, Oct. 23

National Mustard Day, August

National Negro Baseball League was formed in 1920, Feb. 13

National Noodle Month, March

National Nutrition Month, March

National Organization for Women was formed in 1966, Oct. 29

National Park Service was created in 1916, Aug. 25

National Peanut Month, March

National Physical Fitness and Sports Month, May

National Pie Day, Jan. 23

National Pig Day, Mar. 1

National Pizza Month, October

National Popcorn Poppin' Month, October

National Postal Worker Day, July 1

National PTA Founder's Day, Feb. 17

National Recreation and Parks Month, July

National School Lunch Week, October

National School Nurse Day, January

National Science and Technology Week, April

National Skin Safety Month, June

National Soup Month, January

National Spelling Bee, May, June 17

National Tap Dance Day, May 25

National Teacher Appreciation Day, May

National Transportation Week, May

National Weather Observer's Day, May 4

National Weather Vane Day, Sept. 15

National Week of the Ocean, April

National Wild Bird Feeding Month, February

National Wildlife Federation was established in 1936, Feb. 5

National Women's Hall of Fame opened in 1979, July 21

National Women's History Month, March

Native American Day, September

Native Americans were given citizenship in 1924, June 2

Natural Bridges National Monument was dedicated in 1908, Apr. 16

Nauru celebrates a national holiday, Jan. 31

Naval Academy opened in Annapolis, Maryland, in 1845, Oct. 10

Navy Day, Oct. 27

Naylor, Phyllis Reynolds, Jan. 4

Near Miss Day happened in 1989, Mar. 23

Nebraska, Mar. 1, May 30

Nebuchadnezzar died in 1104 B.C., Sept. 6

Nehru, Jawaharlal, Nov. 14

Nelson, Thomas, Dec. 26

Nelson, Willie, Apr. 30

Nepal celebrates National Unity Day, Jan. 11

Neptune, Jan. 28, June 9, Sept. 23

Nero, Dec. 15

Ness, Evaline, Apr. 24

Netherlands, Apr. 27, Apr. 30, July 26, Oct. 3

Nevada, June 11, Oct. 31

New Amsterdam was incorporated in 1653, Feb. 2

Newbery, John, July 19

Newbery Medal was awarded for the first time, June 27

Newcastle Badminton Club was established in 1900, Jan. 24

Newfoundland, June 23, Aug. 5

New Hampshire became the ninth state in 1788, June 21

New Jersey, Nov. 20, Dec. 18

New Mexico became the forty-seventh state in 1912, Jan. 6

Newspaper in Education Week, March

newsreel theater was first opened in 1929, Nov. 2

Newton, Isaac, Dec. 25

Newton, Wayne, Apr. 3

New Year's Day, Jan. 1

New Year's Eve is celebrated, Dec. 31

New York City subway began operating in 1904, Oct. 27

New York Harbor was discovered in 1524, Apr. 17

New York hosted the first performance of an Italian opera, *The Barber of Seville,* in 1825, Nov. 29

New York Knickerbockers became the first baseball team to wear uniforms in 1851, June 3

New York Metropolitan Opera House opened in 1883, Oct. 22

New York Public Library opened in 1911, Oct. 26

New York State, Apr. 6, July 26

New York Stock Exchange, May 17, Sept. 20

New York Times printed its first issue in 1851, Sept. 18

New Zealand, Feb. 6, Dec. 13

Niagara Falls stopped flowing for one day in 1848, Mar. 29

Nicaragua declared its independence from Spain in 1821, Sept. 15

Nicholson, Jack, Apr. 22

Nickelodeon premiered in 1979, Apr. 2

Niger celebrates its Independence Day, Aug. 3

Nigeria celebrates its Independence Day, Oct. 1

Nightingale, Florence, May 12

Nixon, Joan Lowery, Feb. 3

Nixon, Richard Milhous, Jan. 9, Feb. 21, May 22, Aug. 9, Sept. 8

Nixon, Thelma Catherine Patricia Ryan, Mar. 16

Nixon-Kennedy debates began in 1960, Sept. 26

Nobel, Alfred Bernhard, Oct. 21

Nobel Prizes are awarded, Dec. 10

Noguchi, Isamu, Nov. 7

Noonan, Fred, July 2

North, Sterling, Nov. 4

North American Treaty was signed in 1949, Apr. 4

North Carolina became the twelfth state in 1789, Nov. 21

North Dakota became the thirty-ninth state in 1889, Nov. 2

North Star, an abolitionist newspaper, was first printed in 1847, Dec. 3

Northwest Ordinance was created in 1787, July 13

Norton, Mary, Dec. 10

Norway, May 14, May 17, July 29

Numeroff, Laura Joffe, July 14

Nutcracker was performed for the first time in 1892, Dec. 18

Nye, Bill, Nov. 27

nylon stockings were first sold in 1940, May 15

nylon was invented in 1934, May 23

nylon was patented in the United States in 1937, Feb. 16

Oakley, Annie, Mar. 8

Oates, John, Apr. 7

Oatmeal Month, January

Oberlin Institute opened its doors in 1837, Sept. 6

O'Brian, Robert C., Jan. 11

O'Connor, Sandra Day, Mar. 26, Sept. 25

O'Dell, Scott, May 23

Odie, Aug. 8

odometer was invented in 1847, May 12

O'Donnell, Rosie, Mar. 21

Office of Attorney General was created in 1789, Sept. 24

Oglethorpe, James Edward, Dec. 22

Oglethorpe Day, Feb. 12

Ogo 5 was launched in 1968, Mar. 4

Ohio became the seventeenth state in 1803, Mar. 1

Ohm, Georg Simon, Mar. 16

oil was pumped through the Alaska Pipeline for the first time in 1977, July 28

O'Keefe, Georgia, Nov. 15

Oklahoma, Apr. 22, May 2, Nov. 16

Oklahoma City Federal Building was bombed in 1995, Apr. 19

Olajuwon, Hakeem Abdul, Jan. 21

Older Americans Month, May

oleomargarine was patented in 1873, Apr. 8

Olive Branch Petition was signed in 1775, July 8

Olmsted, Frederick Law, Apr. 26

Olsen, Ashley, June 13

Olsen, Mary-Kate, June 13

Olympic Games, Feb. 4, Apr. 6, July 31, Aug. 5, Aug. 9, Sept. 2

Olympic National Park was created in 1938, June 29

Oman celebrates a national holiday, Nov. 18

Onassis, Jacqueline Bouvier Kennedy, July 28

O'Neal, Shaquille, Mar. 6

O'Neill, Eugene Gladstone, Oct. 16

Onizuka, Ellison, Jan. 28, June 24

opera was first performed in America in 1735, Feb. 8

Oregon became the thirty-third state in 1859, Feb. 14

Oreo cookie went on sale in 1912, Mar. 6

Organization of American States was created in 1948, Apr. 30

Orwell, George, June 25

Osbourne, Mary Pope, May 20

Otis, Elisha Graves, Aug. 3

Oughtred, William, Mar. 5

Ousland, Borge, first person to trek to the North Pole alone, Feb. 6

Owens, James Cleveland "Jesse," Aug. 9, Sept. 12

Oz, Frank, May 24

Paca, William, Oct. 31

Paganini, Nicolo, Jan. 17

Paige, Leroy "Satchel," July 7

Paine, Robert Treat, Mar. 11

Paine, Thomas, Jan. 10, Jan. 29

Pakistan celebrates Republic Day, Mar. 23

Palmer, Arnold, Sept. 10

Panama, Jan. 9, Nov. 3, Nov. 4, Dec. 31

Panama Canal, Dec. 31

Pan American Day, Apr. 14

Pan American Health Day, Dec. 2

paper money was used for the first time in 1690, Feb. 3

Papua New Guinea celebrates its Independence Day, Sept. 16

parachute jump was made for the first time in 1797, Oct. 22

Paracutín became an active volcano in Mexico in 1943, Feb. 20

Paraguay, May 14, May 15

Parish, Peggy, July 14

Park, Barbara, Apr. 21

Park, Mungo, Sept. 10

Parker, Charlie, Aug. 29

Parks, Rosa Louise, Feb. 4, Dec. 1

Parry, Sir William Edward, Dec. 19

Pascal, Blaise, June 19

passenger air service began in 1919, May 3

passenger train service began in 1830, May 24

Pasternak, Boris Leonidovich, Feb. 10

Pasteur, Louis, July 6, Dec. 27

Paterson, Katherine, Oct. 31

Pathfinder landed on Mars in 1997, July 4

Patton, George S., Jr., Nov. 11

Pauley, Jane, Oct. 31

Pauling, Linus, Feb. 28

Paulsen, Gary, May 17

Pavarotti, Luciano, Oct. 12

Pavlova, Anna, Feb. 12

Peace Corps was created in 1961, Mar. 1

Peace Officer Memorial Day, May 15

Peale, Anna Claypoole, Mar. 6

Peale, Charles Willson, Apr. 15

Peale, Raphael, Feb. 17
Peale, Rembrandt, Feb. 22
Peale, Sarah Miriam, May 19
Peanut Butter Lovers' Month, November
peanut butter was invented in 1890, Nov. 13
Pearl Harbor was attacked by the Japanese in 1941, Dec. 7
pearl weighing fourteen pounds was removed from a Philippine clam in 1934, May 7
Peary, Robert E., Apr. 6, May 6
Pecan Day, Mar. 25
Peck, Annie Smith, Oct. 19
Peck, Gregory, Apr. 5
Peck, Richard, Apr. 5
Peck, Robert Newton, Feb. 17
Peet, Bill, Jan. 29
Pei, I. M., Apr. 26
Pele, Oct. 23
Pemberton, John Styth, invented Coca-Cola in 1886, May 8
pencil sharpener was patented in 1897, Nov. 23
pencil with eraser was patented in 1858, Mar. 30
Penn, John, Apr. 6
Penn, Sean, Aug. 17
Penn, William, Mar. 4, June 23, Oct. 14, Dec. 12
Pennsylvania, Mar. 4, Dec. 12
Pennsylvania Child Labor Law was passed in 1848, Mar. 28
Pennsylvania Evening Post, first newspaper to be published in the United States, May 30
Peres, Shimon, Feb. 9
Perkins, Carl, Apr. 9
Perkins, Frances, Apr. 10
Perkins, Marlin, Mar. 28
Perlman, Itzhak, Aug. 31
Perot, H. Ross, June 27
Perrault, Charles, Jan. 12
Perry, Matthew Calbraith, Apr. 10, July 15
Perry, Oliver Hazard, Aug. 23
Perry, William "The Refrigerator," Dec. 16
Pershing, John J., Sept. 13
Persia became Iran in 1935, Mar. 21
Persia defeated Athens at the Battle of Marathon in 490 B.C., Sept. 9
Peru, July 28, Aug. 30, Oct. 8
Peshtigo Forest Fire started in 1871, Oct. 8
Peter I of Russia, May 30
Petrified Forest National Park was formed in 1962, Dec. 9
Petty, Richard, July 2
Philadelphia Zoological Society, first U.S. zoo in 1874, July 1
The Philanthropist, first abolitionist newspaper, was printed in 1817, Aug. 29
Philippines, Mar. 24, Apr. 9, May 6, May 14, June 12, July 4, Dec. 30
phonograph was invented in 1877, Aug. 12, Nov. 21
piano was invented in 1796, May 27
Picasso, Pablo, Apr. 26, Oct. 25, Nov. 28
Piccard, Bertrand, Mar. 21
Picket, Bill, Dec. 5
Pi Day, Mar. 14

Pied Piper of Hamelin piped the rats out of the town in 1376, July 22
Pierce, Franklin, Nov. 23
Pierce, Jane Means Appleton, Mar. 12
Pietà was damaged when Lazlo Toth attacked the sculpture in 1972, May 21
Pike, Zebulon, Jan. 5, Nov. 15
Pilgrim's Progress was published in 1678, Feb. 18
pilgrims reached Plymouth Rock in 1620, Dec. 21
Pilkey, Dav, Mar. 4
Pinchot, Gifford, Aug. 11
pineapple was brought to Hawaii for cultivation in 1813, Jan. 21
Pinkham, Lydia Estes, Feb. 9
Pinkney, J. Brian, Aug. 28
Pinkney, Jerry, Dec. 22
Pioneer 7 sent images of Saturn and its rings back to Earth in 1978, July 29
pipe wrench was patented in 1876, Dec. 5
Pippin, Horace, Feb. 22
Pisces astrological sign, Feb. 19–Mar. 20
Pitt, Brad, Dec. 18
Plante, Jacques, invented hockey mask in 1959, Nov. 1
player piano was patented in 1912, June 11
Pledge of Allegiance was read publicly for the first time in 1892, Sept. 8
Plough Day, January
Plunkett, Roy J., Apr. 6, June 26
plutonium was weighed for the first time in 1942, Aug. 20
Pluto was discovered in 1930, Mar. 18
Pocahontas, Mar. 21, Apr. 5
Poe, Edgar Allan, Jan. 19
Poensich, Walter, swam from Cuba to Florida in 1978, July 13
Poinsettia Day, Dec. 12
Pokemon appeared in the United States in 1998, Sept. 28
Polacco, Patricia, July 11
Poland, Jan. 17, May 3
polar bear was put on display in a zoo in 1733, Jan. 18
Polaroid camera was patented in 1947, Feb. 21
police force was created in America in 1658, Aug. 12
Police Week, May
polio vaccine discovery was made known in 1953, Mar. 26
Polk, James Knox, Nov. 2
Polk, Sarah Childress, Sept. 4
Pollock, Jackson, Jan. 28
poll tax was outlawed in 1966, Apr. 8
Polyakov, Valery, Mar. 22
Ponce de Leon discovered Florida in 1513, Apr. 2
Pony Express had its first run in 1860, Apr. 3
Pope John Paul II, May 18, Oct. 16
Popov, Leonid, Apr. 9
porpoise was born in captivity for the first time in 1940, Feb. 14
Porter, Cole, June 9
Porter, Katherine Anne, May 15
Porter, William Sydney, Sept. 11
Portola, Gaspar de, claimed San Francisco Bay for the Spanish in 1769, Nov. 2
Portugal, May 12, June 10, Dec. 1
Post, Emily Price, Oct. 30

Post, Wiley, Nov. 22
postal service between Boston and New York was started in 1673, Jan. 22
Potter, Helen Beatrix, July 6
Powell, Colin, Apr. 5
Powell, Emily, first woman hired to pilot passenger airplanes, June 12
Powell, John Wesley, Mar. 24
Prelutsky, Jack, Sept. 8
Preminger, Otto, Dec. 5
Prescott, William, Feb. 20
presidential elections occurred in America for the first time in 1789, Jan. 7
presidential inaugurations, Jan. 20, Mar. 4
President's Day, February
President's Flag was officially adopted in 1916, May 29
Presley, Elvis, Jan. 8
Prevention of Animal Cruelty Month, April
Previn, Andre, Apr. 6
Price, Leontyne, Feb. 10
Priesand, Sally Jan, became first woman rabbi in 1972, June 3
Priestley, Joseph, Mar. 13, Aug. 1
Prime Meridian was formally agreed to in 1884, Nov. 1
Principals Week, June
Prohibition, Jan. 29, Dec. 5
Prokofiev, Sergei Sergeyevich, Apr. 23
Ptolemy made the first recorded reference to a lunar eclipse in A.D. 72, Mar. 19
Puccini, Giacomo, Dec. 22
Puckett, Kirby, Mar. 14
Puerto Rico, Mar. 2, Mar. 22, July 25, Nov. 19
Pulaski, Casimir, Mar. 4
Pulitzer, Joseph, Apr. 10
Pulitzer Prizes, May 5, June 4
Pullman, George, Mar. 3
Pullman, Philip, Oct. 19
Pure Food Law was enacted in 1881, May 28
Purple Heart was created by George Washington in 1782, Aug. 7
Putin, Vladimir, Oct. 7
Pyle, Ernie, Aug. 3
Pyle, Howard, Mar. 5

Qatar celebrates its Independence Day, Sept. 3
Quackenbush, Robert, July 23
Quantrill, William Clark, Aug. 21
Quebec citizens voted to remain part of Canada in 1995, Oct. 30
Queen Mary made her first voyage in 1936, May 27
Queensboro Bridge was finished in 1909, Mar. 30
Quito, Ecuador, was formed in 1534, Dec. 6

Rachmaninoff, Sergei Vasilievich, Apr. 1
radiation belt was discovered in 1958, Jan. 31
radio broadcasting began on station KDKA in Pittsburgh in 1920, Nov. 2
radio show was broadcast for the first time in 1910, Jan. 13
radio was patented by Marconi in 1898, July 13
radium was isolated in 1902, Apr. 20
Raggedy Ann dolls were patented in 1915, Sept. 7

Railton, George, Mar. 10
Ram, Jagjivan, Apr. 1
Ramon, Ilan, Feb. 1, June 20
Randolph, James Madison, Jan. 17
Randolph, John, June 2
Randolph, Peyton, Oct. 22
Random Acts of Kindness Week, February
Ranger 7 sent back over four thousand pictures of the moon in 1964, July 28
Rankin, Jeannette, June 11, Nov. 7
Raphael Santi, Apr. 6
Raskin, Ellen, Mar. 13
Rather, Dan, Oct. 31
Rathmann, Peggy, Mar. 4
Ratification Day, Jan. 14
Rauschenberg, Robert, Oct. 22
Ravel, Maurice, Mar. 7
Rawlins, Wyoming, experienced a two-foot snowfall in 1889, June 13
Rawls, Wilson, Jan. 24
rayon was patented in 1902, Sept. 30
Read, George, Sept. 18
Reading Is Fun Week, April
Reagan, Nancy Davis, July 6
Reagan, Ronald, Feb. 6
reaping machine was patented in 1834, June 21
"Red Baron" was killed, Apr. 21
Redwood National Park was created in 1968, Oct. 2
Reed, Walter, Sept. 13
refrigeration apparatus was patented in 1879, Nov. 4
refrigerator was patented in 1899, Aug. 8
Rehnquist, William Hubbs, Oct. 1
Reid, Barbara, Nov. 16
Rembrandt Van Rijn, July 15
Remember the *Maine* Day, Feb. 15
Remington, Frederic, Oct. 4
Remsen, Ira, Feb. 10
Renoir, Pierre Auguste, Feb. 25
Republican Party, Feb. 28, July 6, Nov. 7
Resnick, Judith A., Jan. 28, Apr. 5
Responsible Pet Owners Month, February
Retton, Mary Lou, Jan. 24
Revels, Hiram R., first African American to be elected to the Senate, Feb. 25
Revere, Paul, Jan. 1, Apr. 18
Rey, H. A., Sept. 16
Rey, Margaret, May 16
Reynolds, Joshua, July 16
rhinoceros was exhibited for the first time in the United States in 1826, Sept. 13
Rhode Island, Mar. 24, May 4, May 29, June 13
Rhodes, Cecil John, July 1
Rhodes Scholarships were created in 1902, Apr. 4
Richardson, Tacy, rode to warn General Washington of approaching British troops in 1777, Sept. 22
Richard the Lionhearted, Apr. 17, Sept. 8
Richter, Conrad, Oct. 13
Richter Scale Day, Apr. 26
Rickenbacker, Edward, Oct. 8
Riddles, Libby, Apr. 1
Ride, Sally Kristen, May 26, June 18

Riis, Jacob August, May 3
Riley, James Whitcomb, Oct. 7
Rinaldi, Anne, Aug. 27
Ringgold, Faith, Oct. 8
Ringling Brothers Circus performed for the first time in 1884, May 19
Ripken, Cal, Aug. 24
Ripley, Robert, Dec. 25
Rivera, Diego, Dec. 8
rivet was patented in 1794, Mar. 23
Roanoke, North Carolina, colony was started in 1587, July 22
Robbins, Jerome, Oct. 11
Robert, Henry M., May 2
Robertson, Alice, first woman to officiate in the House of Representatives in 1921, June 20
Robert the Bruce, July 11
Robeson, Paul Bustill, Apr. 9
Robinson, Frank, first African American major league baseball team manager, Oct. 3
Robinson, Jackie, Jan. 31
Robinson, Roscoe, Jr., Oct. 11
Robinson Crusoe Day, Feb. 1
Rockwell, Norman, Feb. 3
Rocky Mountain National Park was created in 1915, Jan. 26
Rodgers, Richard, June 28
Rodin, Auguste, Nov. 12
Rodney, Caesar, Oct. 7
Roentgen, Wilhelm Konrad, Mar. 27
Rogers, Fred, Mar. 20
Rogers, Roy, Nov. 5
Rogers, Will, Nov. 4
Roget, Peter, Jan. 18
Rolfe, John, Mar. 21, Apr. 5
roller skates were patented in 1823, Apr. 22
Romania celebrates National Day, Dec. 1
Rome, Apr. 21, July 18
Romeo and Juliet, Mar. 11
Romulus Augustulus was deposed in A.D. 476, Sept. 3
Roosevelt, Alice, Feb. 17, July 29
Roosevelt, Alice Hathaway Lee, July 29
Roosevelt, Anna Eleanor, Oct. 11
Roosevelt, Edith Kermit Carow, Aug. 6
Roosevelt, Franklin Delano, Jan. 14, Jan. 30, Feb. 19, Mar. 5, Mar. 12
Roosevelt, Theodore, Jan. 17, Nov. 9, Nov. 18
root beer was first sold in 1869, June 9
Roquefort Cheese Day, June 4
Rose, Pete, Apr. 14
Rose Bowl, Jan. 1
Ross, Betsy, Jan. 1
Ross, Diana, Mar. 26
Ross, George, May 10
Ross, Nellie Tayloe, Jan. 5, Nov. 29
Rossetti, Christina Georgina, Dec. 5
Rothko, Marcus "Mark," Sept. 25
Rousseau, Henri Julien Felix, May 20
Rowling, J. K., July 31
Royal Greenwich Observatory was established in 1675, June 22

Rubber Eraser Day, Apr. 15
Rubens, Peter Paul, June 28
Rubenstein, Arthur, Jan. 28
Rudolph, Wilma, June 23, Sept. 2
Rulton, Robert, Nov. 14
Runyon, Damon, Oct. 4
Rush, Benjamin, Dec. 24
Russell, Charles, Mar. 19
Russia, Jan. 7, Mar. 4, May 9, June 12, Nov. 7
Rutan, Dick, Dec. 23
Rutgers beat Princeton in the first intercollegiate football game in 1869, Nov. 6
Ruth, George Herman "Babe," Feb. 6, Apr. 22, Aug. 11, Sept. 30
Rutledge, Edward, Nov. 23
Rwanda celebrates its Independence Day, July 1
Ryan, Nolan, Jan. 31
Rylant, Cynthia, June 6
Ryumin, Valery, Apr. 9
Ryun, Jim, broke the mile record in 1979, July 17
Sabin, Albert Bruce, Aug. 26, Oct. 6
Sacagawea golden dollar coins were minted in 1999, Nov. 18
Sacagawea died in 1812, Dec. 20
Sacco and Vanzetti were executed in 1927, Aug. 23
Sachar, Louis, Mar. 20
safety pin was patented in 1849, Apr. 10
safety razor was patented in 1901, Dec. 2
Sagan, Carl, Nov. 9
Sagittarius astrological sign, Nov. 22–Dec. 21
St. Christopher and Nevis celebrate Independence Day, Sept. 19
Saint-Exupery, Antoine de, June 29
Saint George Feast Day, Apr. 23
St. Gotthard Automobile Tunnel opened in 1980, Sept. 5
St. Lasarus's Day, Apr. 1
St. Lawrence Seaway, Apr. 25, July 18
Saint Lucia celebrates its Independence Day, Feb. 22
St. Nicholas Day, Dec. 6
St. Patrick's Day, Mar. 17
Saint-Saens, Camille, Oct. 9
St. Swithin's Day, July 15
St. Valentine's Day, Feb. 14
St. Vincent and the Grenadines celebrate their Independence Day, Oct. 27
Sajak, Pat, Oct. 26
Sakharov, Andrei Dmitriyevich, May 21
Salem witch trials commenced in 1692, Mar. 1
Salinger, J. D., Jan. 1
Salk, Jonas, Mar. 26, Apr. 12, Oct. 28
Salk polio vaccine was allowed to be used for the first time in 1955, Apr. 12
Salvation Army of the United States was created in 1880, Mar. 10
Salyut 6, Apr. 9
Sampson, Deborah, Dec. 17
Sandberg, Ryne, Sept. 18
Sandburg, Carl, Jan. 6
sandpaper was patented in 1834, June 14
sandwich was invented in 1762, Aug. 6
San Francisco earthquake of 1906, Apr. 18

San Francisco earthquake of 1989, Oct. 17
San Marino, Apr. 1, Sept. 3
San Souci, Daniel, Oct. 10
San Souci, Robert, Oct. 10
Santa Fe Trail opened in 1822, Sept. 23
Santa Lucia Day, Dec. 13
Santayana, George, Dec. 16
Santiago, Benito, Mar. 9
sardines were first canned in 1876, Feb. 17
Sargent, John Singer, Jan. 12
Saturnalia was celebrated by the ancient Romans, Dec. 17
Saudi Arabia celebrates the 1932 Kingdom Unification,
    Sept. 23
Savage, Fred, July 9
Save the Rhino Day, Apr. 1
Sawyer, Diane, Dec. 22
Sax, Adolphe, Nov. 6
Scalia, Antonin, Mar. 11
Scarry, Richard, June 5
Schaefer, Jack, Nov. 19
Schawlow, Arthur, Mar. 22
Schembechler, Glenn Edward "Bo," Apr. 1
Schirra, Wally, Mar. 12
Schmidt, Mike, Sept. 27
Schneiderman, Rose, Apr. 6
Schoenberg, Arnold, Sept. 13
Schoolcraft, Henry, found source of Mississippi River in
    1832, July 13
Schubert, Franz, Jan. 31
Schultz, Charles, Nov. 26
Schwarzkopf, Norman, Aug. 22
Schweitzer, Albert, Jan. 14
scientists discovered a satellite circling Venus in 1686,
    Aug. 18
Scieszka, Jon, Sept. 8
Scobee, Francis R., Jan. 28, May 19
Scorpio astrological sign, Oct. 23–Nov. 21
Scotland, Dec. 31
Scotland Yard began operating in 1829, Sept. 29
Scott, David R., July 26, July 31
Scott, Sir Walter, Aug. 15
Scott, Winfield, June 13
screw was patented in 1798, Dec. 14
Sears, Richard Warren, Dec. 7
Seeger, Pete, May 3
Seeing Eye Guide Dog Organization was founded in
    1929, Jan. 29
Seibert, Florence, Oct. 6
Seinfeld, Jerry, Apr. 29
Selden, George, May 14
Seles, Monica, Dec. 2
self-winding clock was patented in 1783, Oct. 6
Selleck, Tom, Jan. 29
Sendak, Maurice, June 10
Senegal celebrates its Independence Day, Apr. 4
Sequoia National Park was created in 1890, Sept. 25
serfdom was prohibited in Russia in 1861, Mar. 4
Serra, Father Junipero, July 16, Nov. 24
"Sesame Street" aired for the first time in 1969, Nov. 10
Sesquicentennial Expo opened in Philadelphia in 1926,
    May 31

Seurat, Georges Pierre, Dec. 2
Seuss, Dr., Mar. 2
Seward, William Henry, May 16
sewing machine was patented in 1846, Sept. 10
Seychelles celebrates its Independence Day, June 29
Shakespeare, William, Mar. 11, Apr. 23
Shakira, Feb. 9
Shamu, Sept. 26
Sharif, Omar, Apr. 10
Sharmat, Marjorie Weinman, Nov. 12
Shaw, George Bernard, July 26
Shays' Rebellion started in 1786, Aug. 29
Shelley, Mary Wollstonecraft, Mar. 11, Aug. 30
Shelley, Percy Bysshe, Aug. 4
Shenandoah National Park was created in 1926, Dec. 26
Shepard, Alan, Feb. 6, May 5, Nov. 18
Sherman, Roger, Apr. 19
Sherman, William Tecumseh, Feb. 8, Nov. 16
shoelaces were invented in 1790, Mar. 27
Shoemaker, Willie, Aug. 19
Shoemaker-Levy comet began crashing into Jupiter in
    1994, July 16
Shostakovich, Dmitri, Sept. 25
shredded wheat was patented in 1892, Aug. 1
Sibelius, Jean, Dec. 8
Siege of Yorktown commenced in 1781, Sept. 28
Sierra, Ruben Angel, Oct. 6
Sierra Club was organized in 1929, May 28
Sierra Leone, Apr. 19, Apr. 27
Sikorsky, Igor, May 25
"Silent Night" was created in 1818, Dec. 24
Silent Spring was published in 1962, Apr. 13
Sills, Beverly, May 25
Silverstein, Shel, Sept. 25
silver was no longer used in minting dimes and quarters
    as of 1965, June 3
Simon, Neil, July 4
Simon, Paul, Oct. 13
Simon, Seymour, Aug. 9
Simplon Tunnel opened in 1898, May 19
Sinatra, Frank, Dec. 12
Sinclair, Upton, Sept. 20
Singapore, Jan. 19, Aug. 9
Singer, Isaac Bashevis, July 14, Oct. 5
Sirani, Elisabetta, Jan. 8
Sis, Peter, May 11
"$64,000 Question" television game show premiered in
    1955, June 7
"Sixty Minutes" was televised for the first time in 1968,
    Sept. 24
Skylab, May 25, July 11, Nov. 16
slavery was abolished in 1865, Feb. 1
slavery was abolished in England in 1807, Mar. 25
slavery was abolished in Vermont in 1777, Feb. 11
Slayton, Donald "Deke," Mar. 1
slinky was patented in 1947, Mar. 4
Slobodkina, Esphyr, Sept. 22
Slovakia celebrates the adoption of its constitution, Sept. 1
Slovenia declared its independence from Yugoslavia in
    1991, June 25
Small, David, Feb. 12

Smith, Bessie, Apr. 15
Smith, Doris Buchanan, June 1
Smith, James, July 11
Smith, Jedediah Strong, Jan. 6
Smith, John, Sept. 10
Smith, J. W., Mar. 22
Smith, Kathryn Elizabeth "Kate," May 1
Smith, Lane, Aug. 25
Smith, Margaret Madeline Chase, Dec. 14
Smith, Michael J., Jan. 28, Apr. 30
Smith, Will, Sept. 25
Smithson, James, June 27
Smithsonian Institute was created in 1846, Aug. 10
Smokey Bear, Aug. 2
smoking was banned on airplane flights lasting two hours or less in 1988, Apr. 23
Snoopy, Oct. 2
Sobol, Donald, Oct. 4
Social Security Act was approved in 1935, Aug. 14
Society for the Relief of Free Negroes Unlawfully Held in Bondage was formed in 1775, Apr. 14
Socrates, June 5
solar eclipse ended a battle between the Lydians and the Medes in 585 B.C., May 26
solar powered battery was invented in 1954, Apr. 25
Solidarity received legal status in Poland, Apr. 17
Solomon Islands celebrates its Independence Day, July 7
Solzhenitsyn, Alexander, Mar. 24
Sondheim, Stephen, Mar. 22
Sosa, Sammy, Nov. 12
SOS became the international distress signal in 1906, Nov. 22
Sousa, John Philip, Sept. 26, Nov. 6
Souter, David H., Sept. 17
South Africa, Apr. 6, Apr. 26, May 31
South Carolina became the eighth state in 1788, May 23
South Dakota became the fortieth state in 1889, Nov. 2
South Pacific opened on Broadway in 1949, Apr. 7
Soviet Union expired in 1991, Dec. 8
Soyuz 4, Jan. 14
Soyuz 5, Jan. 14
Soyuz 9 set a space endurance record in 1970, June 1
Soyuz 13 was launched in 1973, Dec. 18
Soyuz 35 was launched in 1980, Apr. 9
space shuttle program launched its one hundredth mission in 2000, Oct. 11
Spain, Apr. 23, July 17, Oct. 1
Spanish-American War began in 1898, Apr. 21
Spanish-American War ended in 1900, Feb. 6
Spanish conquered Aztecs in 1521, Aug. 13
Speare, Elizabeth George, Nov. 21
Spears, Britney, Dec. 2
speed limit of 55 miles per hour was imposed in 1974, Jan. 2
Spielberg, Steven, Dec. 18
Spier, Peter, June 6
spinach farmers built a statue of Popeye in 1937, Mar. 26
Spinelli, Jerry, Feb. 1
spitting outlawed in New York, New York, in 1896, May 12
Spooner, William Archibald, July 22

Sports Eye Safety Month, April
Sports Illustrated appeared for the first time in 1954, Aug. 16
Spruce Goose flew its first and only flight in 1947, Nov. 2
Sputnik 1 was launched in 1957, Oct. 4
Sputnik 2 was launched in 1957, Nov. 3
Sputnik 5 was launched in 1960, Aug. 19
Sputnik 9 ventured into space in 1961, Mar. 9
Sri Lanka celebrates its Independence Day, Feb. 4
Stafford, Thomas, May 18
Stalin, Joseph Vissarionovich, Dec. 21
Stamp Act was imposed on the colonies by the British in 1765, Nov. 1
Stanley, Henry Morton, Jan. 28, Nov. 10
Stanley Cup, Mar. 18
Stanton, Elizabeth Cady, Nov. 12
stapler was patented in 1868, Mar. 5
Stardust was launched in 1999, Feb. 7
Starr, Ringo, July 7
Stars and Stripes Forever was performed for the first time, May 14
"Star-Spangled Banner," Mar. 3, Sept. 13
"Star Trek" premiered in 1966, Sept. 8
Statue of Liberty, June 19, July 4, Oct. 28
statue of Ramses II was uncovered in Egypt in 1991, Nov. 30
Staub, Rusty, Apr. 1
steamboat, invented by John Fitch, was successfully working in 1787, Aug. 22
"Steamboat Willie" appeared in 1928, Sept. 19, Nov. 18
steam engine was operated for the first time in 1755, Mar. 12
Steichen, Edward, Mar. 27
Steig, William, Nov. 14
Stein, David, created a bubble fifty feet long in 1988, June 6
Stein, Gertrude, Feb. 3
Steinbeck, John, Feb. 27
Stengel, Charles Dillon "Casey," July 30
Stephens, Alexander, Feb. 9
Stephenson, George, June 9
Steptoe, John, Sept. 14
Stern, Isaac, July 21
Steuben, Friedrich Wilhelm von, Sept. 17
Stevens, John Paul, Apr. 20
Stevenson, Robert Louis, Nov. 13
Stewart, Jimmy, May 20
Still, William, created the Underground Railroad in 1850, Aug. 2
Stine, R. L., Oct. 8
stock market crashed in 1929, Oct. 29
Stockton, Richard, Oct. 1
Stojko, Elvis, Mar. 22
Stone, Lucy, Aug. 13
Stone, Thomas, Oct. 5
Stourbridge Lion was the first steam locomotive to run in 1829, Aug. 9
Stowe, Harriet Beecher, Mar. 20, June 14
Stratemeyer, Edward, Oct. 4
Strauss, Johann, Oct. 25
Strauss, Levi, Feb. 26

Strauss, Richard Georg, June 11

Stravinsky, Igor Fyodorovich, June 17

Streisand, Barbra, Apr. 24

Stuart, Gilbert Charles, Dec. 3

Stuyvesant, Peter, May 11, Sept. 8

Sudan celebrates its Independence Day, Jan. 1

Suez Canal, Mar. 7, Apr. 25, Nov. 17

Sullivan, Anne Mansfield, Apr. 14

Sullivan, Sir Arthur, May 13

Sullivan, Ed, Sept. 28

Sullivan, Kathryn D., Oct. 11

Sun Yat-Sen, Nov. 12

Super Bowl I was played in 1967, Jan. 15

Superman comic was issued for the first time in 1938, June 1

supernova was observed in 1006, May 1

Supreme Court, Feb. 1, Mar. 6, Mar. 18, May 17, June 13, Sept. 25, October, Dec. 12

Suriname, Feb. 25, Nov. 25

Surveyor 3 was launched in 1967, Apr. 17

Surveyor 7 made a landing on the surface of Mars in 1968, Jan. 9

Susan B. Anthony dollars were first issued in 1979, July 2

Sutter, John Augustus, Jan. 24, Feb. 15

swallows leave Capistrano for the winter, Oct. 23

swallows return to San Juan Capistrano, California, Mar. 19

Swan Lake opened in 1895, Jan. 15

Swaziland celebrates Somhlolo, its independence day, Sept. 6

Sweden, Apr. 30, June 6, Nov. 6, Dec. 13

Swift, Jonathan, Nov. 30

Swigert, John L., Apr. 11

Switzerland, Mar. 1, Apr. 6, Aug. 1

synthetic detergent was invented in 1933, Oct. 10

synthetic rubber was first fabricated in 1930, Apr. 10

Syrian Arab Republic celebrates its Independence Day, Apr. 17

Taback, Simms, Feb. 13

Tabei, Junko, first woman to climb Mount Everest, May 23

tabulating machine patented in 1889, Jan. 8

Taft, Helen Herron, Jan. 2, Mar. 27

Taft, William Howard, Sept. 15

Tagore, Rabindranath, Apr. 6

Taiwan, Mar. 29, Apr. 29, Sept. 28, Oct. 25

Tajikistan celebrates its Independence Day, Sept. 9

Take Our Daughters and Sons to Work Day, April

Tallchief, Maria, Jan. 24

Tanner, Henry Ossawa, June 21

Tanzania celebrates Union Day, Apr. 26

Tarbell, Ida Minerva, Nov. 5

Tasman, Abel, discovered New Zealand in 1642, Dec. 13

Taurus astrological sign, Apr. 20–May 20

Taylor, George, Feb. 23

Taylor, Margaret MacKall Smith, Sept. 21

Taylor, Mildred D., Sept. 13

Taylor, Theodore, June 23

Taylor, Zachary, Nov. 24

Tchaikovsky, Peter, May 7

Teddy bear was created in 1902, Nov. 18

teflon was discovered in 1938, Apr. 6

telephone was invented in 1876, Mar. 10

television began featuring regular programs in 1939, Apr. 30

Tell, William, shot the famous apple from his son's head in 1307, Nov. 18

Teller, Edward, Jan. 15

Temple, Shirley, Apr. 23

Tennessee became the sixteenth state in 1796, June 1

Tennyson, Alfred, Aug. 6

ten women's rights campaigners were arrested outside the White House in 1917, Aug. 28

Tereshkova, Valentina, first woman to travel in space, June 16

Texas, Mar. 2, Mar. 30, Oct. 22, Dec. 29

Thailand, Apr. 6, May 5, Oct. 23, Dec. 10

Thanksgiving, November, Nov. 26, Dec. 4

Thank You School Librarian Day, Apr. 17

Thatcher, Margaret Hilda Roberts, Oct. 13

Third Millennium officially started on January 1, 2001, Jan. 1

Thomas, Clarence, June 23

Thomas, Dylan, Jan. 17

Thomas, Joyce Carol, May 25

Thomas, Lowell, Apr. 6

Thompson, Kay, Nov. 9

Thomson, Charles, Nov. 29

Thoreau, Henry David, July 12

Thornton, Matthew, June 24

Thorpe, James Francis, May 28

Three Mile Island experienced a nuclear power plant disaster in 1979, Mar. 28

Thurber, James Grover, Dec. 8

Tiananmen Square Massacre occurred in 1989, June 4

Tiburzi, Bonnie, first woman pilot for a U.S. airline, June 4

Time magazine published its first issue in 1923, Mar. 2

tin can processing of food was patented in 1825, Jan. 19

tin-type camera was patented in 1856, Feb. 19

Titanic, Apr. 15, July 18, Sept. 1

Titanic Memorial Maritime Act was created in 1986, Oct. 21

Togo, Jan. 24, Apr. 27

Tolkien, J. R. R., Jan. 3

Tolstoy, Leo, Sept. 9

Tombaugh, Clyde W., Feb. 18, Mar. 18

Tomb of the Unknown Soldier was created in 1921, Nov. 11

Tom Thumb, Jan. 4

Tonga, June 4, Nov. 4

Toomey, Bill, Jan. 10

toothpaste tube was invented by Dr. Washington Sheffield in 1892, May 22

top quark was discovered in 1994, Apr. 23

Toscanini, Arturo, Mar. 25

Toulouse-Lautrec, Henri de, Nov. 24

Tournament of Roses Parade, Jan. 1

Towne, Charles, Mar. 22

traffic light was patented in 1923, Nov. 20

transatlantic radio and telephone service began in 1926, Mar. 7

transatlantic telephone calls could be made for the first time in 1927, Jan. 7

transcontinental railroad was finished in 1869, May 10

transcontinental telephone link was connected between New York City and San Francisco in 1914, July 29

transcontinental television premiered in 1951, Sept. 4

transistor was invented in 1947, Dec. 23

Travers, P. L., Aug. 9

Travolta, John, Feb. 18

Treaty of Guadalupe Hidalgo was signed in 1848, Feb. 2

Treaty of Paris ended the Spanish-American War in 1898, Dec. 10

Treaty of Paris was signed in 1783, Sept. 3

Treaty of Versailles was signed in 1919, June 28

Trinidad and Tobago, Aug. 1, Aug. 31

Trinidad was sighted by Columbus in 1498, July 31

Tripp, Valerie, Sept. 12

Truman, Elizabeth "Bess" Virginia Wallace, Feb. 13

Truman, Harry, Jan. 21, Mar. 27, May 8, Oct. 5

Truth, Sojourner, Nov. 26

Tuba Day, May 3

Tubman, Harriet, Mar. 10

Tunis, John, Dec. 7

Tunisia, Jan. 18, Mar. 20, Apr. 9, Aug. 13

Turkey, Apr. 23, May 19, Aug. 20, Oct. 29

Turkmenistan celebrates its Independence Day, Oct. 27

Turow, Scott, Apr. 12

Tuscarora Indian War ended in 1713, Mar. 23

Tutu, Desmond, Oct. 7

TV dinner was produced for the first time in 1953, Sept. 10

Twain, Mark, Nov. 30

TWA showed the first in-flight movie in 1961, July 19

Twelfth Night, Jan. 5

Tyler, John, Mar. 29

Tyler, Julia Gardiner, May 4

Tyler, Letitia Christian, Nov. 12

Tyng, James, Apr. 12

typewriter was patented in 1868, June 23

Uganda, Apr. 11, Oct. 9

Ukraine celebrates its Independence Day, Aug. 24

"Uncle Sam," Mar. 13, Sept. 7

Uncle Tom's Cabin was published in 1852, Mar. 20

underground railway opened in London in 1863, Jan. 10

UNESCO was created in 1946, Nov. 4

UNICEF Day, Oct. 31

UNICEF was created in 1946, Dec. 11

Union's first offense engagement took place at Sewall's Point, Virginia, in 1861, May 18

Unitas, Johnny, May 7

United Arab Emirates was formed in 1971, Dec. 2

United Nations Charter was signed in 1945, June 26

United Nations Day, Oct. 24

United Nations General Assembly held its first meeting in 1946, Jan. 10

United States and Canada agreed on a treaty to complete the St. Lawrence Seaway in 1932, July 18

U.S. Army was created in 1775, June 14

U.S. capital was established in New York in 1788, Sept. 13

U.S. Capitol, Apr. 24, Sept. 18, Nov. 17

United States celebrates its Independence Day, July 4

U.S. Customs Service was created in 1789, Aug. 1

United States declared war against Great Britain in 1812, June 18

United States declared war against Japan in 1941, Dec. 8

United States declared war on Algiers in 1815, Mar. 3

United States declared war on Germany in 1917, Apr. 6

United States declared war on Mexico in 1846, May 13

U.S. Department of Agriculture was created in 1862, May 15

U.S. Department of Education was created in 1979, Oct. 17

U.S. Department of Labor was created in 1888, June 13

U.S. Department of State (Department of Foreign Affairs) was created in 1789, July 27

U.S. Department of Veterans Affairs was created in 1989, Sept. 8

United States established uniform time zones in 1883, Nov. 18

U.S. flag with thirteen stripes and a star for each state was adopted in 1818, Apr. 4

U.S. government offered a reward of $100,000 for the capture of Jefferson Davis in 1865, May 2

U.S. Government Printing Office was created in 1860, June 23

United States Holocaust Museum opened in 1993, Apr. 26

United States levied the first income tax, Aug. 5

U.S. men's gymnastics team won a gold medal in the 1984 Summer Olympics, July 31

U.S. Mint stopped producing one-dollar and three-dollar gold pieces, Sept. 26

U.S. Navy was created in 1775, Oct. 13

"United States of America" became our country's official name in 1776, Sept. 9

U.S. Patent Office began operations in 1790, July 31

U.S. Post Office and the office of postmaster general were created in 1789, Feb. 20, Sept. 22

U.S. Secret Service was established in 1861, June 23

U.S. State Department issued the first passport in 1796, July 8

U.S. Surgeon General issued smoking hazard report in 1964, Jan. 11

United States took control of Mexico City in 1847, Sept. 14

U.S. Treasury Department was created in 1789, Sept. 2

United States war bonds were created in 1812, Mar. 14

U.S. War Department was created in 1789, Aug. 7

United States was attacked by Al Qaeda terrorists in 2001, Sept. 11

U.S. Weather Bureau began recording weather observations in 1870, Nov. 1

United States Weather Service was created in 1870, Feb. 9

Univac I was demonstrated for the first time in 1951, June 14

Universal Children's Day, Nov. 20

Universal Human Rights Month, December

Universal Product Codes were put into practice in 1974, June 26

Unser, Al, Apr. 19

Uranus' moons discovered, Jan. 11, Jan. 24

Uranus' rings were discovered in 1977, Mar. 10

Uranus was discovered in 1781, Mar. 13

Uruguay celebrates its Independence Day, Aug. 25

USS *Constitution,* "Old Ironsides," had its maiden voyage in 1797, Sept. 20
USS *Enterprise* was launched in 1960, Sept. 25
USS *Monitor* sank in a storm in 1862, Dec. 30
Ustinov, Peter, Apr. 16
Utah became the forty-fifth state in 1896, Jan. 4
Uzbekistan celebrates its Independence Day, Sept. 1

vacuum cleaner was patented in 1869, June 8
Valentino, Rudolph, Apr. 6
Valenzuela, Fernando, Nov. 1
Valley Forge encampment during the winter of 1777–1778, Dec. 19
Van Allen, James, Jan. 31
Van Allsburg, Chris, June 18
Van Buren, Hannah Hoes, Mar. 8
Van Buren, Martin, Dec. 5
Vancouver located and named Mount Rainier in 1792, May 8
Van Dyck, Sir Anthony, Mar. 22
van Gogh, Vincent, Mar. 30
Vanguard 2 was launched in 1959, Feb. 17
Van Loon, Hendrik, June 27
Vanuatu celebrates its Independence Day, July 30
Vatican City, Feb. 11, June 7, Oct. 22
Vaughn, Sarah, Mar. 27
V-E Day, May 8
Vega I was launched in 1984, Dec. 15
Venera 3 was launched in 1965, Nov. 16
Venera 4 was launched in 1967, June 12
Venera 8 landed on Venus in 1972, Feb. 16
Venezuela, Apr. 19, July 5
Venus 2 was launched in 1978, Aug. 8
Verdi, Giuseppe, Oct. 10
Vereen, Ben, Oct. 10
Vermeer, Jan, Oct. 31
Vermont, Feb. 11, Mar. 4, Aug. 16
Verne, Jules, Feb. 8
Verrazano, Giovanni, discovered New York Harbor in 1524, Apr. 17
Verrazano Narrows Bridge opened in 1964, Nov. 21
Vespucci, Amerigo, Mar. 9
Vesuvius erupted in A.D. 79, Aug. 24
Veterans Day, Nov. 11
video tape recording on magnetic tape was made for the first time in 1958, Sept. 6
videotapes of the sunken *Titanic* were shown in 1986, July 18
Vietnam Conflict started in 1945, Aug. 22
Vietnam Veterans Memorial was unveiled in 1982, Nov. 9
Vietnam War ended in 1973, Jan. 28
Vietnam Women's Memorial was opened in 1993, Nov. 11
Viking I, July 20, Aug. 20
Vining, Elizabeth Gray, Oct. 6
Viola, Frank, Jr., Apr. 19
Viorst, Judith, Feb. 2
Virchow, Rudolf, Oct. 13
Virgil, Oct. 15
Virginia, Jan. 13, June 25
Virginia Company left England in 1606, Dec. 20

Virgin Islands, Mar. 31, Aug. 4
Virgo astrological sign, Aug. 23–Sep. 22
vitamin C was discovered in 1932, Apr. 4
V-Mail began in 1942, June 22
Voigt, Cynthia, Feb. 25
volleyball was invented in 1895, Feb. 9
Volta, Count Alessandro Giuseppe Antonio, Feb. 18
Voltaire, Jean François Marie, Nov. 21
Vostok, Antarctica, experienced the lowest temperature ever recorded in 1983, July 25
Vostok I, Apr. 12
Vostok VI, June 16
Voting Rights Act of 1965 was signed, Aug. 6
Voyager 1 was launched in 1977, Sept. 5
Voyager 2, Jan. 24, Aug. 20
VTOL craft was demonstrated for the first time in 1954, Aug. 3
vulcanized rubber was patented in 1844, June 12

waffle iron was patented in 1869, Aug. 24
Wagner, John Peter "Honus," Feb. 24
Wagner, Richard, May 22
Waitangi Day, Feb. 6
Wald, Lillian D., Mar. 10
Waldseemuller, Martin, Apr. 25
Wales celebrates St. David's Day, Mar. 1
Walker, Alice, Feb. 9
Wallace, Mike, May 9
Wallenberg, Raoul, Aug. 4
Walters, Barbara, Sept. 25
Walton, George, Feb. 2
Ward, Aaron Montgomery, Feb. 17
Warner, Gertrude Chandler, Apr. 16
War of 1812 ended in 1814, Dec. 24
Warren, Robert Penn, Apr. 24
Warsaw was conquered by the Nazis in 1939, Sept. 8
washing machine was patented in 1797, Mar. 28
Washington, Booker Tallaferro, Apr. 5
Washington, Denzel, Dec. 28
Washington, George, Jan. 8, Feb. 4, Feb. 22, Mar. 25, Apr. 5, Apr. 30, Aug. 7, Sept. 19, Sept. 26, Dec. 4, Dec. 25
Washington, Harold, first African American mayor of Chicago, Apr. 11
Washington, Martha Dandridge Custis, June 21
Washington became the forty-second state in 1889, Nov. 11
Washington, D.C., Aug. 24, Dec. 1
Washington Monument was dedicated in 1885, Feb. 21
Washington National Cathedral was completed in 1990, Sept. 29
Watergate Day happened in 1972, June 17
Water Pollution Control Act was passed in 1972, Oct. 18
Watson, James, Apr. 6, Oct. 18
Watt, James, Jan. 19
WAVES was created in 1942, July 30
Wayne, John, May 26
Wayne, "Mad" Anthony, Jan. 1
Weatherperson's Day, Feb. 5
weather reports were issued weekly for the first time in 1878, Feb. 11

Weaver, Robert C., first African American appointed to the Cabinet, Jan. 13

Webber, Andrew Lloyd, Mar. 22

Weber, Bernard, Sept. 27

Webster, Daniel, Jan. 18

Webster, Noah, Apr. 14, Oct. 16

Webster-Ashburton Treaty was finalized in 1842, Aug. 9

Weekly Reader was first published in 1928, Sept. 15

Weems, Parson Mason Locke, Oct. 11

Weights and Measures Day, May 20

Weir, Reginald, first African American to play in the U.S. Tennis Open, Mar. 11

Weissmuller, Johnny, June 2

Weitz, Paul, May 25

Welles, Orson, Apr. 6, Oct. 30

Wells, Herbert George, Sept. 21

Wells, Ida B., July 16

Wells, Rosemary, Jan. 29

West, Benjamin, Oct. 10

Western Samoa celebrates a national holiday, Sept. 5

Westinghouse, George, Oct. 6

Westminster Abbey opened in 1066, Feb. 28

Weston, Martha, Jan. 16

West Side Story premiered in 1957, Sept. 26

West Virginia became the thirty-fifth state in 1863, June 20

WGY became the first station to provide scheduled television broadcasts in 1928, May 11

Whipple, William, Jan. 14

Whistler, James Abbott McNeill, July 10

White, Byron, June 8

White, E. B., July 11

White, Edward, Jan. 27, June 3

White, Peregrine, Nov. 21

White Cane Safety Day, Oct. 15

White House, Jan. 17, Feb. 8, Mar. 23, Apr. 24, Oct. 13, Nov. 1

Whitman, Walt, May 31

Whitney, Eli, Mar. 14, Dec. 8

Whittier, John Greenleaf, Dec. 17

Whymper, Edward, conquered Matterhorn in 1865, July 14

Wiesel, Elie, Sept. 30, Oct. 14

Wiesner, David, Feb. 5

wiffle ball was patented in 1953, Aug. 14

Wiggin, Kate Douglas, Sept. 28

Wilde, Oscar, Oct. 16

Wilder, Laura Ingalls, Feb. 7

Wilder, L. Douglas, Jan. 13, Nov. 7

Wilder, Thornton, Apr. 17

Wilkins, Maurice, Oct. 18

Wilkins, Roy, Aug. 30

Willard, Archibald M., Aug. 22

Willard, Nancy, June 26

William, Prince, June 21

Williams, Esther, Aug. 8

Williams, Hank, Sept. 17

Williams, John, Feb. 8

Williams, Mason, Aug. 24

Williams, Robin, July 21

Williams, Roger, Feb. 5

Williams, Serena, Sept. 26

Williams, Ted, Aug. 30

Williams, Tennessee, Mar. 26

Williams, Venus, June 17

Williams, Vera B., Jan. 28

Williams, William, Apr. 8

Williamsburg, Virginia, began restoration processes in 1926, Nov. 27

William the Conqueror arrived in England in 1066, Sept. 28

Willis, Bruce, Mar. 19

Wilson, Edith Bolling Galt, Oct. 15

Wilson, Ellen Louise Axson, May 15

Wilson, James, Sept. 14

Wilson, Woodrow, Mar. 7, Mar. 15, Dec. 28

Wimbledon tennis championships were held for the first time in 1877, July 19

Winchell, Walter, Apr. 7

Wind Cave National Park was established in 1903, Jan. 9

windshield wiper was patented in 1903, Nov. 10

Winfrey, Oprah, Jan. 29

Winthrop, Elizabeth, Sept. 14

Winthrop, John, Jan. 12

Wisconsin, Jan. 22, May 29

Wisniewski, David, Mar. 21

Witherspoon, John, Feb. 5

Wojciechowska, Maia, Aug. 7

Wolcott, Oliver, Nov. 21

Wolfe, Thomas Clayton, Oct. 3

Women's Equality Day, Aug. 26

Women's Rights Convention was held in Seneca Falls, New York, in 1848, July 19

women were allowed to attend military academies in 1975, Sept. 22

Wonder, Stevie, May 13

Wood, Grant, Feb. 13

Woodhull, Victoria Chaflin, Sept. 23

Woodruff, Elvira, June 19

Woods, Eldrick "Tiger," Dec. 30

Woods, Granville T., Apr. 23

Woodson, Jacqueline, Jan. 12

Woolworth, Frank Winfield, Apr. 13

Wordsworth, William, Apr. 7

World Bank was organized in 1945, Dec. 27

World Court was organized in 1920, June 16

World Cup Soccer began in 1930, July 13

World Day for Water, Mar. 22

World Environment Day, June 5

World Food Day, Oct. 16

World Health Day, Apr. 7

World Meteorological Day, Mar. 23

World Population Day, July 11

world population reached six billion people in 1999, Oct. 11

World Press Freedom Day, May 3

World Red Cross Day, May 8

world's biggest cheese made in 1964, Jan. 22

World Series, Oct. 1, Oct. 13

World Standard Time was accomplished in 1884, Mar. 13

World TB Day, Mar. 24

World Telecommunications Day, May 17

World Turtle Day, May 23

World War II ended in 1945, Aug. 14
World War II started in 1939, Sept. 1
Worthy, James Ager, Feb. 27
Wren, Christopher, Oct. 20
wrench was patented in 1835, Aug. 17
Wright, Frank Lloyd, June 8
Wright, Orville, Aug. 19, Dec. 17
Wright, Wilbur, Apr. 16, Dec. 17
writing can be traced back to Mesopotamia in 4224 B.C.,
    Oct. 18
Wyeth, Andrew, July 12
Wyeth, N. C., Oct. 22
Wynette, Virginia "Tammy," May 4
Wyoming, June 13, July 10, Dec. 10
Wythe, George, June 8

xerographic image was produced for the first time in
    1938, Oct. 22
x-ray photograph was first created in 1896, Jan. 12
x-rays were discovered by Dr. Wilhelm Roentgen in
    1895, Nov. 8

Yale, Linus, Apr. 4
Yale University was created in 1701, Oct. 16
Yamaguchi, Kristi Tsuya, July 12
Yang, Chen Ning, Sept. 22
Yankee Stadium opened in 1923, Apr. 18
Yastrzemski, Carl, Aug. 22
Yeager, Charles "Chuck," Feb. 13, Oct. 14
Yeager, Jeana, Dec. 23
yellow fever vaccine was reported in 1932, Apr. 28
Yellowstone National Park was established in 1872, Mar. 1
Yemen, May 22, Sept. 26, Nov. 30

Yep, Laurence, Mar. 20
Yevtushenko, Yevgeny Aleksandrovich, July 18
YMCA began in London in 1944, June 6
Yolen, Jane, Feb. 11
Yorktown Day, Oct. 19
Yosemite National Park was established in 1864, Oct. 1
Young, Andrew, Mar. 12
Young, Brigham, June 1
Young, Denton True "Cy," Mar. 29, May 5
Young, Ed, Nov. 28
Young, John, Apr. 12, Apr. 16
Yount, Robin, Sept. 16
Youth Art Month, March
Yukon became a Canadian Territory in 1898, June 13

Zaharias, Mildred Ella "Babe" Didrickson, June 26
Zambia, May 25, Oct. 24
ZAM! Zoo and Aquarium Month, April
Zanuck, Darryl F., Sept. 5
Zanzibar remembers its revolution day of 1935, Jan. 12
Zelinsky, Paul O., Feb. 14
Zemach, Margot, Nov. 30
Zeppelin, Ferdinand, Count von, July 8
Zimbabwe celebrates its Independence Day, Apr. 18
Zindel, Paul, May 15
Zion National Park was created in 1919, Nov. 19
ZIP codes were introduced in 1963, July 1
zipper was patented in 1913, Apr. 29
Zola, Emile, Apr. 2
Zolotow, Charlotte, June 26
ZR-1 flew over the Woolworth Tower in 1923, Sept. 11
Zworykin, Vladimir Kosma, July 30